FIRST, DO LESS HARM

FIRST, DO LESS HARM

Harm Reduction as a Principle of Law and Policy

Edited by Vanessa Gruben and Chelsea Cox

University of Ottawa Press
2025

Les Presses de l'Université d'Ottawa
University of Ottawa **Press**

Les Presses de l'Université d'Ottawa / University of Ottawa Press (PUO-UOP) is North America's flagship bilingual university press, affiliated to one of Canada's top research universities. PUO-UOP enriches the intellectual and cultural discourse of our increasingly knowledge-based and globalized world with peer-reviewed, award-winning books.

www.Press.uOttawa.ca

Library and Archives Canada Cataloguing in Publication

Title: First, do less harm : harm reduction as a principle of law and policy / edited by Vanessa Gruben and Chelsea Cox.

Names: Gruben, Vanessa, editor. | Cox, Chelsea, editor.

Series: Health and society (University of Ottawa Press)

Description: Series statement: Health and society | Includes bibliographical references.

Identifiers: Canadiana (print) 20240403061 | Canadiana (ebook) 2024040307X | ISBN 9780776641942 (hardcover) | ISBN 9780776641935 (softcover) | ISBN 9780776641959 (PDF) | ISBN 9780776641966 (EPUB)

Subjects: LCSH: Drug legalization—Canada. | LCSH: Drug abuse—Canada—Prevention. | LCSH: Drug control—Canada. | LCSH: Harm reduction—Canada.

Classification: LCC KE3720.F57 2024 | DDC 345.71/0277—dc23

Legal Deposit: First Quarter 2025
Library and Archives Canada

Production Team

Copy editing	Robbie McCaw
Proofreading	Tanina Drvar
Typesetting	John van der Woude, JVDW Designs
Cover design	Benoit Deneault

Cover Image   Jackijuk, *Reach Out for Hope,* acrylic painting, Shutterstock, 2067746156.

---

uOttawa

The University of Ottawa Press gratefully acknowledges the support extended to its publishing list by the Government of Canada, the Canada Council for the Arts, the Ontario Arts Council, and by the University of Ottawa.

ONTARIO ARTS COUNCIL
CONSEIL DES ARTS DE L'ONTARIO
an Ontario government agency
un organisme du gouvernement de l'Ontario

Ontario

Canada Council   Conseil des arts
for the Arts   du Canada

Canadä

Table of Contents

CHAPTER 1

Decriminalizing Simple Possession of all Drugs:
Developing Harm Reduction Strategies

CHAPTER 2

Protecting Health, Respecting Rights:
Decriminalizing Drug Possession as a Constitutional Imperative

CHAPTER 3

Long Overdue and Still Deficient: The Correctional Service
of Canada's Prison Needle Exchange Program

CHAPTER 4

Ontario's Consumption and Treatment Services Model:
Problematizing Conservative Safe-Consumption Site Policy

List of Figures

List of Tables

Introduction

This edited collection arose from a two-day conference exploring the contemporary debate around harm reduction approaches held in November 2020. The conference was organized by the Ottawa Hub for Harm Reduction in collaboration with the Centre for Health Law, Policy and Ethics and the Faculty of Law at the University of Ottawa. The Ottawa Hub for Harm Reduction serves as a multidisciplinary forum for scholars and community organizations who work on innovative harm reduction strategies.

The focus of the conference, and this book, is on three substances: opioids, tobacco, and cannabis. Harm reduction has been an element of the legal and policy response to all three but has manifested in very different ways. In regard to opioids, harm reductionists emphasize safe-consumption sites and anti-overdose drugs such as naloxone. For cannabis, the legalization and regulation of a product formerly subject to criminal sanction offers a powerful harm reduction case study of the merits and pitfalls of Canada's pioneering approach. Harm reduction is also at the centre of a key debate regarding the use of tobacco, insofar as how to address new technology, such as e-cigarettes, that offer smokers a less harmful alternative but may also create new issues, such as how to address health concerns arising from their uptake by young people without discouraging their harm reduction potential.

The conference and this volume bring together established and emerging scholars from multiple disciplines, frontline organizations working in the area of harm reduction, and people with experience of substance use and harm reduction. These chapters reflect the shared knowledge from different disciplines and best practices from the harm reduction responses from Canada and elsewhere. Developing a shared understanding of harm reduction and, in turn, a deeper appreciation of how harm reduction can be approached in different ways, will ultimately serve to create a stronger foundation for effective policies and laws. This book reflects the concerns that arose at the time of the conference, capturing the key issues and discussions prevalent then. While they have been somewhat updated, they are not comprehensive to the current date but still reflect ongoing issues in the field of harm reduction.

Part I, "Illicit Drugs," focuses on illicit substances and the overdose crisis in Canada. Overdose deaths and harms have been driven by a toxic drug supply, with high levels of fentanyl and analogue substances.[1] The number of overdose deaths has risen substantially and represents one of Canada's most serious public health crises. The first two chapters explore the harms arising from the use of criminal law to prohibit drug possession as well as different strategies to reduce harms related to illicit substances and various law reform options to reduce these harms. They furthermore consider the criminalization of drug possession. In recent years, there have been many calls for governments to decriminalize drug possession for personal use. In Chapter 1, Line Beauchesne considers whether the criminalization of drug possession for personal use violates the constitutional rights of people who use drugs (PWUD) under the *Canadian Charter of Rights and Freedoms*.[2] Her detailed analysis leads her to conclude that prohibiting drug possession for personal use violates section 7 of the Charter. In Chapter 2, Martha Jackman surveys how various countries have decriminalized simple drug possession and examines whether these reforms have reduced criminal proceedings against users and their impact on PWUD. Her study reveals a number of shortcomings associated with the decriminalization model in certain countries, and offers recommendations to ensure that decriminalization of personal possession meets the needs of PWUD. Since the conference in 2020, there have been a number of important developments to address the worsening toxic drug crisis. Most notable was the government of British Columbia's request to Health Canada, on 1 November 2021, for an exemption under section 56(1) of the *Controlled Drugs and Substances Act* to decriminalize PWUD. Health Canada granted the exemption, which authorizes possession of small amounts of certain illicit drugs for personal use and which took effect on 31 January 2023. However, on 26 April 2024, the Province of British Columbia announced that it would ask the federal government to roll back the scope of the exemption. In response, the federal government on 7 May 2024, exempted public spaces from the decriminalization exemption. The spaces where the exemption continues to apply includes private residences, addictions health care facilities, places where people are sheltering lawfully as well as overdose prevention and drug checking sites.

The last two chapters in Part I describe and evaluate two harm reduction strategies in: prison needle exchange programs and safe-consumption sites in prisons. Sandra Ka Hon Chu and Richard Elliott examine the Correctional Service of Canada's prison needle exchange program, an important harm reduction measure that seeks to prevent HIV and HCV transmission in prisons.[3] The authors explore the constitutional challenge brought by former prisoner Steven Simons, the HIV Legal Network, and other organizations which argued that the prohibitions against sterile injection equipment violate prisoners' section 7 and 15 Charter rights. Although the Supreme Court case prompted the correctional service to implement their needle exchange program, the court's decision did not address whether prisoners have a basic constitutional right to sterile injection equipment.[4] The authors conclude that the court's failure to address this issue, together with ongoing opposition to the program by correctional officers and the official opposition, leaves the needle exchange program vulnerable to cancellation.

In Chapter 4, Stephanie Arlt examines Ontario's consumption and treatment services and the underlying discursive assumptions that drive the program. The author's analysis reveals that the program is problematic because it reflects a centre-right political understanding of the overdose crisis as a result of addiction and emphasizes abstinence-based treatment, while failing to acknowledge the unpredictable drug supply and the social determinants of health as contributing factors to the crisis.

Part II considers the challenges and opportunities for harm reduction with cannabis. In October 2018, the Cannabis Act came into effect in Canada.[5] The act established a regulatory framework, legalizing the production, sale, and distribution of cannabis for recreational use. Among the objectives of the Cannabis Act are the protection of public health and the minimization of harms related to illicit cannabis use. Some have questioned whether the act and other laws governing cannabis use have, in fact, minimized harm. In Chapter 5, Joao Velloso and Véronique Fortin examine the impact of the federal legal framework which creates two categories of cannabis: licit and illicit. Their analysis reveals that the Cannabis Act resulted in more laws, more regulations, and more punitive governance. Decriminalization did not result in the end of punitiveness and the prohibitionist approach, which is not always in tune with harm reduction principles.

In Chapter 6, Stephanie Lake and Margot Young examine an emerging concern regarding unequal access to legal cannabis for communities who have historically faced unrelenting criminalization and marginalization related to drug use. Their analysis, grounded in field work conducted by Professor Lake, reveals that cannabis is commonly used to address a range of harm reduction and therapeutic needs for PWUD, and yet the new legalization regime threatens enhanced criminalization of cannabis use for this population. As such, the authors recommend that amending the current laws to allow for equitable access to cannabis for marginalized communities would be of great benefit.

In Chapter 7, Ryan Pusiak examines the various facets of the regulated cannabis industry: from pharmacology to the legal and policy frameworks that govern cannabis in Canada. His analysis reveals important discrepancies and gaps in the current framework and offers a series of recommendations to add these concerns. These recommendations include establishing a defined standard dose of cannabis, creating a validated cannabis-testing methodology, and requiring compositional standards for cannabis products to ensure consumers are well informed.

Part III explores harm reduction and tobacco. Canada's federal government has a long history of regulating tobacco products to reduce the risks associated with smoking.[6] In May 2018, the federal Tobacco and Vaping Products Act, which regulates the manufacture, sale, labelling, and promotion of tobacco products and vaping products sold in Canada, came into force.[7] E-cigarettes and vaping are considered important tools of smoking cessation but there have been concerns about use by non-smokers. In Chapter 8, Marewa Glover adopts a critical Indigenous perspective to explore the potential perverse effects of certain tobacco-control interventions. She demonstrates that such interventions can result in unintended negative economic and social effects for Indigenous Peoples, which, in turn, contravenes the guidelines contained in the United Nations Declaration on the Rights of Indigenous Peoples.[8] She concludes by offering a set of recommendations to reduce tobacco-related harms, which are consistent with the UN resolution.

In Chapter 9, Sam Halabi examines recent tobacco-control legislation in Canada and the United States that establishes regulatory mechanisms for tobacco manufacturers to submit for promotion of non-cigarette tobacco products, which are intended to reduce harm relative to cigarette use. The chapter identifies the strengths and weaknesses of the laws and regulatory review mechanisms, and recommends a series of steps to adopt to ensure that these regimes protect and promote individual and public health.

Finally, in Chapter 10, Alex Clarke offers a personal perspective regarding vaping and his advocacy work as the CEO of the Consumer Advocates for Smoke-free Alternatives Association. The chapter offers valuable insights from a person with lived experience on the role of vaping as a harm reduction tool and the impact of legal regulation on access to harm reduction measures.

References

Legislation

Canadian Charter of Rights and Freedoms, Part 1 of the *Constitution Act, 1982*, being Schedule B to the Canada Act 1982 (UK), 1982, c 11.
Cannabis Act, SC 2018, c 16.
Tobacco and Vaping Products Act, SC 1997, c 13.

Jurisprudence

Simons v Minister of Public Safety, 2020 ONSC 1431.

Publications

Correction Service Canada, News Release "Correctional Service Canada Announces a Prison Needle Exchange Program" (14 May 2018), online: www.newswire.ca/news-releases/correctional-service-canada-announces-a-prison-needle-exchange-program-682556901.html.
Government of Canada, *Opioid- and Stimulant-related Harms in Canada* (Ottawa: Public Health Agency of Canada, last updated 28 June 2024), online: health-infobase.canada.ca/substance-related-harms/opioids-stimulants.
United Nations Declaration on the Rights of Indigenous Peoples, UNGA, 61 Sess, UN Doc A/Res/61/295 (2007) GA Res 61/295 online: www.un.org/development/desa/indigenouspeoples/wpcontent/uploads/sites/19/2018/11/UNDRIP_E_web.pdf

Notes

1   Government of Canada, *Opioid- and Stimulant-related Harms in Canada* (Ottawa: Public Health Agency of Canada, last updated 28 June 2024), online: health-infobase.canada.ca/substance-related-harms/opioids-stimulants/.

2   *Canadian Charter of Rights and Freedoms*, Part 1 of the *Constitution Act, 1982*, being Schedule B to the Canada Act 1982 (UK), 1982, c 11.

3   Correction Service Canada, "Correctional Service Canada Announces a Prison Needle Exchange Program" (14 May 2018), online: www.newswire.ca/news-releases/correctional-service-canada-announces-a-prison-needle-exchange-program-682556901.html.

4   *Simons v Minister of Public Safety*, 2020 ONSC 1431.

5   *Cannabis Act*, SC 2018, c 16.

6   The first federal Tobacco Act was enacted in 1997: *Tobacco Act*, SC 1997, c 13.

7   *Tobacco and Vaping Products Act*, SC 1997, c 13. This Act was enacted in response to House of Commons, Standing Committee on Health, Vaping: *Toward a Regulatory Framework for E-cigarettes*, 41-2, No 9 (10 March 15) (Chair: Ben Lobb), online: www.ourcommons.ca/DocumentViewer/en/41-2/HESA/report-9.

8   *United Nations Declaration on the Rights of Indigenous Peoples*, UNGA, 61 Sess, UN Doc A/Res/61/295 (2007) GA Res 61/295 online: www.un.org/development/desa/indigenouspeoples/wpcontent/uploads/sites/19/2018/11/UNDRIP_E_web.pdf

CHAPTER 1

Decriminalizing Simple Possession of all Drugs

Developing Harm Reduction Strategies

Line Beauchesne

International drug-control conventions allow signatory countries to treat drug possession for personal use (i.e., not for the purpose of trafficking) as a minor offence and to refer problem drug users to treatment facilities instead of subjecting them to penal sanctions.[1]

Decriminalization of drug possession can be a *de jure* decriminalization, where the offence is removed from the criminal code and put under another type of jurisdiction, generally imposing non-penal sanctions, such as community work, fines, mandatory drug-education programs, which is the approach taken by most countries that have instituted decriminalization. Or, it can be a *de facto* decriminalisation, meaning that while possession remains a criminal offence, no criminal sanction is imposed, as is the case in the Netherlands.

This chapter focuses on the question of whether decriminalizing all drug possession, as some countries have done, has reduced criminal proceedings against users and improved care for problem drug users considering the political, social, economic, legal, and judicial context of those countries. Our intent was also to identify the factors that enhance or reduce the possibilities of harm reduction strategies within the framework of decriminalization.

We start by laying out the theoretical grounds of this legal framework, then address the methodological criteria used to select the countries in our analysis. Second, we present our findings, which enable us to identify the elements required for drug-possession decriminalization to become a step toward better harm reduction strategies, with criminal law being a last resort.

Theoretical and Methodological Considerations

This chapter is written from a critical criminological perspective, in which problems relating to drug use are not denied but are addressed in a manner to prevent or treat them using tools other than criminal sanctions.[2] On drug issues, our perspective is also in line with the anti-prohibitionist trend and focuses on harm reduction.

The number of countries that decriminalized the personal possession of drugs varies depending on the criteria that inform the count: some scholars include countries in which only some regions have adopted the policy, or countries where the decriminalization of possession is for certain drugs, mainly cannabis, or countries where possession is a criminal offence but it is *possible* to avoid criminalization under certain conditions (e.g., diversion programs in Australia, in place since 1999).[3] For this chapter, we considered countries that have enacted a nationwide policy decriminalizing possession of all drugs, without condition. Some countries in this category were nevertheless excluded due to insufficient data, data that are key to understanding the influence of varying political, economic, social, legal, and judicial contexts. These excluded countries are Armenia, Chile, Croatia, Estonia, and Paraguay. In addition, Russia, which would otherwise qualify for inclusion, was excluded because decriminalization has been inconsistent and largely unrealized.[4]

Based on these considerations, the countries that were selected in this study are, in Europe, Italy, the Netherlands, Spain, Poland, the Czech Republic, Portugal, and Germany; and, in Latin America, Uruguay, Costa Rica, Peru, Colombia, Brazil, Ecuador, Argentina, and Mexico.

Findings

First Finding: Paradoxically, Decriminalization Can Lead to Criminalization of More Users

Most of the governments that decriminalized personal possession deemed it necessary, in parallel or shortly afterward, to increase penalties for drug possession for the purpose of trafficking. This was done largely to send a message to their domestic population, or to external authorities in the United States (especially in the case of Latin American countries) or the European Union, that decriminalization was not a soft-on-drugs policy. Exceptions to the increase in penalties are Portugal and Germany in Europe and Uruguay and Costa Rica in Latin America.

In addition, in the spirit of not giving the impression of being lax on drugs, personal-use amounts are often specified and very small. Consequently, some users end up in the criminal justice system with even heavier sentences in cases where penalties for possession deemed for the purpose of trafficking were increased via decriminalization. This paradoxical situation is particularly acute in Latin America, due to three factors.

The first is that, to comply with international drug-control conventions signed in the 1960s, the countries concerned tightened sanctions under pressure over the years from a number of authoritarian regimes, as well as from the US government. Pressure from the United Sates resulted in a certification process that conditioned the provision of economic assistance and trade benefits on a tougher response to drugs as evidence that Latin American governments were effectively engaged in the so-called war on drugs:

> In Latin America—where the cocaine and some of the heroin and cannabis consumed in the United States originates—Washington has used its political influence and aid and trade policies to ensure collaboration with its so-called war on drugs. By the late 1980s, the U.S. government was demanding implementation of harsh drug control legislation that included steep sentences and mandatory minimums—and much of the legislation that appeared in fact went beyond the requirements of the UN Conventions. In some cases, such as Law 1008 in Bolivia, the U.S. government was even drafting the proposed laws. By the 1990s, the United States was routinely using arrest and seizure statistics to evaluate levels of Latin American drug-control cooperation. Washington has thus exported its model of harsh drug laws and mandatory minimum sentencing across the region.[5]

For this reason, in most countries where possession is decriminalized, individuals accused of drug offences are not eligible for any sanction other than prison sentences, and they are often held in pretrial custody once charges are laid:

In five of the eight countries studied—Bolivia, Brazil, Ecuador, Mexico and Peru—pre-trial detention is mandatory in drug offences, independent of whether the offences in question are minor or major. Drug offences are classified along with murder, rape, and kidnapping as serious crimes, independent of the degree of one's involvement.[6]

This results in overcrowded prisons in which most detainees, many of whom are simply drug users, are kept in pre-trial custody. Furthermore, to demonstrate greater forcefulness in the US-led war on drugs, a parallel penal justice system developed for drug offences, thus opening the door to violations of human rights. For example, *habeas corpus* has been suspended in several countries in cases of drug-related offences, resulting in the imprisonment of individuals unaware of the charges or cases against them. In addition, in some countries there is no appeal process for drug-related offences. Several countries also apply minimum sentences that preclude consideration of the circumstances of the offence.

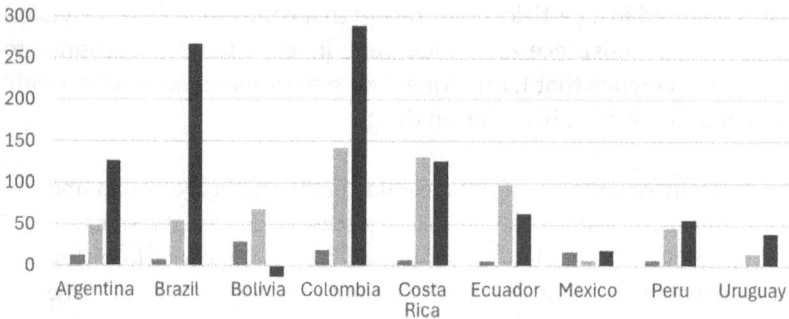

Column 1: Percentage increase in the general population
Column 2: Percentage increase in prison population
Column 3: Percentage increase in the prison population incarcerated for drug offences

FIGURE 1.1. Percentage increase in demography, prison population and prison population incarcerated for drug offences in nine Latin American countries 2001-2014. *Source*: Prepared by CEDD based on World Bank data.

The second factor in Latin America is corruption, which provides an extrajudicial way out of prison for drug lords. Further, when major traffickers do end up in prison, it boosts the illegal market because prisons are hot spots for recruitment into the drug trade. This is partly because many detainees, often drug users, lose everything as a result of their imprisonment and have to find new ways to make money, sometimes illicitly.

The third factor is that in most Latin American countries, where police and other penal institutions are often biased in their practices, the definition of personal possession and possession for the purpose of trafficking is left to the police and courts; it is not codified. Consequently, fundamental human rights of drug users are violated, as they are subjected to extortion, physical abuse, and arbitrary detention.[7]

Second Finding: "Law and Order" Government and Decriminalization

Decriminalization policies remain fragile in a prohibitionist-policy context. For example, reports of drug-related scandals in the media can create public pressure for harsher sentences. "Law and order" governments tend to be especially responsive to such public pressure. As a result, decriminalization policies can quickly be changed or diluted, sometimes to the point of being meaningless.

In Italy, where decriminalization was implemented in 1975, there was an initial attempt to avoid user imprisonment as much as possible. Personal possession referred to two-to-three times the daily dose. Subsequently, the legislation was amended to drop minor charges related to problem drug use for those who agreed to treatment. However, treatment was often slow in coming. The public disorder that occurred as a result of the presence of untreated users prompted Italian Socialist Party leader Bettino Craxi to call for a return to the criminalization of personal possession, which was reinstated in 1990. In 1993, following a referendum, the government reverted to a policy of decriminalization and stepped up care services.[8] In 2006, Silvio Berlusconi, president of the Council of Ministers (the Italian cabinet), who was opposed to decriminalization, reduced the maximum substance amount allowed for private use. It was left up to the police to decide, on a case-by-case basis, whether to invoke an administrative sanction or to refer the offender to the criminal justice system. In addition, drug users who refused treatment were penalized. Moreover, measures became stricter for possession of cannabis and cannabis cultivation for personal use. Consequently, whether drug users incurred penal sanctions or not became a result of factors such as the extent of police activity in the various regions, users' attitudes and degree of "repentance," users' nationality (foreigners being arrested more often than Italians), and users' socio-economic status, with poorer individuals being more likely to be arrested. Between 2006 and 2014, criminal sanctions against users were on the rise, even for cannabis, for which the Berlusconi government had tripled the sentence. In February 2014, the Italian Constitutional Court repealed the 2006 legislation on the basis that the penalty must correspond to the gravity of the offence, without challenging the right of the police to determine the gravity.[9]

In Spain, possession was decriminalized in 1983. On 26 March 2015, the Citizen Safety Act was changed to limit demonstrations in public squares. The attempt to regain governmental control of public squares also resulted in lower tolerance for the presence of undocumented migrants, sex workers, and drug users. The negative reaction to the development of cannabis social clubs, non-profit co-operatives, whose existence was permitted by regional governments and cities but opposed by the conservative government, contributed to the change in attitudes about drug possession.[10] As a result, for users, the possibility of enrolling in a rehabilitation program instead of receiving fines for personal possession was taken away, and fines for use and personal possession increased considerably for people arrested in public (often on their way back from the aforementioned clubs, carrying cannabis).

The lack of clarity surrounding decriminalization holds true even for the Netherlands, which decriminalized possession in 1976. In the 1990s, European agreements on police and judicial co-operation brought about a transfer of the drug-policy budget from the Dutch Ministry of Health to the Ministry Justice. This led to tougher penalties for drug-related offences, increasingly resembling the sanctions implemented in neighbouring countries.[11] In addition, with the arrival of Mark Rutte's centre-right government in 2010, police enforcement of drug users who commit offences such as public disorder or exceeding the number of authorized cannabis plants, increased considerably. In addition, enforcement related to addicts involved in criminal activity also increased. They are offered treatment, asylum, and specialized residential facilities, and if these fail to produce results, they can be subjected to compulsory medical treatment under the authority of the judiciary.

Poland decriminalized personal possession in 1985. Under the presidency of Aleksander Kwaśniewski, the government, to fulfill an election promise, reversed thev decriminalization of personal possession, a law that was considered too permissive and was invoked to explain the rise of violence linked to illegal drugs. First, in 1988, quantities defining personal possession were drastically reduced, and, in 2000, decriminalization was abolished. The effects of these changes in the law were seismic: over the course of the year 2000, some two thousand people were charged for personal possession; in 2006, more than thirty thousand were charged.[12]

After the fall of the Communist regime, in 1989, several amendments were subsequently made to the Criminal Code of the Czech Republic, including the decriminalization of drug possession for personal use. However, an increase in drug use during the 1990s generated much debate, with many demanding a return to the criminalization of personal possession to dissuade people from using illegal drugs. This led, in 1998, to a nebulous amendment in the Criminal Code that reintroduced penalties for possession. The law creates criminal sanctions only for those whose possession is "greater than small. [...] No further criteria were provided for determining quantity thus leaving interpretation to judicial practice."[13] The law changed nothing in terms of consumption, generated no public health benefits, and its application has proved extremely costly for the country.[14] Moreover, the lack of definition of what constitutes a "greater than small" amount has been the subject of much controversy. Finally, that the sentences of people charged with more than personal possession were the same, regardless of the amount of drugs they carried, was also questioned. As a result, to clarify the matter, in 2001 the Czech government asked the ministries of justice and health to classify drugs according to their social and health risk. In 2009, the law was rewritten yet again in response to these concerns, and a new one came into force in January 2010. Penalties for cannabis became less than other drugs if the quantity possessed was "greater than small." To end the controversy about what constitutes possession, in 2009 the government issued Regulation 467 to clarify what "small" means: 2 g of methamphetamine, 1.5 g of heroin, 1 g of cocaine, 4 tablets of ecstasy, 0.4 g of MDMA, 15 g of dried cannabis, 5 g of hashish, 40 g of hallucinogenic whole mushrooms, and 5 tablets, blotters, or microdots of LSD. Growing a cannabis plant is not considered a criminal offence, but growing more than five plants is punishable by a fine of up to €600. In practice, however, if this maximum of five plants is adhered to by growers, a policy of tolerance prevails.[15] This decriminalization, in order not to appear soft, instituted minimum prison sentences for drug trafficking, including the trafficking of cannabis, which has resulted in more people in the penal system.[16] In July 2013, in a case that challenged regulation 467, the Czech Constitutional Court ruled in favour of the plaintiff and annulled the regulation, as only criminal law, and not a government regulation, can give rise to criminal sanctions. In March 2014, in order to standardize the practice of the courts, the Czech Supreme Court unanimously adopted the definition of a "greater than small" quantity, which should generally be understood as a quantity that, depending on the health risks of the drug concerned, is several times higher than the daily dose of a typical user. In addition, in assessing cases, courts must consider whether the individual is a first- or long-time user, as well as other factors that may pose a threat to public health. As an appendix to this decision, the Supreme Court reintroduced the quantities as specified in regulation 467 as a guide for judges, lowering even the quantity considered minimal for methamphetamines to 1.5 g and to 10 g for dried cannabis. The latter is currently being challenged in the courts as the plaintiffs wish to return to the measure of five cannabis plants for personal cultivation.[17]

This saga bears witness to the lack of consensus on the issue of decriminalizing simple possession, which has resulted in a narrow margin of manoeuvre to avoid criminal sanction. In fact, experts consulted by the government were divided into two groups: those who believed that taking recreational drugs was problematic per se, and those who believed that experimenting with common recreational drugs was not unusual:

> While both paradigms are present in the declarations as well as practices of contemporary drug policy in many countries, the former enjoys the institutional advantage of the UN drug control regime, with most resources globally devoted to criminal prohibition of the production, supply and possession of scheduled substances.[18]

This echoes what has happened in several European countries during parliamentary debates on decriminalization.

Third Finding: Perpetuation of Stigma against Drug Users

To send the message that drug use remained socially unacceptable, most countries that had decriminalized drugs nevertheless adopted administrative sanctions—fines, community service—to replace penal sanctions against drug users. This perpetuates the stigma placed on drug users, and their social and economic vulnerability, partly because fines are difficult to pay for many such individuals, who are then more likely to join criminal networks.[19]

Fourth Finding: Harm Reduction Strategies Depend on Governmental Will

Many researchers and stakeholders who support the implementation of harm reduction strategies for drug users view the decriminalization of drug possession as a positive step. This position is held by several UN institutions, such as the World Health Organization (WHO), the Joint United Nations Programme on HIV/AIDS (UNAIDS), and the Office of the United Nations High Commissioner for Human Rights (OHCHR). However, in countries that have decriminalized possession, decriminalization did not automatically lead to the implementation of harm reduction strategies or to increased access to care. There are several reasons for this. First, governments must have the economic capacity to adequately fund these strategies, which is problematic in many Latin American countries. Further, governments must also be willing to invest in a range of effective harm reduction strategies and deal with the problem of unequal access to care. Even in Europe, disparities exist in the implementation of harm reduction strategies and access to care both among and within countries. In addition, investment in any given country often fluctuates over time and is sometimes considerably diminished with the election of centre-right governments. This means that the implementation of harm reduction strategies and the increase in access to care are not automatic results of the decriminalization of possession. It would be more accurate to say that when governments choose to make the necessary investment, decriminalization of possession makes it easier to implement harm reduction strategies and to improve access to care for problematic users.

The Portuguese Exception

Regarding both improved care and reduced enforcement, Portugal is an exception. This can be explained partly by that, from the outset, the debate on decriminalizing personal possession and expanding harm reduction strategies for problematic drug users involved actors of three key sectors: justice, health care, and policy. This led to consensus in the National Strategy for the Fight Against Drugs, adopted in 1999, and funding for implementation across the country. Furthermore, decriminalization in Portugal was not offset by a corresponding toughening of sanctions for other drug offences. On the contrary, the legislation takes into consideration the individual's involvement in the drug market, which contributes to lighter penal sanctions for smaller players in the drug market.[20] However, in the context of prohibition, the consequence was to force arrested drug users to appear before the Comissões para a Dissuasão da Toxicodependência (CDT), Portugal's commission for the dissuasion of drug abuse, which can apply administrative sanctions:

> The CDTs are regional panels made up of three people, including lawyers, social workers and medical professionals. Alleged offenders are referred by the police to the CDTs, who then discuss with the offender the motivations for and circumstances surrounding their offence and are able to provide a range of sanctions, including community service, fines, suspensions on professional licences and bans on attending designated places. However, their primary aim is to dissuade drug use and to encourage dependent drug users into treatment. Towards this end, they determine whether individuals are dependent or not. For dependent users, they can recommend that a person enters a treatment or education programme instead of receiving a sanction. For non-dependent users, they can order a provisional suspension of proceedings, attendance at a police station, psychological or educational service, or impose a fine. The panel members of the CDTs are supported by staff employed by the Instituto da Droga e da Toxicodependência (IDT, the Institute for Drugs and Drug Addiction), the central government agency on drugs.[21]

To date, the data have shown that prevention and help are the preferred approach, and sanctions are rarely applied during follow-up with users.[22]

Discussion

Analysis of the situation in countries that decriminalized drug possession shows that this policy remains fragile against the backdrop of prohibition.

Although some Latin American countries have decriminalized personal possession of all drugs, or consider doing so, we should not expect much in terms of fewer users in the penal system or more harm reduction strategies. What is at stake is the vulnerability of Latin American countries in international trade agreements and development aid, which requires they comply with international conventions and demonstrate forcefulness in enforcement. Added to this are police, judicial, and political corruption, as well as underdevelopment, which limit the capacity of these countries to provide care and harm reduction strategies for problem drug users.

However, US pressure on Latin American countries on this front has eased in recent years. It is important that decriminalization goes hand in hand with putting an end to parallel justice systems with drug offences. This means making available avenues other than imprisonment, ensuring that sentences are proportional to the offence, abolishing mandatory minimum sentencing, ending automatic pretrial detention, allowing sentences and charges to be appealed, and considering blanket amnesty or pardons for all individuals detained for drug use or possession of small amounts. This would reduce overcrowding in jails and allow decriminalization of personal possession to genuinely translate into fewer harsh enforcement measures and, eventually, more effective harm reduction strategies.

As far as European countries are concerned, our study shows that because users continue to be perceived negatively, when high-profile drug scandals are exploited politically or centre-right governments come to power, the amounts constituting possession are lowered and public disorder and minor offences associated with drug use are penalized more severely. This leads to renewed criminalization of drug users, sometimes more severely than prior to decriminalization. Though Portugal is an exception, this comes at the expense of normalizing use, even for non-problem drug users.

In view of the results in countries where personal possession of all drugs has been decriminalized, certain conditions appear to be necessary to ensure that this legal avenue becomes a positive step toward less criminalization and more care and harm reduction strategies for problem drug users:

1. In legislation, personal possession must be defined as possession of drugs for a purpose other than trafficking as a lucrative activity, rather than according to an arbitrarily set amount that does not allow for a flexible definition of personal use (e.g., an individual might store a larger amount of drugs at home for use over time). This would prevent amendments to lower the amount of a drug that defines

possession in the law as a result of conservative shifts in the political landscape or as a political response to public concerns induced by high-profile drug scandals.

2. On the ground, police should be given clear guidelines that would enable them to make decisions to help users avoid criminal proceedings, in particular pre-trial detention, before deciding whether to classify a case as personal possession. It is important to spare users criminal proceedings, and especially a criminal record, considering the negative consequences.

3. No alternative sanctions should be applied (fines, community service, etc.) for personal possession because penalties, whether criminal or administrative, maintain the stigma on drug users and diminish decriminalization.

4. If users experience problems, they must not be subjected to forced treatment as a substitute for sanctions because they may not be ready for treatment, which is then likely to be ineffective, or they may submit to treatment only to avoid sanctions, not because they need it. It is better to provide them with support that would help them reduce the risk of drug-related harm.

5. In cases outside the scope of personal possession, criminal measures for possession for the purpose of trafficking must distinguish between degrees of participation in the market and consider whether violence was committed. This is necessary to maintain the proportionality between sanction and offence; also, we must take into account problem drug users, for whom participation in the market may result from desperation to get money in order to buy drugs:

> [D]ecriminalization when implemented effectively does appear to direct more people who use drugs problematically into treatment, reduce criminal justice costs, improve public health outcomes, and shield many drug users from the devastating impact of a criminal conviction. Decriminalization when coupled with investment in harm reduction, and health

and social services, can have an extremely positive effect on both individuals who use drugs and society as a whole.[23]

Conclusion

Our analysis of decriminalizing personal possession of all drugs shows that, as long as international drug-control conventions maintain prohibition and perpetuate the stigmatization of illicit drug users, political decisions aimed at reducing the criminalization of users and increasing harm reduction strategies will remain fragile and subject to political, social, and economic hazards and vagaries. To improve this state of affairs, governments should (i) define personal possession such that all users can avoid the penal justice system, (ii) avoid any judicial procedures for drug use, and (iii) make the necessary investment in care for problematic drug users.

References

Agra, Cândido da, "Requiem pour la guerre à la drogue : L'expérimentation portugaise de décriminalisation" (2009) 33:1 Déviance et Société 27.

Belackova, Vendula et al, "Assessing the Concordance between Illicit Drug Laws on the Books and Drug Law Enforcement: Comparison of Three States on the Continuum from 'Decriminalised' to 'Punitive'" (2017) 41 Intl J Drug Policy 148.

Belackova, Vendula et al, "'Should I Buy or Should I Grow?' How Drug Policy Institutions and Drug Market Transaction Costs Shape the Decision to Self-supply with Cannabis in the Netherlands and the Czech Republic" (2015) 26:3 Intl J Drug Policy 296.

Campedelli, Massimo & Dominique Férault, "Entre répression, indifférence et réduction des risques" (1996) 62:1 Communications 67.

Cesoni, Maria Luisa, "Usage de stupéfiants : les variations de la politique criminelle italienne" (1999) 23:2 Déviance et Société 221.

Chaparro, Sergio, Catalina Pérez Correa & Coletta Youngers, *Irrational Punishment: Drug Laws and Incarceration in Latin America* (Mexico: Colectivo de Estudios Drogas y Derecho, 2017).

Chatwin, Caroline, "UNGASS 2016: Insights from Europe on the Development of Global Cannabis Policy and the Need for Reform of the Global Drug Policy Regime" (2017) 49 Intl J Drug Policy 80.

Correa, Catalina Pérez, Rodrigo Uprimny & Sergio Chaparro, "Regulation of Possession and the Criminalization of Drug Users in Latin America" in

John Collin, ed, *After the Drug Wars: Report of the LSE Expert Group on the Economics of Drug Policy* (London, UK: London School of Economics, 2016) 30.

Dupras, Daniel, *Canada's International Obligations under the Leading International Conventions on the Control of Narcotic Drugs* (Ottawa: Library of Parliament, 1998).

Eastwood, Niamh, Edward Fox & Ari Rosmarin, *A Quiet Revolution: Drug Decriminalization across the Globe* (London, UK: Release, March 2016), online: www.release.org.uk/sites/default/files/pdf/publications/A%20Quiet%20Revolution%20-%20Decriminalisation%20Across%20the%20Globe.pdf.

Global Commission on Drug Policy, *Advancing Drug Policy Reform: A New Approach to Decriminalization* (Geneva, Switzerland: Global Commission on Drug Policy, 2016), online: www.globalcommissionondrugs.org/wp-content/uploads/2016/11/GCDP-Report-2016-ENGLISH.pdf.

Gonçalves, Ricardo, Ana Lourenço, and Sofia Nogueira da Silva, "A Social Cost Perspective in the Wake of the Portuguese Strategy for the Fight Against Drugs" (2015) 26:2 Intl J Drug Policy 199. Hughes, Caitlin, "Portuguese Drug Policy" in Renaud Colson & Henri Bergeron, eds, *European Drug Policies: The Ways of Reform* (London, UK: Routledge, 2017).

Hugues, Caitlin Elizabeth & Alex Stevens, "What Can We Learn from the Portuguese Decriminalization of Illicit Drugs?" (2010) 50:6 British J Criminology 999.

——, "A Resounding Success or a Disastrous Failure: Re-examining the Interpretation of Evidence on the Portuguese Decriminalization of Illicit Drugs" (2012) 31:1 Drug & Alcohol Rev 101.

Hulsman, LHC & Jacqueline Bernat de Célis, *Peines perdues : le système pénal en question* (Paris, France: Centurion, 1982).

Krajewski, Krzysztof, "How Flexible Are the United Nations Drug Conventions?" (1999) 10:3 Intl J Drug Policy 329.

Laqueur, Hannah, "Uses and Abuses of Drug Decriminalization in Portugal" (2015) 40:3 L & Soc Inquiry 746.

Malinowska-Sempruch, Kasia, "Shaping Drug Policy in Poland" (2016) 31 Intl J Drug Policy 32.

Marks, Amber, "The Legal and Socio-political Landscape for Cannabis Social Clubs in Spain" (2015) Observatorio Civil De Drogas.

Martineau, Hélène & Émilie Gomart, *Politiques et expérimentations sur les drogues aux Pays-Bas* Report (Paris, France: Observatoire français des drogues et des toxicomanies, 2000).

Metaal, Pien & Coletta Youngers, *Systems Overload—Drug Laws and Prisons in Latin America* (Washington, DC: WOLA, 2011).

Mravcik, Viktor, "(De) Criminalisation of Possession of Drugs for Personal Use—A View from the Czech Republic" (2015) 26:7 Intl J Drug Policy 705.

Nekola, Martin & Jan Moravek, "Regulating New Psychoactive Substances in the Czech Republic: Policy Analysis under Urgency" (2015) 17:3 J Comparative Policy Analysis: Research and Practice 232.

Nougier, Marie, "The Portuguese Model for Decriminalizing Drug Use" in WOLA, ed, *Gender and Drug Policy: Exploring Global Innovative Approaches to Drug Policy and Incarceration* (Washington, DC: WOLA, 2017), online www.wola.org/wp-content/uploads/2017/05/DONE-12-Portuguese-decriminalisation_ENGFINAL.pdf.

Pisapia, G, "La législation italienne en matière de stupéfiants" in Maria Luisa Cesoni, ed, *Usages de stupéfiants : politiques européennes* (Geneva, Switzerland: Georg Editeur, 1996) 113.

Summers, Diana L & Emil W Plywaczewski, "The Polish Context: Examining Issues of Police Reform, Drug Use and Drug Trafficking in a Transitioning Democracy" (2012) 35:2 Policing: an Intl J of Police Strategies & Management 231.

Zuffa, Grazia, "Italian Drug Policy" in Renaud Colson & Henri Bergeron, eds, *European Drug Policies: The Ways of Reform* (London, UK: Routledge, 2017) 114.

Notes

1   See Daniel Dupras, *Canada's International Obligations under the Leading International Conventions on the Control of Narcotic Drugs*, (Ottawa: Library of Parliament, 1998); see also Krzysztof Krajewski, "How Flexible Are the United Nations Drug Conventions?" (1999) 10:3 Intl J Drug Policy 329.

2   See LHC Hulsman & Jacqueline Bernat de Célis, *Peines perdues : le système pénal en question*, (Paris, France: Centurion, 1982).

3   See Niamh Eastwood, Edward Fox & Ari Rosmarin, *A Quiet Revolution: Drug Decriminalization across the Globe* (London, UK: Release, March 2016), online: www.release.org.uk/sites/default/files/pdf/publications/A%20Quiet%20Revolution%20-%20Decriminalisation%20Across%20the%20Globe.pdf.

4   *Ibid.*

5   See Pien Metaal & Coletta Youngers, *Systems Overload—Drug Laws and Prisons in Latin America* (Washington, DC: WOLA, 2011) at 9.

6   *Ibid* at 6.

7   See Catalina Pérez Correa, Rodrigo Uprimny & Sergio Chaparro, "Regulation of Possession and the Criminalization of Drug Users in Latin America" in John Collin, ed, *After the Drug Wars: Report of the LSE Expert Group on the Economics of Drug Policy* (London, UK: London School of Economics, 2016) 30; see also: Chaparro, Sergio, Catalina Pérez Correa & Coletta Youngers, *Irrational Punishment: Drug Laws and Incarceration in Latin America* (Mexico: Colectivo de Estudios Drogas y Derecho, 2017) at 23.

8   See Massimo Campedelli & Dominique Férault, "Entre répression, indifférence et réduction des risques" (1996) 62 Communications 67; see also Maria Luisa Cesoni, "Usage de stupéfiants : les variations de la politique criminelle italienne" (1999) 23:2 Déviance et Société 221; see also G Pisapia, "La législation italienne en matière de stupéfiants" in Maria Luisa Cesoni, ed, *Usages de stupéfiants : politiques*

européennes (Geneva, Switzerland: Georg Editeur, 1996) 113; see also Grazia Zuffa, "Italian Drug Policy" in Renaud Colson & Henri Bergeron, eds, *European Drug Policies: The Ways of Reform* (London, UK: Routledge, 2017) 114.

9   See Zuffa, *supra* note 8.

10   See Amber Marks, "The Legal and Socio-political Landscape for Cannabis Social Clubs in Spain" (2015) Observatorio Civil De Drogas.

11   See Caroline Chatwin, "UNGASS 2016: Insights from Europe on the Development of Global Cannabis Policy and the Need for Reform of the Global Drug Policy Regime" (2017) 49 Intl J Drug Policy 80; see also Hélène Martineau & Émilie Gomart, *Politiques et expérimentations sur les drogues aux Pays-Bas* Report (Paris, France: Observatoire français des drogue et des toxicomanies, 2000).

12   See Kasia Malinowska-Sempruch, "Shaping Drug Policy in Poland" (2016) 31 Intl J Drug Policy 32; see also Diana L Summers & Emil W Plywaczewski, "The Polish Context. Examining Issues of Police Reform, Drug Use and Drug Trafficking in a Transitioning Democracy" (2012) 35:2 Policing: an Intl J of Police Strategies & Management 231.

13   See Viktor Mravcik, "(De) criminalisation of Possession of Drugs for Personal Use—A View from the Czech Republic" (2015) 26:7 Intl J Drug Policy 705.

14   *Ibid.*

15   See Vendula Belackova et al, "'Should I Buy or Should I Grow?' Hot Drug Policy Institutions and Drug Market Transaction Costs Shape the Decision to Self-supply with Cannabis in the Netherlands and the Czech Republic" (2015) 26:3 Intl J Drug Policy 296.

16   See Vendula Belackova et al, "Assessing the Concordance between Illicit Drug Laws on the Books and Drug Law Enforcement: Comparison of Three States on the Continuum from 'Decriminalised' to 'Punitive'" (2017) 41 Intl J Drug Policy 148.

17   See Mravcik, *supra* note 13.

18   See Martin Nekola & Jan Moravek, "Regulating New Psychoactive Substances in the Czech Republic: Policy Analysis under Urgency" (2015) 17:3 J Comparative Policy Analysis: Research and Practice 232.

19   See Global Commission on Drug Policy, *Advancing Drug Policy Reform: A New Approach to Decriminalization* (Geneva, Switzerland: Global Commission on Drug Policy, 2016), online: www.globalcommissionondrugs.org/wp-content/uploads/2016/11/GCDP-Report-2016-ENGLISH.pdf.

20   See Cândido da Agra, "Requiem pour la guerre à la drogue : L'expérimentation portugaise de décriminalisation" (2009) 33:1 Déviance et Société 27; see also Ricardo Gonçalves, Ana Lourenço & Sofia Nogueira da Silva, "A Social Cost Perspective in the Wake of the Portuguese Strategy for the Fight against Drugs" (2015) 26:2 Intl J Drug Policy 199; see also Caitlin Hughes, "Portuguese Drug Policy" in Renaud Colson & Henri Bergeron, eds, *European Drug Policies: The Ways of Reform* (London, UK: Routledge, 2017); see also Hannah Laqueur, "Uses and Abuses of Drug Decriminalization in Portugal" (2015) 40:3 L & Soc Inquiry 746.

21   See Caitlin Elizabeth Hugues & Alex Stevens, "A Resounding Success or a Disastrous Failure: Re-examining the Interpretation of Evidence on the Portuguese Decriminalization of Illicit Drugs" (2012) 31:1 Drug & Alcohol Rev 101.

22   *Ibid*; see also Hughes, "Portuguese Drug Policy," *supra* note 20; see also Caitlin Elizabeth Hugues & Alex Stevens, "What Can We Learn from the Portuguese Decriminalization of Illicit Drugs?" (2010) 50:6 British J Criminology 999; see also Marie Nougier, "The Portuguese Model for Decriminalizing Drug Use" in WOLA, ed, *Gender and Drug Policy: Exploring Global Innovative Approaches to Drug Policy and*

Incarceration (Washington, DC: WOLA, 2017), online: www.wola.org/wp-content/
uploads/2017/05/DONE-12-Portuguese-decriminalisation_ENGFINAL.pdf.
23   See Eastwood, *supra* note 3 at 7.

CHAPTER 2

Protecting Health, Respecting Rights

Decriminalizing Drug Possession as a Constitutional Imperative

Martha Jackman

This chapter is dedicated to my niece, Miranda Berglund, and to Finnley English. The author thanks Diana Majury, Sandra Ka Hon Chu, and Margot Young for their helpful comments and suggestions. Portions of this chapter previously appeared in the RSC Working Group on Harm Reduction Policy brief: Vanessa Gruben, Elaine, Hyska; Matthew Bonn; Chelsea Cox; Marilou Gagnon; Adrian Guta; Martha Jackman; Jason, Mercredi; Akia, Munga; Eugene, Oscapella; Carol Strike; Hakique, Virani, "Urgent and Long Overdue: Legal Reform and Drug Decriminalization in Canada" (2024) Facets https://doi.org/10.1139/facets-2022-0080

Well before COVID-19, an epidemic of overdose injuries and deaths was afflicting families and communities in every corner of Canada.[1] COVID-19 deepened this health and human-rights crisis:[2] "People are losing their children, siblings, spouses, parents, friends and co-workers. The impact of these losses is devastating for the individuals involved and for the community, not least because these deaths are preventable."[3] It has long been clear that the non-response by Canadian governments to drug use—namely, criminalization—is causing, rather than reducing, harm at both an individual and a societal level. Simply put, "[a]n overwhelming body of evidence demonstrates that the continued emphasis on drug prohibition—from policing to prosecution to prisons—is failing to achieve both the stated public health and public safety goals of prohibition, and resulting in costly damage to the public purse, to public health and to human rights in Canada."[4]

Numerous governmental and non-governmental organizations, health and human-rights experts, and advocates agree it is past time for Canada to abandon the failed "war on drugs."[5] The UN Committee on Economic, Social and Cultural Rights;[6] the UN Committee on the Elimination of Discrimination Against Women;[7] the Canadian Civil Society Working Group on UN Drug Policy;[8] the Canadian Mental Health Association;[9] the Canadian Public Health Association;[10] the Nurses and Nurse Practitioners of British Columbia and the Harm Reduction Nurses Association;[11] the chief public health officers of British Columbia, the Yukon, Quebec, Toronto, Vancouver, and Montreal;[12] the Canadian Association of Chiefs of Police;[13] and the House of Commons Standing Committee on Health,[14] among many others,[15] have called for a different approach. The HIV Legal Network, a Toronto-based human-rights organization, articulates this growing consensus:

> Canada is in urgent need of [a] comprehensive harm reduction policy that jettisons the failed costly model of drug prohibition that has ravaged so many lives, from fueling the spread of HIV and hepatitis C virus (HCV), to contributing to over-incarceration, to creating conditions for the ongoing epidemic of overdose fatalities. [...] Drug policy must be guided by evidence, public health objectives and a commitment to upholding the human rights of people who use drugs.[16]

Between 1969 and 1972, the Royal Commission of Inquiry into the Non-Medicinal Use of Drugs (often referred to as the Le Dain Commission) undertook a comprehensive study of Canadian drug laws, exposing their negative effects and recommending that Canada move away from criminalizing people who use drugs (PWUD).[17] Fifty years later, drug prohibition remains firmly in place, and the numbers speak for themselves: over 29,000 overdose deaths from opioids alone between January 2016 and December 2021,[18] and an unprecedented stagnation in Canadian life expectancy attributed to the overdose crisis.[19] Criminalizing drug use by prohibiting possession for personal use is highly problematic from a public health perspective. It is also, I contend, unconstitutional. To support this claim, I first briefly review the current approach to illegal drug use in Canada. In light of the Supreme Court of Canada's decision in *Canada (Attorney General) v. PHS Community Services Society* and related cases,[20] I proceed to argue that prohibiting drug possession for personal use under section 4(1) of the Controlled Drug and Substances Act (CDSA)[21] violates section 7 of the Canadian Charter of Rights and Freedoms.[22] Given the overwhelming evidence of the arbitrary and discriminatory impact of this criminalization, I submit that section 4(1) of the CDSA can in no way be justified under section 1 of the Charter.[23] I will conclude that Canadian governments must abandon criminalization and adopt a human-rights and health-based approach to drug use as a matter of constitutional imperative.

Canada's Approach to Drug Use

Ensuring access to health care for those who need it is one of our country's defining social values, given effect by the Canada Health Act and provincial and territorial health insurance programs and services.[24] While universal drug coverage is not included within medicare, the federal Liberal government has committed to introducing a national "pharmacare" plan.[25] In the meantime, age- and income-targeted programs at the federal level and in most provinces and territories provide at least some degree of publicly funded drug coverage.[26] Through the Food and Drugs Act, and related regulatory measures, the federal government also oversees the safety of the pharmaceutical supply and safeguards the health of users.[27] Our collective commitment to those seeking drugs and therapeutics within the publicly funded system is in sharp contrast to our total disregard for the health and safety of people who use prohibited drugs in Canada. Far from equal protection or concern, they face criminalization, stigma, and social exclusion. Toronto Public Health describes this parallel reality: "People are denied or are afraid to use the services and supports they need. People are evicted from their housing and have their children taken away. They are also forced into unsafe spaces and behaviours which can lead to overdose and blood-borne infections."[28]

In her 2019 report calling for decriminalization of PWUD in British Columbia, Provincial Health Officer Bonnie Henry outlines the evolution of Canada's drug laws over the past century.[29] The criminal regime first put in place under the 1908 Opium Act was, as she notes, rooted in racism and moral panic.[30] And, "despite drug use emerging as a public health issue during the 1960s," the 1961 Narcotics Control Act maintained or increased criminal penalties for drug possession and trafficking.[31] A decade later, the Le Dain Commission "highlighted that the harms caused by the application of criminal law—especially for people who use drugs—were more serious than the harms associated with substance use."[32] However, the Le Dain Commission's recommendations for a shift away from criminalization were not adopted.[33] The CDSA,[34] which replaced the Narcotics Control Act in 1996, brought little change.[35] Possession of a wide range of drugs, including opioids, cocaine, ecstasy, speed, hallucinogens, and heroin, among others, remains an offence under section 4(1) of the CDSA, and those convicted risk imprisonment for a period up to seven years or a fine of up to $2,000.[36]

As Henry recounts, in 2003 the federal minister of health granted Vancouver Coastal Health and the PHS Community Services Society an exemption under section 56 of the CDSA,[37] to allow the creation of Insite, North America's first supervised drug-use site, in Vancouver's Downtown Eastside.[38] The Harper government's refusal to renew that exemption was successfully challenged in the 2011 *Canada (Attorney General) v. PHS Community Services Society*—widely known as the *Insite* case.[39] In 2016, the recently elected Liberal government of Justin Trudeau announced the Canadian Drugs and Substances Strategy.[40] This new strategy sets out a "four-pillar approach," focussing on prevention, treatment, enforcement, and harm reduction (an objective abandoned in the previous Conservative government's 2007 National Anti-Drug Strategy).[41] Subsequent federal measures included streamlining the approval process for safe-injection sites and other overdose-prevention services, increasing access to naloxone to counter the effects of opioid overdose, and expanding treatment options for people who depend on opioids.[42]

In 2017, the federal government enacted the Good Samaritan Drug Overdose Act to protect those calling for emergency assistance from being charged under section 4(1) of the CDSA.[43] In 2018, cannabis was removed from the CDSA following enactment of the Cannabis Act.[44] Regulations, first introduced under the CDSA in 2001 to allow access to cannabis for medical purposes, were also replaced.[45] Under the new legislation, possession by an adult of up to 30 g of legally obtained dried cannabis (or its non-dried equivalent) is permitted, as are edible cannabis, cannabis extracts, and cannabis topicals.[46] At the same time, significant criminal penalties for non-compliance with the new regime were put in place, including imprisonment for up to five years, less a day, for possession over the prescribed limit, and for up to 14 years for illegal distribution and sale.[47]

In February 2021, the federal minister of justice introduced An Act to amend the Criminal Code and the Controlled Drugs and Substances Act (Bill C-22).[48] In addition to repealing mandatory minimum sentences for all drug offences and increasing the availability of conditional sentences, Bill C-22 provides alternatives to criminal charges in the form of "warnings" to people found in possession of drugs for personal use, and "referrals" to community programs and services.[49] Bill C-22 does not, however, repeal section 4(1) of the CDSA, and drug possession for personal use remains a criminal offence subject to prosecution and imprisonment.[50]

Aside from the new cannabis regime, Canada's approach to illegal drugs has barely shifted over the past century. Notwithstanding increasing government acknowledgement of the importance of harm reduction as an objective of Canadian drug policy, most recently in the language of Bill C-22, drug use continues to be treated as a matter of crime rather than health. The current Liberal government has taken a more permissive approach to granting exemptions under section 56 of the CDSA.[51] However, the current application process for an exemption is an onerous one, requiring consultation with a wide variety of community interests,[52] and provincial and local support and government funding are in no way assured.[53] The availability of over-the-counter naloxone has been increased,[54] and restrictions on prescriptions of some controlled substances have been reduced in response to the COVID-19 pandemic.[55] But, in contrast to the safeguards in place with regards to prescription drugs, government measures to ensure drug safety for people who use illegal drugs are non-existent in most parts of the country.[56] Access to treatment within the publicly funded system, for health concerns relating to drug use, is also grossly inadequate.[57]

Criminalizing Possession Violates Section 7 Rights to Life, Liberty, and Security of the Person

Section 7 of the Charter guarantees everyone "the right to life, liberty and security of the person and the right not to be deprived thereof except in accordance with the principles of fundamental justice."[58] In the *Insite* case, the claimants relied in part on section 7 to challenge the federal health minister's refusal to renew the exemption under section 56 the CDSA that enabled staff to provide supervised injection services to Insite's clients.[59] The Supreme Court found that, without such an exemption, Insite's staff was at risk of imprisonment for illegal possession of drugs—an infringement of their right to liberty.[60] In the case of Insite's clients, the court ruled that "[t]o prohibit possession by drug users *anywhere* engages their liberty interests."[61] The court also held that the government had violated the claimants' section 7 rights to life and to security of the person.[62] Chief Justice McLachlin affirmed that "[w]here a law creates a risk to health [...] a deprivation of the right to security of the person is made out. [...] Where the law creates a risk not just to the health but also to the lives of the claimants, the deprivation is even clearer."[63]

Criminalizing Possession Violates the Right to Liberty

Each year, thousands of people across the country are charged with possession of drugs for personal use and face the threat of imprisonment for a period of up to seven years under section 4(1) of the CDSA. Statistics Canada figures show in excess of 540,000 drug offences in Canada between 2014 and 2019, over two-thirds of those are drug possession for personal use.[64] According to Statistics Canada, in 2019 alone there were 6,732 police-reported drug offences for possession of cocaine, 10,849 for methamphetamine, 231 for ecstasy, 2,342 for heroin, 2,346 for opioids other than heroin, and 7,965 for possession of other drugs.[65] In 2018–2019, there were 6,374 drug-possession cases in adult criminal courts in Canada, of which 3,330 resulted in a guilty verdict,[66] 623 in imprisonment.[67] The Supreme Court's ruling in *Insite*, as well as its earlier judgment in *R v. Malmo-Levine; R v. Caine*,[68] establishes that the threat of imprisonment for drug possession for personal use at any location under section 4(1) of the CDSA, without more, infringes the right to liberty under section 7 of the Charter.[69]

Criminalizing Possession Violates the Right to Life and to Security of the Person

Those imprisoned for contravening section 4(1) of the CDSA suffer not only a deprivation of liberty but immediate and longer-term harms to life and security of the person.[70] Canada's correctional investigator found that, in 2014, 80 percent of federal prisoners had serious substance-use problems and over half reported a link between alcohol or drug use and their crimes.[71] As the Canadian Mental Health Association explains: "Contrary to the logic of criminalization, incarceration does not result in the cessation of substance use, nor does it prevent harm." [72] Drug use in prison is much riskier because federal, provincial, and territorial prison authorities do not provide prisoners with adequate harm reduction services, including sterile equipment for drug consumption, which contributes to higher incidences of HIV and HCV (hepatitis C virus).[73] Lack of access to opioid agonists (such as methadone and buprenorphine-naloxone) therapy is also a concern in prisons, as are high rates of poisonings due to fentanyl and fentanyl analogue contamination.[74] The association notes that, beyond an immediate risk to life and health, "incarceration poses a significant barrier to recovery from substance use disorders, given that access to treatment is often limited for Canadians behind bars."[75]

Other serious threats to the life and security of the person of those imprisoned for drug possession include exposure to physical violence and criminal subculture, trauma, aggravated mental illness, inadequate medical care, and internalized stigma "which can cause acute mental suffering."[76] After leaving prison, the negative consequences of criminalization persist, including a greatly increased risk of overdose death in the period immediately following release.[77] Over the longer term, "incarceration presents barriers to re-entry into general society, and increases a wide range of challenges from employment [...] to housing (that can directly and negatively affect health and well-being.)"[78]

Damage to life and security of the person extends well beyond those who are imprisoned, to include persons who are charged and convicted but not incarcerated, and those who use drugs more generally.[79] William Bogart, University of Windsor distinguished professor of law emeritus, explains: "If something is a criminal act, individuals are reluctant to admit to doing it for fear that they will be apprehended and punished. Prohibiting an activity can also stigmatize those engaged in such actions. Criminalizing [drug use] has driven users into the margins and created barriers to them receiving counselling and treatment they may need."[80] In the context of Canada's toxic illegal drug supply, criminalization has done more than hinder access by PWUD to health and other services, it has significantly increased their risk of serious injury and death: "Some people in possession of illegal drugs will not seek out supervised consumption, overdose prevention, or treatment services for fear of being arrested; instead, they will use drugs alone, increasing their risk of dying from a potential overdose."[81] When contrasted with the government's approach to prescription drugs, the impact of criminalization on the life and security of those who use illegal drugs is glaringly obvious:

> [H]ospitals dispense opioids every day to relieve pain. These drugs are not killing people because the quality of the supply is regulated, the dosages are managed, ingestion is overseen and, should a problem arise, there are trained people on hand who can intervene and who are not made afraid by the spectre of criminalization and stigma. Proponents of harm reduction argue that context matters and shunting drug consumption out of sight while criminalizing and stigmatizing it does the opposite of keeping people safe.[82]

By any measure, the harm caused by section 4(1) of the CDSA to the physical and mental health and well-being of PWUD constitutes a clear violation of their section 7 rights to life, liberty, and security of the person.

Criminalizing Possession Is not in Accordance with Section 7 Principles of Fundamental Justice

Section 7 of the Charter prohibits any deprivation of life, liberty, or security of the person that is not "in accordance with the principles of fundamental justice."[83] In *Malmo-Levine*, the Supreme Court affirmed that "a criminal law that is shown to be arbitrary or irrational will infringe s. 7."[84] In that case, the court found that prohibiting possession of marijuana under section 4(1) of the CDSA was not fundamentally unjust because, in the majority's view, "criminalization of possession is a statement of society's collective disapproval of the use of a psychoactive drug [...] and [...] the continuing view that its use should be deterred. The prohibition is not arbitrary but is rationally connected to a reasonable apprehension of harm."[85] In its subsequent judgment in *Chaoulli v. Quebec (Attorney General)*, the court set out two standards for determining arbitrariness: first, whether the deprivation of life, liberty or security of the person is "necessary" to achieve the government's objectives, and, second, whether it is "inconsistent" with those objectives.[86] In the *Insite* case, the court held that the minister's failure to grant Insite an exemption under section 56 of the CDSA was arbitrary under either approach, since it undermined rather than furthered the government's objectives of maintaining and promoting public health and safety.[87] In particular, the court noted that criminal prohibitions had done little to reduce drug use and that, while Insite was operating, the risk to drug users of death and disease had been reduced.[88]

In *Malmo-Levine*, the court rejected the claimants' argument that the prohibition on possession of marijuana violated the principles of fundamental justice because its adverse effects were "grossly disproportionate" to its purposes.[89] In the majority's view, the impact of section 4(1) of the CDSA on accused persons, including the possibility of imprisonment and of having a criminal record, did not trigger a finding of gross disproportionality in that case.[90] In contrast, in the *Insite* case, the court concluded that the minister of health's failure to grant Insite an exemption from the CDSA was fundamentally unjust because the harm caused to Insite's clients was "grossly disproportionate to the benefit that Canada might derive from presenting a uniform stance on possession of narcotics."[91]

In *R v. Morgentaler*, Justice Wilson ruled that an interference with life, liberty, or security of the person "which has the effect of infringing a right guaranteed elsewhere in the Charter cannot be in accordance with the principles of fundamental justice."[92] Justice Wilson found that criminalizing women's access to abortion was fundamentally unjust because it violated their right to freedom of conscience under section 2(a) of the Charter.[93] The parallel argument, that discriminatory violations of life, liberty, and security of the person are fundamentally unjust in light of section 15's equality guarantee, is reinforced by Justice L'Heureux-Dubé's affirmation, in *New Brunswick (Minister of Health and Community Services) v. G (J)*, that "[t]he rights in s. 7 must be interpreted through the lens of ss. 15 and 28, to recognize the importance of ensuring that our interpretation of the Constitution responds to the realities and needs of all members of society."[94]

As outlined below, criminalizing possession of drugs for personal use under section 4(1) of the CDSA violates section 7 principles of fundamental justice because it is an arbitrary, grossly disproportionate and systemically discriminatory infringement of the life, liberty, and security of the person of those who use drugs.

Criminalizing Possession Is Arbitrary and Grossly Disproportionate

Almost 20 years after the Supreme Court's decision relating to marijuana in *Malmo-Levine*, and consistent with its findings in regard to restrictions on access to supervised injection services in *Insite*, it is evident that prohibiting drug possession for personal use is not only unnecessary to achieve but is totally inconsistent with the CDSA's objectives of reducing the harms of illegal drug use and safeguarding individual and public health and safety. Health, human-rights, and lived experts have long argued, and more than half of Canadians now agree, that "[i]f the intention of a prohibition-based system was to protect individuals from harms inherent to substance use, then this policy approach has significantly failed to achieve this goal at an individual or population level. Evidence shows that this approach has had the opposite effect and has substantially increased harms."[95] In a 2020 report on decriminalization, the Canadian Association of Chiefs of Police concluded: "We must adopt new and innovative approaches if we are going to disrupt the current trend of overdoses impacting communities across Canada. Merely arresting individuals for simple possession of illegal drugs has proven to be ineffective."[96] Canada's chief public health officer, Dr. Theresa Tam, is even more direct: "You cannot arrest your way out of an opioid crisis."[97]

There is no debate that criminalization "is the major cause of stigma related to drug use," and that, by creating and reinforcing social, structural, and internalized stigma, section 4(1) of the CDSA seriously undermines the act's public health and safety purposes.[98] Toronto Public Health's overdose action plan, created in 2017, points out that "[s]tigma is not a deterrent to drug use, it simply pushes people farther into isolation, marginalization and further harm."[99] Its impact, as Sandra Ka Hon Chu and Cécile Kazatchkine document, is deeply gendered: "Canadian scholars have observed that women who use criminalized drugs 'have long been vilified as more deviant than men who use similar drugs.' [...] Such stigma has fuelled the regulation of women, especially poor, indigenous and racialized women, and intersected with 'the regulation of sexuality, reproduction, mothering and drug consumption.'"[100] The damaging effects of stigma caused by criminalizing drug possession are exacerbated in the context of Canada's toxic drug supply. Dr. Henry explains:

Stigma matters because it undermines the response to the overdose crisis […] at every turn. It negatively impacts the lives of people and the ability of some individuals to receive or access basic health [needs] […] and […] influences public support for evidence-based strategies that save lives and link people to treatment, such as supervised consumption services."[101]

In the words of Vancouver addiction medicine specialist Dr. Derek Chang, "addiction does not kill a person on its own. Stigma does."[102]

The Canadian government has itself acknowledged that "[r]educing stigma is key to effectively addressing problematic substance use, and is a critical step in recognizing the fundamental rights and dignity of all Canadians, including those who use substances."[103] In 2018, Canada co-sponsored the UN Commission on Narcotic Drugs resolution 61/11: Promoting non-stigmatizing attitudes to ensure the availability of, access to and delivery of health, care and social services for drug users.[104] In introducing that resolution, Canada argued "the stigmatisation of people who use drugs runs counter to health and human rights, which should underpin responses to drug use."[105] The "Declaration of principles" for "evidence-based diversion measures," set out under section 10.1 of Bill C-22, likewise affirms that

(a) problematic substance use should be addressed primarily as a health and social issue;

(b) interventions should be founded on evidence-based based practices and should aim to protect the health, dignity and human rights of individuals who use drugs and to reduce harm to those individuals, their families and their communities;

(c) criminal sanctions imposed in respect of the possession of drugs for personal use can increase the stigma associated with drug use and are not consistent with established public health evidence […].[106]

Whatever the facts before the Supreme Court of Canada in *Malmo-Levine* on the issue of whether prohibiting the possession of marijuana was an arbitrary violation of the claimants' section 7 liberty rights in 2003, the irrational impact of section 4(1) of the CDSA in Canada is incontrovertible. As discussed above, a direct line has been drawn between criminalization and the national epidemic of overdose injuries and deaths that began well before COVID-19, and that has only worsened since.[107] Criminalizing drug possession for personal use undermines, rather than protects, the "health, dignity and human rights" of PWUD, and criminalization increases, instead of reducing, harm to "those individuals, their families and their communities."[108] Given the federal government's avowal, under Bill C-22, that criminalization stigmatizes people who use illegal drugs, and that criminal sanctions are "not consistent with established public health evidence,"[109] it is no longer possible to maintain that section 4(1) is consistent with, let alone necessary to, advance the health and safety purposes of the CDSA.

Maintaining, *versus* abandoning, the criminal prohibition against drug possession for personal use under section 4(1) of the CDSA is an arbitrary means of realizing the government's objectives. In the words of the Canadian Mental Health Association: "The evidence strongly suggests that policies that punish and criminalize people who use illegal substances are ineffective [...] decriminalization will help treat problematic substance use as a health issue rather than a criminal one, will redirect resources from the criminal justice system into health care and will begin to address the stigma that acts as a barrier to treatment."[110] Put more simply: "Decriminalization is the first step towards reconciling a drug strategy that is at odds with itself."[111]

In addition to being arbitrary, section 4(1) of the CDSA contravenes section 7 principles of fundamental justice because, in the language of *Malmo-Levine*, criminalizing drug possession for personal use is "grossly disproportionate in its effects on accused persons, when considered in light of the objective of protecting them from the harm caused" by drug use.[112] The Canadian Public Health Association makes the point that "[c]riminalization does not reduce the likelihood of illegal psychoactive substance use, and often results in stigmatization and other harms to those caught in possession of small amounts of substances for personal use. The effect of this criminalization often does not reflect the severity of the crime." [113] Henry decries the situation in her province: "The current regime has resulted in the criminalization of hundreds of thousands of British Columbians whose only 'crimes' were the desire or need to use illegal substances."[114] Instead of protecting them from harm, section 4(1) of the CDSA has resulted in increased illness, suffering, and countless needless deaths of PWUD across the entire country—a grossly disproportionate effect that in no way accords with the section 7 principle of fundamental justice.

In the *Insite* case, the Supreme Court found that, while the federal government's failure to grant Insite an exemption under section 56 of the CDSA violated section 7 principles of fundamental justice, the criminalization of drug possession under section 4(1) did not. In the court's view:

> Section 56 gives the Minister of Health a broad discretion to grant exemptions from the application of the Act [...]. The availability of exemptions acts as a safety valve that prevents the CDSA from applying where such application would be arbitrary, overbroad, or grossly disproportionate in its effects. [...] If there is a *Charter* problem, it lies not in the statute but in the Minister's exercise of the power the statute gives him to grant appropriate exemptions.[115]

As noted, while the federal Liberal government has been more permissive than its Conservative predecessor in granting exemptions for supervised injection services, "the expansion of SCS in Canada continues to be limited by a legislative regime [... that] treats SCS as exceptional rather than as health vital services."[116] For applicants, the section 56 exemption application process also "continues to be exceedingly time- and resource-intensive."[117] Among other documentation, applicants must provide a "Community Consultation Report" describing the "consultation activities that were undertaken for the proposed site [and] results [...] including all feedback and comments that were received" in order to enable Health Canada "to understand the efforts that have been made to engage with the community to inform them of the proposal and ensure that the voices of community members have been heard."[118] The politicization of the exemption process, as University of Alberta School of Public Health Professor Elaine Hyshka underscores, is problematic from both a health and human-rights perspective: "[W]hen governments approach supervised consumption and other harm reduction services through a political lens focused on public support, it can have negative effects on people who use substances [...] it sends the message that they're not deserving of care and [...] that it's appropriate to stigmatize people who use substances or have addictions."[119]

Many applicants seeking an exemption from the CDSA continue to face strong opposition from provincial governments and local communities.[120] While there are currently seven authorized safe-consumption sites in British Columbia, five in Alberta, nineteen in Ontario, and four in Quebec, there is only one in Saskatchewan, and none in Manitoba, New Brunswick, Nova Scotia, Prince Edward Island, Newfoundland, Nunavut, the Yukon, or the Northwest Territories.[121] When a Winnipeg community resource centre presented a report outlining the benefits of supervised consumption services to Manitoba Premier Brian Pallister, he reportedly tossed it to the ground.[122] In Alberta, the United Conservative Party government "has been critical of harm reduction services and is reviewing the province's existing sites after ordering a report that criticized them as a blight on neighbourhoods."[123] Ontario Premier Doug Ford has expressed similarly negative views and, following the election of his Progressive Conservative government, several approved sites were put on pause, defunded, or closed, with the premier explaining at one news conference that "if I put one beside your house, you'd be going ballistic."[124] In Saskatchewan, the province's only safe-consumption site is operating without government funding or support. In the words of the Prairie Harm Reduction Executive Director Jason Mercredi, "[w]e need some leadership [...] from government. [...] It shouldn't be up to us selling T-shirts to stop people from dying."[125]

The political and public hostility facing many section 56 applicants is in sharp contrast to the situation described by the Supreme Court in the *Insite* case—one of broad support for Insite and its safe-consumption services. The court noted that "Insite was the product of cooperative federalism. Local, provincial and federal authorities combined their efforts to create it. [...] The Vancouver police support Insite. The city and provincial government want it to stay open."[126] Against this factual backdrop, the Supreme Court concluded that prohibiting personal possession under section 4(1) of the CDSA did not violate Charter section 7 principles of fundamental justice because of the ministerial power to grant exemptions under section 56.[127] A decade after *Insite*, the suggestion that the section 56 "safety valve" of the CDSA provides an adequate safeguard for the life, liberty, and security rights of PWUD can no longer be sustained. In the context of Canada's toxic drug supply, the impact of section 4(1) on the Charter rights of PWUD, not only in Vancouver's Downtown Eastside but in every part of the country, is exponentially worse. Leaving aside the numerous other health and human-rights harms caused by the continued criminalization of drug possession, Canada's overdose death toll alone belies the argument that section 56 remains an answer to the arbitrary and grossly disproportionate effects of section 4(1) of the CDSA.

Criminalizing Possession is Fundamentally Unjust Because it is Discriminatory

By perpetuating, reinforcing, and exacerbating stigma, social exclusion, and disadvantage on a number of prohibited grounds of discrimination under section 15 of the Charter,[128] section 4(1) of the CDSA violates the Charter's section 7 principle of fundamental justice that deprivations of life, liberty, and security of the person cannot violate other rights.[129] Most obviously, prohibiting possession for personal use has an adverse impact on people who depend on illegal drugs. The Supreme Court noted in *Insite* that the federal government has itself recognized that drug dependence is an illness, bringing it within the section 15 enumerated ground of disability.[130] The Le Dain Commission observed that "[t]he application of the criminal law against simple possession or use by one who is dependent on a drug [...] is akin to making dependence itself a crime."[131] Toronto's overdose plan underscores the reality that "[t]here is no other group of people who are treated so poorly because of a health issue."[132]

A 2019 report of the House of Commons Standing Committee on Health, on the impacts of methamphetamine use in Canada, identified the grounds of disadvantage that are most directly related to illegal drug use.[133] In particular, the committee noted the co-occurrence between drug use and dependence and both diagnosed and un-diagnosed metal-health disorders, such as schizophrenia and related psychotic disorders, bipolar disorder, anxiety, and depression.[134] Witnesses testifying before the committee explained that "prior or ongoing trauma is common" in PWUD and that, in many cases, drug use "is a direct response to experiences of physical and sexual abuse and trauma,"[135] including childhood experiences of sexual abuse, emotional and physical abuse, neglect, and violence, substance use, mental illness, and incarceration within the household.[136] For Indigenous people, the committee heard that drug use is a product of colonialism and intergenerational trauma arising from residential school experiences, the assimilative "Sixties Scoop," foster care, violence, incarceration, forced dislocation, and cultural, social, and economic disempowerment.[137] Experts also explained that homeless individuals use drugs to address unmet health care and other needs, such as women who are homeless using methamphetamine to stay awake at night to protect themselves.[138]

The systemically racist effects of the CDSA are well documented. The Canadian Public Health Association points out that, with respect to the criminalization of possession, "the current structure of fines and incarceration causes most harm to those at the lower end of the social gradient, which results in greater health inequity […] furthermore, these approaches have been demonstrated to systematically perpetuate socio-economic harm, especially against racialized communities."[139] The HIV Legal Network and the Centre on Drug Policy and Evaluation's joint submission to the UN High Commissioner for Human Rights—on the disproportionate impact of drug criminalization on Black people in Canada[140]—points, among other evidence, to the 2017 concluding observations of the international Committee on the Elimination of Racial Discrimination (CERD)[141] and to the Ontario Human Rights Commission's 2020 report on racial profiling by the Toronto Police. Among its recommendations, the CERD called on Canada to "[a]ddress the root causes of overrepresentation of African-Canadians and indigenous peoples at all levels of the justice system […] by […] re-examining drug policies." For its part, the Ontario Human Rights Commission reports that the disproportionate numbers of Black people accused of drug offences "raise concerns of systemic racism and anti-Black racial bias, because the over-representation of Black people in drug possession charges does not align with what is known about drug use within Black communities."[142]

The relationship between drug use and mental illness, abuse, and trauma, compounds the gendered impact of criminalization under the CDSA.[143] Research suggests not simply a correlation but a causal relationship between women's experiences of physical and sexual violence and pre-existing and subsequent mental-health and substance-use issues.[144] The stigma and risk of being criminalized for drug use have distinct gender impacts, particularly for women who are mothers, and especially for women who are Indigenous, Black or racialized, and/or living in poverty.[145] Canada's correctional investigator has reported that federally incarcerated women are "twice as likely [as men] to be serving a sentence for drug-related offences"[146] and "Indigenous and Black women are more likely than White women to be in prison for that reason."[147] Dr. Bonnie Henry makes the point that incarcerating women with addictions "negatively impacts their families and children in a much greater way than incarcerating men" and that separating women from their children has both immediate and longer term destabilizing effects.[148] Women who are pregnant and dependent on drugs face particular difficulties if they are held in custody, even for a short time, and, for street-involved women especially, conditions restricting where they can go and what they can do after they are released isolates them from social-safety networks and puts them at increased risk of violence, illness, and death.[149]

Youth are also adversely impacted by Canada's approach to drug use. A 2018 Health Canada consultation document reports that youth have the highest rate of problematic substance use nationally and are more likely than older adults to experience harms related to substance use.[150] High rates of substance use have been documented among Indigenous and Black youth, homeless or street-involved youth, youth in custody, and youth with co-occurring mental-health problems,[151] as well as among lesbian, gay, and bisexual youth, "linked to social stigma, homophobic discrimination and violence."[152] Youth with a history of child-welfare involvement "are particularly at risk, as the initial transition out of foster care is associated with increased rates of problematic substance use."[153] The BC Centre on Substance Use notes, with specific reference to crystal meth, that the limited public health interventions currently available for youth "are embedded within a highly criminalized approach to drug use [… that is] not effective and can lead to enhanced harms."[154] As is the case for other section 15 protected groups, "[d]rug prohibition has not only failed to protect [their] wellbeing […] it has also failed to subvert rates of youth substance abuse."[155]

The Canadian Civil Society Working Group on UN Drug Policy summarizes the reasons why multiple international health and human-rights agencies have called for decriminalization of possession:

> There is now copious evidence of the harms of criminalizing simple possession particularly to vulnerable people. Since criminalization of drug possession directly leads to both individual and systemic stigma, it supports discrimination against people who use drugs and prevents people from seeking services. It also undermines the development of health services because needed resources are diverted to the criminal justice system (including correctional facilities) and because people with problematic drug use, when regarded as criminals, are not seen as deserving of services.[156]

As outlined above, evidence in Canada supports these findings. In addition to being arbitrary and grossly disproportionate, section 4(1) of the CDSA violates Charter section 7 principles of fundamental justice because it is systemically discriminatory based on race, colour, sex, age, and disability, among other grounds protected under section 15 of the Charter.

Criminalizing Possession Is not Justified under the Charter

Section 1 of the Charter says that rights are guaranteed "subject only to such reasonable limits prescribed by law as can be demonstrably justified in a free and democratic society."[157] In its decision in *R v. Oakes*, the Supreme Court set out a four-part test for determining whether a rights violation can be justified under section 1.[158] In order to be upheld, the rights-violating measure must have a sufficiently important objective; it must be rationally connected to that objective; it must impair the Charter right as little as possible; and its harms must not be disproportionate to its benefits.[159] The court has suggested that a section 7 violation "will be saved by section 1 only in cases arising out of exceptional conditions, such as natural disasters, the outbreak of wars, epidemics, and the like,"[160] and that "it would be rare for a violation of the fundamental principles of justice to be justifiable under s. 1."[161] In the *Insite* case, Chief Justice McLachlin concluded: "If a s. 1 analysis were required, a point not argued, no s. 1 justification could succeed. The goals of the CDSA, as I have stated, are the maintenance and promotion of public health and safety. The Minister [of Health]'s decision to refuse an exemption bears no relation to those objectives; therefore they cannot justify the infringement of the complainant' s. 7 rights."[162]

The objective of the CDSA—to maintain and promote public health and safety—is unquestionably of sufficient importance to meet the first requirement of the *Oakes* test. But the Supreme Court has questioned "whether an arbitrary provision, which by reason of its arbitrariness cannot further its state objective, will ever meet the rational connection test under *R v Oakes*."[163] In the same way that its arbitrariness and gross disproportionately violate section 7 principles of fundamental justice, section 4(1) fails the second, rational connection, as it does the fourth, proportionality, requirement of section 1. As Henry recaps:

> The current prohibitionist approach to drug policy has failed to achieve its stated ends: to prevent the growth of illegal drug markets,

to curtail use of illegal substances, and to prevent harms associated with the use of these substances. Instead, harms have been magnified through the creation, in reaction to interdiction, of a highly toxic illegal drug supply, and the criminalization, stigmatization, and marginalization of individuals—many of whom have opioid use disorder, a known chronic, relapsing health condition. In addition, massive profits have been generated for violent criminal enterprises involved in the illegal drug market.[164]

In terms of the requisite proportionality between its salutary and deleterious effects,[165] weighing against section 4(1)'s non-existent benefits are the health harms and stigma caused by criminalizing drug possession, its role in creating and maintaining Canada's illegal drug trade, and its lost productivity, health care, criminal justice, and other economic costs, amply documented by Henry and others.[166]

Nor can section 4(1) be justified as a minimal impairment of the section 7 rights of PWUD, as the third part of the *Oakes* test demands. This is true whether or not Bill C-22 is ultimately adopted. As described above, Bill C-22 grants police and prosecutors the power to "consider whether it would be preferable" to use "warnings" or "referrals" to community programs or services, instead of charging and prosecuting those found in possession of illegal drugs for personal use.[167] Critics have pointed out that police and prosecutors must keep a record of such warnings and referrals, and can still choose to charge and prosecute violations of section 4(1), with the systemic racism and other resulting risks this discretion creates.[168] While Bill C-22 may enable some drug users to avoid imprisonment, and even criminal charges, it does not remove the threat and does nothing to address the pervasive stigma of criminalization. The HIV Legal Network's executive director, Richard Elliott, summarizes the problem: "There will continue to be the threat of surveillance, interrogation, detention, prosecution and other harms."[169]

In the criminal-law context, particularly where a vulnerable group is being harmed rather than protected, no deference is owing to the government's unreasonable belief that maintaining a rights violation is justified.[170] Twenty years after *Malmo-Levine* and a decade after *Insite*, the evidence is beyond dispute. Section 4(1) of the CDSA does not achieve the government's health and safety objectives in a manner that causes the least possible harm to the rights of those who use drugs. Prohibition does not advance those objectives at all. Instead, it impairs drug users' health and human rights with no benefit to society, much less a proportionate one. Criminalizing drug possession for personal use deprives those who use drugs of their rights to life, liberty, and security of the person. That deprivation is not in accordance with the principles of fundamental justice, it cannot be justified under section 1, and it is therefore unconstitutional.

Conclusion: Protecting Health, Respecting Rights

In place of prohibition, section 7 of the Charter calls for an approach to drug use that protects the health, and respects the human rights, of PWUD. Decriminalizing drug possession is the starting point because, as the Global Commission on Drug Policy, a lobbying group of former political leaders, declares, "criminalization [...] is, in effect, a policy of harm maximization."[171] Repealing section 4(1) of the CDSA is not only necessary to reduce overdose deaths, it is a precondition for the effectiveness of any other public health measures directed at addressing threats to life, liberty, and security of the person that are related to drug use. In the words of Chang, "decriminalization [...] is the single most important change our society can take to stop the stigma of addiction. It is also an essential step to end this heartbreaking overdose crisis."[172] To fully safeguard the health and human rights of PWUD, decriminalizing possession is, however, only a first step.[173] The Canadian Public Health Association explains:

> The alternative to criminalization is a public health approach that seeks to maintain and improve the health of populations based on the principles of social justice, attention to human rights and equity, evidence-informed policy and practice, and addressing underlying determinants of health. Such an approach places health promotion, health protection, population health surveillance, and the prevention of death, injury and disability as the central tenets of all related initiatives. [...] This approach finds its basis in the *Canadian Charter of Rights and Freedoms* as well as several United Nations (UN) agreements.[174]

UN human-rights monitoring bodies have urged Canadian governments to bring this country's drug laws and practices into alignment with Canada's health and human-rights obligations under the

International Covenant on Economic, Social and Cultural Rights and other international agreements ratified by Canada.[175] In its 2016 concluding observations on Canada's compliance with the right to health guarantees under article 12 of the covenant, the UN Committee on Economic, Social and Cultural Rights expressed concern "that drug users face barriers in access to health-care services" and it exhorted Canada to ensure its national drug law and strategy "incorporate a public-health approach and be harm-reduction-based."[176] In particular, the committee called upon Canada to "take effective measures to facilitate access to appropriate health care, psychological support services and rehabilitation for drug users."[177] In its own concluding observations the same year, the UN Committee on the Elimination of Discrimination Against Women also recommended that Canada "define harm reduction as a key element" in its drug strategy, and that it "reduce the gap in health service delivery related to women's drug use, by scaling-up and ensuring access to culturally appropriate harm reduction services."[178] Following his visit to Canada in 2018, the UN special rapporteur on the right to health, Dr. Dainius Pūras, underlined the gravity of the overdose crisis, which he likened to the HIV epidemic.[179] Pūras decried the continued criminalization of drug use, and he advised the Canadian government that the supervised consumption and overdose-prevention services available in Vancouver should be extended throughout British Columbia and across the country.[180]

The Canadian Association of People who Use Drugs explains the importance of including safe supply as a key feature of a health and human-rights-based approach to drug use:

> For many decades, the drug using community has had to risk overdose, poisoning, infection, disease transmission, and death because it has been forced to rely on the illicit drug market. Meaningful and purposeful expansion of the provision of safe and regulated drugs to compete with the black market will significantly curtail these harms, and it is a necessary step to stop the ongoing overdose crisis ... [and] to end the stigmatization of drug use and drug users.[181]

Among many others, the House of Commons Standing Committee on Health has underscored the importance of access to treatment, including withdrawal management and long-term community-based, residential, and on-the-land treatment programs, as a core component of governments' approach to drug use.[182] The committee reported in

2019 that it "heard from all witnesses that there is an urgent need for federal, provincial and territorial governments to provide substantial additional funding to expand the availability of and provide timelier access to treatment services for substance use and addiction across the country."[183]

UN treaty-monitoring bodies have reminded successive Canadian governments in relation to socio-economic rights, generally, that the right to health and to access health services based on need is an international human-rights obligation that must be given domestic effect, including through the interpretation and application of section 7 and other Canadian Charter rights.[184] It is also, as suggested at the outset of the chapter, a defining Canadian value. Yet, the dehumanizing stigma created by a century of criminalization has resulted in the exclusion of PWUD from this collective commitment. As outlined above, disadvantaged groups—especially those who depend on drugs—have been disproportionately harmed by Canada's approach to drug use. They, unlike other people seeking drugs and treatment for acute and chronic illnesses in Canada, have neither the assurance of safe drugs nor an expectation of publicly funded drug-related care or services, much less without discrimination or judgment. In addition to decriminalizing drug possession for personal use, a health and human-rights approach to drug use—one that respects the Charter's promise of life, liberty, and security of the person, and equal protection and benefit of the law—must include access to safe drugs. It must also provide timely, appropriate, publicly funded treatment for health concerns related to drug use for those seeking it.

Finally, the determinants of health that are most directly associated with drug use and dependence, and the need for concerted government action to address them, must be explicitly recognized.[185] Tam stated: "Broad interventions that improve socio-economic conditions and early childhood development will improve overall community and individual health and resilience in a manner that reduces the risk of problematic substance use in the future. These types of interventions target the 'causes of the causes' of societal health problems."[186] The measures required to attenuate certain risk factors, such as aging out of care for youth[187] or being released from prison into homelessness,[188] are obvious. The failure to address these known threats to individual health and safety, like the failure to decriminalize drug possession itself, is indefensible from a health and human-rights perspective. And while colonialism, racism, poverty, and gender-based violence, among other more systemic determinants of health associated with drug use, are not amenable to simple solutions, inclusion of people with lived expertise presents the clearest way forward in the design and implementation of drug policies and programs that respect and promote domestic and international human-rights principles.[189]

A May 2019 *Globe and Mail* editorial captures why section 4(1) of the CDSA can no longer be justified as a reasonable limit on Charter rights:

> Treating drug users as criminals isn't working [...]. It's expensive to arrest people, put them on trial and send them to prison. The return on investment appears to be nil, or negative [...]. And the looming threat of criminal prosecution for drug possession scares people away from seeking help, while also encouraging dangerous behaviour, such as doing drugs alone. [...] Decriminalizing drugs is not a magic bullet that will end drug addiction. But it can be part of a broader harm reduction strategy that includes many other steps. More money for treatment. Less money spent on prosecution. And a clearer-eyed focus on this national tragedy, and addiction generally, as a health crisis.[190]

After more than a century of harm to individuals, families, communities, and Canadian society as a whole, moving from criminalization to a health and human-rights approach to drug use is not simply better public health policy, it is what our Constitution demands.

References

Legislation

Bill C-22, *An Act to amend the Criminal Code and the Controlled Drugs and Substances Act*, 2nd Sess, 43rd Parl, 2021 (first reading 18 February 2021).

Canada Health Act, RSC 1985, c C-6.

Cannabis Regulations, SOR/2018-144, Part 14.

Controlled Drugs and Susbtances Act, SC 1996, c 19.

Food and Drugs Act, RSC 1985, c F-27.

Good Samaritan Drug Overdose Act, SC 2017, c-4.

Narcotics Control Act, RSC 1985, c-N-1.

Opium Act, SC 1908, c-50.

Part 1 of the *Constitution Act, 1982*, being Schedule B to the *Canada Act 1982* (UK), 1982, c 11.

Jurisprudence

Canada (AG) v PHS Community Services Society, 2011 SCC 44.

Chaoulli v Quebec (Attorney General), 2005 SCC 35.

Dagenais v Canadian Broadcasting Corp, [1994] 3 SCR 835 at 887, 120 DLR (4th) 12.

Irwin Toy Ltd v Quebec (AG), [1989] 1 SCR 927 at 993-994, 58 DLR (4th) 577.

Malmo-Levine; R v Caine, 2003 SCC 74.

New Brunswick (Minister of Health and Community Services) v G (J), [1999] 3 SCR 46 at 115, 177 DLR (4th) 124.

R v Morgentaler, [1988] 1 SCR 30 at 175, 44 DLR (4th) 385.

R v Oakes, [1986] 1 SCR 103, 26 DLR (4th) 200.

Reference re s 94(2) of the Motor Vehicle Act (BC), [1985] 2 SCR 486 at 518, 60 DLR (4th) 397.

Suresh v Canada, 2002 SCC 1 at para 78, [2002] 1 SCR 3.

United States v Burns, 2001 SCC 7 at para 133, [2001] SCR 283.

Publications

Alberta Health, *Opioid-related Deaths in Alberta in 2017: Review of Medical Examiner Data* (Edmonton: Alberta Health, 8 July 2019) at 15, online: open.alberta.ca/publications/9781460143421.

Angus Reid Institute, "Canada's Other Epidemic: As Overdose Deaths Escalate, Majority Favour Decriminalization of Drugs" (24 February 2021), online: angusreid.org/opioid-crisis-covid/.

BC Coroners Service Death Review Panel, *A Review of Illicit Drug Overdoses, Report to the Coroner of British Columbia* (Victoria: BC Coroners Service Death Review Panel, 5 April 2018), online: www2.gov.bc.ca/assets/gov/birth-adoption-death-marriage-and-divorce/deaths/coroners-service/death-review-panel/bccs_illicit_drug_overdose_drp_report.pdf

Bodkin, Claire, Matthew Bonn & Sheila Wildeman, "Fuelling a Crisis: Lack of Treatment for Opioid Use in Canada's Prisons and Jails," *The Conversation* (4 March 2020) online: theconversation.com/fuelling-a-crisis-lack-of-treatment-for-opioid-use-in-canadas-prisons-and-jails-130779.

Bogart, WA, *Off the Street: Legalizing Drugs* (Toronto: Dundurn Press, 2006) at 35.

Bonn, Matthew et al, "Addressing the Syndemic of HIV, Hepatitis C, Overdose, and COVID-19 Among People Who Use Drugs: The Potential Roles for Decriminalization and Safe Supply" (2020) 81 J Stud Alcohol Drugs 556.

Bonn, Matthew et al, *Securing Safe Supply During COVID-19 and Beyond: Scoping Review and Knowledge Mobilization* (Ottawa: Canadian Institutes of Health Research, 12 January 2021) at 4, online: cihr-irsc.gc.ca/e/52043.html.

British Columbia, Office of the Provincial Health Officer, *Stopping the Harm: Decriminalization of People who Use Drugs in BC*, (Special Report) (Victoria: Office of the Provincial Health Officer, 2019) at 10–16, online: www2.gov.bc.ca/assets/gov/health/about-bc-s-health-care-system/

office-of-the-provincial-health-officer/reports-publications/special-reports/stopping-the-harm-report.pdf

Brochu, Serge, "Our Responses to Youth Substance Abuse" in Canadian Centre for Substance Use, ed, *Substance Abuse in Canada: Youth in Focus* (Ottawa: Canadian Centre for Substance Use, 2007).

Brownlee, Nicole, "Supervised Consumption Services Face Host of Difficulties in Prairie Provinces," *The Globe and Mail* (30 May 2021), online: www.theglobeandmail.com/canada/alberta/article-supervised-consumption-services-face-host-of-difficulties-in-prairie/.

Canadian Association of Chiefs of Police Special Purpose Committee on the Decriminalization of Illicit Drugs, "Decriminalization for Simple Possession of Illicit Drugs: Exploring Impacts on Public Safety & Policing" (July 2020), online: www.cacp.ca/index.html?asst_id=2189.

Canadian Association of People who Use Drugs, "Safe Supply: Concept Document" (February 2019), online: static1.squarespace.com/static/5ef3cdaf47af2060a1cc594e/t/608c29e8d9137244ec7da81f/1619798507472/CAPUD+safe+supply+English+March+3+2019.pdf

Canadian Centre on Substance Abuse, *Concurrent Disorders: Substance Abuse in Canada* (Ottawa: Canadian Centre on Substance Abuse 2009), online: www.ccsa.ca/sites/default/files/2019-04/ccsa-011811-2010.pdf

Canadian Civil Society Working Group on UN Drug Policy, "Supporting Health and Human Rights in Drug Policy: Brief to the Minister of Health and Canadian Delegation to the UN Commission on Narcotic Drugs" (21 January 2019), online: www.drugpolicy.ca/wp-content/uploads/2019/02/HLM-Brief-2019-FINAL.pdf

Canada, Commission of Inquiry into the Non-Medical Use of Drugs, *Final Report of the Commission of Enquiry into the Non-Medical Use of Drugs / Gerald Le Dain, Chairman*, (monograph), Catalogue No H21-5370/2E-PDF (Ottawa: Information Canada, 1973), online: publications.gc.ca/site/eng/9.699765/publication.html [Le Dain Commission].

Canadian Drug Policy Coalition, "Drug Policy and Harm Reduction" (2016), online: drugpolicy.ca/wp-content/uploads/2016/12/CDPC-Harm Reduction-Brief-Final-Web.pdf

Canadian HIV/AIDS Legal Network et al, *Harm Reduction in Canada: What Governments Need to Do Now* (12 May 2017) at 2, online: www.aidslaw.ca/site/harm-reduction-in-canada-what-governments-need-to-do-now/?lang=en.

Canadian Institute for Health Information, *Opioid-Related Harms in Canada* (Ottawa: Canadian Institute for Health Information, December 2018), online: www.cihi.ca/sites/default/files/document/opioid-related-harms-report-2018-en-web.pdf

Canadian Mental Health Association, *Care Not Corrections: Relieving the Opioid Crisis in Canada* (Toronto: Canadian Mental Health Association, April

2018) at 2, online: cmha.ca/wp-content/uploads/2018/04/CMHA-Opioid-Policy-Full-Report_Final_EN.pdf

Canadian Public Health Association, "Decriminalization of Personal Use of Psychoactive Substances: Position Statement" (October 2017), online: www.cpha.ca/sites/default/files/uploads/policy/positionstatements/decriminalization-positionstatement-e.pdf

Canadian Women's Foundation & BC Society of Transition Houses, *Report on Violence against Women, Mental Health and Substance Use* (Vancouver: Canadian Women's Foundation, 2011) at 9, online: www.canadianwomen.org/wp-content/uploads/2018/03/PDF-VP-Resources-BCSTH-CWF-Report_Final_2011_-Mental-Health_Substance-use.pdf

CBC News, "Change Your Stance on Overdose Prevention Sites, Health Groups Urge Ford" (30 August 2018), online: www.cbc.ca/news/canada/toronto/change-your-stance-on-overdose-prevention-sites-health-groups-urge-ford-1.4804099.

——, "Province Cut Some Injection Sites Because Area Residents 'Upset,' Ford Says" (1 April 2019), online: www.cbc.ca/news/canada/toronto/province-cut-some-injection-sites-because-area-residents-upset-ford-says-1.5079616.

Chang, Derek, "Dr. Derek Chang: We Must Make Drug Decriminalization a Federal Election Issue" *Vancouver Sun* (4 September 2019), online: vancouversun.com/opinion/op-ed/dr-derek-chang-we-must-make-drug-decriminalization-a-federal-election-issue.

Chu, Sanda Ka Hon & Cécile Kazatchkine, *Gendering the Scene: Women, Gender Diverse People and Harm Reduction in Canada* (Toronto: HIV Legal Network, 12 May 2020), online: www.hivlegalnetwork.ca/site/gendering-the-scene-women-gender-diverse-people-and-harm-reduction-in-canada-full-report/?lang=en.

Commission on the Future of Health Care in Canada, *Building on Values: The Future of Health Care in Canada: Final Report*, Catalogue No CP32-85/2002E-IN (Ottawa: National Library of Canada, 1 November 2002), online: publications.gc.ca/collections/Collection/CP32-85-2002E.pdf

Concluding Observations on the Combined Eighth and Ninth Periodic Reports of Canada, UN Committee on the Elimination of Discrimination Against Women, 65th Sess, UN Doc CEDAW/C/CAN/CO/8-9 (18 November 2016).

Concluding Observations on the Combined Twenty-first to Twenty-third Periodic Reports of Canada, UN Committee on the Elimination of Racial Discrimination, 93rd Sess, UN Doc CERD/C/CAN/CO/21-21 (2017).

Concluding Observations on the Sixth Periodic Report of Canada, UN Committee on Economic, Social and Cultural Rights, 57th Sess, UN Doc E/C.12/CAN/CO/6 (23 March 2016).

Correctional Investigator of Canada, *Annual Report 2013-2014 of the Office of the Correctional Investigator*, Catalogue No PS100-2014E-PDF (Ottawa:

Correctional Investigator of Canada, 27 June 2014), online: oci-bec.gc.ca/sites/default/files/2023-06/annrpt20132014-eng.pdf

——, *Annual Report 2014-2015 of the Office of the Correctional Investigator*, Catalogue No PS100E-PDF (Ottawa: Correctional Investigator, 26 June 2015), online: www.oci-bec.gc.ca/cnt/rpt/pdf/annrpt/annrpt20142015-eng.pdf

——, *Profile of Federally Sentenced Women Drug Offenders*, by Renée Gobeil, (Ottawa: Correctional Services Canada, May 2009), online: publications.gc.ca/collections/collection_2010/scc-csc/PS83-3-204-eng.pdf

——, *Summary of Emerging Findings from the 2007 National Inmate Infectious Diseases and Risk-Behaviours Survey*, by Dianne Zakaria et al (Ottawa: Correctional Service of Canada, March 2010), online: www.csc-scc.gc.ca/005/008/092/005008-0211-01-eng.pdf

——, *Women Offenders, Substance Use, and Behaviour*, by Shanna Farrell Macdonald et al, Catalogue No Ps83-3/358E-PDF (Ottawa: Correctional Service Canada, January 2015), online: publications.gc.ca/site/eng/9.840538/publication.html.

Cox, Chelsea & Matthew Herder, "Pharmaceutical Regulation and Public Health" in Tracey M Bailey, C Tess Sheldon & Jacob J Shelley, eds, *Public Health Law and Policy in Canada*, 4th ed (Toronto: LexisNexis Canada Inc, 2019).

Csete, Joanne & Richard Elliott, "Consumer Protection in Drug Policy: The Human Rights Case for Safe Supply as an Element of Harm Reduction" (2021) 91 Intl J Drug Policy 102976.

Dale, Laura, "Decriminalizing Drug Use Isn't a Slippery Slope—It's a Proven Path Forward" *The Tyee* (19 July 2019), online: thetyee.ca/Opinion/2019/07/19/Decriminalizing-Drug-Use-Path-Forward/.

——, "Here's What Drug Legalization Should Really Look Like" *The Tyee* (13 March 2020), online: thetyee.ca/Opinion/2020/03/13/What-Drug-Legalization-Should-Really-Look-Like/.

Delisle, Raina, "It's a Risky Time for People with Substance Use Issues" *The Tyee* (14 April 2020), online: thetyee.ca/News/2020/04/14/How-A-Pandemic-Affects-Substance-Use/.

Editorial, "How Drug Decriminalization Could Help Stem an Epidemic of Drug Overdoses" *The Globe and Mail* (26 May 2019), online: www.theglobeandmail.com/opinion/editorials/article-how-drug-decriminalization-could-help-stem-an-epidemic-of-drug/.

Elliott, Richard, "Statement: Bill C-22 Introduces Welcome Drug Policy Amendments but Falls Short, Advocates Say" (18 February 2021), online: www.hivlegalnetwork.ca/site/statement-bill-c-22-introduces-welcome-drug-policy-amendments-but-falls-short-advocates-say/?lang=en.

Erickson, Patricia G, "Neglected and Rejected: A Case Study of the Impact of Social Research on Canadian Drug Policy" (1998) 23 Canadian J Sociology 263.

Flader, Suzy, "Fundamental Rights for All: Toward Equality as a Principle of Fundamental Justice under Section 7 of the *Charter*" (2020) 25 Appeal 43.

Foreman-Mackey, Annie & Cécile Kazatchkine, "Overdue for a Change: Scaling up Supervised Consumption Services in Canada" (19 February 2019) at 3-4, 7-10, online: www.hivlegalnetwork.ca/site/overdue-for-a-change-full-report/?lang=en.

Froc, Kerri, "Constitutional Coalescence: Substantive Equality as a Principle of Fundamental Justice" (2011) 42 Ottawa L Rev 41.

Gibson, Shane, "Drug Overdose Deaths Spiked 87 Per Cent in Manitoba Last Year" *Global News* (22 April 2021), online: globalnews.ca/news/7778633/drug-overdose-deaths-manitoba-2020/.

Global Commission on Drug Policy, *Taking Control: Pathways to Drug Policies that Work* (Geneva, Switzerland: Global Commission on Drug Policy, September 2014), online: www.globalcommissionondrugs.org/reports/taking-control-pathways-to-drug-policies-that-work.

Government of Canada, *Budget* 2019: *Moving Forward on Implementing National Pharmacare* (Ottawa: Government of Canada, 19 March 2019), online: www.budget.canada.ca/2019/docs/themes/pharmacare-assurance-medicaments-en.html.

Hamilton, Jonnette Watson, "Cautious Optimism: *Fraser v Canada (Attorney General)*" (2021) 30:2 Const Forum Const 1.

Harvey, Alexandra, "The Pandemic Is Intensifying the Opioid Crisis" *The Walrus* (20 September 2020), online: thewalrus.ca/the-pandemic-is-intensifying-the-opioid-crisis/.

Health Canada, Advisory Council on the Implementation of National Pharmacare, *A Prescription for Canada: Achieving Pharmacare for All*, Catalogue No H22-4/18-2019E (Ottawa: Health Canada, June 2019) at 29–34, online: www.canada.ca/content/dam/hc-sc/images/corporate/about-health-canada/public-engagement/external-advisory-bodies/implementation-national-pharmacare/final-report/final-report.pdf/

Health Canada, "Apply to Run a Supervised Consumption Site: What You Need Before You Start," (28 January 2019), online: www.canada.ca/en/health-canada/services/substance-use/supervised-consumption-sites/apply/before-you-start.html.

——, "Backgrounder: The New Canadian Drugs and Substances Strategy," (12 December 2016), online: www.canada.ca/en/health-canada/news/2016/12/new-canadian-drugs-substances-strategy.html.

——, "Backgrounder: Royal Assent of Bill C-37—An Act to amend the Controlled Drugs and Substances Act and to make related amendments to other Acts," (18 May 2017), online: www.canada.ca/en/health-canada/news/2017/05/royal_assent_of_billc-37anacttoamendthecontrolleddrugsandsubstan.html.

——, "Supervised Consumption Sites: Status of Applications," (5 July 2021), online: www.canada.ca/en/health-canada/services/substance-use/supervised-consumption-sites/status-application.html#a1.

HIV Legal Network, "Submission to the High Commissioner", *supra* note 73 at 4, citing Ontario Human Rights Commission, *A Disparate Impact: Second Interim Report on the Inquiry into Racial Profiling and Racial Discrimination of Black Persons by the Toronto Police Services* (Toronto: Ontario Human Rights Commission, 10 August 2020), online: www.ohrc.on.ca

——, "Submission to the United Nations High Commissioner for Human Rights pursuant to HRC Res. 43/1 on the Promotion and protection of the human rights and fundamental freedoms of Africans and of people of African descent against excessive use of force and other human rights violations by law enforcement officers" (2 December 2020), online: www.hivlegalnetwork.ca/site/submission-to-the-united-nations-high-commissioner-for-human-rights-by-hln-and-cdpe/?lang=en.

——, *Decriminalizing People Who Use Drugs: Making the Ask, Minimizing the Harms—A Primer for Municipal and Provincial Governments* (Toronto: HIV Legal Network, 12 November 2020), online: www.hivlegalnetwork.ca/site/decriminalizing-people-who-use-drugs-a-primer-for-municipal-and-provincial-governments/?lang=en.

HIV Legal Network, Pivot Legal Society & the Canadian Drug Policy Coalition, "Letter to Canadian Government: Decriminalize Simple Drug Possession Immediately" (3 March 2021), online: www.hivlegalnetwork.ca/site/letter-to-canadian-government-decriminalize-simple-drug-possession-immediately/?lang=en.

House of Commons, *Impacts of Methamphetamine Abuse in Canada: Report of the Standing Committee on Health*, 42 Parl, 1st sess, Chair Bill Casey (Ottawa, ON: House of Commons: 2019) at 59.

Huncar, Andrea, "Indigenous Women Nearly 10 Times More Likely to be Street Checked by Edmonton Police, New Data Shows ," *CBC News* (27 June 2017), online: www.cbc.ca/news/canada/edmonton/street-checks-edmonton-police-aboriginal-black-carding-1.4178843.

Iftene, Adelina, "COVID-19 in Canadian Prisons: Policies, Practices and Concerns" in Colleen M Flood et al, eds, *Vulnerable: The Law, Policy and Ethics of COVID-19* (Ottawa: University of Ottawa Press, 2020) 367 at 371.

International Centre for Human Rights and Drug Policy et al, *International Guidelines on Human Rights and Drug Policy* (New York: UNDP, 6 November 2020), online: www.undp.org/content/undp/en/home/librarypage/hiv-aids/international-guidelines-on-human-rights-and-drug-policy.html.

International Covenant on Economic, Social and Cultural Rights, 16 December 1966, 993 UNTS 3 art 12(1) (entered into force 3 January 1976, accession by Canada 19 May 1976).

International Drug Policy Consortium, *The 2018 Commission on Narcotic Drugs: Report of Proceedings* (London, UK: IDPC, 19 June 2018) at 14, online: fileserver.idpc.net/library/CND-Proceedings-Report-2018_18.06.pdf

Ireland, Nicole, "Life Expectancy In Canada May Be Decreasing As Opioid Crisis Rages On," *CBC News* (23 October 2018), online: www.cbc.ca/news/health/life-expectancy-canada-decrease-opioid-crisis-1.4874651.

Jackman, Martha, "Law as a Tool for Addressing Social Determinants of Health" in Tracey M Bailey, C Tess Sheldon & Jacob J Shelley, eds, *Public Health Law and Policy in Canada*, 4th ed (Toronto: LexisNexis Canada Inc, 2019) at 112–115.

Jeffries, Fiona, "The Right to Safety in the City: Vancouver, Ottawa, Toronto, Thunder Bay, Guelph, Montreal and Beyond Tells an Extraordinary Story of Grassroots Activists Creating Infrastructures of Care Beyond the State" (1 January 2019), online: www.policyalternatives.ca/publications/monitor/right-safety-city.

Jesseman, Rebecca & Doris Payer, *Decriminalization: Options and Evidence* (Ottawa: Canadian Centre on Substance Use and Addiction, June 2018) at 10, online: www.ccsa.ca/sites/default/files/2019-04/CCSA-Decriminalization-Controlled-Substances-Policy-Brief-2018-en.pdf

Klein, Alana, "Criminal Law and the Counter-Hegemonic Potential of Harm Reduction" (2015) 38 Dal LJ 447 at 469.

Knaak, Stephanie et al, *Stigma and the Opioid Crisis: Final Report* (Ottawa: Mental Health Commission of Canada, 2019) at 11, online: www.mentalhealthcommission.ca/sites/default/files/201907/Opioid_Report_july_2019_eng.pdf

Korzinski, David, "Mandatory Treatment? Decriminalization? As Opioid Epidemic Rages, Canadians Seek Extreme Measures to Save Lives" (14 February 2019), online: angusreid.org/wp-content/uploads/2019/02/2019.02.06-opioid-release.pdf

Kouyoumdjian, Fiona et al, "Health Status of Prisoners in Canada: Narrative Review" (March 2016) 62:3 J Canadian Family Physician 215, online: www.cfp.ca/content/cfp/62/3/215.full.pdf

Lawrence, Sonia, "Equality and Anti-Discrimination" in Peter Oliver, Patrick Macklem & Nathalie DesRosiers, eds, *The Oxford Handbook of the Canadian Constitution* (New York: Oxford University Press, 2017) 815 at 841.

Ling, Justin, "Canada's Drug Crisis Has a Solution: Politicians Don't Like It" (29 September 2019), online: foreignpolicy.com/2019/09/29/canadas-drug-crisis-has-a-solution-politicians-dont-like-it/.

——, "Seven Chief Public Health Officers Call for Drug Decriminalization, But Justin Trudeau Isn't Budging," *Vice* (2 September 2020), online: www.vice.com/en/article/935j58/seven-chief-public-health-officers-call-for-drug-decriminalization-but-justin-trudeau-isnt-budging.

———, "Canada's Top Cop Says Criminalizing Drugs Doesn't Work, but He'll Keep Doing It Anyway," *Vice* (9 September 2020), online: www.vice.com/en/article/935je7/canada-bill-blair-criminalizing-drugs.

———, "Houses of Hate: How Canada's Prison System Is Broken," *Maclean's* (28 February 2021), online: www.macleans.ca/news/canada/houses-of-hate-how-canadas-prison-system-is-broken/.

Lowik, AJ et al, *Side by Side: A Community Summit on Meth—Findings and Recommendations* (Vancouver: British Columbia Centre on Substance Use, 2020) at 12.

McGuire, Tara, "I Want to Tell You How This Feels" *The Tyee* (5 May 2021), online: thetyee.ca/Analysis/2021/05/05/I-Want-To-Tell-You-How-This-Feels/.

Modjeski, Morgan, "Supervised Consumption Site Advocates Say Kimberly Squirrel's Death Could Have Been Prevented," *CBC News* (25 April 2021), online: www.cbc.ca/news/canada/saskatoon/autopsy-results-on-squirrel-tragedy-1.5999888.

National Inquiry into Missing and Murdered Indigenous Women and Girls, *Reclaiming Power and Place: The Final Report of the National Inquiry into Missing and Murdered Indigenous Women and Girls Volume 1a* (Ottawa: National Inquiry into Missing and Murdered Indigenous Women and Girls, 2019) at 637, online: www.mmiwg-ffada.ca/wp-content/uploads/2019/06/Final_Report_Vol_1a-1.pdf

Nurses and Nurse Practitioners of British Columbia & Harm Reduction Nurses Association, Press Release "Nurses and Nurse Practitioners of British Columbia (NNPBC) and the Harm Reduction Nurses Association (HRNA) Call for the Decriminalization of People Who Use Drugs in B.C." (8 August 2019), online: www.nnpbc.com/pdfs/media/press-releases/PR-HRNA-NNPBC-Statement.pdf

Nunavut, NVision Insight Group, *Addictions and Trauma Treatment in Nunavut: Executive Summary*, (Ottawa: NVision Insight Group, August 2018) at 1, online: www.gov.nu.ca/sites/default/files/gn_att_executive_summary_summary_report-final-english.pdf

Ontario Drug Policy Research Network et al, *Preliminary Patterns in Circumstances Surrounding Opioid-Related Deaths in Ontario during the COVID-19 Pandemic* (Toronto: Ontario Drug Policy Research Network, 2020), online: www.publichealthontario.ca/-/media/documents/o/2020/opioid-mortality-covid-surveillance-report.pdf?la=en.

Ottawa Public Health, *Ottawa Community Action Plan: Comprehensive Mental Health and Substance Use Strategy—Focus on Opioids* (Ottawa: Ottawa Public Health, 12 September 2019) at 2, online: https://www.ottawapublichealth.ca/en/reports-research-and-statistics/resources/Documents/Mental_Health_Substance_Use_focus_on_opiods_-_Community_Action_Plan_Public_Version_FINAL-ua.pdf.

Owusu-Bempah, Akwasi & Alex Luscombe, "Race, Cannabis and the Canadian War on Drugs: An Examination of Cannabis Arrest Data by Race in Five Cities" (2021) 91 Intl J Drug Policy 102937.

Passafiume, Alessia, "Critics of Alberta's New Rules for Supervised Consumption Sites Say They Will Curb Access for Vulnerable Clients," *The Globe and Mail* (4 June 2021), online: www.theglobeandmail.com/canada/alberta/article-critics-of-albertas-new-rules-for-supervised-consumption-sites-say/.

PIVOT, "Canada's Safe Consumption and Overdose Prevention Sites" (15 January 2021), online: www.pivotlegal.org/scs_ops_map.

Porter, Bruce, "International Human Rights in Anti-poverty and Housing Strategies: Making the Connection" in Martha Jackman & Bruce Porter, eds, *Advancing Social Rights in Canada* (Toronto: Irwin Law, 2014) 33 at 33.

Potter, Andrew & Daniel Weinstock, eds, *High Time: The Legalization and Regulation of Cannabis in Canada* (Kingston and Montreal: McGill-Queen's University Press, 2019).

Proctor-Simms, Michelle et al, "Transitioning from Incarceration to the Community: Reducing Risks and Improving Lives of People Who Use Substances" (23 November 2020), online: blog.catie.ca/2020/11/23/transitioning-from-incarceration-to-the-community-reducing-risks-and-improving-lives-of-people-who-use-substances/.

Public Health Agency of Canada, *Preventing Problematic Substance Use in Youth: The Chief Public Health Officer's Report on the State of Public Health in Canada 2018*, Catalogue No HP2-10E-PDF (Ottawa: Public Health Agency of Canada, 23 October 2018) at 23-24, online: www.canada.ca/content/dam/phac-aspc/documents/corporate/publications/chief-public-health-officer-reports-state-public-health-canada/2018-preventing-problematic-substance-use-youth/2018-preventing-problematic-substance-use-youth.pdf

——, *Addressing Stigma—Towards a More Inclusive Health System: The Chief Public Health Officer's Report on the State of Public Health in Canada, 2019* (Ottawa: Public Health Agency of Canada, December 2019), online: www.canada.ca/content/dam/phac-aspc/documents/corporate/publications/chief-public-health-officer-reports-state-public-health-canada/addressing-stigma-what-we-heard/wwh-2019-12-17.pdf.

Pūras, Dainius, "Preliminary Observations—Country Visit to Canada, 5 to 16 November 2018" (16 November 2018) online: www.ohchr.org/en/NewsEvents/Pages/DisplayNews.aspx?NewsID=23896&LangID=E> [Special Rapporteur].

Ratchford, Sarah, "Canada Made Weed Legal. But for Who?" *The Walrus* (25 October 2019), online: thewalrus.ca/canada-made-weed-legal-but-for-who.

Report on the 61st Session (8 December 2017 and 12–16 March 2018), United Nations Commission on Narcotic Drugs, 61st Sess, UN Doc E/CN.7/2018/13 (2018) at 28.

Saewyc, Elizabeth M, "Substance Use Among Non-mainstream Youth" in Canadian Centre for Substance Use, ed, *Substance Abuse in Canada: Youth in Focus* (Ottawa: Canadian Centre for Substance Use, 2007) at 15-17.

Senate Special Committee on Illegal Drugs, *Cannabis: Our Position for a Canadian Public Policy: Report of the Senate Special Committee on Illegal Drugs* (Ottawa: Senate of Canada, September 2002) (Chair: Pierre Claude Nolin) at 245-263, online: sencanada.ca/Content/SEN/Committee/371/ille/rep/repfinalvol2-e.pdf

Sharpe, Robert J & Kent Roach, *The Charter of Rights and Freedoms*, 6th ed (Toronto: Irwin Law, 2017) at 48–65.

Special Advisory Committee on the Epidemic of Opioid Overdoses, "Opioids and Stimulant-Related Harms in Canada" (last visited 25 July 2022), online: health-infobase.canada.ca/substance-related-harms/opioids-stimulants.

Statistics Canada, *Adult Criminal Courts, Guilty Cases by Type of Sentence, Table 35-10-0030-01*, (Ottawa: Statistics Canada, 28 May 2012), online: www150.statcan.gc.ca.

——, *Adult Criminal Courts, Number of Cases and Charges by Type of Decision, Table 35-10-0027-01*, (Ottawa: Statistics Canada, 28 May 2012), online: www150.statcan.gc.ca.

——, *The Daily—Life Tables, 2016/2018*, (Ottawa: Statistics Canada, 28 January 2020) online: www150.statcan.gc.ca/n1/en/daily-quotidien/200128/dq200128a-eng.pdf?st=S9IFYKvw.

——, *Police-Reported Crime Statistics in Canada, 2019, Table 3: Police-Reported Crime for Selected Drug Offences, Canada, 2018 And 2019*, (Ottawa: Statistics Canada, 29 October 2020), online: www150.statcan.gc.ca/n1/pub/85-002-x/2020001/article/00010/tbl/tbl03-eng.htm.

Taylor, Stephanie, "Saskatchewan Rejected Funding Despite Advice that Supervised Consumption Sites Save Lives, Documents Show," *CBC News* (6 April 2021), online: www.cbc.ca/news/canada/saskatchewan/advance-consumption-sites-funding-1.5976434.

Toronto Public Health, "Toronto Overdose Action Plan: Prevention and Response" (March 2017) at 4, online: www.toronto.ca/wp-content/uploads/2017/08/968f-Toronto-Overdose-Action-Plan.pdf

Truth and Reconciliation Commission, *Honouring the Truth, Reconciling for the Future: Summary of the Final Report of the Truth and Reconciliation Commission of Canada* (Winnipeg: Truth and Reconciliation Commission, 2015) at 161-162, online: ehprnh2mwo3.exactdn.com/wp-content/uploads/2021/01/Executive_Summary_English_Web.pdf

Tsicos, Stephanie, "Tossed Report on Safe Consumption Spaces Causes Stir in Manitoba Legislature," *CTV News* (8 April 2019), online: winnipeg.ctvnews.ca/tossed-report-on-safe-consumption-spaces-causes-stir-in-manitoba-legislature-1.4371338.

Woo, Andrea, "As Canada's Overdose Deaths Soar, the Safe-Supply Debate Enters a New and Urgent Phase," *The Globe and Mail* (18 February 2021), online: www.theglobeandmail.com/canada/article-as-canadas-overdose-deaths-soar-the-safe-supply-debate-enters-a-new/.

Wright, Teresa, "Talks Needed on Decriminalizing Hard Drugs to Address Opioid Crisis, Tam Says," *CTV News* (22 August 2020), online: www.ctvnews.ca/health/talks-needed-on-decriminalizing-hard-drugs-to-address-opioid-crisis-tam-says-1.5075176.

Wyton, Moira, "BC's Opioid Substitution System Isn't a System at All, Say Frontliners" *The Tyee* (8 June 2021), online: thetyee.ca/News/2021/06/08/BC-Opioid-Substitution-System-Not-System-At-All-Say-Front-Liners/.

Young, Margot, "Sleeping Rough and Shooting Up: Taking British Columbia's Urban Justice Issues to Court" in Martha Jackman & Bruce Porter, eds, *Advancing Social Rights in Canada* (Toronto: Irwin Law, 2014) 413 at 441.

——, "Section 7: The Right to Life, Liberty and Security of the Person" in Peter Oliver, Patrick Macklem & Nathalie DesRosiers, eds, *The Oxford Handbook of the Canadian Constitution* (New York: Oxford University Press, 2017) 777 at 794.

Notes

1   See Tara McGuire, "I Want to Tell You How This Feels" (5 May 2021), online: thetyee.ca/Analysis/2021/05/05/I-Want-To-Tell-You-How-This-Feels/; see also HIV Legal Network, *Decriminalizing People Who Use Drugs: Making the Ask, Minimizing the Harms—A Primer for Municipal and Provincial Governments* (12 November 2020) at 2, online: www.hivlegalnetwork.ca/site/decriminalizing-people-who-use-drugs-a-primer-for-municipal-and-provincial-governments/?lang=en [HIV Legal Network, *Making the Ask*]; see also David Korzinski, "Mandatory Treatment? Decriminalization? As Opioid Epidemic Rages, Canadians Seek Extreme Measures to Save Lives" (14 February 2019), online: angusreid.org/wp-content/uploads/2019/02/2019.02.06-opioid-release.pdf; see also Canadian Mental Health Association, *Care Not Corrections: Relieving the Opioid Crisis in Canada* (Toronto: Canadian Mental Health Association April 2018) at 2, online: cmha.ca/wp-content/uploads/2018/04/CMHA-Opioid-Policy-Full-Report_Final_EN.pdf [CMHA]; see also Nicole Ireland, "Life Expectancy in Canada May Be Decreasing as Opioid Crisis Rages On" (23 October 2018), online: www.cbc.ca/news/health/life-expectancy-canada-decrease-opioid-crisis-1.4874651; see also Dainius Pūras, "Preliminary Observations—Country Visit to Canada, 5 to 16 November 2018" (16 November 2018) at 5–6, online: www.ohchr.org/en/NewsEvents/Pages/DisplayNews.aspx?NewsID=23896&LangID=E [Special Rapporteur].

2   See Matthew Bonn et al, "Addressing the Syndemic of HIV, Hepatitis C, Overdose, and COVID-19 among People Who Use Drugs: The Potential Roles for Decriminalization and Safe Supply" (2020) 81 J Stud Alcohol Drugs 556 [Bonn et al, "Syndemic"]; see also Alexandra Harvey, "The Pandemic Is Intensifying

the Opioid Crisis" (20 September 2020), online: thewalrus.ca/the-pandemic-is-intensifying-the-opioid-crisis/; see also Raina Delisle, "It's a Risky Time for People with Substance Use Issues" (14 April 2020), online: thetyee.ca/News/2020/04/14/How-A-Pandemic-Affects-Substance-Use/; see also Ontario Drug Policy Research Network et al, *Preliminary Patterns in Circumstances Surrounding Opioid-Related Deaths in Ontario During the COVID-19 Pandemic* (Toronto: Public Health Ontario, 2020), online:www.publichealthontario.ca/-/media/documents/0/2020/opioid-mortality-covid-surveillance-report.pdf?la=en.

3   See Toronto Public Health, "Toronto Overdose Action Plan: Prevention and Response" (March 2017) at 4, online: www.toronto.ca/wp-content/uploads/2017/08/968f-Toronto-Overdose-Action-Plan.pdf [Toronto Public Health].

4   See Canadian HIV/AIDS Legal Network et al, "Harm Reduction in Canada: What Governments Need to Do Now" (12 May 2017) at 2, online: www.aidslaw.ca/site/harm-reduction-in-canada-what-governments-need-to-do-now/?lang=en [HIV Legal Network, "Harm Reduction"]; see also Sanda Ka Hon Chu & Cécile Kazatchkine, "Gendering the Scene: Women, Gender Diverse People and Harm Reduction in Canada" (12 May 2020) at 3, online: www.hivlegalnetwork.ca/site/gendering-the-scene-women-gender-diverse-people-and-harm-reduction-in-canada-full-report/?lang=en [Ka Hon Chu & Kazatchkine]; see also WA Bogart, *Off the Street: Legalizing Drugs* (Toronto: Dundurn Press, 2006) at 35 [Bogart, *Off the Street*].

5   HIV Legal Network, Pivot Legal Society & the Canadian Drug Policy Coalition, "Letter to Canadian Government: Decriminalize Simple Drug Possession Immediately" (3 March 2021), online: www.hivlegalnetwork.ca/site/letter-to-canadian-government-decriminalize-simple-drug-possession-immediately/?lang=en [HIV Legal Network, "Letter to Canadian Government"]; at the international level, see Canadian Civil Society Working Group on UN Drug Policy, "Supporting Health and Human Rights in Drug Policy: Brief to the Minister of Health and Canadian Delegation to the UN Commission on Narcotic Drugs" (21 January 2019), online: www.drugpolicy.ca/wp-content/uploads/2019/02/HLM-Brief-2019-FINAL.pdf [Civil Society Working Group]; see also Global Commission on Drug Policy, *Taking Control: Path-ways to Drug Policies that Work* (Geneva, Switzerland: Global Commission on Drug Policy, September 2014), online: www.globalcommissionondrugs.org/reports/taking-control-pathways-to-drug-policies-that-work [Global Commission on Drug Policy].

6   See *Concluding Observations on the Sixth Periodic Report of Canada*, UNCESR 57th Sess, UN Doc E/C.12/CAN/CO/6 (23 March 2016) at paras 49, 50.

7   See *Concluding Observations on the Combined Eighth and Ninth Periodic Reports of Canada*, UNHRC Committee on the Elimination of Discrimination Against Women, 65th Sess, UN Doc CEDAW/C/CAN/CO/8-9 (18 November 2016) at para 45 [CEDAW, Concluding Observations, 2016].

8   See Civil Society Working Group, *supra* note 5.

9   See CMHA, *supra* note 1.

10   See Canadian Public Health Association, "Decriminalization of Personal Use of Psychoactive Substances: Position Statement" (October 2017), online: www.cpha.ca/sites/default/files/uploads/policy/positionstatements/decriminalization-positionstatement-e.pdf [CPHA].

11   See Nurses and Nurse Practitioners of British Columbia & Harm Reduction Nurses Association, "Nurses and Nurse Practitioners of British Columbia (NNPBC) and the Harm Reduction Nurses Association (HRNA) Call for the Decriminalization of People Who Use Drugs in B.C." (8 August 2019), online: www.nnpbc.com/pdfs/media/press-releases/PR-HRNA-NNPBC-Statement.pdf [NNPBC & HRNA].

12   See Justin Ling, "Seven Chief Public Health Officers Call for Drug Decriminalization, but Justin Trudeau Isn't Budging" (2 September 2020), online: www.vice.com/en/article/935j58/seven-chief-public-health-officers-call-for-drug-decriminalization-but-justin-trudeau-isnt-budging.

13   See Canadian Association of Chiefs of Police Special Purpose Committee on the Decriminalization of Illicit Drugs, "Decriminalization for Simple Possession of Illicit Drugs: Exploring Impacts on Public Safety & Policing" (July 2020), online: www.cacp.ca/index.html?asst_id=2189 [Canadian Chiefs of Police].

14   See House of Commons, *Impacts of Methamphetamine Abuse in Canada: Report of the Standing Committee on Health* 42 Parl, 1st sess, Chair Bill Casey (Ottawa, ON: House of Commons: 2019) at 59 [Standing Committee on Health].

15   See Justin Ling, "Canada's Drug Crisis Has a Solution: Politicians Don't Like It" (29 September 2019), online: foreignpolicy.com/2019/09/29/canadas-drug-crisis-has-a-solution-politicians-dont-like-it/; see also Editorial, "How Drug Decriminalization Could Help Stem an Epidemic of Drug Overdoses" (26 May 2019), online: www.theglobeandmail.com/opinion/editorials/article-how-drug-decriminalization-could-help-stem-an-epidemic-of-drug/ [Globe and Mail Editorial]; see also HIV Legal Network, *Making the Ask, supra* note 1 at 9-10.

16   See HIV Legal Network, "Harm Reduction," *supra* note 4 at 1.

17   See Canada, Commission of Inquiry into the Non-Medical Use of Drugs, *Final Report of the Commission of Enquiry into the Non-Medical Use of Drugs* / Gerald Le Dain, Chairman, (monograph), Catalogue No H21-5370/2E-PDF (Ottawa: Information Canada, 1973) online: publications.gc.ca/site/eng/9.699765/publication.html [Le Dain Commission].

18   See Special Advisory Committee on the Epidemic of Opioid Overdoses, Opioids and Stimulant-Related Harms in Canada (last visited 25 July 2022), online: health-infobase.canada.ca/substance-related-harms/opioids-stimulants [Special Advisory Committee]; the Committee also reported 30,860 opioid-related and 13,575 stimulant-related poisoning hospitalizations during the same period in Canada (excluding Quebec).

19   See Statistics Canada, "The Daily—Life Tables, 2016/2018," (Ottawa: Statistics Canada, 28 January 2020) online: www150.statcan.gc.ca/n1/en/daily-quotidien/200128/dq200128a-eng.pdf?st=S9IFYKvw; see also Laura Dale, "Here's What Drug Legalization Should Really Look Like" (13 March 2020), online: thetyee.ca/Opinion/2020/03/13/What-Drug-Legalization-Should-Really-Look-Like/.

20   2011 SCC 44 [*Insite*].

21   SC 1996, c 19 [*CDSA*].

22   Part I of the *Constitution Act, 1982*, being Schedule B to the *Canada Act 1982* (UK), 1982, c 11 [Charter].

23   *Ibid*, s 1.

24   See *Canada Health Act*, RSC 1985, c C-6; see also Commission on the Future of Health Care in Canada, *Building on Values: The Future of Health Care in Canada: Final Report*, Catalogue No CP32-85/2002E-IN (Ottawa: National Library of Canada, 1 November 2002) at xvi, online: publications.gc.ca/collections/Collection/CP32-85-2002E.pdf.

25   See Government of Canada, *Budget 2019: Moving Forward on Implementing National Pharmacare* (Ottawa: Government of Canada, 19 March 2019), online: www.budget.canada.ca/2019/docs/themes/pharmacare-assurance-medicaments-en.html.

26   See Health Canada, Advisory Council on the Implementation of National Pharmacare, *A Prescription for Canada: Achieving Pharmacare for All*, Catalogue No H22-4/18-2019E (Ottawa: Health Canada, June 2019) at 29-34, online: www.canada.

ca/content/dam/hc-sc/images/corporate/about-health-canada/public-engagement/external-advisory-bodies/implementation-national-pharmacare/final-report/final-report.pdf.

27   See *Food and Drugs Act*, RSC 1985, c F-27; see generally Chelsea Cox & Matthew Herder, "Pharmaceutical Regulation and Public Health" in Tracey M Bailey, C Tess Sheldon & Jacob J Shelley, eds, *Public Health Law and Policy in Canada*, 4th ed (Toronto: LexisNexis Canada Inc, 2019) at 9 [Cox & Herder].

28   See Toronto Public Health, *supra* note 3 at 25.

29   See Province of British Columbia, Office of the Provincial Health Officer, *Stopping the Harm: Decriminalization of People Who Use Drugs in BC*, Special Report (Victoria: Office of the Provincial Health Officer, 2019) at 10-16, online: www2.gov.bc.ca/assets/gov/health/about-bc-s-health-care-system/office-of-the-provincial-health-officer/reports-publications/special-reports/stopping-the-harm-report.pdf [Office of the Provincial Health Officer].

30   See *Opium Act*, SC 1908, c-50; see also Office of the Provincial Health Officer, *supra* note 29 at 10; see also Senate Special Committee on Illegal Drugs, *Cannabis: Our Position for a Canadian Public Policy: Report of the Senate Special Committee on Illegal Drugs* (Ottawa: Senate of Canada, September 2002) (Chair: Pierre Claude Nolin) at 245-263, online: sencanada.ca/Content/SEN/Committee/371/ille/rep/repfinalvol2-e.pdf [Senate Special Committee on Illegal Drugs]; see also Bogart, *Off the Street*, *supra* note 4 at 85-86.

31   See *Narcotics Control Act*, RSC 1985, c-N-1; see also Office of the Provincial Health Officer, *supra* note 29 at 11; see also Senate Special Committee on Illegal Drugs, *supra* note 30 at 268-272.

32   See Office of the Provincial Health Officer, *supra* note 29 at 12.

33   See Office of the Provincial Health Officer, *supra* note 29 at 12; see also Le Dain Commission, *supra* note 17; see also Senate Special Committee on Illegal Drugs, *supra* note 30 at 272-284.

34   See *CDSA*, *supra* note 21.

35   See Office of the Provincial Health Officer, *supra* note 29 at 13; see also Patricia G Erickson, "Neglected and Rejected: A Case Study of the Impact of Social Research on Canadian Drug Policy" (1998) 23 Canadian J Sociology 263; see generally Canadian Foundation for Drug Policy, "The (Heavy Handed) Law in Canada" (14 November 2013), online: www.cfdp.ca/index.htm#background.

36   See *CDSA*, *supra* note 21, s 4. Section 4(1) provides that: "Except as authorized under the regulations, no person shall possess a substance included in Schedule I, II, or III." Schedules I, II and III set out the full list of drugs prohibited under the *CDSA*.

37   *Ibid*, s 56. Section 56 grants the federal Minister of Health the power to grant an exemption from the CDSA "if, in the opinion of the Minister, the exemption is … in the public interest." Insite sought an exemption both from sub-section 4(1) and from sub-section 5(1), which prohibits trafficking.

38   See Office of the Provincial Health Officer, *supra* note 29 at 14.

39   See *Insite*, *supra* note 20; see also Annie Foreman-Mackey & Cécile Kazatchkine, "Overdue for a Change: Scaling Up Supervised Consumption Services in Canada" (19 February 2019) at 3-4, 7-10, online: www.hivlegalnetwork.ca/site/overdue-for-a-change-full-report/?lang=en [Foreman-Mackey & Kazatchkine].

40   See Health Canada, *Backgrounder: The New Canadian Drugs and Substances Strategy*, (Ottawa: Health Canada, 12 December 2016), online: www.canada.ca/en/health-canada/news/2016/12/new-canadian-drugs-substances-strategy.html>; see also Office of the Provincial Health Officer, *supra* note 29 at 15.

41   See Canadian Drug Policy Coalition, "Drug Policy and Harm Reduction" (2016), online: drugpolicy.ca/wp-content/uploads/2016/12/CDPC-HarmReduction-Brief-Final-Web.pdf; see also CMHA, *supra* note 1 at 15-16.

42   See Office of the Provincial Health Officer, *supra* note 29 at 15; see also Standing Committee on Health, *supra* note 14 at 32-35; see also CMHA, *supra* note 1 at 16-17.

43   See *Good Samaritan Drug Overdose Act*, SC 2017, c-4.

44   SC 2018, c-16 [*Cannabis Act*]. See generally Andrew Potter & Daniel Weinstock, eds, *High Time: The Legalization and Regulation of Cannabis in Canada* (Kingston and Montreal: McGill-Queen's University Press, 2019); see also Cox & Herder, *supra* note 27 at 736-747.

45   See *Cannabis Regulations*, SOR/2018-144, Part 14 [*Cannabis Regulations*].

46   *Cannabis Act*, *supra* note 44; *Cannabis Regulations*, *supra* note 45; *Cannabis Regulations*, SOR/2019-206.

47   *Cannabis Act*, *supra* note 44, ss 8, 10; see also Lake & Young's chapter, "Criminality and Inequality under Canada's Legalization of Cannabis: A Study of Vancouver's Downtown Eastside" in this volume; see also Sarah Ratchford, "Canada Made Weed Legal. But for Who?" (25 October 2019), online: thewalrus.ca/canada-made-weed-legal-but-for-who/.

48   See Bill C-22, *An Act to amend the Criminal Code and the Controlled Drugs and Substances Act*, 2nd Sess, 43rd Parl, 2021 (first reading 18 February 2021) [Bill C-22]. Bill C-22 became law and received royal assent on 2022-11-17. S.C. 2022, c. 15.

49   *Ibid*, s 10.2 (1).

50   See Richard Elliott, "Statement: Bill C-22 Introduces Welcome Drug Policy Amendments but Falls Short, Advocates Say" (18 February 2021), online: www.hivlegalnetwork.ca/site/statement-bill-c-22-introduces-welcome-drug-policy-amendments-but-falls-short-advocates-say/?lang=en [Elliot, "Statement Bill C-22"].

51   See Health Canada, "Backgrounder: Royal Assent of Bill C-37—An Act to amend the Controlled Drugs and Substances Act and to make related amendments to other Acts," (18 May 2017), online: www.canada.ca/en/health-canada/news/2017/05/royal_assent_of_billc-37anacttoamendthecontrolleddrugsandsubstan.html ; see also Foreman-Mackey & Kazatchkine, *supra* note 39 at 14-17.

52   See Health Canada, "Apply to Run a Supervised Consumption Site: What You Need Before you Start," (28 January 2019), online: www.canada.ca/en/health-canada/services/substance-use/supervised-consumption-sites/apply/before-you-start.html [Health Canada, "Supervised Consumption Site"].

53   See HIV Legal Network, "Harm Reduction," *supra* note 4 at 1-2; see also Toronto Public Health, *supra* note 3 at 13-14; see also Joanne Csete & Richard Elliott, "Consumer Protection in Drug Policy: The Human Rights Case for Safe Supply as an Element of Harm Reduction" (2021) 91 Intl J Drug Policy 102976 [Csete & Elliott]; see also Fiona Jeffries, "The Right to Safety in the City: Vancouver, Ottawa, Toronto, Thunder Bay, Guelph, Montreal and Beyond Tells an Extraordinary Story of Grassroots Activists Creating Infrastructures of Care Beyond the State" (1 January 2019), online: www.policyalternatives.ca/publications/monitor/right-safety-city [Jeffries].

54   Naloxone, a drug that can reverse overdose symptoms, was removed from the federal government's prescription drug list in 2016 to make it more accessible; see CMHA, *supra* note 1 at 30-32.

55   See Bonn et al, "Syndemic," *supra* note 2 at 558; see also Matthew Bonn et al, *Securing Safe Supply during COVID-19 and Beyond: Scoping Review and Knowledge Mobilization* (Ottawa: Canadian Institutes of Health, 12 January 2021) at 4, online: cihr-irsc.gc.ca/e/52043.html [Bonn et al, *Securing Safe Supply*].

56   See Moira Wyton, "BC's Opioid Substitution System Isn't a System at All, Say Frontliners" (8 June 2021), online: thetyee.ca/News/2021/06/08/BC-Opioid-Substitution-System-Not-System-At-All-Say-Front-Liners/; see also Stephanie Taylor, "Saskatchewan Rejected Funding Despite Advice That Supervised Consumption Sites Save Lives, Documents Show" (6 April 2021), online: www.cbc.ca/news/canada/saskatchewan/advance-consumption-sites-funding-1.5976434; see also Andrea Woo, "As Canada's Overdose Deaths Soar, the Safe-Supply Debate Enters a New and Urgent Phase" (18 February 2021), online: www.theglobeandmail.com/canada/article-as-canadas-overdose-deaths-soar-the-safe-supply-debate-enters-a-new; see also Ka Hon Chu & Kazatchkine, *supra* note 4 at 12-16; see also Bonn et al, *Securing Safe Supply, supra* note 55; see also Rebecca Jesseman & Doris Payer, *Decriminalization: Options and Evidence* (Ottawa: Canadian Centre on Substance Use and Addiction, June 2018) at 10, online: www.ccsa.ca/sites/default/files/2019-04/CCSA-Decriminalization-Controlled-Substances-Policy-Brief-2018-en.pdf [Jesseman & Payer, *Decriminalization*]; see also Special Rapporteur, *supra* note 1; see also CMHA, *supra* note 1 at 36.

57   See CMHA, *supra* note 1 at 21-25; see also Ka Hon Chu & Kazatchkine, *supra* note 4; see also Standing Committee on Health, *supra* note 14 at 34, 44-46; see also Health Canada, *Background Document: Public Consultation on Strengthening Canada's Approach to Substance Use Issues*, Catalogue No H14-266/2018E-PDF, (Ottawa: Health Canada, 5 September 2018) at 15-16, online: www.canada.ca/content/dam/hc-sc/documents/services/substance-use/canadian-drugs-substances-strategy/strengthening-canada-approach-substance-use-issue/strengthening-canada-approach-substance-use-issue.pdf [Health Canada, *Public Consultation*]; see also Office of the Provincial Health Officer, *supra* note 29 at 19; see also Toronto Public Health, *supra* note 3 at 16-18; see also A J Lowik et al, *Side by Side: A Community Summit on Meth—Findings and Recommendations* (Vancouver: British Columbia Centre on Substance Use, 2020) at 12 [A J Lowik et al, *Side by Side*]; see also Special Rapporteur, *supra* note 1 at 5.

58   See *Charter, supra* note 22, s 7; see generally Margot Young, "Section 7: The Right to Life, Liberty and Security of the Person" in Peter Oliver, Patrick Macklem & Nathalie DesRosiers, eds, *The Oxford Handbook of the Canadian Constitution* (New York: Oxford University Press, 2017) 777 at 794.

59   See *Insite, supra* note 20; see generally Margot Young, "Sleeping Rough and Shooting Up: Taking British Columbia's Urban Justice Issues to Court" in Martha Jackman & Bruce Porter, eds, *Advancing Social Rights in Canada* (Toronto: Irwin Law, 2014) 413 at 441.

60   See *Insite, supra* note 20 at paras 87-90.

61   *Ibid* at para 92.

62   *Ibid* at paras 91-92.

63   *Ibid* at para 93.

64   See HIV Legal Network, *Making the Ask, supra* note 1 at 8, n 55.

65   See Statistics Canada, *Police-Reported Crime Statistics in Canada, 2019, Table 3: Police-Reported Crime for Selected Drug Offences, Canada, 2018 and 2019*, (Ottawa: Statistics Canada, 29 October 2020), online: www150.statcan.gc.ca/n1/pub/85-002-x/2020001/article/00010/tbl/tbl03-eng.htm.

66   See Statistics Canada, *Adult Criminal Courts, Number of Cases and Charges by Type of Decision, Table 35-10-0027-01*, (Ottawa: Statistics Canada, 28 May 2012), online: www150.statcan.gc.ca/t1/tbl1/en/tv.action?pid=3510002701&pickMembers%5B0%5D=1.1&pickMembers%5B1%5D=2.37&pickMembers%5B2%5D=3.1&pickMembers%5B3%5D=4.1&pickMembers%5B4%5D=5.2&cubeTimeFrame.startYear=2018+

%2F+2019&cubeTimeFrame.endYear=2018+%2F+2019&referencePeriods=2018010
1%2C20180101.

67   See Statistics Canada, *Adult Criminal Courts, Guilty Cases by Type of Sentence, Table 35-10-0030-01*, (Ottawa: Statistics Canada, 28 May 2012), online: www150.statcan. gc.ca/t1/tbl1/en/tv.action?pid=3510003001&pickMembers%5B0%5D=1.1&pickMe mbers%5B1%5D=2.37&pickMembers%5B2%5D=3.1&pickMembers%5B3%5D=4. 1&pickMembers%5B4%5D=5.1&cubeTimeFrame.startYear=2018+%2F+2019&cub eTimeFrame.endYear=2018+%2F+2019&referencePeriods=20180101%2C20180101; see generally Justin Ling, "Canada's Top Cop Says Criminalizing Drugs Doesn't Work, but He'll Keep Doing It Anyway" (9 September 2020), online: www.vice. com/en/article/935je7/canada-bill-blair-criminalizing-drugs; see also HIV Legal Network, *Making the Ask, supra* note 1 at 8-9.

68   2003 SCC 74 at para 84 [*Malmo-Levine*].

69   See *Insite, supra* note 20 at para 92.

70   See generally Justin Ling, "Houses of Hate: How Canada's Prison System Is Broken" (28 February 2021), online: www.macleans.ca/news/canada/houses-of- hate-how-canadas-prison-system-is-broken/; see also Fiona Kouyoumdjian et al, "Health Status of Prisoners in Canada: Narrative Review" (March 2016) 62:3 J Canadian Family Physician 215, online: www.cfp.ca/content/cfp/62/3/215.full.pdf.

71   See Correctional Investigator of Canada, *Annual Report 2013-2014 of the Office of the Correctional Investigator*, Catalogue No PS100-2014E-PDF (Ottawa: Correctional Investigator of Canada, 27 June 2014) at 22, online: oci-bec.gc.ca/sites/default/ files/2023-06/annrpt20132014-eng.pdf [Correctional Investigator, *Annual Report 2013-2014*]; see also Office of the Provincial Health Officer, *supra* note 29 at 18; see also Correctional Service of Canada, *Women Offenders, Substance Use, and Behaviour*, by Shanna Farrell Macdonald et al, Catalogue No Ps83-3/358E-PDF (Ottawa: Correctional Service Canada, January 2015) online: publications.gc.ca/ site/eng/9.840538/publication.html.

72   See CMHA, *supra* note 1 at 39; see also HIV Legal Network, "Harm Reduction," *supra* note 4; see also Correctional Service Canada, *Summary of Emerging Findings from the 2007 National Inmate Infectious Diseases and Risk-Behaviours Survey*, by Dianne Zakaria et al (Ottawa: Correctional Service of Canada, March 2010), online: www.csc-scc.gc.ca/005/008/092/005008-0211-01-eng.pdf.

73   See CMHA, *supra* note 1 at 37; see also Ka Hon Chu & Kazatchkine, *supra* note 4 at 16-18; see also HIV Legal Network & Centre on Drug Policy and Evaluation, "Submission to the United Nations High Commissioner for human rights pursuant to HRC Res. 43/1 on the 'Promotion and protection of the human rights and fundamental freedoms of Africans and of people of African descent against excessive use of force and other human rights violations by law enforcement officers'" (2 December 2020) at 6-9, online: www.hivlegalnetwork. ca/site/submission-to-the-united-nations-high-commissioner-for-human-rights- by-hln-and-cdpe/?lang=en [HIV Legal Network, "Submission to the High Commissioner"]; see also HIV Legal Network, *Making the Ask, supra* note 1 at 2-3; see also Adelina Iftene, "COVID-19 in Canadian Prisons: Policies, Practices and Concerns" in Colleen M Flood et al, eds, *Vulnerable: The Law, Policy and Ethics of COVID-19* (Ottawa: University of Ottawa Press, 2020) 367 at 371.

74   See HIV Legal Network, Submission to the High Commissioner, *supra* note 73 at 7; see also CMHA, *supra* note 1 at 37; see also Claire Bodkin, Matthew Bonn & Sheila Wildeman, "Fuelling a Crisis: Lack of Treatment for Opioid Use in Canada's Prisons and Jails" (4 March 2020), online: theconversation.com/fuelling-a-crisis- lack-of-treatment-for-opioid-use-in-canadas-prisons-and-jails-130779.

75   See CMHA, *supra* note 1 at 39.

76   See Le Dain Commission, *supra* note 17 at 57; see also Correctional Investigator, *Annual Report 2013-2014, supra* note 71 at 20-21; see also Office of the Provincial Health Officer, *supra* note 29 at 21; see also Stephanie Knaak et al, *Stigma and the Opioid Crisis: Final Report* (Ottawa: Mental Health Commission of Canada, 2019) at 11, online: www.mentalhealthcommission.ca/sites/default/files/2019-07/Opioid_ Report_july_2019_eng.pdf [Knaak et al, *Stigma and the Opioid Crisis*].

77   See Morgan Modjeski, "Supervised Consumption Site Advocates Say Kimberly Squirrel's Death Could Have Been Prevented" (25 April 2021), online: www.cbc. ca/news/canada/saskatoon/autopsy-results-on-squirrel-tragedy-1.5999888; see also BC Coroners Service Death Review Panel, *A Review of Illicit Drug Overdoses, Report to the Coroner of British Columbia* (Victoria: BC Coroners Service Death Review Panel, 5 April 2018) at 19–20, online: www2.gov.bc.ca/assets/gov/birth-adoption-death-marriage-and-divorce/deaths/coroners-service/death-review-panel/bccs_illicit_ drug_overdose_drp_report.pdf; see also Alberta Health, *Opioid-related Deaths in Alberta in 2017: Review of Medical Examiner Data,* (Edmonton: Alberta Health, 8 July 2019) at 15, online: open.alberta.ca/publications/9781460143421; see also CMHA, *supra* note 1 at 37; see also Office of the Provincial Health Officer, *supra* note 29 at 19; see also Toronto Public Health, *supra* note 3 at 4.

78   See CPHA, *supra* note 10 at 4; see also CMHA, *supra* note 1 at 39.

79   See CPHA, *supra* note 10 at 5; see also CMHA, *supra* note 1 at 3; see also Office of the Provincial Health Officer, *supra* note 29 at 20-21; see also Standing Committee on Health, *supra* note 14 at 55; Jeffries, *supra* note 53.

80   See Bogart, *Off the Street, supra* note 4 at 50; see also Health Canada, Public Consultation, *supra* note 57 at 13; see also Office of the Provincial Health Officer, *supra* note 29 at 20; see also Toronto Public Health, *supra* note 3 at 5; see also Canadian Women's Foundation & BC Society of Transition Houses, *Report on Violence Against Women, Mental Health and Substance Use* (Vancouver: Canadian Women's Foundation, 2011) at 9, online: www.canadianwomen.org/wp-content/ uploads/2018/03/PDF-VP-Resources-BCSTH-CWF-Report_Final_2011_-Mental-Health_Substance-use.pdf [CWF, *Report on Violence*].

81   See Office of the Provincial Health Officer, *supra* note 29 at 19; see also Knaak et al, *Stigma and the Opioid Crisis, supra* note 76 at 12-18; see also Jeffries, *supra* note 53; see also Toronto Public Health, *supra* note 3 at 4-5, 12; see also Special Advisory Committee, *supra* note 18; see also Canadian Institute for Health Information, *Opioid-Related Harms in Canada* (Ottawa: Canadian Institute for Health Information December 2018), online: www.cihi.ca/sites/default/files/document/opioid-related-harms-report-2018-en-web.pdf.

82   See Jeffries, *supra* note 53.

83   See *Charter, supra* note 22, s 7.

84   See *Malmo-Levine, supra* note 68 at para 135.

85   *Ibid* at para 136.

86   See *Chaoulli v Quebec (Attorney General)*, 2005 SCC 35 at paras 131-132, 232, [2005] 1 SCR 791 [*Chaoulli*].

87   *Ibid* at paras 131, 132.

88   See *Insite, supra* note 20 at para 131.

89   See *Malmo-Levine, supra* note 68 at 169.

90   *Ibid* at 174-175.

91   See *Insite, supra* note 20 at para 133.

92   See *R v Morgentaler*, [1988] 1 SCR 30 at 175, 44 DLR (4th) 385 [*Morgentaler*].

93   *Ibid* at 175-176.

94   See *New Brunswick (Minister of Health and Community Services) v G (J)*, [1999] 3 SCR 46 at 115, 177 DLR (4th) 124; see generally Kerri Froc, "Constitutional Coalescence: Substantive Equality as a Principle of Fundamental Justice" (2011) 42 Ottawa L Rev 41; see also Suzy Flader, "Fundamental Rights for All: Toward Equality as a Principle of Fundamental Justice under Section 7 of the *Charter*" (2020) 25 Appeal 43.

95   See Office of the Provincial Health Officer, *supra* note 29 at 18; see also HIV Legal Network, "Letter to Canadian Government," *supra* note 5; see also Angus Reid Institute, "Canada's Other Epidemic: As Overdose Deaths Escalate, Majority Favour Decriminalization of Drugs" (24 February 2021), online: angusreid.org/opioid-crisis-covid/.

96   See Canadian Chiefs of Police, *supra* note 13 at 14.

97   See Teresa Wright, "Talks Needed on Decriminalizing Hard Drugs to Address Opioid Crisis, Tam Says" (22 August 2020), online: www.ctvnews.ca/health/talks-needed-on-decriminalizing-hard-drugs-to-address-opioid-crisis-tam-says-1.5075176.

98   See Toronto Public Health, *supra* note 3 at 26; see also Office of the Provincial Health Officer, *supra* note 29 at 20; see also Knaak et al, *Stigma and the Opioid Crisis, supra* note 76 at 18-20; see also Canadian Association of People who Use Drugs, "Safe Supply: Concept Document" (February 2019), online: static1.squarespace.com/static/5ef3cdaf47af2060a1cc594e/t/608c29e8d9137244ec7da81f/1619798507472/CAPUD+safe+supply+English+March+3+2019.pdf [CAPUD]; see also Civil Society Working Group, *supra* note 5 at 10.

99   See Toronto Public Health, *supra* note 3 at 25; see also A J Lowik et al, *Side by Side, supra* note 57 at 6.

100 See Ka Hon Chu & Kazatchkine, *supra* note 4 at 6.

101 See Office of the Provincial Health Officer, *supra* note 29 at 20; see also Knaak et al, *Stigma and the Opioid Crisis, supra* note 76 at 12-18; see also PHAC, *State of Public Health 2018, supra* note 151 at 28.

102 See Derek Chang, "Dr. Derek Chang: We Must Make Drug Decriminalization a Federal Election Issue" (4 September 2019), online: vancouversun.com/opinion/op-ed/dr-derek-chang-we-must-make-drug-decriminalization-a-federal-election-issue [Chang, "Decriminalization"].

103 See Health Canada, *Public Consultation, supra* note 57 at 13.

104 See *Report on the 61st Session (8 December 2017 and 12-16 March 2018)*, United Nations Commission on Narcotic Drugs, 61st Sess, UN Doc E/CN.7/2018/13 (2018) at 28.

105 See International Drug Policy Consortium, *The 2018 Commission on Narcotic Drugs: Report of Proceedings*, (London, UK: IDPC, 19 June 2018) at 14, online: idpc.net/publications/2018/06/the-2018-commission-on-narcotic-drugs-report-of-proceedings.

106 See Bill C-22, *supra* note 48, s 10(1).

107 See HIV Legal Network, "Letter to Canadian Government," *supra* note 5; see also Bonn et al, "Syndemic," *supra* note 2.

108 See HIV Legal Network, "Letter to Canadian Government," *supra* note 5.

109 *Ibid*.

110 See CMHA, *supra* note 1 at 40-41; see also Canadian Chiefs of Police, *supra* note 13 at 14.

111 See Laura Dale, "Decriminalizing Drug Use Isn't a Slippery Slope—It's a Proven Path Forward" (19 July 2019), online: thetyee.ca/Opinion/2019/07/19/Decriminalizing-Drug-Use-Path-Forward [Dale, "Path Forward"].

112 See *Malmo-Levine, supra* note 68 at para 169.

113 See CPHA, *supra* note 10 at 6.

114 See Office of the Provincial Health Officer, *supra* note 29 at 21.

115 See *Insite, supra* note 20 at paras 113, 114.

116 See Foreman-Mackey & Kazatchkine, *supra* note 39 at 17; see also Ka Hon Chu & Kazatchkine, *supra* note 4 at 12-16; see also Special Rapporteur, *supra* note 1 at 5-6.

117 See Foreman-Mackey & Kazatchkine, *supra* note 39 at 18; see also Health Canada, "Supervised Consumption Site," *supra* note 52; see also HIV Legal Network, "Harm Reduction," *supra* note 4; see also Ka Hon Chu & Kazatchkine, *supra* note 4 at 8.

118 See Health Canada, "Supervised Consumption Site," *supra* note 52; see also Foreman-Mackey & Kazatchkine, *supra* note 39 at 20-21.

119 See Nicole Brownlee, "Supervised Consumption Services Face Host of Difficulties in Prairie Provinces" (30 May 2021), online: www.theglobeandmail.com/canada/alberta/article-supervised-consumption-services-face-host-of-difficulties-in-prairie/ [Brownlee]; see also Foreman-Mackey & Kazatchkine, *supra* note 39 at 20-21.

120 See Foreman-Mackey & Kazatchkine, *supra* note 39 at 18; see also Toronto Public Health, *supra* note 3 at 13-14; see also Jeffries, *supra* note 53; see also CMHA *supra* note 1 at 36; see also Alessia Passafiume, "Critics of Alberta's New Rules for Supervised Consumption Sites Say They Will Curb Access for Vulnerable Clients" (4 June 2021), online: www.theglobeandmail.com/canada/alberta/article-critics-of-albertas-new-rules-for-supervised-consumption-sites-say/; see also Shane Gibson, "Drug Overdose Deaths Spiked 87 Per Cent in Manitoba Last Year" (22 April 2021), online: globalnews.ca/news/7778633/drug-overdose-deaths-manitoba-2020/.

121 See Health Canada, "Supervised Consumption Sites: Status of Applications," (5 July 2021), online: www.canada.ca/en/health-canada/services/substance-use/supervised-consumption-sites/status-application.html#a1;   see   also   PIVOT, "Canada's Safe Consumption and Overdose Prevention Sites" (15 January 2021), online: www.pivotlegal.org/scs_ops_map; see also CBC News, "Change Your Stance on Overdose Prevention Sites, Health Groups Urge Ford" (30 August 2018); online: www.cbc.ca/news/canada/toronto/change-your-stance-on-overdose-prevention-sites-health-groups-urge-ford-1.4804099.

122 See Stephanie Tsicos, "Tossed Report on Safe Consumption Spaces Causes Stir in Manitoba Legislature" (8 April 2019), online: winnipeg.ctvnews.ca/tossed-report-on-safe-consumption-spaces-causes-stir-in-manitoba-legislature-1.4371338.

123 See Brownlee, *supra* note 119.

124 See CBC News, "Province Cut Some Injection Sites Because Area Residents 'Upset,' Ford Says" (1 April 2019), online: www.cbc.ca/news/canada/toronto/province-cut-some-injection-sites-because-area-residents-upset-ford-says-1.5079616.

125 See Brownlee, *supra* note 119.

126 See *Insite, supra* note 20 at para 19.

127 *Ibid* at para 114; see also Alana Klein, "Criminal Law and the Counter-Hegemonic Potential of Harm Reduction" (2015) 38 Dal LJ 447 at 469.

128 Section 15(1) provides that: "Every individual is equal before and under the law and has the right to the equal protection and equal benefit of the law without discrimination and, in particular, without discrimination based on race, national or ethnic origin, colour, religion, sex, age or mental or physical disability." In *Fraser v Canada (Attorney General)*, 2020 SCC 28 at para 50: "To prove discrimination under s. 15(1), claimants must show that a law or policy creates a distinction based on a protected ground, and that the law perpetuates, reinforces or exacerbates disadvantage." See generally Sonia Lawrence, "Equality and Anti-Discrimination" in Peter Oliver, Patrick Macklem & Nathalie DesRosiers, eds, *The Oxford Handbook of the Canadian Constitution* (New York: Oxford University Press, 2017) 815 at 841;

see also Jonnette Watson Hamilton, "Cautious Optimism: *Fraser v Canada (Attorney General)*" (2021) 30:2 Const Forum Const 1.

129 See *Morgentaler, supra* note 92.

130 See *Insite, supra* note 20 at paras 99, 101.

131 See Le Dain Commission, *supra* note 17 at 53.

132 See Toronto Public Health, *supra* note 3 at 25.

133 See Standing Committee on Health, *supra* note 14 at 22; see also CMHA, *supra* note 1 at 8-10; see also Office of the Provincial Health Officer, *supra* note 29 at 18-19; see also Health Canada, Public Consultation, *supra* note 57 at 10; see also Global Commission on Drug Policy, *supra* note 5 at 21.

134 See Standing Committee on Health, *supra* note 14 at 22; see also CMHA, *supra* note 1 at 11; see also Ottawa Public Health, *Ottawa Community Action Plan: Comprehensive Mental Health and Substance Use Strategy—Focus on Opioids* (Ottawa: Ottawa Public Health, 12 September 2019) at 2, online: www.ottawapublichealth.ca/en/reports-research-and-statistics/resources/Documents/Mental_Health_Substance_Use_focus_on_opiods-Community_Action_Plan_Public_Version_FINAL-ua.pdf; see also Health Canada, Public Consultation, *supra* note 57 at 24; see also Canadian Centre on Substance Abuse, *Concurrent Disorders: Substance Abuse in Canada* (Ottawa: Canadian Centre on Substance Abuse, 2009) at 2, online: www.ccsa.ca/sites/default/files/2019-04/ccsa-011811-2010.pdf [CCSA, *Concurrent Disorders*].

135 See Standing Committee on Health, *supra* note 14 at 23; see also CMHA, *supra* note 1 at 10; see also Toronto Public Health, *supra* note 3 at 23.

136 See Standing Committee on Health, *supra* note 14 at 23-24; see also Ka Hon Chu & Kazatchkine, *supra* note 4 at 6; see also CMHA, *supra* note 1 at 10.

137 See Standing Committee on Health, *supra* note 14 at 25; see also Truth and Reconciliation Commission, *Honouring the Truth, Reconciling for the Future: Summary of the Final Report of the Truth and Reconciliation Commission of Canada* (Winnipeg: Truth and Reconciliation Committee, 2015) at 161-162, online: ehprnh2mwo3.exactdn.com/wp-content/uploads/2021/01/Executive_Summary_English_Web.pdf [Truth and Reconciliation Commission]; see also Ka Hon Chu & Kazatchkine, *supra* note 4 at 6; see also Public Health Agency of Canada, *Addressing Stigma—Towards a More Inclusive Health System: The Chief Public Health Officer's Report on the State of Public Health in Canada, 2019* (Ottawa: Public Health Agency of Canada, December 2019) at 9, 13, online: www.canada.ca/content/dam/phac-aspc/documents/corporate/publications/chief-public-health-officer-reports-state-public-health-canada/addressing-stigma-what-we-heard/wwh-2019-12-17.pdf [PHAC, *State of Public Health 2019*]; see also CMHA, *supra* note 1 at 10; see also Nunavut, NVision Insight Group, *Addictions and Trauma Treatment in Nunavut: Executive Summary* (Ottawa: NVision Insight Group, August 2018) at 1, online: www.gov.nu.ca/sites/default/files/gn_att_executive_summary_summary_report_-_final_-_english.pdf [NVision Insight Group]; see also Health Canada, Public Consultation, *supra* note 57 at 21-22, 24; see also CMHA, *supra* note 1 at 10; see also Special Rapporteur, *supra* note 1 at 5.

138 See Standing Committee on Health, *supra* note 14 at 26; see also Health Canada, Public Consultation, *supra* note 57 at 24.

139 See CMHA, *supra* note 1 at 4; see also CAPUD, *supra* note 98.

140 See HIV Legal Network, "Submission to the High Commissioner," *supra* note 73; see also A J Lowik et al, *Side by Side, supra* note 57 at 6; see also CESCR, *Concluding Observations*, 2016, *supra* note 6 at para 49.

141 See *Concluding Observations on the Combined Twenty-first to Twenty-third Periodic Reports of Canada*, UN Committee on the Elimination of Racial Discrimination, 93rd Sess, UN Doc CERD/C/CAN/CO/21-21 (2017) at para 16(d).

142 See HIV Legal Network, "Submission to the High Commissioner," *supra* note 73 at 4, citing Ontario Human Rights Commission, *A Disparate Impact: Second Interim Report on the Inquiry into Racial Profiling and Racial Discrimination of Black Persons by the Toronto Police Services* (Toronto: Ontario Human Rights Commission, 10 August 2020), online: www.ohrc.on.ca/sites/default/files/A%20Disparate%20Impact%20 Second%20interim%20report%20on%20the%20TPS%20inquiry%20executive%20 summary.pdf#overlay-context=en/disparate-impact-second-interim-report-inquiry-racial-profiling-and-racial-discrimination-black.

143 See CWF, *Report on Violence, supra* note 80; see also Ka Hon Chu & Kazatchkine, *supra* note 4 at 7.

144 See CWF, *Report on Violence, supra* note 80 at 5; see also Ka Hon Chu & Kazatchkine, *supra* note 4 at 5-6.

145 See CWF, *Report on Violence, supra* note 80 at 9, 14-15; see also CESCR, *Concluding Observations, 2016, supra* note 6 at para 49; see also Ka Hon Chu & Kazatchkine, *supra* note 4 at 6, 9-11, 16-18.

146 See Correctional Investigator of Canada, *Annual Report 2014-2015 of the Office of the Correctional Investigator,* Catalogue No PS100E-PDF (Ottawa: Correctional Investigator, 26 June 2015) at 50, online: www.oci-bec.gc.ca/cnt/rpt/pdf/annrpt/annrpt20142015-eng.pdf.

147 *Ibid* at 51; see also CMHA, *supra* note 1 at 39; see also National Inquiry into Missing and Murdered Indigenous Women and Girls, *Reclaiming Power and Place: The Final Report of the National Inquiry into Missing and Murdered Indigenous Women and Girls Volume 1a* (Ottawa: National Inquiry into Missing and Murdered Indigenous Women and Girls 2019) at 637, online: www.mmiwg-ffada.ca/wp-content/uploads/2019/06/Final_Report_Vol_1a-1.pdf; see also Correctional Services of Canada, *Profile of Federally Sentenced Women Drug Offenders,* by Renée Gobeil, (Ottawa: Correctional Services Canada, May 2009), online: publications. gc.ca/collections/collection_2010/scc-csc/PS83-3-204-eng.pdf>; see also CEDAW, *Concluding Observations, 2016, supra* note 7 at para 45; see also HIV Legal Network, "Submission to the High Commissioner," *supra* note 73 at 6-7.

148 See Office of the Provincial Health Officer, *supra* note 29 at 18; see also Standing Committee on Health, *supra* note 14 at 29-30.

149 See Office of the Provincial Health Officer, *supra* note 29 at 18-19; see also Toronto Public Health, *supra* note 3 at 12; see also CMHA, *supra* note 1 at 39; see also Ka Hon Chu & Kazatchkine, *supra* note 4 at 15-17.

150 See Health Canada, *Public Consultation, supra* note 57 at 23.

151 See HIV Legal Network, "Submission to the High Commissioner," *supra* note 73 at 4; see also *Public Health Agency of Canada, Preventing Problematic Substance Use in Youth: The Chief Public Health Officer's Report on the State of Public Health in Canada 2018,* Catalogue No HP2-10E-PDF (Ottawa: Public Health Agency of Canada, 23 October 2018) at 23-24, online: www.canada.ca/content/dam/phac-aspc/documents/ corporate/publications/chief-public-health-officer-reports-state-public-health-canada/2018-preventing-problematic-substance-use-youth/2018-preventing-problematic-substance-use-youth.pdf [PHAC, *State of Public Health 2018*].

152 See CMHA, *supra* note 1 at 10; see also Elizabeth M Saewyc, "Substance Use Among Non-mainstream Youth" in Canadian Centre for Substance Use, ed, *Substance Abuse in Canada: Youth in Focus* (Ottawa: Canadian Centre for Substance Use, 2007) at 15-17; see also PHAC, *State of Public Health 2018, supra* note 151 at 24.

153 See Health Canada, *Public Consultation, supra* note 57 at 23.

154 See A J Lowik et al, *Side by Side, supra* note 57 at 6; see also Serge Brochu, "Our Responses to Youth Substance Abuse" in Canadian Centre for Substance Use, ed,

Substance Abuse in Canada: Youth in Focus (Ottawa: Canadian Centre for Substance Use, 2007) at 25.

155 See Civil Society Working Group, *supra* note 5 at 15.

156 *Ibid* at 9.

157 See *Charter, supra* note 22, s 1.

158 See *R v Oakes*, [1986] 1 SCR 103, 26 DLR (4th) 200.

159 See generally Robert J Shape & Kent Roach, *The Charter of Rights and Freedoms*, 6th ed (Toronto: Irwin Law, 2017) at 48-65.

160 See *Suresh v Canada*, 2002 SCC 1 at para 78; see also Reference re s 94(2) of the *Motor Vehicle Act* (BC), [1985] 2 SCR 486 at 518, 60 DLR (4th) 397.

161 See *United States v Burns*, 2001 SCC 7 at para 133.

162 See *Insite, supra* note 20 at para 137.

163 See *Chaoulli, supra* note 86 at para 155.

164 See Office of the Provincial Health Officer, *supra* note 29 at 35.

165 See *Dagenais v Canadian Broadcasting Corp*, [1994] 3 SCR 835 at 887, 120 DLR (4th) 12.

166 See Office of the Provincial Health Officer, *supra* note 29 at 18-22; see also Civil Society Working Group, *supra* note 5 at 8; see also Bogart, *Off the Street, supra* note 4 at 39-52; see also Standing Committee on Health, *supra* note 14 at 20; see also Dale, "Path Forward," *supra* note 111.

167 See Bill C-22, *supra* note 48, ss 10(2), 10(3).

168 *Ibid*, s 10(4), 10(5); see also Elliott, "Statement Bill C-22," *supra* note 50; see also Akwasi Owusu-Bempah & Alex Luscombe, "Race, Cannabis and the Canadian War on Drugs: An Examination of Cannabis Arrest Data by Race in Five Cities" (2021) 91 Intl J Drug Policy 102937; see also Andrea Huncar, "Indigenous Women Nearly 10 Times More Likely to Be Street Checked by Edmonton Police, New Data Shows" (27 June 2017), online: www.cbc.ca/news/canada/edmonton/street-checks-edmonton-police-aboriginal-black-carding-1.4178843.

169 See Elliott, "Statement Bill C-22," *supra* note 50.

170 See *Irwin Toy Ltd v Quebec (AG)*, [1989] 1 SCR 927 at 993-994, 58 DLR (4th) 577.

171 See Global Commission on Drug Policy, *supra* note 5 at 21.

172 See Chang, "Decriminalization," *supra* note 102.

173 See HIV Legal Network, "Harm Reduction," *supra* note 4; see also Toronto Public Health, *supra* note 3; see also Civil Society Working Group, *supra* note 5; see also Jesseman & Payer, *Decriminalization, supra* note 56; see also International Centre for Human Rights and Drug Policy et al, "International Guidelines on Human Rights and Drug Policy" (6 November 2020), online: www.undp.org/content/undp/en/home/librarypage/hiv-aids/international-guidelines-on-human-rights-and-drug-policy.html.

174 See CPHA, *supra* note 10 at 4.

175 See *International Covenant on Economic, Social and Cultural Rights*, 16 December 1966, 993 UNTS 3 art 12(1) (entered into force 3 January 1976, accession by Canada 19 May 1976); see generally Martha Jackman, "Law as a Tool for Addressing Social Determinants of Health" in Tracey M Bailey, C Tess Sheldon & Jacob J Shelley, eds, *Public Health Law and Policy in Canada*, 4th ed (Toronto: LexisNexis Canada Inc, 2019) at 112-115 [Jackman, "Determinants of Health"].

176 See CESCR, *Concluding Observations*, 2016, *supra* note 6 at paras 49, 50.

177 *Ibid* at para 50.

178 See CEDAW, *Concluding Observations*, 2016, *supra* note 7 at paras 44, 45(a).

179 See Special Rapporteur, *supra* note 1 at 5-6.

180 *Ibid*.

181 See CAPUD, *supra* note 98 at 5; see also Csete & Elliott, *supra* note 53; see also Bonn et al, *Securing Safe Supply, supra* note 55; see also Standing Committee on Health, *supra* note 14 at 39-44.

182 See Standing Committee on Health, *supra* note 14 at 44.

183 *Ibid*; see also HIV Legal Network, Harm Reduction, *supra* note 4; see also NVision Insight Group, *supra* note 137 at 1; see also CWF, *Report on Violence, supra* note 80 at 16-19; see also CCSA, *Concurrent Disorders, supra* note 134 at 2; see also CMHA, *supra* note 1 at 5-6, 20-25.

184 See Jackman, "Determinants of Health," *supra* note 175 at 112-115; see also Csete & Elliott, *supra* note 53 at 2-3; see also Special Rapporteur, *supra* note 1; see also Bruce Porter, "International Human Rights in Anti-poverty and Housing Strategies: Making the Connection" in Martha Jackman & Bruce Porter, eds, *Advancing Social Rights in Canada* (Toronto: Irwin Law, 2014) 33 at 33.

185 See CMHA, *supra* note 1 at 5-6; see also CPHA, *supra* note 10 at 4; see also Toronto Public Health, *supra* note 3 at 23-24; see also NNPBC & HRNA, *supra* note 11.

186 See PHAC, *State of Public Health 2018, supra* note 151 at 32.

187 See A J Lowik et al, *Side by Side, supra* note 57 at 12; see also Health Canada, *Public Consultation, supra* note 57 at 23.

188 See Michelle Proctor-Simms et al, "Transitioning from Incarceration to the Community: Reducing Risks and Improving Lives of People Who Use Substances" (23 November 2020), online (blog): blog.catie.ca/2020/11/23/transitioning-from-incarceration-to-the-community-reducing-risks-and-improving-lives-of-people-who-use-substances/; see also Toronto Public Health, *supra* note 3 at 23-24.

189 See HIV Legal Network, "Harm Reduction," *supra* note 4; see also Bonn et al, *Securing Safe Supply, supra* note 55 at 21-22; see Foreman-Mackey & Kazatchkine, *supra* note 39 at 24-25; see HIV Legal Network, *Making the Ask, supra* note 1; see also International Network of People who Use Drugs, "Drug Decriminalization: Progress or Political Red Herring?" (12 April 2021) at 31-32, online: www.inpud. net/en/drug-decriminalisation-progress-or-political-red-herring; see also Truth and Reconciliation Commission, *supra* note 137 at 160-164.

190 See *Globe and Mail* Editorial, *supra* note 15.

CHAPTER 3

Long Overdue and Still Deficient

The Correctional Service of Canada's
Prison Needle Exchange Program

Sandra Ka Hon Chu and Richard Elliott

In May 2018, the Correctional Service of Canada (CSC) announced its plan to implement a prison needle exchange program (PNEP) in federal prisons, beginning with a "phased approach to strengthen its ongoing efforts to prevent and manage infectious disease in federal penitentiaries and in the community," before rolling out the program.[1]

This announcement followed more than two decades of advocacy by prison-health and human-rights organizations across Canada, and shortly before the long-delayed hearing of a lawsuit initiated in the Ontario Superior Court of Justice in 2012 to compel the CSC to make sterile injection equipment available to federal prisoners. While the roll-out of the PNEP is a historic development, representing the first prison-based needle and syringe program (PNSP) in the Americas, concerns remain about the accessibility of the CSC program, which prioritizes unfounded threats to security over clinical need and violates prisoners' confidentiality in numerous ways without reasonable justification, and whether the PNEP will withstand changing political environments.

Background

In Canada and many other countries, the prevalence of HIV and HCV in prison populations is significantly higher than in the population as a whole. Recent studies indicate the prevalence of HIV among people in federal prisons is 0.9% compared to 0.2% for the general population, while HCV prevalence is 3.2%, compared to 0.6% in the population as a whole.[2] Indigenous prisoners are particularly affected, and Indigenous women in federal prisons are reported to have prevalence of HIV and HCV of 11.7% and 49.1%, respectively.[3]

Research over many years and from a range of jurisdictions has demonstrated the nexus between such infections and injection drug use, a result of the prevalence of HIV and HCV infections among people who inject drugs in the wider community, the high rates of incarceration of people who use drugs (PWUD), and a lack of access to harm reduction measures in prisons equivalent to those available outside. In a recent national survey, 3.6% of federal prisoners reported injecting drugs within the past six months; among them, approximately half reported using a previously used needle to inject, or passing their needle to someone else after they injected.[4] In 2014, the Office of the Correctional Investigator reported that, upon admission, 80% of federally sentenced men had a substance-use problem;[5] in a 2017 CSC study, 92% of all federally sentenced Indigenous women were assessed as having moderate or high substance-use needs.[6]

Despite the penalties for their use and the significant resources spent by prison systems on drug-interdiction efforts such as canine detecting units, ion scanners, X-ray machines, mandatory drug testing, and the employment of security officers to contain availability,[7] prohibited drugs do get into prisons, and prisoners use them. Yet, the scarcity of sterile injection equipment and the punitive consequences of being found in possession of drugs mean prisoners resort to using non-sterile injecting equipment.[8] A needle (or a makeshift "rig" for injection) may circulate among large numbers of prisoners who inject drugs, thereby increasing the risk of HIV and HCV transmission because of the presence of blood in the equipment after injection[9]—a risk further compounded by the higher prevalence of both HIV and HCV among prisoners. In the 2010 CSC survey, 17% of men and 14% of women acknowledged injecting drugs in prison, roughly half of those prisoners used a contaminated needle, and roughly one-third shared a needle with someone who had HIV, HCV, or an unknown infection status.[10] A study in Vancouver estimated that incarceration more than doubled the risk of HIV infection for PWUD, and estimated that 21% of all HIV infections among people in Vancouver who inject drugs may have been acquired in prison.[11] As the correctional investigator of Canada has concluded, "[d]rug interdiction can only go so far in reducing the rate of infection among [prisoners]."[12]

Significantly higher prevalence of HIV and HCV in prison populations must also be considered against a backdrop of the mass incarceration of Indigenous and Black people incarcerated in Canada. Not only are Black and Indigenous communities disproportionately policed, arrested, and jailed for drug offences,[13] they are also disproportionately exposed to the risks brought on by the lack of harm reduction services behind prison walls. While accounting for approximately 5% of the adult population, Indigenous peoples account for 32% of all individuals in custody, and Indigenous women account for 50% of all federally incarcerated women.[14] Similarly, while accounting for only 3% of the total Canadian population, Black people represent 9% of the federal prison population.[15] Since 2010, the number of Indigenous people in prison has increased by 43.4%, whereas the non-Indigenous prison population has declined by 13.7% over the same period.[16]

Harm reduction measures aimed at preventing HIV and HCV transmission in prisons are neither new nor ground-breaking in Canada. Prison systems including the CSC have implemented, to varying degrees, forms of harm reduction such as condoms, bleach, and opioid agonist treatment. However, until 2018, no jurisdiction in Canada had implemented a PNSP.[17] Outside of Canada, and at the time of writing, PNSPs had been implemented and are operating in Armenia, Germany, Kyrgyzstan, Luxembourg, Macedonia, Moldova, Romania, Spain, Switzerland, and Tajikistan.[18] No matter the context studied, and in diverse environments and under differing circumstances, evaluations of these programs—including in 2006 by the Public Health Agency of Canada, at the CSC's request—have consistently demonstrated that they:

- reduce needle sharing,
- do not lead to increased drug use or injecting,
- reduce drug overdoses,
- facilitate referrals of users to drug treatment programs,
- have not resulted in needles or syringes being used as weapons against staff or other people in prison,
- have been effective in a wide range of institutions, and
- have effectively employed different methods of needle distribution, such as peer distribution by people in prison,

hand-to-hand distribution by prison health-care staff or outside agencies, and automatic dispensing machines.[19]

Notably, in more than more than three decades of functioning PNSPs, there has not been a single reported incident of assault with needles from such programs anywhere in the world. As early as 1999, a group of experts convened by the CSC reported that providing access to sterile injection equipment through a PNSP "is an effective and well-proven method of reducing the harms associated with injection drug use, and would be an effective way for the CSC to meet its legislative obligation under the [Corrections and Conditional Release Act] to do everything possible to ensure public protection in the treatment and release of [prisoners]."[20] The group recommended an immediate multi-site PNSP pilot in CSC prisons. In his 2003–2004 annual report, the correctional investigator of Canada reported "no movement" on this issue and recommended introduction of a PNSP by March 31, 2005, and, failing compliance, that the responsible minister direct implementation of that program.[21] Since then, the ombudsman's office has made repeated recommendations to implement PNSPs,[22] as have a range of health and human-rights organizations in Canada, including the Canadian and Ontario Medical Associations.[23] At the same time, numerous international organizations have called for PNSPs as a matter of both sound public health policy and human rights, including UN agencies such as the Joint United Nations Programme on HIV/AIDS (UNAIDS), the Office of the United Nations High Commissioner for Human Rights (OHCHR),[24] the World Health Organization (WHO), and the United Nations Office on Drugs and Crime (UNODC).[25]

Constitutional Challenge

In 2012, after successive governments in Canada had refused to implement a PNSP, despite years of recommendations from a growing body of experts, the HIV Legal Network (then the Canadian HIV/AIDS Legal Network), three other HIV organizations, and former prisoner Steven Simons launched a court challenge against the Canadian government. The co-applicants argued that prohibitions against sterile injection equipment (i.e., the prohibitions in the federal Corrections and Conditional Release Act [CCRA] on "contraband" and "unauthorized items" that prevent federal prisoners from receiving or possessing sterile injection equipment)[26] violated prisoners' rights under the Charter,[27] specifically the rights to life, liberty, and security of the person protected by section 7 and the right to equality protected by section 15, and the CSC's obligations under the CCRA, as well as being contrary to Canada's obligations under international human-rights law. Simons, who had spent more than a decade in a federal penitentiary before his release in 2010, tested positive for HCV after another prisoner used his injection equipment without his knowledge.

The co-applicants contended that the prohibitions established by the CCRA against prisoners' receipt and possession of sterile injection equipment for drug use force prisoners who inject drugs to use in unsafe circumstances. The threat of discipline if detected means injection is furtive and often hurried, and the scarcity of injection equipment compels the sharing of injection equipment by many in a population known by the CSC to have a high prevalence of drug use and dependence, and a much higher prevalence of HIV and HCV. This occurs in circumstances where the CSC exercises absolute control over prisoners' access to health care and living conditions, and the CSC is expressly mandated under the CCRA to use "the least restrictive measures" in carrying out sentences,[28] to provide "essential health care" and "reasonable access to non-essential health care" that shall "conform to professionally accepted standards," and otherwise to take all reasonable steps to ensure prisoners' "safe, healthful and humane living conditions."[29]

The CCRA's blanket prohibitions against the receipt and possession of injection equipment for drug use thus infringe the security of the person and life of federal prisoners who inject drugs by preventing their access to sterile injection equipment (a form of essential health care) and denying them the ability to make fundamental personal choices with respect to their health and bodily integrity, thereby putting their health at grave risk of harm and increased risk of death. The penal consequences of being found with prohibited injection equipment further violate prisoners' liberty interests. Such deprivation is arbitrary, overbroad, and grossly disproportionate to the legislative objectives of protecting prisoners' health and safety, the maintenance of institutional security, and the protection of public health and safety. The co-applicants also argued that CSC's failure to provide access to sterile injection equipment to people who inject drugs in prisons violates section 15 of the Charter by denying prisoners—many of whom are dependent on drugs (recognized as a disability in Canadian law for purposes of protection against discrimination) and are also dis-proportionately women and Indigenous—the right to equal protec-tion and benefit of the law.

International human rights standards were also key elements of the co-applicants' legal arguments. In particular, the United Nations Standard Minimum Rules for the Treatment of Prisoners (known as the Nelson Mandela Rules, which Canada adopted in a unanimous vote of UN General Assembly members) affirm that prisoners retain all the rights enjoyed by all other members of society except those that are lawfully and necessarily removed or restricted as a con-sequence of the sentence.[30] This includes the right to health under article 12 of the International Covenant on Economic, Social and Cultural Rights, which has been recognized by the UN committee of independent experts that monitors states' progress in implementing the agreement as obligating states to refrain from "denying or limit-ing equal access for all persons, including prisoners or detainees [...] to preventive, curative and palliative health services."[31] The Mandela Rules also affirm that prisoners "should enjoy the same standards of health care that are available in the community" (generally referred to as the "principle of equivalence"), and that "[h]ealth-care ser-vices should be organized in close relationship to the general public health administration and in a way that ensures continuity of treat-ment and care, including for HIV, tuberculosis and other infectious diseases, as well as for drug dependence."[32] The co-applicants fur-ther highlighted specific recommendations to Canada by expert UN human-rights bodies tasked with monitoring states' compliance with the Convention on the Elimination of All Forms of Discrimination against Women and the Convention on the Elimination of All Forms of Racial Discrimination, both of which addressed the issue of pris-oner health with respective recommendations to Canada to "[e]xpand care, treatment and support services to women in detention living with or vulnerable to HIV, including by implementing prison-based needle and syringe programmes,"[33] and to "implement key health and harm reduction measures across all prisons."[34]

CSC's Flawed Prison Needle Exchange Program

Six years after the court challenge was initiated—after several delays during which the applicants made good faith, but ultimately unsuccessful, efforts to settle the matter by securing a firm commitment by the CSC to implement a well-designed program—and mere months before the initial hearing date, the CSC announced its plan in May 2018 to implement a PNEP in federal prisons, beginning in two institutions in June 2018, followed by a national rollout in January 2019.[35] The announcement was met by strident opposition from the Union of Canadian Correctional Officers, whose members denounced the program on the basis that "handling needles" (which they were not asked to do) is "not [their] job" and would put members' safety at risk,[36] and vociferously protested the PNEP through numerous demonstrations in front of federal penitentiaries and by lobbying federal policy-makers, including the minister of public safety, to cancel the program.[37] Following the announcement, the CSC also sought to dismiss the court application, arguing, solely on the basis of this political statement by the minister of the plan to implement a PNEP, that the Charter challenge had been rendered moot.

The Superior Court rejected this claim, but on the basis of the government's promise, unfortunately adjourned the hearing for one year, despite the previous years-long and ongoing daily denial of access to this health service to thousands of prisoners in federal prisons. The court chose not to address the past breaches of constitutional rights and to defer the question of whether there was a constitutional obligation to ensure access to this harm reduction measure. Despite submissions regarding the breaches that had already occurred and were continuing, the court chose instead to wait for more evidence on the promised PNEP before making a judgment. The original and ongoing underlying issue of prisoners' constitutional rights to access this health service were, ultimately, left unaddressed by the court, which focussed its analysis entirely—and erroneously—on whether the program introduced by the CSC was constitutionally adequate, which represented only one of the two claims put forward by the co-applicants.

While the Canadian government's decision to implement a PNEP was historic, representing the first such program in the Western hemisphere, a closer examination of the program reveals serious deficiencies that are not in keeping with public health principles or professionally accepted standards for such programs—deficiencies the co-applicants argued continue to violate prisoners' Charter rights. Most fundamentally, the correctional service's PNEP violates prisoners' confidentiality in numerous ways without reasonable justification.

For example, the PNEP is based on a model employed for EpiPens and diabetic insulin injection in federal correctional institutions, involving a "threat/risk" assessment of each individual prisoner that requires a warden or deputy warden to approve each prisoner's participation based on security considerations rather than clinical need. This process requires prisoners who need access to sterile injection equipment to protect themselves against HIV, HCV, or other bloodborne infection to identify themselves to the head of the institution as engaging in the use of illegal drugs—without any guarantee of participation being approved. As the co-applicants contended, while this model may be appropriate to manage injection equipment for medication used to treat allergies and diabetes, these are not stigmatized, criminalized health conditions and do not imply a prisoner's involvement in a prohibited activity that risks punishment. Moreover, prisoners who are not authorized to carry an EpiPen or insulin self-injection equipment have alternative means of access to this medical intervention, which is not the case for prisoners who are denied access to the CSC's PNEP. For those prisoners, there is no option but to continue to reuse drug injection equipment, some of it makeshift rigs fashioned out of other available materials, with all the risks that this entails.

The correctional service's PNEP also requires daily "visual inspections" to verify accountability for the equipment distributed, a significant intrusion that breaches participants' confidentiality, including vis-à-vis other prisoners, with the attendant risk of institutional disciplinary, criminal, and other repercussions should trace amounts of prohibited substances be found on the equipment. This is contrary to accepted PNEP practice established in other jurisdictions, where—in the absence of any evidence of security risks—participating prisoners remain subject only to the same checks as other prisoners. (The CSC also originally maintained that a prisoner's participation in the PNEP could be disclosed to the Parole Board of Canada when considering parole applications, a further disincentive to participation, given the risk that this admission of use of prohibited drugs would undermine chances of successfully being paroled. During the course of the litigation, the CSC ultimately abandoned this provision, at least on paper.)

These breaches of confidentiality are contrary to national and international standards of medical ethics and conduct, public health principles, the international experience of effective PNSPs, and best practices as described in UN guidance and elsewhere. As the UNODC has underscored in its handbook on PNSPs:

Trust and confidentiality are essential elements of a successful programme. Without trust people will not participate in the programme. It is challenging to gain prisoner's trust, especially if prison staff, including health staff, are directly involved in the distribution of injecting materials. Prisoners will not be willing to register in a programme if they fear it could be used as proof that they continue to use drugs in prisons and therefore lead to a denial of conditional release.[38]

At the same time, equipment is only distributed via CSC health-care staff in a one-for-one exchange—a restrictive model that is no longer employed in needle and syringe programs in the community (further indicating a failure on the part of the CSC to provide health care that is equivalent to that available outside prison). Best practice in public health requires program accessibility to avoid placing prisoners in circumstances where they will resort to sharing used equipment. Among the recommendations of a 2016 study of various PNSP models in Canada, and former federal prisoners' perspectives on the necessary features of an effective program, was that the correctional service adopt a "hybrid or multi-model approach to distribution within each institution."[39] This entails confidential access to sterile injection equipment via multiple access points, including at least two modes of delivery in each penitentiary involving, for example, hand-to-hand distribution (by CSC health-care staff, outreach workers, and/or community-based harm reduction service providers) and/or automated dispensing machine, and the supply of equipment determined by need (i.e., not limited to one-for-one exchange).

One year after its rollout, Canada's prison watchdog expressed concerns about the approach the CSC had adopted. As he noted in his 2019 annual report, "[h]arm reduction strategies can only be successful if there is uptake on the part of users, and the way that the PNEP has been developed and implemented thus far seems to have built-in restrictions to enrollment. As of April 2019, perhaps not surprisingly, there were only a handful of individuals enrolled in the program."[40] In particular, the ombudsman criticized the one-to-one syringe exchange, which "does not necessarily respect clinical need or demand,"[41] the threat/risk assessment, the lack of multiple access and distribution points, and various breaches of confidentiality. In his view, "[t]oo much of what should be an exclusively health and harm reduction program has been shaped by security concerns."[42] As such, he recommended that "CSC revisit its Prison Needle Exchange Program purpose and participation criteria in consultation with inmates and staff with the aim of building confidence and trust, and look to international examples in how to modify the program to enhance participation and effectiveness."[43] Despite this, the CSC maintained the criticized elements of the PNEP and merely responded that the program would "continue to be developed and implemented according to scientific evidence."[44]

Ontario Superior Court Decision

In 2020, eight years after the court case was launched, and at a time when the PNEP had only been implemented in a handful of federal prisons, the Ontario Superior Court of Justice rendered its decision and declined to find that the PNEP, as implemented by the CSC, breached prisoners' constitutional rights. Such a conclusion, the court stated, would be "premature" because the rollout of the current program was only partially complete—after CSC's implementation was far slower than previously represented to the court—and the program continued to evolve, making it too early, in the court's view, to draw any conclusion as to its efficacy and adequacy.

The court did observe that the litigation had "raised important prison and public health issues and may well have prompted the CSC to implement the PNEP," and also acknowledged expressly that when the case was launched in 2012—at a time when the CSC had a complete prohibition on possession of sterile injection equipment by prisoners who use drugs—there were "compelling constitutional arguments" supporting access to sterile injection equipment as "essential health care." Regrettably, however, the court erred by failing to undertake any substantive constitutional analysis of this original, underlying, and still live question of whether the CSC could legally maintain a complete prohibition on possession of injection equipment, despite that, at the time of its decision, prohibition remained in place in the large majority of CSC institutions, and which the co-applicants had urged the court to address. The court chose to solely address the question of whether the PNEP program being implemented breached prisoners' Charter rights, failing to address whether prisoners have a basic constitutional right to sterile injection equipment, aside from the merits or demerits of the specific program introduced by the CSC.[45]

The court's failure to address this underlying question of the state's constitutional obligation to ensure prisoners have effective access to sterile injection equipment leaves the current (flawed) program in a precarious position. In 2019, in response to an election questionnaire posed by the Union of Canadian Correctional Officers, the Conservative Party of Canada indicated that "Conservatives have long opposed the prison needle exchange program. We do not believe that prisoners should have access to drugs while behind bars. And we also don't think that giving convicted criminals a weapon like a needle is smart policy. That is why a Conservative Government [...] will end the prison needle exchange program."[46] Moreover, at the time of the Ontario Superior Court decision, the PNEP was only operating in nine federal prisons and had been suspended in response to the COVID-19 pandemic,[47] with no indication of when the program rollout would resume. Already, a March 2020 interim evaluation of the PNEP revealed low rates of participation: of the nine federal prisons in which the program had been implemented, only four had any participants, and three institutions had not received a single expression of interest in the program. As the evaluation highlighted: "The fact that the majority (56 percent) of institutions with a PNEP have no active participants is of concern and needs to be examined in further detail in order to identify any potentially modifiable problems and challenges preventing participation."[48]

Low uptake, ongoing opposition to the program from correctional officers and the official opposition in Parliament, and the indefinite suspension of the PNEP during the COVID-19 pandemic means the program remains vulnerable to cancellation. If this were to occur, it would not be the first time that the CSC dismantled a proven harm reduction measure. In 2006, even though a draft evaluation indicated that CSC's pilot project in six prisons on safer tattooing practices "demonstrated potential to reduce harm," the federal (Conservative) public safety minister terminated the program even before completing and releasing a final evaluation.[49]

Conclusion

As detailed above, previous research in Canada centring on the perspectives of people with federal prison experience has underscored the importance of ensuring easy, confidential access to sterile injection supplies via a "hybrid or multi-model" approach, prisoners' active role in determining the specific model(s) to be implemented in each institution, and ongoing meaningful consultation with relevant stakeholders to ensure the accessibility and positive health outcomes of the program.[50] Moreover, the co-applicants in the constitutional challenge against the CSC have urged the service to reconsider the threat/risk assessment, one-for-one approach to equipment exchange, lack of multiple access and distribution points, and various breaches of confidentiality. Troublingly, the CSC has not addressed any of these recommendations and there is little indication that it plans to do so.

Programs meant to protect prisoners' health must be guided by scientific evidence and human-rights principles, not dictated by speculative claims about security risks—claims that have not been borne out in the evidence from more than 30 years of PNSPs in other jurisdictions. People in prison already experience marginalization and disproportionate illness, and bear the negative health consequences of policies and programs that do little to address a clear need. As the Ontario Superior Court acknowledged, the PNEP would not likely exist had there been no litigation. But for the PNEP to have tangible benefits, prisoners must have meaningful access to the program. And as co-applicant Steve Simons said: "For years, CSC has failed to provide adequate access to proven harm reduction programs. With this decision, I'm worried that prisoners will continue to lack access to injection equipment, which means people will continue to share needles and rigs."[51] Prison health and human rights advocates must continue to press for changes to the program model to address the shortcomings of the PNEP and for the corrections service to complete implementation of the PNEP in all federal prisons without further delay so the program is available and accessible to all prisoners. In the face of extensive evidence of the manifold benefits of an effective program, it is critical that the CSC not turn its back on prisoners yet again.

References

Legislation

Corrections and Conditional Release Act, SC 1992, c 20, ss 2(1), 40(i)-(j).
Part I of the *Constitution Act, 1982*, being Schedule B to the *Canada Act 1982* (UK), 1982, c 11.

SOR/92-620. Enforced by disciplinary and summary conviction offences under section 45 of the CCRA.

Jurisprudence

Simons et al v Minister of Public Safety, 2020 ONSC 1431.

Publications

Canadian Agency for Drugs and Technology in Health, *Needle Exchange Programs in a Correctional Setting: A Review of the Clinical and Cost-Effectiveness* (Ottawa: Canadian Agency for Drugs and Technology in Health, 2015).

Canadian Human Rights Commission, *Protecting Their Rights: A Systemic Review of Human Rights in Correctional Services for Federally Sentenced Women* (Ottawa: Canadian Human Rights Commission, 2004).

Committee on the Elimination of Discrimination Against Women, *Concluding Observations on the Combined Eighth and Ninth Periodic Reports of Canada*, UN Doc CEDAW/C/CAN/CO/8-9 (25 November 2016) at para 49(c).

Committee on the Elimination of Racial Discrimination, *Concluding Observations on the Twenty-First to Twenty-Third Periodic Reports of Canada*, UN Doc CERD/C/CAN/CO/21-23 (25 August 2017) at para. 16(3).

Convention on the Elimination of All Forms of Discrimination against Women, 18 December 1979, 1249 UNTS 13 (entered into force 3 September 1981), ratified by Canada on 10 December 1981.

Convention on the Elimination of All Forms of Racial Discrimination, 21 December 1965, 660 UNTS 195 (entered into force 4 January 1969).

Correctional Service Canada, *Final Report of the Study Group for the Risk Management of Infectious Diseases* (Ottawa: Correctional Service of Canada, 1999).

——, News Release, "Correctional Service Canada Announces a Prison Needle Exchange Program" (14 May 2018), online: www.newswire.ca/ news-releases/correctional-service-canada-announces-a-prison-needle-exchange-program-682556901.html.

——, *Prevalence of Injection Drug Use among Male Offenders*, by Shanna Farrell et al, *No*. RS-10-02, (Ottawa: Correctional Service of Canada, 2010).

——, *Summary of Emerging Findings from the 2007 National Inmate Infectious Diseases and Risk-Behaviours Survey*, by Dianne Zakaria et al, No. R-211 (Ottawa: Correctional Service of Canada, March 2010).

——, *Correctional Service Drug Detection Strategies: International Practices within Correctional Settings*, by Serenna Dastouri, Sara Johnson & Andrea Moser, No. R-258 (Ottawa: Addictions Research Centre Correctional Service of Canada, January 2012).

——, *Research Brief: Comparing Lifetime Substance Use Patterns of Men and*

Women Offenders, by L Kelly & Shanna Farrell MacDonald, No. RIB 14-44, (Ottawa: Correctional Service of Canada, March 2015).

——, *Reliability and Validity of the Dynamic Factors Identification and Analysis — Revised,* by Lynn Stewart et al, *No. R-395,* (Ottawa: Correctional Service of Canada, May 2017).

Dolan, Kate et al, "Prison-based Syringe Exchange Programmes: A Review of International Research and Development" (2003) 98 Addiction 153.

Elliott, Richard, "Deadly Disregard: Government Refusal to Implement Evidence-based Measures to Prevent HIV and Hepatitis C Virus Infections in Prisons" (2007) 177:3 CMAJ.

Graveland, Bill, "Guards Union Says Prison Needle Exchange Expansion on Hold Amid Coronavirus Crisis," *The Globe and Mail* (22 March 2020), online: www.theglobeandmail.com/canada/article-guards-union-says-prison-needle-exchange-expansion-on-hold/.

Hagan, Holly, "The Relevance of Attributable Risk Measures to HIV Prevention Planning" (2003) 17:6 AIDS 911.

Harm Reduction International, "Harm Reduction and Prisons: Global State of Harm Reduction 2018 Briefing" (2018), online: www.hri.global/files/2019/03/29/prisons-harm-reduction-2018.pdf

HIV Legal Network and Centre on Drug Policy Evaluation, "Submission to the United Nations High Commissioner for Human Rights pursuant to HRC Res. 43/1 on the 'Promotion and protection of the human rights and fundamental freedoms of Africans and of people of African descent against excessive use of force and other human rights violations by law enforcement officers'" (December 2020).

HIV Legal Network, *Decriminalizing People Who Use Drugs: Making the Ask, Minimizing the Harms* (Toronto: HIV Legal Network, 2020).

Jürgens, R, *Interventions to Address HIV/AIDS in Prisons: Needle and Syringe Programmes and Decontamination Strategies* (Geneva: WHO, UNODC and UNAIDS, 2007).

Khenti, A, "The Canadian War on Drugs: Structural Violence and Unequal Treatment of Black Canadians" (2014) 25:2 Intl J Drug Policy 190.

Kouyoumdjian, Fiona et al, "Health Status of Prisoners in Canada" (2016) 62 Canadian Family Physician 215.

Leonard, Lynne, *Evaluation of the Prison Needle Exchange Program Interim Report* (Ottawa: University of Ottawa, March 2020).

Lines, Rick, "From Equivalence of Standards to Equivalence of Objectives: The Entitlement of Prisoners to Health Standards Higher than those Outside Prisons" (2006) 2:4 Intl J Prisoner Health 269.

Milloy, MJ et al, "Incarceration Experiences in a Cohort of Active Injection Drug Users" (2008) Drug and Alcohol Rev 1.

Needle, Richard et al, "HIV Risk Behaviors Associated with the Injection Process: Multiperson Use of Drug Injection Equipment and Paraphernalia in Injection Drug User Networks" (1998) 33:12 Substance Use & Misuse 2403.

Nelles, Joachim et al, "Provision of Syringes: The Cutting Edge of Harm Reduction in Prison?" (1998) 317:7153 British Medical J 270.

——, *Prevention of Drug Use and Infectious Diseases in the Realta Cantonal Men's Prison: Summary of the Evaluation* (Berne: University Psychiatric Services, 1999).

Office of the Correctional Investigator, *Office of the Correctional Investigator Annual Report 2003-2004* (Ottawa: Office of the Correctional Investigator, 2004).

——, *Office of the Correctional Investigator Annual Report 2005-2006* (Ottawa: Office of the Correctional Investigator, 2006).

——, *Office of the Correctional Investigator Annual Report 2006-2007* (Ottawa: Office of the Correctional Investigator, 2007).

——, *Office of the Correctional Investigator Annual Report 2009-2010* (Ottawa: Office of the Correctional Investigator, 2010).

——, *Office of the Correctional Investigator annual report 2013-2014* (Ottawa: Office of the Correctional Investigator, 2014).

——, *Office of the Correctional Investigator Annual Report 2015-2016* (Ottawa: Office of the Correctional Investigator, 2016).

——, *Office of the Correctional Investigator Annual Report 2016-2017* (Ottawa: Office of the Correctional Investigator, 2017).

——, *Office of the Correctional Investigator Annual Report 2018-2019* (Ottawa: Office of the Correctional Investigator, 2019).

Office of the High Commissioner on Human Rights and UNAIDS, *International Guidelines on HIV/AIDS and Human Rights, Consolidated Version*, UN Doc HR/PUB/06/9 (2006) Guideline 4 at para 21(e).

Ontario Medical Association, *Improving Our Health: Why Is Canada Lagging Behind in Establishing Needle Exchange Programs in Prisons? A Position Paper by the Ontario Medical Association* (Toronto: Ontario Medical Association, 2004).

Public Health Agency of Canada, *Prison Needle Exchange: Review of the Evidence* (Ottawa: Public Health Agency of Canada, 2006).

Sanz, J et al, "Syringe-Exchange Programmes in Spanish Prisons" (2003) 13 Connections: The Newsletter of the European Network Drug Services in Prison & Central and Eastern European Network of Drug Services in Prison 9.

Shah, SM et al, "Detection of HIV-1 DNA in Needle/Syringes, Paraphernalia, and Washes from Shooting Galleries in Miami: A Preliminary Laboratory Report" (1996) 11:3 J Acquired Immune Deficiency Syndrome & Human Retrovirology 301.

Simons, Steve, "I Contracted Hepatitis C in Federal Prison. A Proper Prison Needle and Syringe Program Will Ensure That Others Don't" (17 August

2020), online (blog): www.hivlegalnetwork.ca/site/former-prisoner-steve-simons-writes-why-a-prison-needle-exchange-program-is-needed/?lang=en.

Small, Will et al, "Incarceration, Addiction and Harm Reduction: Inmates Experience Injecting Drugs in Prison" (2005) 40 Substance Use and Misuse 831.

Stöver, Heino & Joachim Nelles, "10 Years of Experience with Needle and Syringe Exchange Programmes in European Prisons: A Review of Different Evaluation Studies" (2003) 14 Intl J Drug Policy 437.

UN Committee on Economic, Social and Cultural Rights, *General Comment 14: The Right to the Highest Attainable Standard of Health*, 22nd Sess, UN Doc E/C.12/2000/4 (2000).

Union of Canadian Correctional Officers, "Elections 2019—Questions to the Political Parties" (15 October 2019), online (blog): ucco-sacc-csn.ca/news/elections-2019-questions-to-the-political-parties/.

———, "Prison Needle Exchange Program (PNEP)" (last visited on 22 July 2022), online (blog): ucco-sacc-csn.ca/files/prison-needle-exchange-program-pnep/.

———, Press Release, "Prison Needle Exchange Program: Handling Needles: Not Our Job!" (7 June 2019), online: ucco-sacc-csn.ca/assets/uploads/2019/06/2019-06-07-PNEP-Press-Release-ENG.pdf

United Nations Office on Drugs and Crime, *A Handbook for Starting and Managing Needle and Syringe Programmes in Prisons and Other Closed Settings* (Vienna: UNODC, 2015).

United Nations Standard Minimum Rules for the Treatment of Prisoners (the *Nelson Mandela Rules*), GA Res 70/175, UN Doc A/RES/70/175 (17 December 2015), at rules 3 and 5.

van der Meulen, Emily et al, *On Point: Recommendations for Prison-Based Needle and Syringe Programs in Canada* (Toronto: Ryerson University, Canadian HIV/AIDS Legal Network & PASAN, 2016).

Wood, Evan et al., "Recent Incarceration Independently Associated with Syringe Sharing by Injection Drug Users" (2005) 120 Public Health Reports 150.

Notes

1   Correctional Service Canada, "Correctional Service Canada Announces a Prison Needle Exchange Program" (14 May 2018), www.newswire.ca/news-releases/correctional-service-canada-announces-a-prison-needle-exchange-program-682556901.html.

2   See Fiona Kouyoumdjian et al, "Health Status of Prisoners in Canada" (2016) 62 Canadian Family Physician 215.

3   Correctional Service Canada, *Research Report 477: Infectious Diseases, Risk Behaviours, and Harm-Reduction Approaches: A Summary of Findings from the 2022 National Health Survey*, 2024 (Ottawa: Correctional Service of Canada, March 2010) [Zakaria].

4   Correctional Service Canada, Research Report 477: *Infectious Diseases, Risk Behaviours, and Harm-Reduction Approaches: A Summary of Findings from the 2022 National Health Survey, 2024.*

5   See Office of the Correctional Investigator, *Office of the Correctional Investigator Annual Report 2013-2014* (Ottawa: Office of the Correctional Investigator, 2014).

6   See Correctional Service of Canada, *Reliability and Validity of the Dynamic Factors Identification and Analysis—Revised*, by Lynn Stewart et al, *No. R-395*, (Ottawa: Correctional Service of Canada, May 2017).

7   See Correctional Services Canada, *Correctional Service Drug Detection Strategies: International Practices within Correctional Settings*, by Serenna Dastouri, Sara Johnson & Andrea Moser, No. R-258 (Ottawa: Addictions Research Centre Correctional Service of Canada, January 2012).

8   See, e.g., MJ Milloy et al, "Incarceration Experiences in a Cohort of Active Injection Drug Users" (2008) Drug and Alcohol Rev 1; see also Evan Wood et al., "Recent Incarceration Independently Associated with Syringe Sharing by Injection Drug Users" (2005) 120 Public Health Reports 150; see also Will Small et al, "Incarceration, Addiction and Harm Reduction: Inmates Experience Injecting Drugs in Prison" (2005) 40 Substance Use and Misuse 831.

9   See, e.g., SM Shah et al, "Detection of HIV-1 DNA in Needle/Syringes, Paraphernalia, and Washes from Shooting Galleries in Miami: A Preliminary Laboratory Report" (1996) 11:3 J Acquired Immune Deficiency Syndrome & Human Retrovirology 301; see also Richard Needle et al, "HIV Risk Behaviors Associated with the Injection Process: Multiperson Use of Drug Injection Equipment and Paraphernalia in Injection Drug User Networks" (1998) 33:12 Substance Use & Misuse 2403.

10   See Zakaria, *supra* note 3.

11   See Holly Hagan, "The Relevance of Attributable Risk Measures to HIV Prevention Planning" (2003) 17:6 AIDS 911.

12   See Office of the Correctional Investigator, *Office of the Correctional Investigator Annual Report 2006-2007* (Ottawa: Office of the Correctional Investigator, 2007).

13   See, e.g., A Khenti, "The Canadian War on Drugs: Structural Violence and Unequal Treatment of Black Canadians" (2014) 25:2 Intl J Drug Policy 190; see also HIV Legal Network and Centre on Drug Policy Evaluation, "Submission to the United Nations High Commissioner for Human Rights pursuant to HRC Res. 43/1 on the 'Promotion and protection of the human rights and fundamental freedoms of Africans and of people of African descent against excessive use of force and other human rights violations by law enforcement officers'" (December 2020); see also HIV Legal Network, *Decriminalizing People Who Use Drugs: Making the Ask, Minimizing the Harms* (Toronto: HIV Legal Network, 2020).

14   Public Safety Canada, Parliamentary Committee Notes: Overrepresentation (Indigenous Offenders), March 9, 2023, online: https://www.publicsafety.gc.ca/cnt/trnsprnc/brfng-mtrls/prlmntry-bndrs/20230720/12-en.aspx.

15   Department of Justice Canada, *State of the Criminal Justice System: Impact of COVID-19 on the Criminal Justice System, 2022*. Online: https://www.justice.gc.ca/eng/cj-jp/state-etat/2022rpt-rap2022/p5.html

16   See Office of the Correctional Investigator, *2018-2019 Report, supra* note 15.

17   The term "prison needle and syringe program" is used to refer to any program that provides sterile injection equipment to prisoners who inject drugs, whether in a one-for-one exchange of a used needle for a sterile needle or in a less restrictive

manner. Unless otherwise indicated explicitly, or by context, the terms "needle" and "syringe" mean a device used to inject fluids into the body, and are used interchangeably throughout this chapter.

18 See Harm Reduction International, "Harm Reduction and Prisons: Global State of Harm Reduction 2018 Briefing" (2018), online: www.hri.global/files/2019/03/29/prisons-harm-reduction-2018.pdf.

19 See, e.g., Public Health Agency of Canada, *Prison Needle Exchange: Review of the Evidence* (Ottawa: Public Health Agency of Canada, 2006); see also Canadian Agency for Drugs and Technology in Health, *Needle Exchange Programs in a Correctional Setting: A Review of the Clinical and Cost-Effectiveness* (Ottawa, Canadian Agency for Drugs and Technology in Health, 2015); see also Heino Stöver & Joachim Nelles, "10 Years of Experience with Needle and Syringe Exchange Programmes in European Prisons: A Review of Different Evaluation Studies" (2003) 14 Intl J Drug Policy 437; see also Joachim Nelles et al, "Provision of Syringes: The Cutting Edge of Harm Reduction in Prison?" (1998) 317:7153 British Medical J 270; see also Kate Dolan et al, "Prison-Based Syringe Exchange Programmes: A Review of International Research and Development" (2003) 98 Addiction 153; see also Joachim Nelles et al, *Prevention of Drug Use and Infectious Diseases in the Realta Cantonal Men's Prison: Summary of the Evaluation* (Berne: University Psychiatric Services, 1999); see also J Sanz et al, "Syringe-Exchange Programmes in Spanish Prisons" (2003) 13 Connections: The Newsletter of the European Network Drug Services in Prison & Central and Eastern European Network of Drug Services in Prison 9.

20 See Correctional Service Canada, *Final Report of the Study Group for the Risk Management of Infectious Diseases* (Ottawa: Correctional Service of Canada, 1999).

21 See Office of the Correctional Investigator, *Office of the Correctional Investigator Annual Report 2003-2004* (Ottawa: Office of the Correctional Investigator, 2004).

22 *Ibid*; see also Office of the Correctional Investigator, *Office of the Correctional Investigator Annual Report 2005-2006* (Ottawa: Office of the Correctional Investigator, 2006); see also Office of the Correctional Investigator, *2006-2007 Report*, *supra* note 13; see also Office of the Correctional Investigator, *Office of the Correctional Investigator Annual Report 2009-2010* (Ottawa: Office of the Correctional Investigator, 2010); see also Office of the Correctional Investigator, *Office of the Correctional Investigator Annual Report 2015-2016* (Ottawa: Office of the Correctional Investigator, 2016).

23 See Canadian Medical Association, Resolution 26 of 17 August 2005; see also Ontario Medical Association, *Improving Our Health: Why Is Canada Lagging Behind in Establishing Needle Exchange Programs in Prisons? A Position Paper by the Ontario Medical Association* (Toronto: Ontario Medical Association, 2004); see also Canadian Human Rights Commission, *Protecting Their Rights: A Systemic Review of Human Rights in Correctional Services for Federally Sentenced Women* (Ottawa: Canadian Human Rights Commission, 2004).

24 See Office of the High Commissioner on Human Rights and UNAIDS, *International Guidelines on HIV/AIDS and Human Rights*, Consolidated Version, UN Doc HR/PUB/06/9 (2006) Guideline 4 at para 21(e).

25 See, e.g., R Jürgens, *Interventions to Address HIV/AIDS in Prisons: Needle and Syringe Programmes and Decontamination Strategies* (Geneva: WHO, UNODC and UNAIDS, 2007).

26 See Corrections and Conditional Release Act, SC 1992, c 20, ss 2(1), 40(i)-(j) [CCRA]; see also SOR/92-620. Enforced by disciplinary and summary conviction offences under section 45 of the CCRA.

27   Part I of the Constitution Act, 1982, being Schedule B to the Canada Act 1982 (UK), 1982, c 11.

28   See CCRA, *supra* note 27, s 4(c).

29   *Ibid*, ss 86, 70.

30   See United Nations Standard Minimum Rules for the Treatment of Prisoners (the Nelson Mandela Rules), GA Res 70/175, UN Doc A/RES/70/175 (17 December 2015), at rules 3 and 5 [Nelson Mandela Rules].

31   UN Committee on Economic, Social and Cultural Rights, General Comment 14: The Right to the Highest Attainable Standard of Health, 22nd Sess, UN Doc E/C.12/2000/4 (2000), at para 34.

32   See Nelson Mandela Rules, *supra* note 31, at rule 24; see also Rick Lines, "From Equivalence of Standards to Equivalence of Objectives: The Entitlement of Prisoners to Health Standards Higher than Those Outside Prisons" (2006) 2:4 Intl J Prisoner Health 269.

33   See Convention on the Elimination of All Forms of Discrimination against Women, 18 December 1979, 1249 UNTS 13 (entered into force 3 September 1981), ratified by Canada on 10 December 1981; see also Committee on the Elimination of Discrimination Against Women, Concluding Observations on the Combined Eighth and Ninth Periodic Reports of Canada, UN Doc CEDAW/C/CAN/CO/8-9 (25 November 2016) at para 49(c).

34   See Convention on the Elimination of All Forms of Racial Discrimination, 21 December 1965, 660 UNTS 195 (entered into force 4 January 1969); see also Committee on the Elimination of Racial Discrimination, Concluding Observations on the Twenty-First to Twenty-Third Periodic Reports of Canada, UN Doc CERD/C/CAN/CO/21-23 (25 August 2017) at para. 16(3).

35   See Correctional Service Canada, "Correctional Service Canada announces a Prison Needle Exchange Program" (14 May 2018), online: www.newswire.ca/ news-releases/correctional-service-canada-announces-a-prison-needle-exchange-program-682556901.html.

36   See Union of Canadian Correctional Officers, Press Release "Prison Needle Exchange Program: Handling Needles: Not Our Job!" (7 June 2019), online: ucco-sacc-csn.ca/assets/uploads/2019/06/2019-06-07-PNEP-Press-Release-ENG.pdf.

37   See Union of Canadian Correctional Officers, "Prison Needle Exchange Program (PNEP)" (last visited on 22 July 2022), online (blog): ucco-sacc-csn.ca/files/ prison-needle-exchange-program-pnep/.

38   See United Nations Office on Drugs and Crime, *A Handbook for Starting and Managing Needle and Syringe Programmes in Prisons and Other Closed Settings* (Vienna: UNODC, 2015).

39   See Emily van der Meulen et al, *On Point: Recommendations for Prison-Based Needle and Syringe Programs in Canada* (Toronto: Ryerson University, Canadian HIV/AIDS Legal Network & PASAN, 2016).

40   See Office of the Correctional Investigator, *2018-2019 Report*, *supra* note 15.

41   *Ibid.*

42   *Ibid.*

43   *Ibid.*

44   *Ibid.*

45   See *Simons et al v Minister of Public Safety*, 2020 ONSC 1431.

46   See Union of Canadian Correctional Officers, "Elections 2019—Questions to the Political Parties" (15 October 2019), online (blog): ucco-sacc-csn.ca/news/ elections-2019-questions-to-the-political-parties/.

47   See Bill Graveland, "Guards Union Says Prison Needle Exchange Expansion on Hold amid Coronavirus Crisis" (22 March 2020), online: www.theglobeandmail.com/canada/article-guards-union-says-prison-needle-exchange-expansion-on-hold/.

48   See Lynne Leonard, *Evaluation of the Prison Needle Exchange Program Interim Report* (Ottawa: University of Ottawa, March 2020).

49   See Richard Elliott, "Deadly Disregard: Government Refusal to Implement Evidence-Based Measures to Prevent HIV and Hepatitis C Virus Infections in Prisons" (2007) 177:3 CMAJ.

50   See van der Meulen, *supra* note 40.

51   See Steve Simons, "I Contracted Hepatitis C in Federal Prison. A Proper Prison Needle and Syringe Program Will Ensure That Others Don't" (17 August 2020), online (blog): www.hivlegalnetwork.ca/site/former-prisoner-steve-simons-writes-why-a-prison-needle-exchange-program-is-needed/?lang=en.

CHAPTER 4

Ontario's Consumption and Treatment Services Model

Problematizing Conservative Safe-Consumption Site Policy

Stephanie Arlt

Canada's drug-policy agenda sits at a complex intersection of evidence-based paradigms and strongly held ideological convictions surrounding drug use and addiction. In recent years, Canadian politicians have embraced the language of harm reduction but have not implemented policy in accordance with harm reduction philosophy.[1] Years into an overdose crisis—more accurately described as a toxic illicit-drug-supply crisis[2]—the implementation of these services has not reflected the urgency of the situation. Numerous research studies support the effectiveness of harm reduction services, including safe-consumption sites (SCS) and overdose-prevention sites (OPS).[3] The disconnect between the core values of harm reduction and implementation of formal drug policy is evident in the Ontario Progressive Conservative government's consumption and treatment services (CTS) policy. The policy change was announced on October 22, 2018, via two documents: a backgrounder, "Review of Supervised Consumption Services and Overdose Prevention Sites–Key Findings,"[4] and a news release, "Ontario Government Connecting People with Addictions to Treatment and Rehabilitation."[5] The backgrounder highlighted the key findings of the provincial review of

SCS and OPS. The press release introduced anticipated changes under the heading "Quick Facts." Both documents emphasized a new direction in provincial drug policy and the adoption of harm reduction language. Yet, the recommended changes entrench long-held convictions about addiction, drug use as a criminal matter, and a preference for abstinence-based treatment. Former research has demonstrated that common beliefs about drug use and people who use drugs (PWUD), within both policy and law, have resulted in experiences of stigma and barriers to health care.[6] The switch from existing SCS and OPS to the CTS model necessitates an analysis of the discursive elements within the CTS policy to illuminate some of the underlying values and tensions under the Ontario government's reform of SCS policy.

The following analysis of the CTS policy draws upon a critical policy-as-discourse framework by applying political scientist Carol Bacchi's work on the construction and representation of social "problems" in policy.[7] When referring to policy as discourse, discourse can be defined as a set of concepts and ideas that form an agenda to accomplish change. Discourse analysis demonstrates that it is through language that politicians and policy-makers communicate ideas and promote policies, illuminating the presence of dominant ideologies in the policy-making process.[8] Problematization is the process of identifying and framing an issue within a policy, and it is integral to the solutions policy-makers decide to implement. Interrogating the social construction of problems is useful to analyze the CTS policy in two ways: the deconstruction of the representation of a problem provides an opportunity to expose taken-for-granted truths by analyzing the framing of social issues, and this approach identifies how the representations of the target population are reproduced through policy.[9] Taken-for-granted truths are beliefs and rationalities assumed as a given and resist critical interpretation. Identifying and examining the language used in the CTS-policy announcement reveals that social issues are conveyed and constructed through discourse and from the values held by different interest groups.[10] In the first part of this chapter, I explain how policies construct representations of social phenomenon as a problem. In the second part, I identify the underlying discursive assumptions that shape the CTS-policy problem. I conclude with an examination of three thematic discursive and subjective effects reproduced through the CTS policy.

Meet the Policy

In Ontario, the election of Doug Ford's Progressive Conservatives entailed a shift from Liberal Party public policy in the province. Notably, Ford has stated he is "dead against safe injection facilities," and during the first Ontario leadership debate in 2018 he announced he would not "have injection sites in neighbourhoods."[11] Ford's remarks align with past Canadian Conservative governments' approaches to SCS.[12] Once Ford was declared Ontario's premier, a reform to SCS was uneasily anticipated. The policy change was announced on 22 October 2018, and the CTS reform drew criticism from frontline workers, activists, researchers, and opposition politicians.[13] The concerns noted an explicit shift from the current low-threshold models toward a rehabilitation-focused service, and the dismissal of the effectiveness and merits of SCS as they currently operated. The shift in operations required existing SCS to reapply under new guidelines to maintain funding,[14] while instating a cap to the province's sites at 21 services.[15] Many viewed this as an attack on SCS, as the new restrictions lacked sufficient research to justify their implementation.

Policy as Discourse

The "what's the problem represented to be" (WPR) policy-analysis framework is useful in deconstructing the language of problems within the CTS-policy announcement. To effectively analyze the underlying discourse present in the CTS policy, it is necessary to move beyond methodological approaches that simply consider policies as evidence-based, value-neutral mechanisms that address "problems" and critically engage with the process of problematizations. Bacchi's approach has been previously applied to drug-policy problematizations with insightful contributions to the understanding of the significance of discourse in drug policy.[16] Policy is intended to be productive, and therefore gives shape and meaning to problems.[17] Problems do not simply exist, predefined in the natural world; rather, the character and boundaries of a problem arise through the act of conceiving said problem. What is seen to be problematic, what is left silent, and how drug consumption and its subsequent treatment is framed have important lived consequences and provide a starting point to highlight how knowledge in policy is intertwined with mechanisms of power. This analysis intends to illuminate the underlying presuppositions that the Ford administration's CTS model is situated in by addressing the first five of the WPR framework's six questions:

1. What is the "problem" represented to be in a specific policy?
2. What presuppositions or assumptions underlie this representation of this "problem"?
3. How has this representation of the "problem" come about?
4. What is left unproblematic in this "problem" representation? Where are the silences? Can the "problem" be thought about differently?
5. What effects (discursive, subjectification, and lived) are produced by this representation of the "problem"?
6. How and where has this representation of the "problem" been produced, disseminated, and defended? How has it been and/or can it be questioned, disrupted, and replaced?

Drawing upon social constructionism, an interpretivist lens reveals the taken-for-granted truths within so-called problems, while illuminating the structural power relations inherent within policy and their resulting solutions. At its essence, social representations are created through practices that give shape and meaning. The documents examined in this analysis include the aforementioned "Review of Supervised Consumption Services and Overdose Prevention Sites–Key Findings" and "Ontario Government Connecting People with Addictions to Treatment and Rehabilitation," released by the then Ontario Ministry of Health and Long-Term Care in 2018. By limiting the inquiry to these documents, the analysis is focussed on analyzing proximal harm reduction efforts under a Conservative government. The documents are the first policy reform to SCS under the Ford administration that account for the primary findings and logic reported to the media by this administration regarding the change to the province's drug and harm reduction policies. For these reasons, along with their potential to reach a wider audience, these two documents were selected to analyze the assumptions made in the policy.

Rather than a problem-solving emphasis found in conventional policy-analysis models that simply accepts the "shape" of a problem as given, the WPR framework shifts toward problem questioning and observes problems as endogenous to the policy process.[18]

Policy as discourse seeks to demonstrate how discourse regulates the prevailing knowledge that gets integrated and then reproduced in public policy, demonstrating how politicians and policy-makers use language to regulate knowledge of the world, thus constructing our shared understanding of events.[19] Policy is intended to make proposals for change, and every policy proposal contains within it an implicit construction of what the problem is represented to be.[20] Discourse, therefore, shapes a collective understanding of a "problem" while also illuminating the power relationships and dominant ideologies within policy-making.[21] In Canada, rarely do PWUD get the opportunity to publicly influence the way the general public sees drugs and how we address solutions.[22] Thus, policy as discourse demonstrates how social action can be shaped by the dominant cultural and political contexts in which they take place, and how discourse further privileges certain voices, while creating and maintaining shared knowledge of events.[23]

How Are Addiction, Safe-Consumption Services, and those who Seek Services Constituted as Problems in the CTS-Policy Announcement?

The foremost problem represented within the CTS policy is addiction. The "opioid crisis" and addiction are referenced interchangeably, giving the impression that addressing addiction will result in ending the opioid crisis. Not all substance use results in dependence, and the focus on addiction, rather than drug use per se, situates the representation of the problem as pathological and therefore in the domain of medicine. The emphasis on biomedical-related solutions are palpable throughout the document; for example: "Combatting the opioid crisis will require a comprehensive and coordinated strategy beginning with prevention, through to connecting affected individuals to treatment."[24] Within the policy, treatment is coded to mean abstinence-based care, or a trajectory toward abstinence such as opioid antagonist therapies. Further, while addiction is situated in the realm of medicine, it is done so in a way that assumes those labelled as addicts are in need of behavioural management. The representation of the problem as addiction leads to an emphasis on medical solutions that target addiction, particularly in line with conservative beliefs of abstinence-oriented treatment.

The second problem identified is the function of SCS. Supervised consumption services are problematized to enable addiction, as demonstrated by this passage: "The sites are not sufficient as standalone entities disconnected from other services; sites should support individuals to seek addictions treatment as well as other health and social services."[25] The wording of this passage frames SCS as incapable of progressing addiction treatment and diminishes the role of SCS in connecting individuals to a variety of services. Thus, the weight given to treatment, aptly demonstrated by the change in name to "consumption and treatment services," is a logical approach to addressing the problem of addiction. The emphasis on a particular form of treatment that is claimed to be absent in current SCS solidifies the criticism of SCS as an ineffective measure to address the overdose crisis and, therefore, of solving addiction.

The final problem is the behaviour of the people who visit SCS. The backgrounder positions the people who use SCS services in contrast to other community members. The dichotomy between valued community members and PWUD is evident in the language used to express concern for local residents and their "quality of life," allegedly negatively affected by the presence of SCS. The boundary is aptly demonstrated by this passage: "There are divided opinions on the community impacts of Supervised Consumption Services and Overdose Prevention Sites in terms of crime increase, drug trafficking or public disorder (such as vandalism and discarded syringes) or their effects on the quality of life for local residents."[26] It is clear the passage is not describing the concern about the quality of life for the people visiting the site. Rather, the passage is concerned with how SCS visitors are perceived by fellow community members, suggesting one is in opposition with the other. Focusing on these "problematic" behaviours allegedly associated with persons using SCS positions these health care services as inherently associated with increased crime, drug trafficking, and vandalism. The problem here is thus represented as the behaviour of SCS visitors, characterizing them as agents of social disorder. This characterization is based on the distinct factor that one group is problematized as addicted to illicit substances. Closely aligned with prohibitionist values about substance use, the Ontario government problematizes SCS as not sufficiently addressing addiction's behavioural ramifications. Addiction is established as the problem that contributes to the alleged social disorder surrounding SCS while these spaces are unable to rectify what is considered the cause of the problem.

Taken-for-Granted Truths

By interrogating the identified problematizations further, numerous assumptions and underlying beliefs surface about SCS, addiction, and PWUD. Deconstructing the assumed problem of addiction in CTS illuminates the significance of discourse behind the policy's conceptualization.

The first is the assumption that SCS are trying to solve addiction and that ending drug use should be the primary goal of site operations. Within the policy proposal, SCS are not validated as effective health care services if they do not encourage the succession of drug use. This belief is evident within this passage: "The new delivery model would not only be equipped to reverse overdoses, it would also include an enhanced and necessary focus on connecting people who use drugs to primary care, treatment and rehabilitation, and other health and social services."[27] The overall tone in the document is that SCS are not doing the "real" work, or at least the work that matters within a prohibitionist framework. The phrasing "would not *only* be equipped to reverse overdoses" suggests a minimization of the act of reversing overdoses in comparison to the "necessary" focus on connection to services such as treatment and rehabilitation. Furthermore, the passage suggests that addiction persists because there is a lack of effort to promote treatment at SCS, and that SCS either divert people from seeking treatment or do not effectively connect people to treatment. Underpinning the CTS policy's problematization of SCS is the belief that SCS contribute to the social and medical harms associated with addiction, which is linked to the core assumptions about the nature of drug use and the expectation of services that seek to address addiction.

The second assumption is that drug use is the genesis of addiction, and within this assumption addiction is believed to result in social disorder by those who are labelled as addicted. Drug use is considered inherently problematic and deleterious. A service that allows people to freely use drugs is viewed as condoning the practice, which would enable rather than address addiction. If the consumption of a drug is assumed to be the core problem, SCS would further entrench drug problems. Sustaining these assumptions is the idea that drug use should be sought to be discouraged at SCS because drug use contributes to public disorder and a decline in health. The belief of drug use as fostering public disorder is conveyed in the passage referring to crime and disorder from the previous section, as well as "[t]he current supervised consumption services and overdose prevention site models require changes to adapt their scope, especially to address public concerns that have been raised about them."[28] The expectation in the CTS policy that SCS must address public concerns legitimizes misrepresentations of SCS as a space that fosters public disorder and crime. This framing reduces the health service to simply a place to engage in drug use, an activity that should be avoided, therefore casting SCS as ineffective services to solve the issue of addiction. However, addiction is much more complex than solely injecting drugs, and conveying addiction as such would be a gross oversimplification. The assumption that drug use is leading to addiction also encourages increased medicalization of the sites as integral to better care.

The third assumption is that the increased medicalization of SCS will rectify the service's inability to produce abstinent service users. The previous sections have established the framing of the problem as addiction; therefore, the policy's emphasis on solutions derived from the medical paradigm are most logically suited to produce abstinence. The passage "[t]he new model would continue to feature life-saving overdose prevention and harm reduction services, as well as a new focus on connecting people with treatment and rehabilitation services"[29] demonstrates the ideal changes to the existing model. The increased emphasis on traditional pathways to abstinence within SCS can be read as an attempt to "legitimize" the services within a medical framework, filling the perceived gap within the existing models.

What Are the Origins of the Representations of Addiction and Drug Use?

The pathways that led to the change in policy are twofold. First, there are the competing, and often partisan, models of knowledge present within the discourse of drug use and addiction in Canada. The second is the change of party in the provincial government from Liberal to Conservative.

An important consideration of the problematization of drugs within the CTS policy are the multiple competing frameworks that seek to dominate health-policy decisions regarding drug use and

PWUD. Many people argue that using drugs is the problem that needs to be addressed. Others argue that environmental factors, such as social systems that create inequality for certain populations, cause addiction. Within the first position there is a moral aversion to drug use, but the logic of drugs being bad is present within the disease model of addiction as well.[30] The CTS policy reflects a mix of the disease and moral models of addiction, each supporting and reinforcing the premises of the other. SCS clients are dually labelled as "sick" by the medical community, and "criminal" based on their substance use. The environmental position is not significantly present within the CTS policy. The moral model is present with the emphasis on increased crime and individual behavioural management. The medical model is evident with the explicit change in title, "Consumption and Treatment Services would replace the former Supervised Consumption Services and Overdose Prevention Site models."[31]

The change in government is relevant because the CTS-policy reform reflects Tory beliefs about drug use and law and order, as indicated by Premier Ford's remarks on the campaign trail and previous opposition to SCS by the federal Conservatives.[32] While there is a significant amount of evidence demonstrating the efficacy of SCS, the Ontario government requested a review of the evidence for SCS.[33] Through this action, the Ontario Ministry of Health was able to cultivate a representation of evidence that fit within a conservative-based framework. It is worth noting that two years later, Alberta's Conservative government embarked on a similar path with their review of SCS.[34] As with Ontario, Alberta's report emphasized "social disorder,"[35] suggesting the emphasis on public disorder is an arguably partisan move to appease Tory voters. It is unclear why a variety of stakeholders, such as local business representatives and police, were required to meet for health authorities to continue the site operations. While the documents explicitly frame addiction as a health issue, there is an internal inconsistency demonstrated by the significant amount of attention paid to enforcement-based approaches. The overemphasis on public disorder reinforces individual behavioural management and the association of PWUD with crime as a core problematization within the policy. The contradictory nature of the document is present in the aforementioned passages about public disorder and the need for the SCS to adapt their scope to address community concerns.

Absences and Silences in the CTS Policy

The silences within the WPR framework are the perspectives and factors that are omitted from the policy that engender the representation of the problem. By acknowledging the silences, this section creates the space to discuss how the problem can be thought of differently.

The operational language of the Ontario government's backgrounder and press release places the responsibility onto PWUD and frontline workers while leaving silent the contributions to this problem made by policy and the broader social determinants of health. The expressed goal of individual behavioural management takes the place of a more useful discussion of the social dimensions of health. Although the backgrounder references inadequate housing and mental-health supports, and thus cannot be viewed as completely silent on the social determinants of health, it is not fully actualized as a significant focus in the policy solution as it only states the issue: "There are inadequate addictions treatment, mental health services and supportive housing options available for individuals using drugs."[36] The press release offers a solution to the lack of addictions treatment: "Ontario is planning to expand access to addiction treatment by creating more detox beds in high need communities";[37] however, there is no parallel to the latter two gaps in care referenced in the backgrounder. What purpose does mentioning these concerns serve within the policy? The external factors that contribute to drug use are not named within the policy, even though it has been established that drug use is a symptom of larger issues within one's social environment.[38]

A glaring omission in the policy concerns the role of the toxic drug supply. The presence of fentanyl, and fentanyl analogues, are becoming the norm within the drug supply. In 2016, fentanyl or fentanyl analogues were present in 68% of all opioid-related deaths in Ontario, compared with 45% the previous year.[39] With no sign of this trend decreasing, in 2017 fentanyl and fentanyl analogues contributed to nearly three-quarters of deaths (71.2%).[40] Without acknowledging the role of a unpredictable drug supply, a policy formulated to address the overdose crisis reinforces the assumption that drug use is the targeted problem. The selected framing of the problem abdicates the Ontario government from conducting a necessary analysis of the prohibitionist policies that make controlling the purity and strength of these drugs impossible, and further entrench abstinence-based solutions as best practice.

The final silence lays in the minimization of the numerous successes SCS have had in connecting people with a variety of services. There is an explicit recognition "that Supervised Consumption Services improve the health of those who use drugs, are cost-effective and reduce the strain on the healthcare system."[41] However, the documents are contradictory in their nature because this praise is minimized by the dominant framing that "[t]he sites are not sufficient as standalone entities disconnected from other services; sites should support individuals to seek addictions treatment as well as other health and social services."[42] A related disconcerting silence within the criticism of SCS operation is the lack of recognition of the successes of peer-run sites. The aforementioned successes of improved health are regarded as insufficient in contrast to the preferred objective of addictions treatment.

Discussion

The following discussion is guided by the fifth question in the WPR framework: what effects (discursive, subjectification, or lived) are produced by this representation of the "problem"? Answering this question provides fertile ground to critically discuss the effects of the representation of the problem within the CTS policy and its impacts on CTS visitors. The discursive effects are those that influence, limit, construct, and regulate our shared understanding of a phenomenon. The concept of "subject position" refers to the kind of potential "subject" that is created in specific discourses/knowledges. The analysis emphasizes the discursive and subject-making effects, while lived effects requires additional research. This analysis exposes three prominent themes: (a) an "othering" through the label of addiction, (b) the reinforced notion of abstinence as best practice, and (c) CTS as an innovative solution to end problematic substance use.

Othering through the Label of Addiction

The concept of "other" has been used across race, gender, and citizenship lines.[43] Othering is the result of "not in my back yard" attitudes that have frequently applied to PWUD,[44] particularly in Ontario.[45] Within the CTS policy, othering is enacted through the legitimization of vocalized opposition from residents and businesses who share a community with the SCS.[46] The concept of "othering" provides a useful tool to understand whose voice is counted in the formation of harm reduction debates and policies. SCS provide a contact point for community residents to seek health and social services, providing the means to improve one's quality of life. However, the framing of the key points in the new policy documents excludes SCS clients from the community by constructing clients as others and not including them in the privileges granted to "local residents." The divide is evident in the language used to refer to "quality of life for local residents." The deployment of an us-and-them dichotomy within the policy establishes that PWUD are not seen to be community members, and their needs and concerns are held in contrast to the needs of a community who fear an assumed risk associated with the presence of illicit drug use. This division results in a hierarchy of community member needs. The result is the exclusion of PWUD from community membership. This exclusion minimizes the benefits of full and equal cultural citizenship, and a person's ability to access health care services. Documented as a key point and published by the Ontario government, concerns of public disorder demonstrate elevation of privileged community members' needs, even when contradicting research has been established for over a decade.[47]

The decision to include prevailing concerns from other residents about the deviation from standardized norms acts as a form of governmentality. The emphasis on the need to rectify service users' behaviour in the documents' passages reinforces a narrative of PWUD as agents of risk, neglecting the role of the environment in the creation of risk. The individualization of risk leads to an individual burden of responsibility to manage that risk, with expectations of management determined by the state's assessments.[48] By explicitly describing addiction within the context of "crime" and "public disorder," persons accessing safe-consumption services—regardless of individual circumstance—are conceptualized as problematic and in need of management. Thus, while drug use is not explicitly problematized, it is implied that drug use is an origin of these social and medical problems that can be ameliorated through solutions that pull from the medical and criminal model of addiction.

Abstinence as Best Practice

Rebranded as the CTS model, the news release and the backgrounder refer to "treatment" sixteen times and "rehabilitation" six. The prioritization of abstinence is clear. The assumption that drug use is the starting point of the problem has led to abstinence-based treatment championed as the solution in CTS reform, all while the focus on abstinence divorces the social context of addiction from the individual. Therefore, the construction of the problem emphasizes medical discourses while eschewing social and environmental discourses, explicitly drawing attention to a solution that necessitates treatment and rehabilitation. Abstinence is central to the idea of a "pragmatic approach to overdose prevention, rooted in a relentless focus on getting people the help that they need by connecting them to treatment."[49] The Ontario government represents "treatment" as an overdose-prevention tactic and the "true" form of help they need. This framing negates the success SCS and OPS have had in treating the harms associated with drug use while further shaping a binary distinction between successful (abstinence) and unsuccessful (harm reduction) mechanisms of help.

The backgrounder and news release draw upon the values present in prohibitionist policies by using notions of safety and security, both historically wielded in support of increased criminalization.[50] With an emphasis on individual behaviour—couched within the discursive framework of social disorder—both documents employ a narrative of PWUD as agents of risk, neglecting the role of the social determinants of health. The medical framework serves to progress the view that SCS are enabling drug use by asserting the belief that individuals who become addicted are unable to stop because their brain chemistry has been altered by substance use.[51] The portrait constructed from these narratives, and specifically their proposed "solutions," suggests persons using SCS require assertive policies aimed at "pragmatically" resolving the overdose crisis via rehabilitation. In this view, allowing for individuals to continue using these substances would be the opposite of help. Often conceptualized as opposite from one another, or as a testament to progress in understanding addiction, the medical and criminal models coexist within the CTS policy to produce a particular representation of addiction, SCS, and their visitors. Interestingly, while advocating for health-based solutions, much weight is given to criminal consequences. The moral/criminal framing of addiction is inextricably linked to the solutions—abstinence-oriented treatment— provided by the medical framing of addiction.

Innovative Health Treatment Response

By constructing the problems of SCS as one of pre-existing inefficiencies it is a political signage that Ontario's Conservative government has control over the identified problem and can eradicate it through their "new and enhanced" model. The government fails to describe how the new model will "focus on connecting people who use drugs to primary care, treatment and rehabilitation," or how current harm reduction services fail to meet these expectations. Where the Tory government describes an "enhanced" treatment model it assumes that existing SCS do not adequately provide care to PWUD. The evidence of SCS in supporting clients in numerous ways prior to the CTS reform is clear—these services improve health, save lives, and connect individuals to a variety of treatment options.[52] The connection to the services mentioned in the new policy have been present in SCS since their conception: one study found elevated rates of withdrawal management service use for over 30% of participants after the opening of SCS.[53] A fundamental limitation of the CTS policy is what constitutes success. In order to identify what counts as success, we need to separate facts and values. The successes can be found in reports of the number of overdoses reversed, needles given out, and drugs tested. The value of these successes are diminished under the discourse of abstinence as best practice.

Described as an "enhanced" model of care, the discursive effect employed in the CTS model prioritizes abstinence-based models of care, delegitimizes harm reduction models as therapeutic, and undermines the role SCS and OPS play in supporting *both* safe use and abstinence.[54] Additionally, the identified underlying assumptions of the policy and the proposed solution of an enhanced focus on abstinence reflect long-standing prohibitionist values of law and order. Thus, while the policy repeatedly refers to an innovative approach, the reality reproduced is not that of innovation but of existing social dispositions around drug use and PWUD. In fact, efforts to divert SCS from their harm reduction origins in an attempt to neutralize individuals and practices that are perceived to harm community were identified almost two decades prior. In Canada, the desire to control and surveil "high risk" populations to foster secure public spaces has been observed since the 1960s.[55] This framing renders service users as dangerous and yet dependant on state-intervention to ameliorate the behaviours that make them such.

Conclusion

The application of the policy-as-discourse method highlights the political and social context that influenced the problematization of SCS,

PWUD, and drug use in the 2018 Ontario CTS policy. The problematization is the result of a conservative political understanding of substance use that represents the overdose crisis as a result of addiction, a condition brought on by drug use, and only effectively addressed if SCS increase their emphasis on abstinence-based treatment. The omission of the role of an unpredictable drug supply and the social determinants of health contributes to the position and framing that drug use is the problem and the succession of drug use the solution. A significant portion of the policy focuses on SCS visitors' behaviours, subjugating them as isolated from the surrounding community and justifying the emphasis on treatment by suggesting that abstinence will rectify one of the policy's primary concerns, the perceived social disorder brought on by these sites. Within the CTS policy, the characterization of addiction as a social threat and the resulting othering is inalienable from the shift to a focus on treatment. The increased emphasis on abstinent-based treatment is deeply intertwined with identifying a community that is in need of fixing and determining that SCS prior to the CTS reform were incapable of succeeding in that task. Ontario's Conservative government claims that this is an innovative approach to the overdose crisis. Given the conflicting knowledge frameworks present, and the deep historical roots of racism in the war on drugs, it would be fruitful for complementary future work to consider the opioid crisis within the wicked-problem framework.[56]

References

Alberta Health, *Impact: A Socio-Economic Review of Supervised Consumption Sites in Alberta* (Edmonton: Government of Alberta, March 2020), online: open.alberta.ca/dataset/dfd35cf7-9955-4d6b-a9c6-60d353ea87c3/resource/11815009-5243-4fe4-8884-11ffa1123631/download/health-socio-economic-review-supervised-consumption-sites.pdf

Bacchi, Carol, "Why Study Problematizations? Making Politics Visible" (2012) 2:1 Open J Political Science 1.

——, "Problematizations in Health Policy: Questioning How Problems Are Constituted in Policies" (2016) 6:2 Sage Open 1.

——, "Drug Problematizations and Politics: Deploying a Poststructural Analytic Strategy" (2018) 45:1 Contemporary Drug Problems 3.

Beattie, Samantha, "GTA Do Supervised Injection Sites Bring Crime and Disorder? Advocates and Residents Disagree," *Toronto Star* (last modified 17 August 2018), online: www.thestar.com/news/gta/2018/08/15/do-supervised-injection-sites-bring-crime-and-disorder-advocates-and-residents-disagree.html.

Boyd, Susan, Connie Carter & Donald Macpherson, *More Harm Than Good: Drug Policy in Canada* (Canada: Fernwood Publishing, 2016).

Didenko, Eugena & Nicole Pankratz "Substance Use: Pathways to Homelessness? Or a Way of Adapting to Street Life" (2007) 4:1 Visions: BC's Mental Health & Addictions J 9.

Fischer, Benedikt et al, "Drug Use, Risk and Urban Order: Examining Supervised Injection Sites (Siss) As 'Governmentality'" (2004) 15:5-6 Intl J Drug Policy 357.

Government of Canada, *National Report: Apparent Opioid-Related Deaths in Canada* (Ottawa: Government of Canada, March 2018), online: www.canada.ca/en/public-health/services/publications/healthy-living/national-report-apparent-opioid-related-deaths-released-march-2018.html#td.

Hyshka, Elaine et al, "Harm Reduction in Name, but Not Substance: A Comparative Analysis of Current Canadian Provincial and Territorial Policy Frameworks" (2017) 14:1 Harm Reduction J 1.

Johnson, Joy L et al, "Othering and Being Othered in the Context of Health Care Services" (2004) 16:2 Health Communication 255.

Kennedy, Mary Clare, Mohammad Karamouzian & Thomas Kerr, "Public Health and Public Order Outcomes Associated with Supervised Drug Consumption Facilities: A Systematic Review" (2017) 14:5 Current HIV/AIDS Reports 16.

Kerr, Thomas et al, "Supervised Injection Facilities in Canada: Past, Present, and Future" (2017) 14:1 Harm Reduction J.

Kerr, Thomas et al, "The Potential Use of Safer Injection Facilities Among Injection Drug Users in Vancouver's Downtown Eastside" (2003) 169:8 CMAJ 1.

Kolla, Gillian et al, "Canada's Overdose Crisis: Authorities Are Not Acting Fast Enough" (2019) 4:4 The Lancet Public Health 180.

Kolla, Gillian et al, "Risk Creating and Risk Reducing: Community Perceptions of Supervised Consumption Facilities for Illicit Drug Use" (2017) 19:1-2 Health, Risk & Society 91.

Lancaster, Kari, "Social Construction and the Evidence-Based Drug Policy Endeavour" (2014) 25:5 Intl J Drug Policy 948.

Lancaster, Kari, Karen Duke & Allison Ritter, "Producing The 'Problem Of Drugs': A Cross National-Comparison Of 'Recovery' Discourse in Two Australian and British Reports" (2015) 26:7 Intl J Drug Policy 617.

Malleck, Daniel, *When Good Drugs Go Bad: Opium, Medicine, and the Origins of Canada's Drug Laws* (Vancouver: UBC Press, 2015).

Maloney, Ryan, "Doug Ford Digs in against Safe Injection Sites at First Debate," *HuffPost Canada* (7 May 2018), online: www.huffingtonpost.ca/2018/05/07/doug-ford-safe-injection-sites-debate_a_23429304/.

Milloy, MLS et al, "Estimated Drug Overdose Deaths Averted by North America's First Medically-Supervised Safer Injection Facility" (2008) 3:10 PLoS One 3351.

Nowell, Magnus, "Safe Supply: What Is It and What Is Happening in Canada" (9 February 2021), online: www.catie.ca/en/pif/spring-2021/safe-supply-what-it-and-what-happening-canada.

Ontario Ministry of Health and Long-Term Care, News Release, "Ontario Government Connecting People with Addictions to Treatment and Rehabilitation" (October 22 2018), online: news.ontario.ca/en/release/50237/ontario-government-connecting-people-with-addictions-to-treatment-and-rehabilitation.

——, *Consumption and Treatment Services: Application Guide* (Toronto: Ministry of Health and Long-Term Care, October 2018), online: https://peterboroughcurrents.ca/wp-content/uploads/2022/03/CTS_application_guide_en.pdf.

——, "Backgrounder Review of Supervised Consumption Services and Overdose Prevention Sites - Key Findings" (22 October 2018), online: news.ontario.ca/en/backgrounder/50238/review-of-supervised-consumption-services-and-overdose-prevention-sites-key-findings.

Pienaar, Kiran & Micheal Savic, "Producing Alcohol and Other Drugs as a Policy 'Problem': A Critical Analysis of South Africa's 'National Drug Master Plan'(2013–2017)" (2016) 30 Intl J Drug Policy 35.

Public Health Ontario, *Opioid Mortality Surveillance Report Analysis of Opioid-Related Deaths in Ontario July 2017–June 2018* (Toronto: Public Health Ontario, 2019), online: www.publichealthontario.ca/-/media/documents/o/2019/opioid-mortality-surveillance-report.pdf?sc_lang=en.

Quirion, Bastein, "From Rehabilitation to Risk Management: The Goals of Methadone Programmes in Canada" (2003) 14:3 Intl J Drug Policy 247.

Rittel, Horst W & Melvin M Webber, "Dilemmas in a General Theory of Planning" (1973) 4:2 Policy Sciences 155.

Shaw, Sara E & Trisha Greenhalgh, "Best Research–for What? Best Health–for Whom? A Critical Exploration of Primary Care Research Using Discourse Analysis" (2008) 66:12 Soc Science & Medicine 2506.

Shaw, Sara E, "Reaching the Parts That Other Theories and Methods Can't Reach: How and Why a Policy-as-Discourse Approach Can Inform Health-Related Policy" (2010) 14:2 Health 196.

Strike, Carol, Ted Myers & Margaret Millson, "Finding a Place for Needle Exchange Programs" (2004) 14:3 Critical Public Health 261.

Tyndall, Mark W et al, "Attendance, Drug Use Patterns, and Referrals Made from North America's First Supervised Injection Facility" (2006) 83:3 Drug & Alcohol Dependence 193.

Urbanoski, Karen et al, "It Is Time to End Canada's Simplistic Approach to Drug Policy," *The Tyee* (3 October 2019), online: thetyee.ca/Opinion/2019/10/03/ End-Canada-Simplistic-Drug-Policy-Approach/.

van der Eijk, Yvette & Susanne Uusitalo, "Towards a 'Sociorelational' Approach to Conceptualizing and Managing Addiction" (2016) 9:2 Public Health Ethics 198.

Wallace, Bruce, Flora Pagan & Bernie Pauly, "The Implementation of Overdose Prevention Sites as a Novel and Nimble Response During an Illegal Drug Overdose Public Health Emergency" (2019) 66 Intl J Drug Policy 64.

Watson, Tara Marie et al, "Critical Studies of Harm Reduction: Overdose Response in Uncertain Political Times" (2020) 76 Intl J Drug Policy 102615.

Wood, Evan et al, "Changes in Public Order After the Opening of a Medically Supervised Safer Injecting Facility for Illicit Injection Drug Users" (2004) 171:7 CMAJ 731.

——, "Rate of Detoxification Service Use and Its Impact Among a Cohort of Supervised Injecting Facility Users" (2007) 102:6 Addiction 916.

Notes

1   See Elaine Hyshka et al, "Harm Reduction in Name, but Not Substance: A Comparative Analysis of Current Canadian Provincial and Territorial Policy Frameworks" (2017) 14:1 Harm Reduction J 1.

2   See Magnus Nowell, "Safe Supply: What Is It and What Is Happening in Canada" (9 February 2021), online: www.catie.ca/en/pif/spring-2021/safe-supply-what-it-and-what-happening-canada.

3   See Thomas Kerr et al, "The Potential Use of Safer Injection Facilities Among Injection Drug Users in Vancouver's Downtown Eastside" (2003) 169:8 CMAJ 1; see also MLS Milloy et al, "Estimated Drug Overdose Deaths Averted by North America's First Medically-Supervised Safer Injection Facility" (2008) 3:10 PLoS One 3351; see also Mark W Tyndall et al, "Attendance, Drug Use Patterns, and Referrals Made from North America's First Supervised Injection Facility" (2006) 83:3 Drug & Alcohol Dependence 193; see also Bruce Wallace, Flora Pagan & Bernie Pauly, "The Implementation of Overdose Prevention Sites as a Novel and Nimble Response During an Illegal Drug Overdose Public Health Emergency" (2019) 66 Intl J Drug Policy 64.

4   See Ontario Ministry of Health and Long-Term Care, "Review of Supervised Consumption Services and Overdose Prevention Sites–Key Findings" (Toronto: Ministry of Health and Long-Term Care, 22 October 2018), online: news.ontario. ca/en/backgrounder/50238/review-of-supervised-consumption-services-and-overdose-prevention-sites-key-findings [Backgrounder].

5   See Ontario Ministry of Health and Long-Term Care, News Release, "Ontario Government Connecting People with Addictions to Treatment and Rehabilitation," (22 October 2018), online: news.ontario.ca/en/release/50237/ontario-government-connecting-people-with-addictions-to-treatment-and-rehabilitation [Ont Gov, News Release].

6   See Kari Lancaster, Karen Duke & Allison Ritter, "Producing the 'Problem of Drugs': A Cross National-Comparison of 'Recovery' Discourse in Two Australian and British Reports" (2015) 26:7 Intl J Drug Policy 617; see also Kiran Pienaar &

Micheal Savic, "Producing Alcohol and Other Drugs as a Policy 'Problem': A Critical Analysis of South Africa's 'National Drug Master Plan' (2013–2017)" (2016) 30 Intl J Drug Policy 35.

7   See Carol Bacchi, "Why Study Problematizations? Making Politics Visible" (2012) 2:1 Open J Political Science 1; see also Carol Bacchi, "Problematizations in Health Policy: Questioning How "Problems" Are Constituted in Policies" (2016) 6:2 Sage Open 1 [Bacchi, "Problemizations"]; see also Carol Bacchi, "Drug Problematizations and Politics: Deploying a Poststructural Analytic Strategy" (2018) 45:1 Contemporary Drug Problems 3 [Bacchi, "Poststructural"].

8   See Sara E Shaw, "Reaching the Parts that Other Theories and Methods Can't Reach: How and Why a Policy-as-Discourse Approach Can Inform Health-Related Policy" (2010) 14:2 Health 196.

9   See Kari Lancaster, "Social Construction and the Evidence-Based Drug Policy Endeavour" (2014) 25:5 Intl J Drug Policy 948.

10   See Sara E Shaw & Trisha Greenhalgh, "Best Research–for What? Best Health–for Whom? A Critical Exploration of Primary Care Research Using Discourse Analysis" (2008) 66:12 Soc Science & Medicine 2506 [Shaw, "Best Research"].

11   See Ryan Maloney, "Doug Ford Digs in Against Safe Injection Sites at First Debate" (7 May 2018), online: www.huffingtonpost.ca/2018/05/07/doug-ford-safe-injection-sites-debate_a_23429304/.

12   See Thomas Kerr et al, "Supervised Injection Facilities in Canada: Past, Present, and Future" (2017) 14:1 Harm Reduction J [Kerr, "Past, Present, Future"].

13   See Gillian Kolla et al, "Canada's Overdose Crisis: Authorities Are Not Acting Fast Enough" (2019) 4:4 The Lancet Public Health 180 [Kolla, "Crisis"].

14   See Ontario Ministry of Health and Long-Term Care, *Consumption and Treatment Services: Application Guide* (Toronto: Ministry of Health and Long-Term Care, October 2018), online: health.gov.on.ca/en/pro/programs/opioids/docs/CTS_application_guide_en.pdf [*Application Guide*].

15   See Yara Marie Watson et al, "Critical Studies of Harm Reduction: Overdose Response in Uncertain Political Times" (2020) 76 Intl J Drug Policy 102615.

16   See "Backgrounder," *supra* note 4; see also Ont Gov, News Release, *supra* note 5.

17   See "Backgrounder," *supra* note 4.

18   *Ibid.*

19   See Bacchi, "Problemizations," *supra* note 7.

20   *Ibid.*

21   *Ibid.*

22   Susan Boyd, Connie Carter & Donald Macpherson, *More Harm than Good: Drug Policy in Canada* (Canada: Fernwood Publishing, 2016).

23   See Bacchi, "Problemizations," *supra* note 7; see also Bacchi, "Poststructural," *supra* note 7.

24   See "Backgrounder," *supra* note 4.

25   See *Application Guide, supra* note 14.

26   *Ibid.*

27   See Boyd, *supra* note 22.

28   See *Application Guide, supra* note 14.

29   *Ibid.*

30   See Daniel Malleck, *When Good Drugs Go Bad: Opium, Medicine, and the Origins of Canada's Drug Laws* (Vancouver: UBC Press, 2015).

31   See Ont Gov, News Release, *supra* note 5.

32   See Shaw, "Best Research," *supra* note 10.

33   See Kerr, "Past, Present, Future," *supra* note 12.

34   See Alberta Health, *Impact: A Socio-Economic Review of Supervised Consumption Sites in Alberta* (Edmonton: Government of Alberta, March 2020), online: open.alberta. ca/dataset/dfd35cf7-9955-4d6b-a9c6-60d353ea87c3/resource/11815009-5243-4fe4-8884-11ffa1123631/download/health-socio-economic-review-supervised-consumption-sites.pdf.

35   See Malleck, *supra* note 30.

36   See *Application Guide, supra* note 14.

37   See Boyd, *supra* note 22.

38   See Eugena Didenko & Nicole Pankratz "Substance Use: Pathways to Homelessness? Or a Way of Adapting to Street Life" (2007) 4:1 Visions: BC's Mental Health & Addictions J 9.

39   See Government of Canada, *National Report: Apparent Opioid-Related Deaths In Canada* (Ottawa: Government of Canada, March 2018), online: www.canada.ca/en/public-health/services/publications/healthy-living/national-report-apparent-opioid-related-deaths-released-march-2018.html#td.

40   See Public Health Ontario, *Opioid Mortality Surveillance Report Analysis of Opioid-Related Deaths in Ontario July 2017–June 2018* (Toronto: Public Health Ontario, 2019), online: www.publichealthontario.ca/-/media/documents/o/2019/opioid-mortality-surveillance-report.pdf?sc_lang=en.

41   See *Application Guide, supra* note 14.

42   *Ibid.*

43   See Joy L Johnson et al, "Othering and Being Othered in the Context of Health Care Services" (2004) 16:2 Health Communication 255.

44   See Carol Strike, Ted Myers & Margaret Millson, "Finding a Place for Needle Exchange Programs" (2004) 14:3 Critical Public Health 261; see also *ibid.*

45   See Gillian Kolla et al, "Risk Creating and Risk Reducing: Community Perceptions of Supervised Consumption Facilities for Illicit Drug Use" (2017) 19:1-2 Health, Risk & Society 91.

46   See Samantha Beattie, "GTA Do Supervised Injection Sites Bring Crime and Disorder? Advocates and Residents Disagree" (last modified 17 August 2018), online: www.thestar.com/news/gta/2018/08/15/do-supervised-injection-sites-bring-crime-and-disorder-advocates-and-residents-disagree.html.

47   Evan Wood et al, "Changes in Public Order After the Opening of a Medically Supervised Safer Injecting Facility for Illicit Injection Drug Users" (2004) 171:7 CMAJ 731.

48   See Benedikt Fischer et al, "Drug Use, Risk and Urban Order: Examining Supervised Injection Sites (Siss) As 'Governmentality'" (2004) 15:5-6 Intl J Drug Policy 357.

49   See Boyd, *supra* note 22.

50   See Kolla, "Crisis," *supra* note 13.

51   See Yvette van der Eijk & Susanne Uusitalo, "Towards a 'Sociorelational' Approach to Conceptualizing and Managing Addiction" (2016) 9:2 Public Health Ethics 198.

52   See Mary Clare Kennedy, Mohammad Karamouzian & Thomas Kerr, "Public Health and Public Order Outcomes Associated with Supervised Drug Consumption Facilities: A Systematic Review" (2017) 14:5 Current HIV/AIDS Reports 16.

53   See Evan Wood et al, "Rate of Detoxification Service Use and Its Impact among a Cohort of Supervised Injecting Facility Users" (2007) 102:6 Addiction 916.

54   See Karen Urbanoski et al, "It Is Time to End Canada's Simplistic Approach to Drug Policy" (3 October 2019), online: thetyee.ca/Opinion/2019/10/03/End-Canada-Simplistic-Drug-Policy-Approach/.

55 See Bastein Quirion, "From Rehabilitation to Risk Management: The Goals of Methadone Programmes in Canada" (2003) 14:3 Intl J Drug Policy 247.

56 See Horst W Rittel & Melvin M Webber, "Dilemmas in a General Theory of Planning" (1973) 4:2 Policy Sciences 155.

CHAPTER 5

Governance of Recreational Cannabis Users in Canada

Jurisdictional Shifts, Punitive Decriminalization, and Challenges for Harm Reduction

Joao Velloso and Véronique Fortin

In December 2015, the Canadian government committed to enacting legislation to legalize cannabis for non-medical use.[1] In June 2016, the ministers of Justice, of Health, and of Public Safety jointly announced the creation of the Task Force on Cannabis Legalization and Regulation.[2] The task force was composed by members with different expertise (health professionals, academics, politicians, and police officers). Their report, *A Framework for the Legalization and Regulation of Cannabis in Canada*,[3] was released by Health Canada in December 2016, not by Justice or Public Safety, or jointly with them, even if they were implicated in this process.[4] The report is strongly marked by harm reduction principles and public health rationales.[5] Its second chapter ("Minimizing Harms of Use") is essentially a discussion on how to reduce harms and makes recommendations to the federal government in this sense. This idea of "minimizing harms" is present throughout the report and is framed as a strictly regulated market, meaning that an unregulated criminal market under a prohibitionist approach is harmful. The same can be said of an unregulated legal market. Figure 5.1 summarizes this rationale.[6]

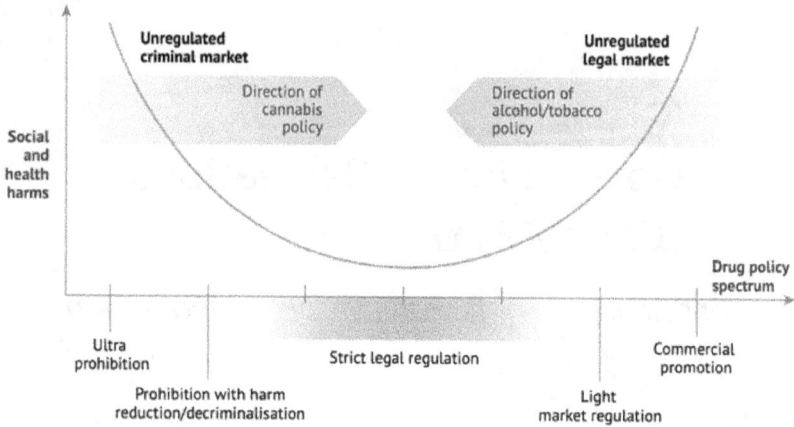

FIGURE 5.1. Social and health harms of drug policies.
Source: S Rolles & G Murkin, *How To Regulate Cannabis: A Practical Guide* (2016).

The 2016 report was intended to be the basis of Bill C-45,[7] which became the Cannabis Act and has been law since October 2018.[8] The Cannabis Act created a legal framework to control the production, distribution, sale, and possession of cannabis in Canada. It is the "central" piece of legislation in a broad legal framework that goes beyond federal jurisdiction. We should note that harm reduction principles from the task force's report were already quite diluted in the first reading of Bill C-45, sponsored by the minister of Justice, and they are arguably inexistant in the Cannabis Act. Prohibitionist overtones subsist: the Cannabis Act did not fully decriminalize the substance, and criminal offences with regards to cannabis still exist and are even now governed through a more punitive criminal-law framework, arguably increasing social and health harms instead of minimizing them. Alana Klein argued in a similar sense in her influential chapter on the place of harm reduction in such law reform.[9] In this chapter, we aim to push this debate further by arguing that the multiplication of norms governing cannabis users through other realms of law and jurisdictions (the "strict legal regulation" in figure 5.1) makes the effective implementation of harm reduction rationales and strategies even more difficult. Theoretically, as illustrated in the model cited in the report, strict regulation should reduce social and health harms. But as socio-legal scholars have long demonstrated, law in action is always more complicated. As we will see, the Cannabis Act created two categories of cannabis, licit and illicit, and the federal legislative changes did not come with less law, but more. More laws, more regulations, more punitive governance both within criminal law (federal jurisdiction) and other areas of law (mostly other jurisdictions). This new plethora of jurisdictions, norms, and actors governing cannabis use is not always in tune with harm reduction principles. Somehow the rationale of "minimizing harms of use" through legal regulation created a paradox, where the conditions to reduce harms are also those that create obstacles to harm reduction initiatives. The problem is not legal regulation in itself but the punitiveness of this regulation and how it was translated into multiple jurisdictions and countless frameworks of regulation that are not necessarily coherent.

This chapter is organized in three parts, followed by a short conclusion. In the first, "The Treachery of Legalization: *Ceci n'est pas la décriminalisation*," paraphrasing René Magritte's masterpiece *La trahison des images* (better known as *Ceci n'est pas une pipe*), we argue that the Cannabis Act harshened the criminal regime used to control users of illegal cannabis. Using the harm reduction rationale summarized in figure 5.1 as reference, we argue that the new framework brought on by the Cannabis Act oscillates between "strict legal regulation" and "ultra prohibition" on the drug-policy spectrum. In the second part, "Opening Pandora's Box: From Criminalization to Multiple Regimes," we discuss the idea of punitive decriminalization.[10] Building on our past research on penalization of migrants,[11] homelessness,[12] and protesters,[13] we show that "licit cannabis" is punitively governed by other jurisdictions, outside the criminal-law field. This questions a second aspect of the rationale presented in figure 5.1: strict regulation beyond criminal law does not necessarily reduce "social and health harms" when punitive and prohibitionist rationales are at play; quite the contrary. Finally, in the third, "Rare Syzygy: Difficulties in Aligning Multiple Norms and Jurisdictions," we borrow the astronomical notion of syzygy (a straight-line configuration of three or more celestial bodies within the same celestial system) and discuss the complexity of syzygy regimes that govern uses of recreational cannabis and how the alignments within the same system matter. We argue that the model of minimizing harms through strict regulation actually corresponds to particular syzygies; that is, harm reduction is not guaranteed in a multi-jurisdictional context such as Canada. We conclude the chapter by underlining the importance of paying attention to the new modes of governance, and their impact, when studying legislative reforms.

The Treachery of Legalization: *Ceci n'est pas la décriminalisation*

It is generally admitted that a prohibitionist criminal regime of drug uses is contradictory to a harm reduction approach. This reasoning is quite clear in the *Final Report of the Task Force on Cannabis Legalization and Regulation* which confirms that the prohibitionist approach is associated with more social and health harms because of criminalization and unregulated criminal markets (interactions, accessibility, quality of the substance, etc.). In Canada, the criminalization of cannabis failed to prevent its use: 14.9% of Canadians aged 15 or older had used cannabis before its legalization for recreational use.[14] The criminalization of cannabis pushed a large portion of the population into illegality, occasioning encounters with drug dealers and potential police interactions that triggered criminal records for about 1.5 million Canadians, disproportionately impacting Black, Indigenous, and people of colour.[15] In addition, cannabis users prior to legalization were using a product that was not always safe.

As early as the end of the 1960s, with the Le Dain Commission,[16] the Canadian government openly studied whether criminal law should be used in the field of non-medical drug use.[17] Ironically, in the 1970s, Prime Minister Pierre Elliott Trudeau did not carry out the recommendations of the commission, which included the decriminalization of simple possession of cannabis, whereas 45 years later his son, Prime Minister Justin Trudeau, legalized recreational cannabis.[18]

A distinction is often made between decriminalization and legalization: decriminalization implies an end to the possibility of criminal prosecution and criminal sanctions, while legalization implies, in addition to decriminalization, quality control and adequate supply sources.[19] In the context of cannabis specifically, even though an adult of a certain age (18 to 21, depending on the province) can legally buy a small quantity of cannabis in cannabis shops, the decriminalization of the substance, in terms of an end to the possibility of criminal prosecution and punishment, has been partial at best.

In fact, Parliament took two distinct approaches in the Cannabis Act. On one hand, it kept the status quo of criminalizing illicit cannabis, harshening penalties associated with it and creating new offences. On the other, it created the category "licit cannabis" for recreational use.[20] But even with regards to licit cannabis, criminal sanctions are possible (e.g., for possessing an amount exceeding the allowed threshold, or sharing with minors). The very piece of legislation that allegedly decriminalized and legalized cannabis is clear about the continuing punishment of illicit activities in relation to cannabis, to the dismay of long-time advocates of reform.[21]

Table 5.1 lists some illicit activities in relation to cannabis (quantity, source, distribution, sale, but excluding offences related to driving under the influence of cannabis) that can lead to criminal offences for adults, and the potential procedures and punishment associated with these offences. Note that the Cannabis Act is different from the Controlled Drugs and Substances Act (CDSA) in two distinct ways.[22] First, it introduced a legal regime for the distribution and sale of cannabis to individuals under 18 years of age. Second, it sets a distinction between distributing (giving for free, sharing) and selling cannabis,[23] whereas under the CDSA, selling, administering, giving, transferring, transporting, sending, or delivering a prohibited substance (e.g., cannabis) all amounts to trafficking.

It is important to also mention that the maximum penalty of 14 years in prison classifies those offences as "serious criminality" under the Immigration and Refugee Protection Act (IRPA),[24] which have important consequences on immigration status (including deportation). This maximum penalty of 14 years in prison also removes the offences from eligibility to conditional sentencing.[25]

TABLE 5.1. Actions that Remain Illicit Following Cannabis Legalization

Offence	Procedures,[*] Maximum Punishment and Immigration Consequences[†]
Possession of a quantity of cannabis surpassing the allowed threshold *or* possession of illicit cannabis.[‡]	Tickets for small quantities (more than 30 g and up to 50 g of dried licit cannabis; or up to 50 g of dried illicit cannabis) (s 51(2)(a) CA). • $200 + victim surcharge + fees (s 51(4)(a) CA). Offence punishable on summary conviction • Fine of no more than $5,000 or imprisonment for no more than 6 months, or both (s 8(2)(b)(i) CA). Indictable offence • Imprisonment for no more than 5 years (s 8(2)(a)(i) CA). Immigration: detention + potential deportation on grounds of criminality

Distribution, to an adult, of a quantity of cannabis surpassing the allowed threshold
 	
or
 	
Distribution, to an adult, of illicit cannabis
	Tickets for small quantities (more than 30 g and up to 50 g of dried licit cannabis; or up to 50 g of dried illicit cannabis) (s 51(2)(a) CA).
	  • $200 + victim surcharge + fees (s 51(4)(a) CA).
	
	Offence punishable on summary conviction
	  • Fine of no more than $5,000 or imprisonment for no more than 6 months, or both (s 9(5)(b)(i) CA).
	
	Indictable offence
	  • Imprisonment for no more than 14 years (s 9(5)(a)(i) CA).
	
	Immigration: detention + deportation on grounds of serious criminality

Selling cannabis to an adult	Tickets for small quantities (up to 50 g of dried licit or illicit cannabis) (s 51(2)(d) CA).
	  • $200 + victim surcharge + fees (s 51(4)(a) CA).
	
	Offence punishable on summary conviction
	  • Fine of no more than $5,000 or imprisonment for no more than 6 months, or both (s 10(5)(b)(i) CA).
	
	Indictable offence
	  • Imprisonment for no more than 14 years (s 10(5)(a) CA).
	
	Immigration: detention + deportation on grounds of serious criminality

Distribution or sale of cannabis to an individual who is under 18 years old	Offence punishable on summary conviction
	  • Fine of no more than $15,000 or imprisonment for no more than 18 months, or both (s 9(5)(b)(ii) and 10(5)(b)(ii) CA).
	
	Indictable offence
	  • Imprisonment for no more than 14 years (s 9(5)(a)(i) and 10(5)(a) CA).
	
	Immigration: detention + deportation on grounds of serious criminality

*   The selected procedure is the result of a discretionary choice by the peace officer or the Crown prosecutor.

†   See "Grounds for Detention Reviews" (last modified 30 May 2022), online: *Immigration and Refugee Board of Canada* irb.gc.ca/en/statistics/detentions-reviews/Pages/detenGr.aspx (Immigration consequences always take the maximum punishment for indictable offences into consideration, regardless of the sentence imposed or whether it has been prosecuted summarily when it is a hybrid offence. Conviction is not necessarily required, especially for detention. Detention in immigration is not an end, but a means to ensure that the foreigner will be present

in future examination, hearing, proceeding or removal from Canada. Unlikely to appear [flight risk] is by far the main ground for immigration detention in Canada [usually over 70% of reviews], distantly followed by security reasons [usually below 13%]).

‡   *Cannabis Act, supra* note 8, s 2(1) (in 2018 Illicit cannabis is defined as: "that is or was sold, produced or distributed by a person prohibited from doing so under this Act or any provincial Act or that was imported by a person prohibited from doing so under this Act").

As may be seen in Table 5.1, cannabis use remains subject to criminal prosecution and punishment, even as concerns licit cannabis. Indeed, criminal sanctions exist for controlled substances; for example, for possession of illicit tobacco or distilling spirits without a licence.[26] However, the criminalization of cannabis remains much harsher than controlled substances like alcohol or tobacco; there is no legal limit to the number of bottles of wine one can possess, unlike the cannabis user, who must abide by a threshold rule. Also, giving alcohol or tobacco to minors is not a criminal offence but a provincial regulatory one, punishable by a fine. Nearly four years after legalization,[27] cannabis users remain stigmatized, criminalized, and punished.

We note the opening sentence of a Government of Canada press release on October 17, 2018, the day the Cannabis Act came into force: "The old approach to cannabis did not work."[28] Yet, as observed in Table 5.1, the legal regime surrounding cannabis continues to rely on significant criminal penalties in certain circumstances, sometimes more so than under the previous law. The old approach to cannabis remains in large portions, and the act does not adopt a harm reduction model, one based on stigma reduction and non-judgment, as a true public health approach would have required.[29] As Alana Klein noted:

The Cannabis Act reflects an ambivalent relationship to harm reduction. On the one hand, it is rooted in a recognition that prohibition has failed, and seeks to eliminate harms caused by criminalization. Its purposes of "provid[ing] access to a quality-controlled supply of cannabis" recall prescription heroin, a well-supported harm reduction intervention that seeks to avoid risks associated with black market opiates by ensuring access to a licit product with a predictable strength that meets users' needs without exposing them to an increased risk of overdose. The objective of "enhanc[ing] public awareness of the health risks associated with cannabis use" is basic public health policy, but compatible with harm reduction's focus on pragmatism and scientism, and its rejection of stigma, dogma, and demonization of drug use. But in important ways, the new law and the policy supporting it remain within the logic of zero tolerance.[30]

The new legal regime of licit cannabis tried to limit those negative impacts of the prohibitionist regime, but in some sense the Cannabis Act represents little more than a tempering of the prohibitionist paradigm with both public health and commercial overtones present.[31] With the partial decriminalization and legalization of cannabis, Parliament, as illustrated in figure 5.1, moved in opposite directions on the drug-policy spectrum; it moved toward strict regulation but it also moved in the opposite direction, toward ultra-prohibition, by creating new criminal offences and harshening criminal punishment.

The next section explores how the legalization and partial decriminalization of cannabis in Canada did not bring with it the end of punitive governance. To the contrary, legalization and partial decriminalization opened a punitive Pandora's Box that undermined efforts to minimize social and health harms of use.

Opening Pandora's Box:
From Criminalization to Multiple Regimes

As Parliament created a new legal regime for licit recreational cannabis, provinces, municipalities, and private actors (including landlords and employers) took over the regulatory role left and enacted multiple norms (laws, regulations, or other) with which to regulate and punish; for example, the legal age of possession and where cannabis can be used, sold, and grown.

And if Alana Klein asks *what* jurisdiction for harm reduction, we ask *how*. How these jurisdictions, including normative arrangements beyond state law, are well aligned, or not, toward harm reduction? We understand jurisdictions to be the governing assemblage of authorities, territories, and matters, but as Mariana Valverde puts it, "[j]urisdiction, however, distinguishes more than territories, and authorities, more than the where and the who of governance. Jurisdiction also differentiates and organizes the 'what' of governance—and most importantly because of its relative invisibility, the 'how' of governance."[32] In this sense, the shift from federal jurisdiction (criminal law) to other jurisdictions, and the types of law within, is not a guarantee of less punitiveness or more inclusive practices. Quite the contrary, in fact. And, as we will see, normative schemes emerging from these other jurisdictions often create obstacles for harm reduction. In other words, the "strict legal regulation" framework for drug policy that theoretically brings down "social and health harms" is rather diverse, plural, messy, and still harmful.

The image of opening Pandora's Box—borrowing from Greek mythology to refer to an action that causes unforeseen problems—is not exaggerated. The process of cannabis legalization in Canada was about moving from the relatively predictable criminalization framework—with all the detrimental effects we know stem from it—to a form of social control related to multiple legal orders and their law-enforcing agencies and agents. Before 2018, a recreational user juggled with basically two legal orders: criminal law and illegal markets,[33] which also includes their enforcing sides (police officers, drug dealers, etc.). Since partial decriminalization and legalization in 2018, a recreational user must handle countless state and non-state legal orders, and their enforcing mechanisms, including the old ones, as illicit cannabis, illegal markets, and criminal offences still exist, and the latter are sometimes applicable to licit cannabis. The legal orders governing licit and illicit cannabis are everywhere, with many operating in the same time and space. The same can be said about punitive outcomes.[34] Legal punishment is fairly predictable in the criminalization framework. Non-criminal sanctions are more fluid and, paradoxically, are sometimes harsher under the new regimes (the Cannabis Act and "strict legal regulation"). Figure 5.2 maps the different areas of law and jurisdictions governing cannabis in Canada today.

Figure 5.2 summarizes the relationships among different types of semi-autonomous areas of law (gray circles) and the realm of formal punitiveness (white circle).[35] Arrows represent relationships and how one subsystem may influence the other(s) or how they relate to punishment ("sanctioning" instead of sentencing), both in one direction or mutually influenced. Dashed lines represent possibilities of, depending on the context/case, and solid lines (trans)systemic certainty; their thickness simply represents how a given area is more or less determinant in "sanctioning." This graphic does not represent all the legal orders involved in the governance of cannabis users in Canada, and the same thing can be said about legal regimes and norms. However, it illustrates how messy "strict legal regulation" is. Coherence is not only a matter of similar content or principles present in a given norm or policy. Functionally differentiated areas of law generally do not frame conflicts in the same way, their rationales and institutional practices are not the same, etc.; different jurisdictions and laws creates incoherency in the governance of cannabis users across Canada.

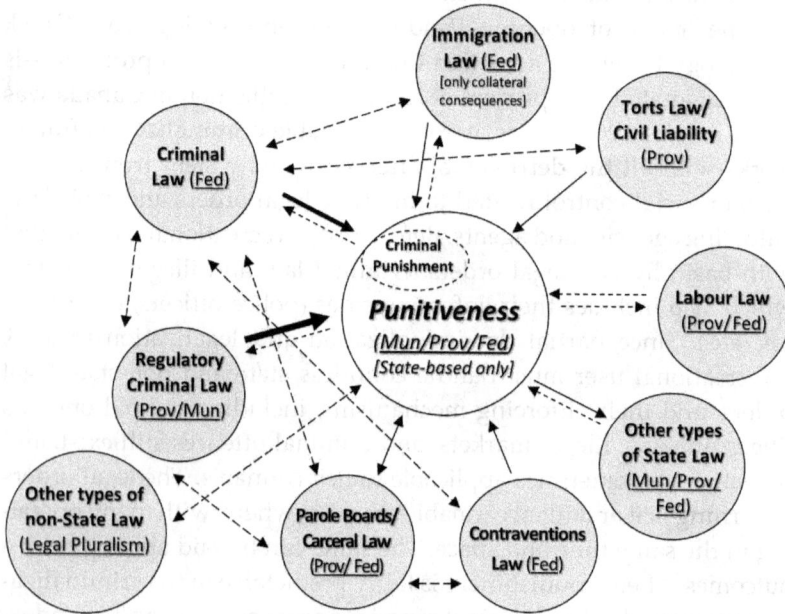

FIGURE 5.2. Areas of law and jurisdictions governing cannabis in Canada. *Source:* Joao Velloso and Véronique Fortin.

We realize this is a broad scheme to describe the actual regime governing cannabis users in the country, and that some of these spheres of interaction need to be nuanced. For instance, labour law may play a role in the social control of the workplace; for example, by regulating the drug testing of employees and the potential disciplinary measures for possession of cannabis on work premises, or in defining substance use as a disability.[36] Immigration law, as noted, may trigger detention or deportation via collateral consequences of criminal justice. The contraventions regime may be mobilized against users in particular contexts related to federal jurisdiction, such as parks and lands, federal workplaces, seaways or seaway properties, and the military (facilities and persons), among other situations present in the Contraventions Regulations.[37] Family law may also enter into play with regards to child custody when one parent is deemed to be using cannabis.[38] Our past research on the social control of vulnerable populations suggests that regulatory regimes and criminal justice will be, and actually is, playing a major role in punitive social control (the thicker arrows in the graphic), mostly through municipal jurisdictions (alone or shared with provinces) and their management of zoning and spaces of consumption (or cultivation).[39] Several non-state entities (e.g., condominium associations, mall owners, university administrations) also regulate cannabis use, creating legal pluralistic dynamics that vary greatly across the country. Interestingly, torts or civil liability may also be mobilized by users against licit growers and vendors, including claims of punitive damages, as legal action can be taken to solve disputes within the legal market (e.g., quality control,[40] mislabelling), opening new venues for harm reduction advocacy.[41]

The point of this graphic is to show how complex, functionally differentiated, fluid, and adaptive the governance of cannabis is in Canada. There is no "cannabis law" for the country. The social control of users is situational, varying from case to case and per the individuals involved. It is not possible to state, in general, what the legal framework is for licit cannabis in Canada; one has to analyze the different layers of jurisdictional law on a case-by-case basis. Every province, and almost every municipality, has their own regulations on cannabis. For instance, every province has two or three different laws on smoking or vaping in public spaces, and major cities in provinces that allow such use have multiple respective bylaws.[42] Interestingly, in Montreal, before the province of Quebec prohibited smoking or vaping cannabis in public spaces, regulations would vary even by borough, with different restrictions and fines across the city.[43] Finally, we should also add non-state norms applicable to private spaces. Sanctions for cannabis uses on the campus of Université Laval, for example, take into consideration the collective labour agreements (professors and staff); any contract, regulation, policy or procedure in force; and a disciplinary code for students.[44] Some condominiums have different rules for owners and tenants, and some tenants also face contractual restrictions via their leases. Again, the situational context is not only a matter of where but of whom, as the applicable legal framework is sometimes contingent on the legal status of the person using cannabis.

The multiplication of legal orders governing various aspects of cannabis use also raises issues of social control. As we will see in the next section, jurisdictional dances may not be as harmonious as a tango, considering that the resulting chimera regimes are somewhat incoherent.[45] Moreover, we must stress that the overuse of regulatory or administrative-based regimes, such as the ticket regime in the Cannabis Act, reifies law-enforcement encounters and has a net-widening effect regarding the social control of users. In other words, such legal orders strengthen police discretion, which may reinforce prohibitionism and create difficulties for harm reduction initiatives, in addition to opening old and new doors to racial and social profiling.

This proliferation of norms and jurisdictions is not just the result of a scale shift—cannabis uses (and users) would now be governed at the local level rather than the federal. As Mariana Valverde warned several years ago, those scale shifts are not a zero-sum game.[46] Multiple scales and jurisdictions do coexist on a single space/time unit, each operating with their own logics, sometime contradictorily:

> The legal mechanism of jurisdiction—which sets limits on the scale shifting that authorities can do, and which in turn generates many scalar effects—has many uses and produces many effects. As has been suggested in the preceding paragraphs, jurisdiction is extremely useful for the workings of governance generally (not only of the formal law) because it manages the epistemological conflicts among heterogeneous logics of governance by sorting different kinds of governance into different boxes.[47]

The effects of jurisdictions are to make them seem "natural."[48] The multiplication of jurisdictions after partial decriminalization makes the punitive effect more difficult to grasp, obfuscating the workings of the numerous new norms. And with this densification of norms and proliferation of jurisdictions comes a legal governance that maintains the stigmatization of users and perpetuates the harmful effects of punishment.[49] In other words, punishment is merely taking new forms and strict regulation does not necessarily reduce or minimize the social and health harms of use, especially for those already in vulnerable positions.

We now turn to how this new legal governance brings additional challenges for harm reduction, and, possibly, opportunities.

Rare Syzygy: Difficulties in
Aligning Multiple Norms and Jurisdictions

As described, despite cannabis decriminalization, criminal prosecution and punishment remain threats for cannabis users. The licit cannabis regime is so complex, heterogeneous, and situational that it may well create more confusion than clarity among users. The only general scenario in which one is allowed to legally smoke or vape cannabis across Canada is the use of licit cannabis by those aged 21 and up, who do not share with anyone under 21, in their own detached house. All other situations depend on one or multiple variables. One's own detached house not bound by some homeowners association rules would be the only guaranteed perfect alignment of all norms and jurisdictions. If one is a co-owner, other restrictive norms may apply. If one is a tenant, contractual restrictions may apply. If one wants to use outdoors, on the public domain (e.g., public streets) or on private lands (e.g., university campus), private policies and municipal or provincial regulations may apply. We will forgo mapping all scenarios wherein one is allowed to smoke or vape cannabis. Our objective in this section is to discuss two examples where we can visualize these different layers of norms and jurisdictions at play and problematize the difficulties (and possibilities) in aligning multiple norms and jurisdictions. The first example is Mario, a hypothetical, regular user from Montreal; the second is a comparison between the two largest universities in Ottawa, Carleton University and the University of Ottawa.

For this, we borrow the astronomical concept of syzygy as it is more precise than the idea of alignment and better captures the complexity of the legal arrangements we are analyzing. The term "alignment" actually refers to only two celestial bodies in a near straight-line configuration, whereas syzygy involves three or more celestial bodies in such configuration. In this sense, syzygy is more complex than alignment, and it is a phenomenon that grows rarer when an observer considers a system with higher numbers of celestial bodies or objects. The idea of syzygy is useful when thinking of the governance of licit cannabis. Legal arrangements become more complex given more norms, policies, and jurisdictions. And the more challenging it is to align the rationales of such norms and policies, particularly regarding harm reduction and health-oriented strategies. In other words, as the examples will illustrate, one layer of norms or policies with a prohibitionist or punitive orientation is enough to upset the almost perfect alignment required for effective harm reduction outcomes. The opposite could also be argued: that is, a more local harm reduction strategy could dilute the penalization of cannabis users; however, the status quo is, unfortunately, already oriented toward criminalization and penal populism, meaning that it is still more difficult to have syzygies oriented toward harm reduction than toward punitivism and prohibitionism.

Imagine Mario, a retired construction worker living in the Montreal area who has used illicit cannabis since his youth, either recreationally or for chronic pain. Since legalization, he uses both licit and illicit cannabis. Mario's consumption is governed by a superposition of different regulations in his everyday life, most of which he is unaware of (see figure 5.3).

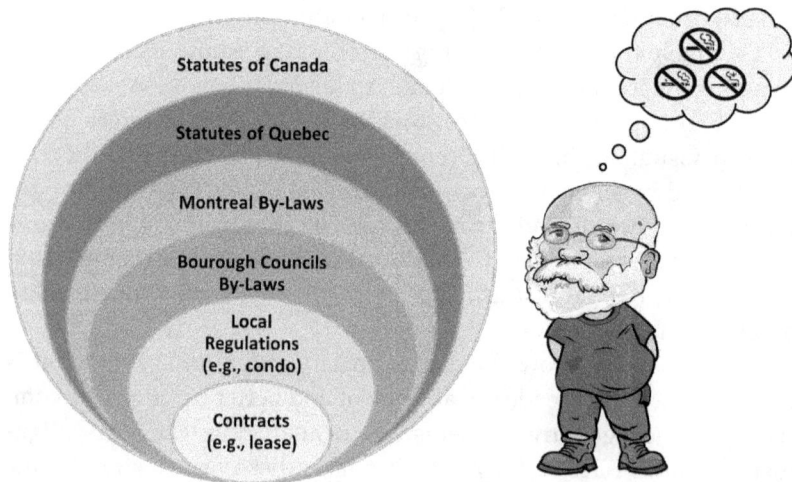

FIGURE 5.3. Various layers of norms governing cannabis use in Montreal.
Source: Joao Velloso and Véronique Fortin.

As mentioned in the previous section, the situation in Montreal was especially chaotic in October 2018. Consumption in public spaces was allowed by provincial legislation and different bylaws were applicable across the city. Public consumption was possible in 14 of the 19 boroughs while the regulations varied in other municipalities on the Island of Montreal. For instance, smoking in public was allowed in Côte Saint-Luc and Montreal West; however, it was illegal in the municipalities of Mount Royal, Hampstead, and Westmount—the fines for which in the first three were "only" $150, but in the latter two could possibly amount to $1,500 and $2,000 respectively. In private spaces, the situation also varied, and local regulations, such as condominium regulations and rental contracts, could add further layers of complexity. During roughly one year, there was some alignment between the statutes of Canada and those of Quebec, but including other jurisdictions and regulations, syzygies—straight alignments of three or more elements—were far more complicated. Where Mario consumed publicly mattered, and a few words in his rental contract or condo rules could prohibit him from using in his private space. Quebec passed An Act to tighten the regulation of cannabis in November 2019, forbidding the smoking or vaping of cannabis in public places, indoor and out.[50] This change on the provincial level made syzygies toward public consumption almost impossible in Quebec, compromising harm reduction efforts, especially among vulnerable populations and those without access to private spaces of consumption.

The second example concerns smoking on campus at the University of Ottawa and Carleton University. Both universities are subject to the same law (under federal, provincial, and municipal jurisdictions), though one can smoke and vape cannabis recreationally on campus at the University of Ottawa, but not at Carleton (see figure 5.4).

Regardless of the favourable syzygy within jurisdictions to consume in private spaces accessible to the public, local regulations and policies from each university substantially change the framework of cannabis uses on campus. The University of Ottawa adopted the same framework used for tobacco, thus licit recreational cannabis can be smoked or vaped in the same areas where one can consume tobacco.[51] Carleton University has some designated areas for tobacco consumption, but cannabis is prohibited on campus.[52] Curiously, the consumption of edible cannabis products is prohibited on both campuses. This prohibitionist approach on edibles raises some harm reduction concerns, as users will more likely hide their consumption (as a way to minimize social harms), make their own unregulated edibles, or simply remove edibles from their distinct packaging, which may increase health harms for users and non-users alike.

Smoking or Vaping on Campus in Ottawa?

FIGURE 5.4. Various layers of norms governing cannabis use on universities' campuses in Ottawa.
Source: Joao Velloso and Véronique Fortin.

Social harms are also an issue, as punitive or restrictive consequences may stigmatize individuals, notably students, and affect their access to resources, even campus.

Conclusion

The partial decriminalization and legalization of cannabis in Canada did not bring with it the end of punishment, as criminal law still regulates the use of illicit and licit cannabis, and the "strict legal regulation" framework implemented is often punitive and restrictive. Nor did it bring the end of stigmatization of cannabis users and the reduction of social harms associated with stigmatization. In the best-case scenario, the overall reduction of social and health harms was undermined by the harshening of criminal-law sanctions and prohibitionist approaches still embedded in the messy regulation framework. In the worst case, the new regime paradoxically increased social and health harms. One could argue that the partial decriminalization of cannabis targeted the most privileged members of Canadian society, making it legal for those who were using under the prohibition but were not risking criminal jeopardy. Allegedly, the White middle-aged home-owner who smoked a cannabis joint at home on Saturday nights was no more likely to be punished before legalization than they are now. However, individuals who used to get arrested for cannabis-related offences might continue to be. Although limited data are available, Akwasi Owusu-Bempah and Alex Luscombe found that in 2015 (pre-legalization) cannabis users were more or less equally distributed across racial groups, however: "Black Canadian and Indigenous people are more likely to be arrested for cannabis possession than White people. This pattern was true in all five cities except Halifax, where only Black people were over-represented in arrests."[53] And in 2019, Owusu-Bempah, Luscombe, and Brandon Finlay cautioned us about the continued punitiveness of cannabis legislation, post-legalization:

> It is important to note that cannabis legalization does not mean an end to law and its enforcement; there are now more laws regulating cannabis following "legalization" than under prohibition. The increased focus on, and enhanced penalties for, cannabis-impaired driving, possession of "illicit cannabis," trafficking to young people, and youthful possession—which will come as a result of legalization—may just as easily reproduce existing racial disparities in the Canadian post-legal landscape. As such, drug legalization will amount to racial justice only if the broader forces that promote injustice in Canada's law enforcement apparatus are addressed.[54]

As we have shown, it is important to pay attention to the varying punitive effects of jurisdictional shifts and modes of governance because decriminalization does not always mean the end of punitiveness and the prohibitionist approaches. Although more research is necessary, it seems like legalization did bring a drastic drop in police arrests for criminal possession, from a yearly average of 50,000 arrests between 1998 and 2017 to around 1,500 in 2019 and 2020 respectively.[55] From a harm reduction perspective, that is a good thing. But the spectre of prohibition still haunts Canada: sometimes through criminal law, but mostly via non-federal jurisdictions. Our two examples suggest that alignments toward harm reduction are quite complex and that syzygies can easily be disrupted by jurisdiction, whether state-based or not. This may sound pessimistic, and in a certain way it is, but the examples also highlight possibilities of intervention and policy reform that may disturb prohibitionist approaches. Harm reduction should be pursued in every jurisdiction. And changes, even if small and/or local, may alter the broader picture and influence other jurisdictions accordingly.

References

Legislation

An Act to tighten the regulation of cannabis, SQ 2019, c 21.

Bill C-22, *An Act to amend the Criminal Code and the Controlled Drugs and Substances Act*, 2nd Sess, 43rd Parl, 2021 (first reading 18 February 2021).

Bill C-45, *An Act respecting cannabis and to amend the Controlled Drugs and Substances Act, the Criminal Code and other Acts*, 1st Sess, 42nd Parl, 2017 (assented to 21 June 2018).*Controlled Drugs and Substances Act*, SC 1996, c 19.

Conventions Regulations, SOR/96-313.

Excise Act, RSC 1985, c E-14.

Immigration and Refugee Protection Act, SC 2001, c 27.

Publications

Beauchesne, Line, *De la criminalisation à la légalisation des drogues : de Charybde en Scylla ?* (1989) 22:1 Criminologie 67.

———, *La légalisation du cannabis au Canada : entre commercialisation et prohibition 2.0*, (Montreal: Bayard Canada, 2020) at 13.

Bellot, Céline & Marie-Ève Sylvestre, *La judiciarisation de l'itinérance à Montréal : les dérives sécuritaires de la gestion pénale de la pauvreté.* (2017) 47 RGD 11.

Bellot, Céline et al, *La judiciarisation de l'itinérance à Montréal : Des données alarmantes témoignent d'un profilage social accru (2018-2019)* (Montreal: RAPSIM, January 2021), online: rapsim.org/wp-content/uploads/2021/01/VF2_Judiciarisation-de-litinérance-à-Montréal.

Bennett, Russell, *Canada's Cannabis Act. Annotation & Commentary* (Toronto: LexisNexis Canada, 2019) at 26.

Breen, Kerri, "Cannabis Companies Facing Proposed Class-Action Lawsuit over Alleged Mislabelling" *Global News* (18 June 2020), online: globalnews. ca/news/7081677/cannabis-companies-proposed-lawsuit-potency/.

Carleton University, "Tobacco Smoking and Cannabis Consumption on Campus Policy" (last modified October 2020), online: carleton.ca/secretariat/wp-content/uploads/Tobacco-Smoking-and-Consumption-of-Cannabis-on-Campus-Policy.pdf.

Chesnay, Catherine, Céline Bellot & Marie-Eve Sylvestre, "Taming Disorderly People One Ticket at a Time: The Penalization of Homelessness in Ontario and British Columbia" (2013) 55:2 Can J Crim Justice 161.

Crépault, Jean-François, "Legalize It (But Don't Advertise It): The Public Health Case for Cannabis Legalization" in Andrew Potter & Daniel Weinstock, eds, *High Time: The Legalization and Regulation of Cannabis in Canada* (Kingston and Montreal: McGill-Queen's University Press, 2019) 79.

Daudelin, Jean & Jose Luiz Ratton, *Illegal Markets, Violence, and Inequality: Evidence from a Brazilian Metropolis*, (Cham, Switzerland: Palgrave Macmillan, 2018).

DeVillaer, Michael, "Cannabis Legalization: Lessons from Alcohol, Tobacco, and Pharmaceutical Industries" in Andrew Potter & Daniel Weinstock, eds, *High Time: The Legalization and Regulation of Cannabis in Canada* (Kingston and Montreal: McGill-Queen's University Press, 2019) 182 at 195.

Ford, Richard T, "Law's Territory (A History of Jurisdiction)" (1999) 97:4 Michigan L Rev 843.

Fortin, Véronique, "The Control of Public Spaces in Montreal in Times of Managerial Justice" (2018) 15 Champ pénal/Penal field.

Habib, David, "Consommer du cannabis lorsqu'on est parent" (October 2019), online (blog): blogue.soquij.qc.ca/2019/10/08/consommer-du-cannabis-lorsquon-est-parent/.

Health Canada, "Understanding the New Access to Cannabis for Medical Purposes Regulations," (August 2016), online: www.canada.ca/en/health-canada/services/publications/drugs-health-products/understanding-new-access-to-cannabis-for-medical-purposes-regulations.html.

——, *A Framework for the Legalization and Regulation of Cannabis in Canada: The Final Report of the Task Force on Cannabis Legalization and Regulation*, by Ann McLellan et al, (Ottawa: Health Canada, 2016), online: www.canada.ca/en/health-canada/services/drugs-medication/cannabis/laws-regulations/task-force-cannabis-legalization-regulation/framework-legalization-regulation-cannabis-in-canada.html.

——, News Release, "Canada Legalizes and Strictly Regulates Cannabis" (17 October 2018), online: www.canada.ca/en/health-canada/news/2018/10/canada-legalizes-and-strictly-regulates-cannabis.html.

Immigration and Refugee Board of Canada, "Grounds for Detention Reviews" (last modified 21 May 2024), online: irb.gc.ca/en/statistics/detentions-reviews/Pages/detenGr.aspx.

Klein, Alana, "What Jurisdiction for Harm Reduction: Cannabis Policy Reform under Canadian Federalism" in Andrew Potter & Daniel Weinstock, eds, *High Time: The Legalization and Regulation of Cannabis in Canada* (Kingston and Montreal: McGill-Queen's University Press, 2019) 132.

Langlois, Philippe & Annabelle Blais, "Searchable Guide" (20 October 2018), online: www.journaldemontreal.com/2018/10/20/le-grand-guide-du-cannabis.

Makela, Finn, *Le cannabis au travail : aspects juridiques* (Montreal: LexisNexis, 2022).

Owusu-Bempah, Akwasi, "Canada's Legalization of Cannabis Is a Success Story, Despite a Shaky First Act," *The Globe and Mail* (15 January 2022), www.theglobeandmail.com/opinion/article-canadas-legalization-of-cannabis-is-a-success-story-despite-a-shaky/.

Owusu-Bempah, Akwasi & Alex Luscombe, "Race, Cannabis and the Canadian War on Drugs: An Examination of Cannabis Arrest Data by Race in Five Cities" (2021) 91 Intl J Drug Policy 102937.

Owusu-Bempah, Akwasi, Alex Luscombe & Brandon M Finlay, "Unequal Justice: Race and Cannabis Arrests in the Post-Legal Landscape." Andrew Potter & Daniel Weinstock, eds, *High Time: The Legalization and Regulation of Cannabis in Canada* (Kingston and Montreal: McGill-Queen's University Press, 2019) 114.

Potter, Andrew, "In Praise of Political Opportunism, or, How to Change a Policy in Only Fifty Years" in Andrew Potter & Daniel Weinstock, eds, *High Time: The Legalization and Regulation of Cannabis in Canada* (Kingston and Montreal: McGill-Queen's University Press, 2019) 9.

Rocher, Guy, "Pour une sociologie des ordres juridiques" (1988) 29:1 Cahiers de droit 91.

Statistics Canada, *What Has Changed Since Cannabis Was Legalized?*, by Michelle Rotermann (Ottawa: Statistics Canada, February 2020), online: www150.statcan.gc.ca/n1/pub/82-003-x/2020002/article/00002-eng.htm.

Sylvestre, Marie-Eve, "Disorder and Public Spaces in Montreal: Repression (and Resistance) through Law, Politics, and Police Discretion" (2010) 31:6 Urban Geography 803.

——, "Quand le problème, c'est aussi la solution': les gangs de rue et la multiplication des systèmes normatifs de prise en charge pénale" (2010) 40:1 Revue générale de droit 179.

Sylvestre, Marie-Eve, Nicholas Blomley & Céline Bellot, *Red Zones: Criminal Law and the Territorial Governance of Marginalized People* (Cambridge: Cambridge University Press, 2019).

The Commission of Inquiry into the Non-Medical Use of Drugs, *Final Report* (Ottawa: Information Canada, 14 December 1973), online: publications.gc.ca/collections/collection_2014/sc-hc/H21-5370-2-1-eng.pdf.

Thibierge, Catherine et al, *La densification normative—Découverte d'un processus* (Paris: Mare & Martin, 2013).

Université Laval, *Politique sur le cannabis à l'Université Laval* (Rés. CA-2018-154), online: https://www.ulaval.ca/sites/default/files/notre-universite/direction-gouv/BSG/Documents/Politique_sur_le_cannabis_%C3%A0_l%27UL.pdf

University of Ottawa, "Policy 58: Smoking Policy" (last modified 3 April 2019), online: https://www.uottawa.ca/about-us/policies-regulations/policy-58-smoking-policy.

University of Ottawa Office of Risk Management, "Cannabis on Campus" (last visited 27 July 2022), online: orm.uottawa.ca/my-safety/smoking-and-vaping-on-campus/cannabis-on-campus.

Valverde, Mariana, "Jurisdiction and Scale: Legal 'Technicalities' as Resources for Theory" (2009) 18:2 Soc & Leg Stud 139.

——, "Practices of Citizenship and Scales of Governance" (2010) 13:2 New Crim L Rev: An Intl & Interdisciplinary J 216.

——, *Chronotopes of Law. Jurisdiction, Scale and Governance* (New York: Routledge, 2015).

Velloso, Joao, "Sobre O Tratamento Jurídico Dado Ao Trabalho Escravo: O Movimento De Descriminalização" (2006) 59 Revista Brasileira de Ciências Criminais 90.

——, "Au-delà de la criminalisation : L'immigration et les enjeux pour la criminologie" (2013) 46:1 Criminologie 55.

——, "Beyond Criminocentric Dogmatism: Mapping Institutional Forms of Punishment in Contemporary Societies" (2013) 15:2 Punishment & Society 166.

Waddell Phillips Professional Corporation, "Statement of Claim: Lisa Langevin v Aurora Cannabis et al" (last visited 27 July 2022), online : waddellphillips.ca/wp-content/uploads/2020/06/20.06.16-Statement-of-Claim-filed.pdf.

Notes

1   We would like to thank Marie-Eve Sylvestre, with whom we first developed the idea of punitive decriminalization of cannabis (Véronique Fortin, Joao Velloso, Marie-Ève Sylvestre, "Vers une décriminalisation punitive du Cannabis au Canada," Third biennial conference on criminal law, May 2019, University of Montreal). We also thank Benoît Doré-Coulombe, Tasha Stansbury, and Amber Miller, for their research assistance. A big thank-you also to the audience at the "First, Do Less Harm. Harm Reduction Principle as a Principle of Health Policy and Law" Conference. Finally, we are grateful to the anonymous reviewer and the book editors for their helpful comments. We acknowledge the financial support of the Fonds de recherche du Québec Société et culture (FRQSC) and the Social Sciences and Humanities Research Council (SSHRC) for this research.

2   See Health Canada, "Understanding the New Access to Cannabis for Medical Purposes Regulations," (August 2016), online: www.canada.ca/en/health-canada/services/publications/drugs-health-products/understanding-new-access-to-cannabis-for-medical-purposes-regulations.html ("Legal access to dried marijuana for medical purposes was first provided in 1999 using unique section 56 exemptions under the *Controlled Drugs and Substances Act* (CDSA). The decision in *R. v. Parker* in 2000 held that individuals with a medical need had the right to possess marijuana for medical purposes. This led to the implementation of the *Marihuana Medical Access Regulations* (MMAR) in 2001").

3   See Health Canada, *A Framework for the Legalization and Regulation of Cannabis in Canada: The Final Report of the Task Force on Cannabis Legalization and Regulation,* by

Ann McLellan et al, (Ottawa: Health Canada, 2016), online: www.canada.ca/en/health-canada/services/drugs-medication/cannabis/laws-regulations/task-force-cannabis-legalization-regulation/framework-legalization-regulation-cannabis-in-canada.html [McLellan, *Final Report*].

4   See Alana Klein, "What Jurisdiction for Harm Reduction: Cannabis Policy Reform under Canadian Federalism" in Andrew Potter & Daniel Weinstock, eds, *High Time: The Legalization and Regulation of Cannabis in Canada* (Kingston and Montreal: McGill-Queen's University Press, 2019) 132 ("It was the Minister of Health at the time, Jane Philpott—rather than, say, the Minister of Justice—who made the first public legalization announcement on 20 April 2016, at the United Nations General Assembly Special Session on Drugs.").

5   As outlined in its Executive Summary: "In taking a public health approach to the regulation of cannabis, the Task Force proposes measures that will maintain and improve the health of Canadians by minimizing the harms associated with cannabis use."; see McLellan, *Final Report, supra* note 2 at 2.

6   See McLellan, *Final Report, supra* note 2 at 12; figure borrowed from S Rolles & G Murkin, *How To Regulate Cannabis: A Practical Guide*, 2nd ed (Transform Drug Policy Foundation, 2016) at 28-29 (Graphic "A Spectrum of Policy Options Available").

7   See Bill C-45, *An Act respecting cannabis and to amend the Controlled Drugs and Substances Act, the Criminal Code and other Acts*, 1st Sess, 42nd Parl, 2017 (assented to 21 June 2018).

8   See *Cannabis Act*, SC 2018, c 16.

9   See Klein, *supra* note 3 at 133 ("[t]he Cannabis Act (formerly Bill C-45) serves as a key example of how the dominant discourse of criminalization and stigmatization can overtake more progressive objectives").

10   See Joao Velloso, "Sobre O Tratamento Jurídico Dado Ao Trabalho Escravo: O Movimento De Descriminalização" (2006) 59 Revista Brasileira de Ciências Criminais 90; see also Joao Velloso, "Beyond Criminocentric Dogmatism: Mapping Institutional Forms of Punishment in Contemporary Societies" (2013) 15:2 Punishment & Society 166.

11   See Joao Velloso, "Au-delà de la criminalisation : L'immigration et les enjeux pour la criminologie" (2013) 46 :1 Criminologie 55.

12   See Véronique Fortin, "The Control of Public Spaces in Montreal in Times of Managerial Justice" (2018) 15 Champ pénal/Penal field; see also Céline Bellot & Marie-Ève Sylvestre, "La judiciarisation de l'itinérance à Montréal : Les dérives sécuritaires de la gestion pénale de la pauvreté" (2017) 47 RGD 11; see also Céline Bellot et al, *La Judiciarisation de l'itinérance à Montréal. Des Données alarmantes témoignent d'un profilage social accru (2012-2019)* (Montreal: RAPSIM, January 2021) online: rapsim.org/wp-content/uploads/2021/01/VF2_Judiciarisation-de-litinérance-à-Montréal.

13   Véronique Fortin, "The Control of Public Spaces in Montreal in Times of Managerial Justice," *Champ pénal/Penal field* [En ligne], Vol. XV | 2018, mis en ligne le 20 novembre 2018, consulté le 11 novembre 2024. URL : http://journals.openedition.org/champpenal/10115; https://doi.org/10.4000/champpenal.10115. Joao Velloso, "La gouvernance plurinormative des manifestants : reconfigurations pénales, exceptionnalité et dégradation des droits pendant le G20 à Toronto" Canadian Journal of Law and Society / Revue Canadienne Droit et Société. 2022;37(3):365-386. doi:10.1017/cls.2022.24

14   See Statistics Canada, *What Has Changed Since Cannabis Was Legalized?* by Michelle Rotermann (Ottawa: Statistics Canada, February 2020), online: www150.statcan.gc.ca/n1/pub/82-003-x/2020002/article/00002-eng.htm.

15   See Akwasi Owusu-Bempah & Alex Luscombe, "Race, Cannabis and the Canadian War on Drugs: An Examination of Cannabis Arrest Data by Race in Five Cities" (2021) 91 Intl J Drug Policy 102937.

16   See Government of Canada, *Commission of Inquiry into the Non-Medical Use of Drugs, Final Report of the Commission of Inquiry into the Non-Medical Use of Drugs*, (Ottawa: Information Canada, 14 December 1973), online: publications.gc.ca/collections/collection_2014/sc-hc/H21-5370-2-1-eng.pdf. (Chaired by Osgoode Hall dean Gerald Le Dain, it ran from 1969 to 1972. Its final report was quite progressive for the time, especially Marie-Andrée Bertrand's conclusions and recommendations 241.)

17   *Ibid*, Appendix F.2.

18   See Andrew Potter, "In Praise of Political Opportunism, or, How to Change a Policy in Only Fifty Years" in Andrew Potter & Daniel Weinstock, eds, *High Time: The Legalization and Regulation of Cannabis in Canada* (Kingston and Montreal: McGill-Queen's University Press, 2019) 9 at 13.

19   See Jean-François Crépault, "Legalize It (But Don't Advertise It): The Public Health Case for Cannabis Legalization" in Andrew Potter & Daniel Weinstock, eds, *High Time: The Legalization and Regulation of Cannabis in Canada* (Kingston and Montreal: McGill-Queen's University Press, 2019) 79; see also Line Beauchesne, "De la criminalisation à la légalisation des drogues : De Charybde en Scylla?" (1989) 22:1 Criminologie 67.

20   See *Marihuana for Medical Purposes Regulations*, C 2013, as repealed by *Access to Cannabis for Medical Purposes Regulations* C, 2016 as repealed by *Cannabis Act, supra* note 8. (Licit cannabis was already accessible for medical use since 1999, occasion in which the Minister of Health granted special exemption under s 56 of the *Controlled Drugs and Substances Act* to two AIDS patients, Jim Wakeford and Jean-Charles Pariseau, allowing them to grow and use cannabis for medical reasons. A legislative framework came into force in 2001 (*Marihuana Medical Access Regulations*), being repealed over the years through newer legislation.

21   See Michael DeVillaer, "Cannabis Legalization: Lessons from Alcohol, Tobacco, and Pharmaceutical Industries" in Andrew Potter & Daniel Weinstock, eds, *High Time: The Legalization and Regulation of Cannabis in Canada* (Kingston and Montreal: McGill-Queen's University Press, 2019) 182 at 195.

22   SC 1996, c 19 [*CDSA*].

23   See Russell Bennett, *Canada's Cannabis Act. Annotation & Commentary* (Toronto: LexisNexis Canada, 2019) at 26.

24   SC 2001, c 27, s 36(1)(a) [*IRPA*].

25   Bill C-22 was then reintroduced as Bill C-5 in the 44th Parliament, 1st session, and this bill received royal assent on November 17, 2022: *An Act to amend the Criminal Code and the Controlled Drugs and Substances Act*, S.C. 2022, c. 15. This Act abolishes restrictions on conditional sentencing for most offences prosecuted by way of indictment, for which the maximum term of imprisonment is 14 years or life.

26   See *Excise Act*, RSC 1985, c E-14, ss. 240(1) and 158(1).

27   The manuscript of this chapter was completed in the Spring of 2022, but this exclusionary tendency remains much the same.

28   See Health Canada, News Release, "Canada legalizes and strictly regulates cannabis," (17 October 2018), online: www.canada.ca/en/health-canada/news/2018/10/canada-legalizes-and-strictly-regulates-cannabis.html.

29   See Klein, *supra* note 3.

30   *Ibid* at 135.

31   See Line Beauchesne, *La Légalisation du cannabis au Canada : Entre commercialisation et prohibition 2.0*, (Montreal: Bayard Canada, 2020) at 13.

32   See Mariana Valverde, "Jurisdiction and Scale: Legal 'Technicalities' as Resources for Theory" (2009) 18:2 Soc & Leg Stud 139 at 144.

33   Illegal markets can be framed as legal orders operating beyond State Law. See for instance the notion of "marginal legal orders" (*ordres juridiques marginaux*) in Guy Rocher, "Pour une sociologie des ordres juridiques" (1988) 29 :1 Cahiers de droit 91 at 91. See also the interesting description of the legal pluralistic functioning of illegal drug markets regulated by criminals in Pernambuco (Brazil) in Jean Daudelin & Jose Luiz Ratton, *Illegal Markets, Violence, and Inequality: Evidence from a Brazilian Metropolis* (Cham, Switzerland: Palgrave Macmillan, 2018).

34   Note that, for reasons of space, we excluded informal, unofficial or non-state forms of punishment from this chapter.

35   We adopt a plural and mobile shaped conception of social control, inspired by the work of Velloso (2013), *supra* note 9.

36   See Finn Makela, *Le cannabis au travail : aspects juridiques* (Montreal: LexisNexis, 2022).

37   SOR/96-313.

38   See, e.g., David Habib, "Consommer du cannabis lorsqu'on est parent" (October 2019), online (blog): blogue.soquij.qc.ca/2019/10/08/consommer-du-cannabis-lorsquon-est-parent/.

39   See also Marie-Eve Sylvestre, "Disorder and Public Spaces in Montreal: Repression (and Resistance) Through Law, Politics, and Police Discretion" (2010) 31:6 Urban Geography 803; see also Marie-Eve Sylvestre, "'Quand le problème, c'est aussi la solution' : Les gangs de rue et ta multiplication des systèmes normatifs de prise en charge pénale" (2010) 40:1 Revue générale de droit 179; see also Catherine Chesnay, Céline Bellot & Marie-Eve Sylvestre, "Taming Disorderly People One Ticket at a Time: The Penalization of Homelessness in Ontario and British Columbia" (2013) 55:2 Can J Criminol Crim Justice 161; see also Marie-Eve Sylvestre, Nicholas Blomley & Céline Bellot, *Red Zones: Criminal Law and the Territorial Governance of Marginalized People* (Cambridge: Cambridge University Press, 2019).

40   Part 6 of the *Cannabis Regulations*, SOR/2018-144, establishes acceptable limits for pest control products (pesticides) and microbial and chemical contaminants in cannabis products. The growers could be liable to administrative monetary penalties, but also sued for damages.

41   See Kerri Breen, "Cannabis Companies Facing Proposed Class-Action Lawsuit over Alleged Mislabelling" (18 June 2020), online: globalnews.ca/news/7081677/cannabis-companies-proposed-lawsuit-potency; see also Waddell Phillips Professional Corporation, "Statement of Claim: Lisa Langevin v Aurora Cannabis et al" (last visited 27 July 2022), online: waddellphillips.ca/wp-content/uploads/2020/06/20.06.16-Statement-of-Claim-filed.pdf. (A class-action suit filed in Alberta is seeking $500 million plus $5 million in punitive damages from cannabis companies due to mislabelling of THC and CBD levels in licit cannabis.)

42   See relevant legislation applicable to users by province (applicable regulations for each Act are not included). Alberta: *Gaming, Liquor and Cannabis Act*, RSA 2000, c G-1; see also *Tobacco and Smoking Reduction Act*, SA 2005, c T-3.8; British Columbia: *Cannabis Control and Licencing Act*, SBC 2018, c 29; see also *Tobacco and Vapour Products Control Act*, 1 RSBC 1996, c 451; Manitoba: *The Liquor, Gaming and Cannabis Control Act*, 2013, CCSM c L153; see also *Smoking and Vapour Products Control Act*, 1991, CCSM c N92; New Brunswick: *Cannabis Control Act*, SNB 2018, c 2; see also *Smoke-Free Places Act*, RSNB 2011, c 222; Newfoundland and Labrador: *Cannabis Control Act*, SNL 2018, c C-4.1; see also *Smoke-Free Environment Act*, SNL 2005, c S-16.2; Northwest Territories: *Cannabis Products Act*, SNWT 2018, c 6, Sch A; see

also *Cannabis Smoking Control Act*, SNWT 2018, c 6, Sch B; see also *Smoking Control and Reduction Act*, SNWT 2019, c 29; see also *Tobacco and Vapour Products Control Act*, SNWT 2019, c 31; Nova Scotia: *Cannabis Control Act*, SNS 2018, c 3; see also *Smoke-free Places Act*, SNS 2002, c 12; Nunavut: *Cannabis Act*, SNu 2018, c 7, *Cannabis Statutes Amendments Act* (SNu 2018, c 8), *Tobacco Control and Smoke-Free Places Act* (SNu 2003, c 13; Ontario: *Cannabis Control Act*, SO 2017, c 26, Sch 1; see also *Smoke Free Ontario Act*, SO 2017, c 26, Sch 3); Prince Edward Island: *Cannabis Control Act*, 2018, RSPEI 1988; see also *Smoke-Free Places Act*, 2018, RSPEI 1988; Quebec: *Loi encadrant le cannabis*, 2019; CQLR c C-5.3; see also *Loi Sur la Société des alcools du Québec* 1993, 2018, CQLR c S-13; see also *Code de la sécurité routière*, 1986, 2018, CQLR c C-24.2; Saskatchewan: *The Cannabis Control (Saskatchewan) Act*, SS 2018, c C-2.111; see also *Tobacco and Vapour Products Control Act*, SS 2001, c T-14.1; Yukon: *Cannabis Control and Regulation Act*, SY 2018, c 4; see also *Smoke-Free Places Act*, SY 2008, c 8; see also *Tobacco and Vaping Products Control and Regulation Act*, SY 2019, c14.

43   In the days after the Cannabis Act (2018) came into force, the *Journal de Montréal* published a very comprehensive guide on the regulations from 1131 cities and municipalities in Quebec, covering four full pages of the newspaper. See also Philippe Langlois & Annabelle Blais, "Searchable Guide" (20 October 2018), online www.journaldemontreal.com/2018/10/20/le-grand-guide-du-cannabis.

44   See Université Laval, *Politique sur le cannabis à l'Université Laval* (Rés. CA-2018-154), online: https://www.ulaval.ca/sites/default/files/notre-universite/direction-gouv/ BSG/Documents/Politique_sur_le_cannabis_%C3%A0_l%27UL.pdf.

45   See Richard T Ford, "Law's Territory (A History of Jurisdiction)" (1999) 97:4 Michigan L Rev 843.

46   See Valverde, *supra* note 30; see also Mariana Valverde, "Practices of Citizenship and Scales of Governance" (2010) 13:2 New Crim L Rev: An Intl & Interdisciplinary J 216 [Valverde, 2010]; see also Mariana Valverde, *Chronotopes of Law, Jurisdiction, Scale and Governance* (New York: Routledge, 2015).

47   Valverde, 2010, *supra* note 44 at 238.

48   *Ibid.*

49   See Catherine Thibierge et al, *La densification normative—Découverte d'un processus* (Paris: Mare & Martin, 2013) at 1204.

50   SQ 2019, c 21.

51   See University of Ottawa, "Policy 58: Smoking Policy" (last modified 3 April 2019), online: https://www.uottawa.ca/about-us/policies-regulations/policy-58-smoking-policy; see also University of Ottawa: Office of Risk Management, "Cannabis on Campus" (last visited 27 July 2022), online: orm.uottawa.ca/my-safety/smoking-and-vaping-on-campus/cannabis-on-campus (general information included).

52   See Carleton University, "Tobacco Smoking and Cannabis Consumption on Campus Policy" (last modified October 2020), online: carleton.ca/secretariat/wp-content/uploads/Tobacco-Smoking-and-Consumption-of-Cannabis-on-Campus-Policy.pdf.

53   See Owusu-Bempah, *supra* note 14 at 5.

54   See Akwasi Owusu-Bempah, Alex Luscombe & Brandon M Finlay, "Unequal Justice: Race and Cannabis Arrests in the Post-Legal Landscape" in Andrew Potter & Daniel Weinstock, eds, *High Time: The Legalization and Regulation of Cannabis in Canada* (Kingston and Montreal: McGill-Queen's University Press, 2019) 114 at 126.

55   See Akwasi Owusu-Bempah, "Canada's Legalization of Cannabis Is a Success Story, Despite a Shaky First Act" (15 January 2022) online: www.theglobeandmail.com/opinion/article-canadas-legalization-of-cannabis-is-a-success-story-despite-a-shaky.

CHAPTER 6

Criminality and Inequity under Canada's Legalization of Cannabis

A Study of Vancouver's Downtown Eastside

Stephanie Lake and Margot Young

The origin of this chapter speaks to the importance of interdisciplinary collaboration in the development and assessment of public policy. And also to the serendipitous beginnings of interesting inquiries. Indeed, this collaboration was fortuitous: the authors met during the defence of Stephanie Lake's doctoral dissertation. Margot Young was on the examining committee. Young presented a series of epidemiological studies (three of which are summarized here) involving the use of cannabis for therapeutic and harm reduction purposes among marginalized people who use drugs (PWUD) in Vancouver.[1] Young's line of questioning involving the legal implications of Lake's findings spurred the idea to formally outline the potential unintended health and legal consequences of inequitable access to legal cannabis among marginalized PWUD during an intensifying drug poisoning and overdose crisis.

The topic of harm reduction often occasions collaboration across the disciplines of health and law. This also underlines the importance of input from populations directly affected by public policy debates.[2] Indeed, development of harm reduction initiatives across Canada owes much to on-the-ground experience and activism,[3] critically supported by collaborations across health research and legal scholarship.[4] In this chapter, we detail an emerging concern regarding unequal access to now-legal cannabis for communities which have historically faced unrelenting criminalization and marginalization related to drug use.[5] We illustrate our argument with Lake's findings from epidemiological analyses involving PWUD in Vancouver. The affected population we chart consists of PWUD consuming cannabis to support harm reduction and addiction-treatment programs. The picture that emerges from Lake's studies has deep implications for policy and legal questions around the decriminalization and legalization of previously illicit drugs, in particular cannabis. The data are deeply suggestive of what law and society scholars already know well—the intended consequences of legal reform are often undercut by the actual impact of that reform in the real world—in particular for groups already profoundly marginalized in society. An additional observation not unique to us is also reinforced, that "the dominate discourse of criminalization [...] can overtake more progressive objectives."[6] In the words of the Australian scholar John Braithwaite, the "myth of deregulation" casts a shadow over legalization schemes: liberalization of a market often leads to enhancement of state power over (some) individuals.[7] Pre-existing disadvantage often accumulates and deepens in the face of so-called liberalizing legal reform. In this case, individuals most in need of relief from the heavy boot of the state are further embedded, through the legalization regime for cannabis, in a net of illegal access to cannabis. Thus, Canada's legalization regime, ushered in only a few years ago, appears to track "simultaneously along both regulatory and carceral registers."[8] This "bifurcation of governance structures"[9] flows alongside those social, colonial, and economic processes that already pattern structural racism, deep inequalities, and marginalization.[10] Not coincidentally, populations shortchanged by the cannabis legalization rules are those already disproportionately targeted by past penal regimes of drug policy.[11] These individuals, the research suggests, are excluded from the legal cannabis market and caught in a "governance landscape" that "channels them to the residual-yet-expansive domain of the carceral state."[12] The result is one of accumulated disadvantage for PWUD, and pragmatic cannabis policy objectives are discriminatorily delivered and denied.[13]

The field work that grounds our analysis revealed that cannabis is a common tool for PWUD to address a range of harm reduction and therapeutic needs. Yet, with early observations indicating a remarkably low uptake of legal cannabis purchase and consumption by this population, the new legalization regime threatens enhanced criminalization of cannabis use for these people. Thus the research gestures toward "the hierarchies of a law that is expected to be equal," revealing the contingency of how that law plays across existing institutions and socio-economic inequalities.[14] In part, this is a message about the intransigence of structural inequalities in the face of legal reform that purports to lighten the legal load. But it is also yet another illustration of how law in action can have real world consequences that belie the purpose of the law, at least as the government articulates it. And, these legalization reforms share with older forms of drug policy the reinforcement of structural inequalities, along race, disability and class, in particular.[15]

Canada's Step into the Unknown: The Legalization of Cannabis

Canada's history of cannabis regulation is peculiar, at times illustrating a clear lack of rationality in legislation interventions. Canada, in 1923, was among the first countries to criminalize cannabis yet the concerns that this criminalization was to alleviate remain unclear.[16] It appears to have been a "last-minute inclusion" in the Act to Prohibit the Improper Use of Opium and other Drugs.[17] For many years, or up until the early 1960s, cannabis use and its consequent criminalization were not much of an issue in the country. Thus one writer referred to the early legislation as "a solution wandering around in search of a problem."[18] By the late 1960s, however, cannabis-related arrests took off: cannabis use became more mainstream and the prohibition against cannabis came increasingly under criticism. Cannabis is now one of the most widely used psychoactive substances in Canada.[19] Indeed, pre-legalization, Canada had one of the highest rates of cannabis consumption in the world.[20] As part of this emerging historical context, various federal governments since the 1970s have mooted changes to cannabis legislation.[21] Cannabis reform over the second half of the twentieth century has been called a "saga of promise, hesitation and retreat."[22]

Options for policy reform sit along a continuum. At one end lies increased criminalization: a ramp-up of prohibitions, penalties, and enforcement. At the other end is full legalization, with no prohibitions, and full toleration of whatever use individuals choose. Under this second option, there would be simply no or few legal tools focused on cannabis. Some refer to this end of the spectrum as commercialization—that is, a free market in cannabis.[23] Other forms of legalization hover somewhere between the poles, demanding some form of non-criminal regulation of use, production, and sale. For example, as the first country to legalize recreational cannabis use in 2013, Uruguay takes a "middle ground" approach in which adults who wish to use cannabis can select one of the following access options: purchase a limited quantity (40 g per month or 10 g per week) of government-approved cannabis from a participating pharmacy, receive cannabis as a member of a cannabis social club, or grow a limited amount of cannabis (up to six plants) at home.[24] Decriminalization as a policy option typically involves the removal of criminal prohibitions relating to cannabis, and installing, instead, a regulatory regime with civil penalties for failure to observe the rules. Thus, most typically, campaigns of decriminalization retain some legal prohibition and regulation of possession and use, but infringements are met with civil, not criminal, penalties, or with diversion from the criminal-justice system.[25] For example, in an effort to curb rising drug-related harms in the population, Portugal decriminalized simple possession of all drugs, including cannabis, in 2001, replacing criminal sanctions with administrative offences (e.g., fines, community service) and a drug "dissuasion" program that refers a consumer to drug-treatment services depending on their level of "risk," as assessed by health care and social workers.[26] Each type of legal response allows a wide range of options within its model, depending on the specific policy goals and political attitudes of the government; a response might combine non-criminal regulation with criminal sanctions for some aspects of behaviour that fail to conform to the regulatory scheme. There are many points along this policy continuum.[27] Harm reduction approaches sneak in somewhere between criminalization and legalization: they employ methods geared to reducing harm and emphasize pragmatic responses over dogmatic condemnation.[28]

While, as we have noted, cannabis decriminalization was frequently discussed by various federal governments throughout the last decades of the twentieth century, the dam broke with key judicial decisions in the early twenty-first century. Appeal-court rulings found aspects of the criminalization of cannabis to be contrary to the Canadian Charter of Rights and Freedoms.[29] In *R v. Parker*,[30] a key case at the turn of the century, the Ontario Court of Appeal upheld a constitutional challenge to several pieces of federal legislation that limited the applicant, Terrance Parker, in his access to use of cannabis for epilepsy treatment. Charges against Parker for growing and using cannabis were stayed and cannabis laws were declared invalid to the extent they failed to provide exemptions permitting medicinal use. The court stated that, "forcing Parker to choose between his health and imprisonment violates his right to liberty and security of the person."[31] The federal government, as a consequence, inserted the Marihuana Medical Access Regulations[32] into the Controlled Drug and Substances Act,[33] allowing individuals who met the medical criteria to lawfully possess and consume marijuana.[34]

The boundaries of this revised regime were hard to enforce in the face of additional court challenges.[35] As well, workarounds by individual consumers exploiting medical-cannabis exemptions rendered the whole cannabis-regulatory system "something of a farce."[36] As a result, "medical marijuana turned out to be a legal Trojan horse that put into question the entire cannabis regulatory regime."[37]

On 17 October 2018, Canada became the second country in the world to legalize the sale, possession, and non-medical use of cannabis by adults, following legalization of cannabis for medical purposes two decades earlier.[38] A year later, federal legislation was amended to allow for the legal production of edible cannabis, cannabis extracts, and cannabis topicals.[39] The resulting scheme is complex, involving federal law and regulations from provincial and municipal governments. Legalization raises a host of issues: where cannabis use is permitted, public-safety concerns, cross-border issues, compliance with international law, and appropriate evisceration of the illegal market— a market that was thriving at the point at which the legislation was introduced.[40] The process surrounding the new law was, in addition, sharply criticized for its failure to include meaningful consultation with Indigenous leadership.

Commentators were clear, well before the legislation was passed and came into force, that the matter was far from simple. In one scholar's words, it was "a hugely complex and risky venture."[41] With no clear precedents in other jurisdictions in the world for the scheme Canada adopted, it was a venture into "the unknown,"[42] a "stab in the dark."[43] One scholar described it as "a novel and radical policy shift,"[44] another as a "seismic shift."[45]

The federal government chose a particular reform path. Criminal prohibitions against the illegal market connected to cannabis use, possession, and sale were not lifted. Instead, a parallel legal market-place was devised.[46] The resulting statute, the Cannabis Act, combines a regulatory scheme enforced by rigorous penalties to ensure compliance.[47] The framework references three governmental purposes: keeping cannabis from youth, keeping cannabis profits from criminals, and protecting public health and safety by permitting adult access to legal cannabis.[48] Adults 18 years and older are legally able to possess and share up to 30 g of legal cannabis, buy cannabis from a provincially licensed retailer,[49] grow up to four cannabis plants for personal use, and make cannabis products (with some restrictions) at home.[50] In sum, the new legislation permits a variety of forms of legal consumption, production, and sale of cannabis for recreational and medicinal purposes.

On the other side, the legislation maintains a strict regime of sanctions and penalties for those operating outside of the legal framework. The legislation does take away mandatory minimum sentences for cannabis offences, but, in other aspects, the legislation has intensified the state's response to illicit cannabis use. Sanctions start with warnings and tickets, but they quickly ramp up to criminal prosecution and imprisonment. For instance, possession over the limit can mean almost five years in prison,[51] and for illegal distribution or sale, up to fourteen.[52] These are significant, life-altering penalties. Legalization is thus paired with intensified carceral oversight.[53] In sum, legalization and its goals carry greater than before punitive responses to those who pursue cannabis through non-legal means.

Cannabis Legalization in a Federal State

Key to the maze of regulations with legalization and enhanced criminalization is appreciation of how jurisdiction to regulate cannabis and its sale is shared across many levels of government.[54] The federal government has jurisdiction over the legal and illegal status of the substance. It can oversee the supply and production of licit cannabis, and its packaging, quality control, and testing. The criminal provisions in the new legislation are also the domain of the federal government. Provincial jurisdiction extends to distribution, consumer retail, and workplace or public consumption. Federal and provincial governments share (or, in the case of home cultivation, dispute) responsibility with respect to personal production, taxation, public safety, and public health.[55]

Provinces and territories are responsible for determining how cannabis is distributed and sold within their jurisdictions, what products are offered, what packaging is allowed, what potency levels are set, and product pricing.[56] Thus, provinces control the retail framework for the sale of recreational cannabis. Provinces can also add additional regulations that lower possession limits, increase the age at which cannabis use becomes legal, restrict public consumption of cannabis, and further regulate personal cultivation. Indeed, in the words of some experts, the "nuts and bolts" of the legal market have been assigned to the provincial governments to implement.[57] The predictable result is twofold: variety across provincial regimes and internecine squabbling between provinces and the federal governments over details of the scheme. However, provincial governments have largely chosen to slide legal cannabis into existing regulatory frameworks for tobacco and alcohol, although it is subject to stiffer regulation and penalties.[58] Again, as with the federal legislation, provincial regulatory frames emphasize prohibition of actions outside the legal market. One commentator notes: "Prohibition and enforcement appear to be so central to the emerging regime that provincial and municipal authorities have secured 75 per cent of cannabis tax revenues to cover the high costs of legalization resulting from the increased burden on policing."[59]

In British Columbia, cannabis retailing responsibility lies with a government agency, the Liquor and Cannabis Regulation Branch. It is the sole distributor of non-medical cannabis for the province. Retailers are required to receive a retail licence pursuant to BC's Cannabis Control and Licensing Act.[60] The City of Vancouver regulates where cannabis retailers in its jurisdiction may open;[61] cannabis retailers are required to have a municipal development permit and business licence.[62]

We have already mentioned the failure of Canadian governments to consult with Indigenous communities on cannabis legal reform: one prominent legal scholar has stated that "they just didn't deal with how they saw things developing with Indigenous involvement."[63] This is problematic for at least two reasons. First, as mentioned, Indigenous individuals disproportionately bear the burdens of criminalization; in Vancouver, approximately 70 percent of the city's Indigenous residents live in the Downtown Eastside (DTES) neighbourhood, making up about 30–40 percent of the DTES population,[64] which is far above the representation of Indigenous residents in

Vancouver's general population (2.2 percent).[65] Second, the cannabis industry, estimated to be worth upward of $5 billion in 2021,[66] could provide much needed revenue and employment for Indigenous communities.[67] First Nations cannabis-tax and regulatory powers remain open subjects of advocacy.[68] In sum, movement toward establishment of Canada as the multi-juridical state urged by the Truth and Reconciliation Commission[69] requires respecting and creating legal space for Indigenous communities' own law-making authority over cannabis, as well as recognizing nation-to-nation participation in consultations around settler-government cannabis reform that impacts Indigenous Peoples.[70] The current federal structure of Canadian settler government fails to contemplate this.

Case Study: Cannabis Use among Marginalized PWUD in Vancouver

We turn now to the field research that Lake undertook into cannabis use for harm reduction and therapeutic purposes among PWUD in Vancouver.[71] The observations that inspired this chapter are incidental to the motivating focus of the research, but like *obiter dicta* in judicial decisions, these findings allow another, additional conversation of interest: unintended health and social disparities perpetuated by the new cannabis legislation on marginalized communities.

Study Setting

In British Columbia, drug overdoses (the majority of which are driven by contamination of the unregulated drug supply with highly potent synthetic opioids such as fentanyl) were declared a public health emergency in 2016.[72] Nearly five years later, at the time of writing, overdose deaths continue to hit unprecedented levels, with over 1,500 in 2020.[73] The majority of overdose deaths in Vancouver have occurred in the DTES, a highly concentrated urban area widely known for illicit drugs.[74] As summarized by Ryan McNeil et al., "[the DTES] has been shaped by the interplay between entrenched poverty, homelessness, and drug use."[75] Often labelled as "the poorest postal code in Canada,"[76] the neighbourhood is marked by extreme levels of visible poverty and substandard living conditions—densely packed low-income housing, shelters, tent encampments, and street-based homelessness.[77] Many people living or accessing services in the DTES contend with a host of intersecting social and structural adversities (e.g., stigma and discrimination, colonialism and dispossession, criminalization, precarious employment and housing, barriers to accessing necessary health care).[78] These conditions contribute to the high burden of disease and disability within the community. In sum, "the landscape is inner city and urban, a material outlook that is among the poorest in North America, and a symbolic vista that signals the multiple blights of race, gender, culture, and class oppressions of 21st century capitalism."[79] Without doubt, the current DTES is a site of crisis that strikes deeply at the heart.

There is another, less-studied aspect to the DTES, however. The neighbourhood is a place of creative and vigorous community. Strong collective ties and identification equally characterize the DTES, resulting in conditions that are celebratory of difference and forceful in assertion of rights.[80] More specifically, in the 1990s, the DTES was the birthplace in Canada of user-led activism that emerged in response to the dual public health crises of drug overdose and HIV/AIDS deaths among PWUD.[81] This DTES-based activist movement, which remains strong today, ultimately paved the way for Vancouver to adopt progressive harm reduction programming, including supervised consumption and overdose-prevention sites, needle distribution programs, and injectable opioid-treatment programs.[82]

In recent years, as a growing number of studies began investigating the potential role of cannabis in reducing or replacing other substances (particularly in the management of chronic pain),[83] the idea of cannabis as harm reduction took off at the community level. In the years preceding cannabis legalization, at least two models of cannabis distribution to PWUD for harm reduction purposes emerged in the DTES, as detailed by Valleriani et al.[84] The Cannabis Substitution Project originated out of the office of the Vancouver Area Network of Drug Users, the city's prominent user-run advocacy organization.[85] The program began in 2017 as a once-weekly first-come-first-serve service for which community members would line up to receive a pre-packaged preparation of cannabis products supplied by local illicit cannabis growers and distributors.[86] At the time of writing, the program runs twice per week, serving approximately 200 people each day.[87] The High Hopes Foundation, also founded in 2017, operates out of the offices of Vancouver's Overdose Prevention Society.[88] At the time of writing, this program serves a smaller number of registered participants on an informal, per-needs basis.[89] Similar to the substitution project, the availability of products within this program is typically dependent on donations from illicit growers and/or producers.[90] One aim of these DTES programs is to support PWUD to reduce, regulate, or stop their use of hard substances through the use of cannabis. The status of these programs is precarious given the previous classification of cannabis as an illicit drug and the newly illegal status of distributing cannabis that originates outside of the regulatory framework. For example, in the fall of 2020, the Cannabis Substitution Project was evicted from its storefront space and began distributing from a van before being raided by Vancouver police.[91] Unregulated cannabis dispensaries in the DTES have also been known to make accommodations for low-income community members;[92] however, given the illegal nature of these stores, their operational status is continuously in question and under threat.

Study Population

Below, we summarize the findings of three epidemiological studies exploring different research questions involving the use of cannabis by marginalized PWUD in the context of mounting opioid-related harms.[93] (The studies were led by Lake as part of her doctoral dissertation.)[94]

Data for the studies come from two cohorts of PWUD recruited from the DTES: the Vancouver Injection Drug Users Study (VIDUS) and the AIDS Care Cohort to Evaluate Exposure to Survival Services (ACCESS). Recruitment protocols and eligibility requirements are described in detail elsewhere.[95] In both cohorts, participants complete interviewer-administered questionnaires every six months at a study office located in the DTES. The questionnaire covers a range of demographic characteristics, drug-use patterns, behavioural factors (e.g., syringe sharing, public injecting), use of harm reduction strategies (e.g., supervised injection sites), and socio-structural exposures (e.g., experiences of incarceration, police interactions). Measures of cannabis use more broadly (e.g., frequency of use) have been longstanding components of the cohort questionnaires; however, questions designed to elicit more specific information about cannabis use (e.g., reasons for use, modes of administration, preferred products) were added to the cohort questionnaires beginning in 2016. Data collection and study instruments for each cohort are harmonized to allow for pooled analysis of the data. All participants provide written informed consent prior to the first data collection and received a $40 honorarium upon completion of each interview. Both cohort studies were approved by the University of British Columbia's Providence Healthcare Research Ethics Board.

Study 1: Characteristics of PWUD Who Use Cannabis

In the first study, we examined the socio-demographic, substance-use, and health-related characteristics of cannabis-using PWUD in Vancouver, and whether these characteristics differed according to self-reported reasons for cannabis use. In short, we analyzed data from 2,686 interviews conducted among 897 PWUD who reported using cannabis between 1 June 2016 and 30 November 2018 (the final six weeks of the study period occurred post-legalization).[96] Self-reported reasons for cannabis use (see categories in box 1) were recorded each interview.

BOX 1. Reasons for cannabis use

(1) To relieve pain, including multiple sclerosis, arthritis, etc.
(2) To help with sleep
(3) To help with HIV medications and AIDS symptoms
(4) To treat nausea or loss of appetite
(5) To substitute for other substances including heroin, crack, meth, or alcohol
(6) To relieve stress
(7) To treat a mental-health concern other than addiction
(8) For spiritual purposes
(9) For creativity
(10) To get high, recreation, to socialize
(11) To come down off of other drugs
(12) To treat withdrawal

We used these data in a latent class analysis, guiding the identification of four cannabis-use groups: (1) PWUD using cannabis predominantly for intoxication ("recreational" class), (2) PWUD using cannabis predominantly for a therapeutic purposes other than pain ("non-pain therapeutic" class), (3) PWUD using cannabis predominantly for pain management ("pain" class), and (4) PWUD using cannabis predominantly for pain and at least one additional therapeutic purposes ("pain +" class); see table 6.1 for distribution of cannabis-use reasons overall and among classes. Notably, intoxication was the most common reason for cannabis use (reported in over half of interviews); but pain, insomnia, nausea and appetite stimulation, and stress were all common therapeutic motivations (reported in roughly one-third of interviews). Participants also reported using cannabis in an effort to stop or reduce the use of other drugs or alcohol in over 10% of interviews.

TABLE 6.1. Representation of Cannabis Use Motivations Overall and within Latent Classes among 897 PWUD Who Reported Cannabis Use between 1 June 2016 and 30 November 2018

	Overall n = 2686; 100%	Class 1 n = 848; 31.6%	Class 2 n = 1007; 37.5%	Class 3 n = 588; 21.9%	Class 4 n = 243; 9.0%
Cannabis use motivations	**Proportion of observations**				
Intoxication	0.53	**1.00**	0.29	0.26	**0.50**
Pain relief	0.31	<0.01	<0.01	**1.00**	**1.00**
Mental health	0.08	0.02	0.10	0.06	0.21
Insomnia	0.32	0.00	**0.50**	0.22	**0.98**
Substitution	0.12	0.05	0.15	0.12	0.26
Nausea	0.29	0.00	0.45	0.27	**0.65**
Creativity / Spirituality	0.06	0.07	0.07	<0.01	0.12
Stress	0.32	0.13	0.45	0.17	**0.77**
Addiction management	0.04	<0.01	0.06	0.02	0.09
Characterization	NA	Recreational	Non-pain therapeutic	Pain	Pain +

Note: Class-specific proportions ≥0.50 are shown in bold.

Source: S Lake, E Nosova & J Buxton, et al. (2020) "Characterizing Motivations for Cannabis Use in a Cohort of People Who Use Illicit Drugs." PLoS One 15(5): e0233463.

Whereas members who fell into the "recreational" class reported receiving their cannabis primarily from an informal source such as a friend or family member, the three remaining use classes—essentially therapeutic (whether exclusively or in addition to non-therapeutic use)—cited illicit cannabis dispensaries as their primary source of cannabis. Members of the pain class were also more likely than the other respondents to report obtaining cannabis from a non-profit compassion club. It is important to emphasize that fewer than 1% of the participant interviews included reports of obtaining cannabis through legal channels (either medical cannabis or through a legal retailer in the six weeks following legalization).

We used generalized estimating equations to examine characteristics associated with membership in each use class. We observed that daily use of cannabis was reported significantly more by therapeutic users. We also observed that therapeutic users exhibited indicators corresponding with lower quality of physical and mental health. For example, having HIV was significantly associated with membership in the "non-pain therapeutic" class; reporting moderate-to-severe levels of pain, a lifetime mental-illness diagnosis, and low quality of perceived health were significantly associated with membership in the "pain" class; and reporting moderate-to-severe levels of anxiety was significantly associated with membership in the "pain +" class. The results revealed a spectrum of cannabis use among PWUD, from non-medical to therapeutic applications, with much overlap. Our findings also suggest that many PWUD are using cannabis to address physical and mental-health issues that often go under- or untreated in this population.

Study 2: Cannabis Use and Opioid Use among PWUD Living with Pain

Chronic pain is highly prevalent among marginalized PWUD. Extensive research led by Voon et al. in Vancouver has highlighted how PWUD must often source illicit opioids to manage pain after being denied adequate pain management through legal routes.[97] As demonstrated in study 1, pain is a driving motivating factor underlying cannabis use among many PWUD. A comprehensive review of the evidence by the US National Academies of Sciences, Engineering, and Medicine concludes that there is substantial evidence of cannabis' therapeutic benefit for certain kinds of chronic pain commonly experienced among PWUD (e.g., neuropathic pain),[98] and experimental research has begun to demonstrate cannabis' potential to lower the opioid dose required to achieve analgesia (known as an "opioid-sparing effect").[99] Study 2 examined a subgroup of marginalized PWUD living with chronic pain to understand whether the use of opioids was reduced among frequent cannabis users.

We analyzed data from 5,350 interviews conducted among 1,152 cannabis using and non-using PWUD who reported living with

pain between 1 June 2014 and 30 November 2017.[100] At each interview during the study period, we asked participants about their
recent (past six-month) use of cannabis and illicit use of opioids (i.e.,
heroin, counterfeit pharmaceutical opioids, and not-as-prescribed
pharmaceutical opioids). Using a generalized linear mixed-effects
model, we analyzed the association between high-frequency (i.e.,
daily or more use, on average, during the past six months) cannabis and high-frequency illicit opioid use. We found that the odds
of high-frequency illicit opioid use were 50 percent lower among
participants who reported high-frequency cannabis use. In contrast,
participants who reported occasional use (less than daily, on average, during the past six months) did not have significantly lower
odds of frequent illicit opioids use. This finding raises the possibility that PWUD engaging in high-frequency cannabis use are managing pain in a way that reduces their need to use illicit opioids. This
hypothesis was further supported through our sub-analysis that
compared reasons for cannabis use between daily and occasional
users. Here, we noted that high-frequency cannabis users reported
using cannabis for pain-management purposes and additional therapeutic purposes that often co-occur with pain, such as insomnia
and stress, significantly more often than occasional cannabis users
(see figure 6.1).

Study 3: Cannabis Use among PWUD on Methadone Treatment for Opioid-Use Disorder

Methadone, an opioid receptor agonist, is the most common medica-
tion-based treatment of opioid-use disorder. Methadone is meant to
block the subjective (euphoric) effects of illicit opioids, prevent opioid
withdrawal, and supress opioid cravings.[101] Retention in treatment
is critical to reducing illicit opioid use and preventing overdose.[102] It
has been well-established through numerous studies that, at lower
doses, patients are more likely to continue using opioids and discon-
tinue treatment.[103] The use of cannabis to manage symptoms of opioid
dependence, including symptoms of withdrawal such as irritability,
nausea, vomiting, and heightened pain sensitivity was documented
in the medical literature as early as the 1800s.[104] The practice remains
common today, but often as a self-guided strategy.[105]

Study 3 examined whether cannabis use interrupted this well-
established link between lower patient doses and negative treatment
outcomes.

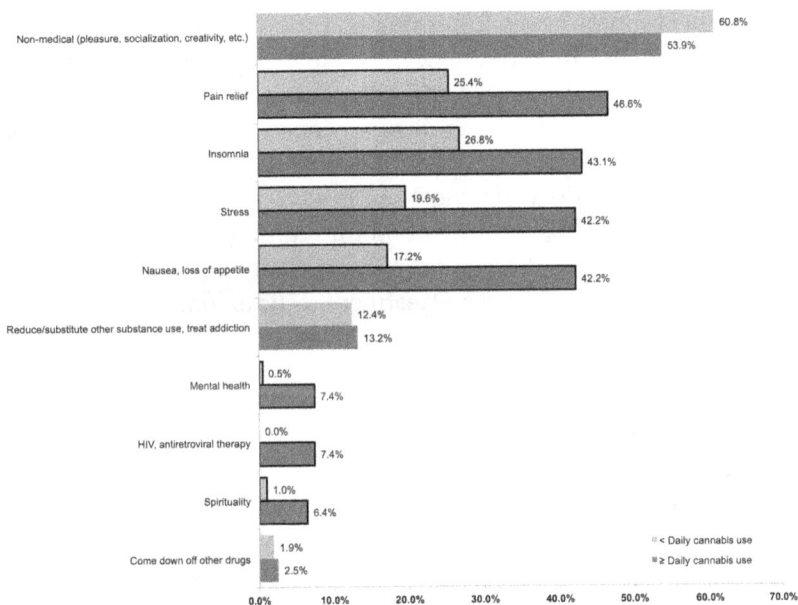

FIGURE 6.1. Self-reported reasons for cannabis use among daily (n = 204) and occasional (n = 210) cannabis-using PWUD with chronic pain, 1 June 2017 to 30 November 2017.

Note: Borders indicate chi-square or Fisher's p < 0.05; Fisher's test used for mental-health and HIV comparisons.

Source: S Lake, Z Walsh & T Kerr, et al. (2019) "Frequency of Cannabis and Illicit Opioid Use Among People Who Use Drugs and Report Chronic Pain." PLoS Medicine 16(11): e1002967.

We analyzed data from over 12,000 interviews conducted among 1,389 non- and cannabis-using PWUD who reported being enrolled in methadone treatment between 1 December 2005 and 30 November 2018.[106] As with study 2, at each interview we asked participants about their recent use of cannabis and illicit opioids. We also asked about their current methadone dose, defining "lower" doses as those below the median dose in the patient sample (90 mg/day).[107] We used generalized estimating equations to analyze the relationship between lower treatment dose and high-frequency illicit opioid use overall and within strata of cannabis use (i.e., high-frequency users and low-frequency/non-users). As expected, lower doses were significantly associated with daily use of illicit opioids during treatment. Within strata of cannabis use, however, the association differed markedly: compared to higher doses, the odds of daily illicit opioid use were

86% higher for patients on lower treatment doses but only 30% higher during periods of high-frequency cannabis use. While the primary finding of this study points to the importance of stabilizing patients on adequate treatment doses, it also signals the potential role of cannabinoids in mitigating negative effects that can arise with sub-therapeutic methadone dosing (e.g., opioid withdrawal and cravings), requiring further investigation through rigorous experimental research. Thus, to emphasize, cannabis use appears to be a common and potentially meaningful co-treatment tactic among patients.

Discussion: Implications of Cannabis Legalization for Marginalized PWUD

As drug-related overdoses continue to rise across British Columbia, the research at the centre of this chapter indicates a range of therapeutic and harm reduction applications of cannabis as it pertains to opioid use. Worth noting (and described in detail within each individual study)[108] are several limitations associated with the design and structure of the studies, including self-reported measures, non-random sampling, and residual confounding, that preclude generalizing these findings to all PWUD and interpreting the reported relationships as being causal. More rigorous experimental research will be needed to formally probe the underlying explanations for the observed relationships between cannabis and opioid use among people at high risk of overdose. However, the current findings reveal a substantial demand for cannabis products for the purpose of harm reduction among PWUD. This observation is further supported by in-depth qualitative research conducted among PWUD both in Vancouver[109] and across a diversity of urban settings in North America.[110] Unlicensed (illegal) dispensaries in the DTES were the primary source of cannabis for the majority of PWUD who used cannabis for therapeutic purposes; legal access routes (either the long-standing medical program or legal non-medical sources in the short period of the study that followed legalization) were virtually inexistent.[111]

A quick scan of the landscape of available legal cannabis sales provides a revealing backdrop to this story. As of March 2021, the City of Vancouver reported 40 licensed cannabis locations, and several additional with developmental approval.[112] Operational retail stores are highly concentrated in certain regions, including the downtown core and its west-end neighbourhood, Kitsilano, and Mount Pleasant. At the time of writing (March 2021), no operational legal stores are situated in the DTES, Chinatown, or Strathcona neighbourhoods—where many of Vancouver's PWUD reside and/or access services. In 2015, despite cannabis' illegality at the federal level, the city moved to regulate the escalating number of illicit cannabis dispensaries. In designing the regulations, stating concern for "vulnerable populations," the city created an exclusion zone on cannabis retail throughout the majority of the DTES.[113] The ban was lifted in June 2019 after council heard testimony from community members, service providers, addiction clinicians, and researchers about the therapeutic potential of cannabis for this population, but the operation of legal cannabis stores in the DTES and surrounding area lags behind other densely populated regions as a result.[114]

Thus, more than two years after cannabis legalization, and more than five years after efforts to regulate retail cannabis at the municipal level, there remains a high level of illicit cannabis retail activity within the city. The BC Ministry of Public Safety does not know how many unregulated cannabis dispensaries operate in the province,[115] but government regulators have described their efforts in containing the prolific and volatile illicit cannabis industry as "fighting a hydra"—that is, as soon as the government closes one illegal shop, another will spring up in the area.[116] Indeed, in the year following legalization, cannabis consumers in British Columbia exhibited both the highest prevalence of illicit product purchase (at 51.4%) and lowest of legal product purchase (at 16.8%) of all the provinces, demonstrating that BC has not transitioned to the legal market at the same rate as other Canadian provinces.[117] A local reporter writes: "The province that was once a global capital of the marijuana world still doesn't have a cannabis retail sector capable of servicing the market, keeping countless unlicensed dealers in business."[118] Municipal regulatory details also confound the spread of legal outlets. For example, concern has been expressed about the high cost of licences for cannabis retailers.[119] The Vancouver city council has moved to address this, with one councillor remarking: "It was quite clear that there's a growing concern that Vancouver's market is actually growing, but in the illegal market."[120]

The pieces connect. The research done by Lake shows a high prevalence of cannabis use—for a wide variety of non-medical and medical purposes—among PWUD living in the DTES. Yet the availability of legal cannabis in that neighbourhood is limited, and the result is a continued and necessary resort to the thriving illegal market and unsanctioned informal cannabis exchanges. The research forces us to think about how legalization regimes, and Canada's in particular, have a disparate impact as they play out in "the context of the uneven distribution of the capacity to comply."[121] The choice available to many of the study participants is illicit use or no use at all.[122] This finding resonates with findings of other researchers, forcing the recognition that "legalization regimes allow for more subtle distinctions whose disparate impact largely rely on the uneven distribution of the capacity to comply."[123]

Other researchers have noted similar obstacles to legal cannabis among marginalized populations; from interviewing clients of recent cannabis-related distribution harm reduction programs in the DTES, Valleriani et al. detailed specific economic, bureaucratic, and societal barriers to access legal cannabis in this population.[124] The cost associated with legal channels emerged as a primary concern.[125] For example, at the time of writing, dried cannabis costs approximately $5 per gram at illicit dispensaries in the DTES, and these stores can weigh out cannabis to match the amount that a community member is able to pay (e.g., half a gram for $2.50),[126] whereas federally regulated dried cannabis flower—subject to minimum pricing schemes established at the provincial level—is sold in prepackaged quantities averaging $10.48 per gram.[127] Thus, even with the eventual establishment of legal cannabis stores in the DTES, the population under study may not have the financial resources to participate in the legal market. Cost-prohibitive prices can have the unintended consequence of supporting a thriving illicit market, running counter to one of the stated aims of cannabis legalization.[128] Additional barriers to access include requirements for government-issued identification (non-medical and medical access), physician authorization (medical access), credit-card payment, and mailing address (medical access).[129] Community-based cannabis distribution programs, including the harm reduction programs described by Valleriani et al., and the more established non-profit cannabis compassion club models, appear to address a number of the reported access gaps for PWUD, but such programs are on shaky ground as they operate outside of a legal framework and must rely on donations of illicit cannabis products.[130] Essentially, they are part of a formally illicit, irregular network of cannabis distribution whose operational status depends on the discretion of local law enforcement. Thus, we return to the key observation that, with few realistic options for accessing legal cannabis, an already marginalized population of PWUD will continue to rely on informal, extra-legal (basically illegal), avenues to procure cannabis for harm reduction and/or therapeutic purposes.

The "retailing and regulatory"[131] issues that are front and centre in how cannabis has been made legally available, the determination of which largely lies with the provinces, raise considerable barriers to accessing the legal market.[132] The legalization regime enhances state control of and scrutiny over consumer cannabis choices. And, while some commentators from a libertarian perspective bemoan such state imposition, our concern is the impact this kind of state regulation has on those most marginalized and typically those already caught in the cross hairs of coercive state oversight.[133]

In sum, PWUD—who already face widespread social and health harms as a direct result of the war on drugs—will not enjoy the many benefits that legalization is touted to bring, including access to quality-tested products, reduced engagement with the illicit drug market, and legalized possession and use. They may even experience enhanced criminalization as a result.

These observations are not surprising. We know that criminalization of cannabis—subjecting cannabis users to criminal penalties and the criminal-justice system—has had disproportionately negative impacts for individuals already subject to toxic mixes of racism, poverty, and colonialism.[134] Canada lags other jurisdictions in collecting racially disaggregated criminal-justice data, but commentators agree that criminalization has had a disparate impact on racialized and Indigenous groups.[135] These groups have had a higher likelihood of arrest and conviction for drug use.[136] In Toronto, "Black people with no history of criminal convictions have been three times more likely to be arrested by Toronto police for possession of small amounts of marijuana than white people with similar backgrounds;"[137] in Vancouver, Indigenous people have been almost seven times as likely to be arrested for simple cannabis possession than their White counterparts.[138] And partial decriminalization is unlikely to effectively and equitably reduce this social burden, and it will not address the structural racism that has configured drug enforcement practices. Moreover, experts assert that "[g]iven that the opportunity for police discretion remains under decriminalization it would likely reproduce and perpetuate the arbitrary and discriminatory law [enforcement] practices" experienced under full criminalization.[139] Criminalization is "not evenly distributed across the population, but [will] focus on racialized minorities."[140] This returns us to our opening argument: legalization schemes "may operate simultaneously along both regulatory and carceral registers."[141] The studies we discuss here reveal a carceral outcome highly likely for PWUD, and especially Black and Indigenous PWUD, living in Vancouver's DTES.

This outcome of intensified criminalization of the most vulnerable is not inevitable, nor is it beyond the control of government regulators. Contrast Canada's situation to California, where cannabis legalization was accompanied by equity measures such as automatic expungement of certain cannabis-related criminal records[142] and cannabis social equity business funding.[143] In Canada, however, very little consideration was paid to social equity[144] in designing the new legislation.[145] Absent are policy measures that address the needs of vulnerable and economically marginalized people who rely on cannabis for therapeutic purposes. Of particular note is the concern already signalled that formulation of the resulting regulatory scheme omitted consideration of and adequate consultation with Indigenous communities, rendering them subordinated stakeholders rather than full partners.[146] Indigenous peoples have had uniquely negative experiences under the previous cannabis regime.[147] And the consequences of past and ongoing colonialism have meant that the population of the DTES that struggles with poverty, substance use, homelessness, and racism is disproportionately Indigenous.[148]

There are many ironies to this tale. The government's "public health" approach to cannabis legalization aimed to dissuade initiation among non-consumers and curb excessive consumption among current consumers by having the provinces and territories set strict controls on product pricing/taxing.[149] Yet it is precisely public health concerns specific to a very disadvantaged group that have taken the hit from the new regime. This is not necessarily to say that the government should implement a blanket loosening of restrictions around cannabis pricing, but considerations should be made to support equitable access for marginalized populations. For example, the federal government recently distributed funding for "safe supply"[150] pilot initiatives to address the opioid crisis.[151] The approval of these programs did not constitute a repeal from the prohibitive laws surrounding non-medical opioids, but they allowed regulated access to opioids for a small subset of the population who met criteria for overdose risk. Local government officials in Vancouver[152] and Victoria[153] have voiced their support for low- and no-cost alternative cannabis distribution models to be integrated into the legal framework. In Vancouver, city council directed municipal staff to research and propose low-barrier models that could act as alternate regulated cannabis access points for marginalized PWUD.[154] With regard to fitting into the existing policy framework, a donor-subsidized gift-card program was the sole identified option.[155] However, a community-run medical-cannabis co-operative (similar to a compassion club) with a sliding cost scale was heavily favoured among PWUD. The then mayor of Vancouver requested support from the federal government in establishing such a site, including an integrated clinical research program.[156] Yet, at present, this type of distribution model would not be permissible under the province's licensing and pricing regulations.[157]

Insofar as the studies presented above point to the use of cannabis as a method of harm reduction, we wish to highlight an important caveat: legal access to a regulated supply of cannabis for marginalized PWUD is not a solitary or comprehensive solution to the current overdose crisis. While cannabis reform tailored to PWUD is a necessary measure, it is merely a supportive one in the growing movement toward decriminalization and legalization of all currently illicit drugs.[158] Thus, our argument in no way detracts from the immediacy and urgency with which a safe and regulated supply of opioids is required to curb the rate of overdose deaths resulting from fentanyl contamination of the drug supply.

Conclusion

If left unchecked, cannabis legalization in Canada is likely to perpetuate existing inequalities, where groups most marginalized in society will not enjoy the societal liberties cannabis legalization is proclaimed to offer. The resulting unequal landscape is complex and intersectional. Those who were targeted by the enforcement of previous cannabis laws—disproportionately Black and Indigenous communities—will have fewer opportunities to profit from the legalization of cannabis.[159] And those without financial means of accessing legal cannabis will be forced to continue engaging with the illicit cannabis market. Using a case study of cannabis use among PWUD during an intensifying drug-poisoning crisis, we argue that marginalized communities stand to benefit the most from legalization, yet they were largely left behind in the design of the legal framework. The old adage is true: "When you focus on the law in action, often we discover important theoretical and policy problems."[160] This vantage point then asks us to look beyond the "hegemonic sight conventions of visuality" to comprehend the experiences of those at the margins of Canadian society.[161] Canada took a big step in repealing cannabis prohibition, but it has much work to do in amending the laws to allow for outcomes that are equitable in access, capacity, and opportunity.

References

Legislation

Canadian Charter of Rights and Freedoms, Part 1 of the *Constitution* Act, 1982, being Schedule B to the *Canada* Act 1982 (UK), 1982, c 11.
Cannabis Act, SC 2018, c. 16.
Cannabis Distribution Act, SBC 2018, c 28.
Controlled Drugs and Substances Act, SC 1996, c 19.
Marihuana Medical Access Regulations, SOR/2001-227.

Jurisprudence

Murray-Hall v Queen (AG), SOC 1923 c 22.
R v Parker, [2000] OJ No 2787, 188 DLR (4th) 385 (CA).

Publications

Akpata, John, "Prometheus Re-Bound" (March 1, 2018) online: www.policyalternatives.ca/publications/monitor/prometheus-re-bound.
Austen, Ian, "2 Years After Legalizing Cannabis, Has Canada Kept Its Promises?" *The New York Times* (last modified 18 April 2021), online: www.nytimes.com/2021/01/23/world/canada/marijuana-legalization-promises-made.html.
Bacchuber, Marcus et al, "Medical Cannabis Laws and Opioid Analgesic Overdose Mortality in the United States, 1999-2010" (2014) 174:10 JAMA Internal Medicine 1668.
Bains, Camille, "Feds Provide $15M to Fund 4 B.C. Pilot Projects Looking into a Safer Drug Supply," *CBC News* (1 February 2021), online: www.cbc.ca/news/canada/british-columbia/feds-provide-15-million-for-safer-bc-drug-supply-1.5896659.
Belle-Isle, Lynne, *Cannabis as Therapy for People Living with HIV/AIDS* (Ottawa: Canadian AIDS Society, 2006), online: sagecollection.ca/en/resources/final-report-cannabis-therapy-people-living-hivaids-our-right-our-choice.

Benoit, Cecilia, Dena Carroll & Munazi Chaudhry "In Search of a Healing Place: Aboriginal Women in Vancouver's Downtown Eastside" (2003) 56 Soc Science & Medicine 821 at 824.

Bergeria, Cecilia L et al, "The Impact of Naturalistic Cannabis Use on Self-Reported Opioid Withdrawal" (2020) 113 J Substance Abuse Treatment 108005.

Berman, Sarah, "Vancouver Projects Give Weed to Curb Overdoses. Police Just Raided One," *The Tyee* (17 November 2020), online: thetyee.ca/News/2020/11/17/Weed-Curbing-Overdoses/.

Bird, Malcolm G, "Legalized Cannabis in Canada: Federalism, Policy, and Politics" in Andrew Potter & Daniel Weinstock, eds, *High Time: The Legalization and Regulation of Cannabis in Canada* (Kingston and Montreal: McGill-Queen's University Press, 2019) 22 at 23.

Blomley, Nick, "Enclosure, Common Right and the Property of the Poor" (2008) 17 Soc Leg Stud 311 at 312.

Boehnke, Kevin F et al, "Medical Cannabis Use Is Associated with Decreased Opiate Medication Use in a Retrospective Cross-Sectional Survey of Patients with Chronic Pain" (2016) 17:6 J Pain 739.

Boeri, Miriam et al, "Green Hope: Perspectives on Cannabis from People Who Use Opioids" (2020) 33:1 Sociological Inquiry 212.

Braithwaite, John, *Regulatory Capitalism: How it Works, Ideas for Making it Work Better* (Cheltenham: Edward Elgar, 2008), as cited in Ely Aaronson & Gil Rothschild-Elyassi, "The Symbiotic Tensions of the Regulatory–Carceral State: The Case of Cannabis Legalization" (2021) 15:S1 Regulation and Governance S23, online: onlinelibrary.wiley.com/doi/pdf/10.1111/rego.12394.

British Columbia Coroners Service, *Illicit Drug Overdose Deaths in BC: Findings of Coroners' Investigations* (Victoria, BC: Ministry of Public Safety and Solicitor General, 27 September 2018), online: www2.gov.bc.ca/assets/gov/birth-adoption-death-marriage-and-divorce/deaths/coroners-service/statistical/illicitdrugoverdosedeathsinbc-findingsofcoronersinvestigations-final.pdf.

——, *Illicit Drug Toxicity Deaths in BC, January 1, 2010—November 30, 2020* (Victoria BC: Ministry of Public Safety and Solicitor General, 2020), online: https://paninbc.ca/wp-content/uploads/2021/02/BC-illicit-drug-deaths-jan1-2010-dec31-2020.pdf.

Browne, Rachel & Arthur White, "Harper Is Waging a War on Drugs in Canada—And Scientists Say He's Clueless," *Vice* (18 December 2015) online: www.vice.com/en/article/43mv99/harper-is-waging-a-war-on-drugs-in-canada-and-scientists-say-hes-clueless.

Cain, Patrick, "Fewer Than 400 People Pardoned Under New System for Erasing Old Weed Convictions," *CTV News* (10 March 2021), online: www.ctvnews.ca/canada/fewer-than-400-people-pardoned-under-new-system-for-erasing-old-weed-convictions-1.5341579.

Campbell, Larry, Neil Boyd & Lori Culbert, *Vancouver's Downtown Eastside and the Fight for Its Future* (Vancouver: Greystone Books, 2009).

Canadian Association of People who Use Drugs, *Safe Supply Concept Document* (Dartmouth, NS: CAPUD, 2019), online: vancouver.ca/files/cov/capud-safe-supply-concept-document.pdf.

Canadian Press, "'Our Own Grey Areas': First Nations Navigate Hazy Cannabis Retail Jurisdictions," *Blue Line* (26 April 2021), online: www.blueline.ca/our-own-grey-areas-first-nations-navigate-hazy-cannabis-retail-jurisdictions/.

Centre for Addiction and Mental Health, *Cannabis Policy Framework,* (Toronto: CAMH, 2014).

Cerdá, Magdalena & Beau Kilmer, "Uruguay's Middle-Ground Approach to Cannabis Legalization" (2017) 42 Int J Drug Policy 118 at 118.

Chayama, Koharu Loulou et al, "The Role of Cannabis in Pain Management Among People Living with HIV Who Use Drugs: A Qualitative Study" (2021) 40:7 Drug & Alcohol Rev 6.

City of Vancouver, *Downtown Eastside Local Area Profile* (Vancouver: City of Vancouver, 2013), online: vancouver.ca/files/cov/profile-dtes-local-area-2013.pdf.

———, "Downtown: Neighbourhood Social Indicators Profile" (2020), online: vancouver.ca/files/cov/social-indicators-profile-downtown.pdf.

———, *Cannabis as an Alternative to Opiates and More Dangerous Drugs on the Downtown Eastside: Report* (Vancouver: City of Vancouver, 6 October 2020), online: council.vancouver.ca/20201020/documents/r1.pdf.

———, "Cannabis Retail Store Business Licence" (2021), online: vancouver.ca/doing-business/cannabis-retail-dealer-business-licence.aspx.

Committee on the Health Effects of Marijuana, *The Health Effects of Cannabis and Cannabinoids: The Current State of Evidence and Recommendations for Research* (Washington, DC: The National Academies Press, 2017).

Cooper, Ziva D et al, "Impact of Co-administration of Oxycodone and Smoked Cannabis on Analgesia and Abuse Liability" (2018) 43:10 NPP 2046 at 2047.

Courtenay, Piper, "Vancouver's City Council Votes to End Cannabis Prohibition in the Downtown Eastside" (27 June 2019), online: www.canncentral.com/vancouvers-city-council-votes-to-end-cannabis-prohibition-in-the-downtown-eastside.

Dole, Vincent P, "A Medical Treatment for Diacetylmorphine (Heroin) Addiction" (1965) 193:8 JAMA 80.

Donovan, Jesse, "Canada Must Respect Indigenous Cannabis Laws" (1 August 2019), online: policyoptions.irpp.org/magazines/august-2019/canada-must-respect-indigenous-cannabis-laws/.

Dubois, Stephanie, "New 'Statement to Police' Card for Indigenous People Released in Alberta," *CBC News* (21 April 2021), online: www.cbc.ca/news/canada/edmonton/statement-to-police-card-1.5997169.

Egan-Elliott, Roxanne, "Harm-Reduction Group Wants Permission to Give Free Cannabis to Opioid Users," *Times Colonist* (3 September 2020), online: www.timescolonist.com/news/local/harm-reduction-group-wants-permission-to-give-free-cannabis-to-opioid-users-1.24196929.

Ejeckam, Chuka "Clearing Pot Charges from Canadians' Records Would Be A Good Start—But It's Not Enough," *Maclean's* (24 October 2018), online: www.macleans.ca/opinion/clearing-pot-charges-from-canadians-records-would-be-a-good-start-but-its-not-enough/.

Ejeckam, Chuka, "The Unbearable Whiteness of Weed: Canada's Booming Cannabis Industry Has a Race Problem," *The Globe and Mail* (2 August 2019), online: www.theglobeandmail.com/opinion/article-the-unbearable-whiteness-of-weed/.

First Nations Tax Commission, "First Nations Cannabis Jurisdiction Update: June 2018," (26 June 2018) online: fntc.ca/first-nation-cannabis-jurisdiction/.

Fumano, Dan, "Regulators Play 'Whac-A-Mole' As Vancouver's Illegal Pot Shops Flourish," *Vancouver Sun* (9 January 2021), online: vancouversun.com/cannabis/cannabis-business/regulators-play-whac-a-mole-as-vancouvers-illegal-pot-shops-keep-sprouting.

Gamage, Michelle, "Vancouver Pot Shops Pay Canada's Highest Licensing Fees. They Don't Have a Straight Answer Why," *Mugglehead Magazine* (30 September 2020), online: mugglehead.com/vancouver-retailers-pay-highest-licensing-fees-in-country/.

Giffen, P James, Shirley Endicott & Sylvia Lambert, *Panic and Indifference: The Politics of Canada's Drug Laws* (Ottawa: Canadian Centre on Substance Abuse, 1991) at 571, quoted in Jean-François Crépault, "Cannabis Legalization in Canada: Reflections on Public Health and the Governance of Legal Psychoactive Substances" (2018) 6:220 Front Public Health at 82.

Government of California, "Cannabis Equity Grants Program for Local Jurisdictions" (2021), online: business.ca.gov/cannabis-equity-grants-program-for-local-jurisdictions/.

Government of Canada, *Canadian Cannabis Survey 2020: Summary* (Ottawa: Cannabis Research and Data, last modified: 12 August 2021), online: www.canada.ca/en/health-canada/services/drugs-medication/cannabis/research-data/canadian-cannabis-survey-2020-summary.html#a6-01.

——, "Cannabis Laws and Regulations: Authorized Cannabis Retailers in the Provinces and Territories" (last modified 26 October 2022), online: www.canada.ca/en/health-canada/services/drugs-medication/cannabis/laws-regulations/provinces-territories.html.

——, "Cannabis Legalization and Regulation" (last visited 24 July 2022), online: www.justice.gc.ca/eng/cj-jp/cannabis/.

Government of Canada, Task Force of Marijuana Legalization and Regulation, *Toward the Legalization, Regulation, and Restriction of Access to Marijuana: Discussion Paper*, (Ottawa: Health Systems and Services, 30 June 2016), online: www.canada.ca/en/health-canada/programs/consultation-toward-legalization-regulation-restriction-access-marijuana/discussion-paper-introduction.html.

Grinspoon, Lester, *Marijuana Reconsidered* (Cambridge: Harvard University Press, 1971).

Health Canada, *Canadian Tobacco, Alcohol and Drugs (CTADS) Survey: 2017 Detailed Tables* (Ottawa: Health Canada, 2018), online: www.canada.ca/en/health-canada/services/canadian-tobacco-alcohol-drugs-survey/2017-summary/2017-detailed-tables.html#t16.

Jozaghi, Ehsan et al, "Activism and Scientific Research: 20 Years of Community Action by the Vancouver Area Network of Drug Users" (2018) 13:1 SATPP 18.

Klein, Alana, "Criminal Law and the Counter-Hegemonic Potential of Harm Reduction" (2015) 38 Dalhousie LJ 447.

——, "What Jurisdiction of Harm Reduction: Cannabis Policy Reform under Canadian Federalism," in Andrew Potter & Daniel Weinstock, eds, *High Time: The Legalization and Regulation of Cannabis in Canada* (Kingston and Montreal: McGill-Queen's University Press, 2019).

——, "Harm Reduction Works: Evidence and Inclusion in Drug Policy and Advocacy" (2020) 28 Health Care Anal 404.

Krausz, Michael & Kerry Jang, "Lessons from the Creation of Canada's Poorest Postal Code" (2015) 2:3 Lancet Psychiatry e5.

Lake, Stephanie "Cannabis Use During an Opioid-Related Public Health Crisis: Implications for Therapeutic Advancements and Harm Reduction Initiatives" (PhD Dissertation, University of British Columbia, 2020), online: open.library.ubc.ca/cIRcle/collections/ubctheses/24/items/1.0395368 .

Lake, Stephanie et al, "Frequency of Cannabis and Illicit Opioid Use Among People Who Use Drugs and Report Chronic Pain: A Longitudinal Analysis" (2019) 16:11 PLoS Med e0233463.

——, "Characterizing Motivations for Cannabis Use in a Cohort of People Who Use Illicit Drugs: A Latent Class Analysis" (2020) 15:5 PLoS One e0233463.

Lakić, Saša, "Cannabis Substitution Project Claims Its Free 'Care Packages' Help Opioid Users Kick" (22 March 2018), online: www.vancourier.com/news/cannabis-substitution-project-claims-its-free-care-packages-help-opioid-users-kick-1.23209946.

Lappalainen, Leslie et al, "Dose-Response Relationship between Methadone Dose and Adherence to Antiretroviral Therapy among HIV-Positive People Who Use Illicit Opioids" (2015) 110:8 Addiction 1330.

Lucas, Philippe et al, "Substituting Cannabis for Prescription Drugs, Alcohol and Other Substances Among Medical Cannabis Patients: The Impact of Contextual Factors" (2015) 35:3 Drug Alcohol Rev 326.

Lupick, Travis, "Decriminalization Is Just the Start of Real Reform—And Drug Users Need to Be Part of the Conversation," *The Globe and Mail* (21 August 2020), online: www.theglobeandmail.com/opinion/article-on-decriminalization-lets-hear-from-drug-users/.

Lupick, Travis, "The Vancouver Area Network of Drug Users Looks Back on 20 Years Fighting for Human Rights" (4 September 2017), online: www.straight.com/news/959286/vancouver-area-network-drug-users-looks-back-20-years-fighting-human-rights.

——, *Fighting for Space: How a Group of Drug Users Transformed One City's Struggle with Addiction* (Vancouver: Arsenal Pulp Press, 2018).

Macauley, Stewart, "Wisconsin's Legal Tradition" (1994) 24 Gargoyle 6 at 9.

Maghsoudi, Nazlee et al, "How Diverse Is Canada's Legal Cannabis Industry" (last visited 24 July 2022), online: cdpe.org/wp-content/uploads/dlm_uploads/2020/10/How-Diverse-is-Canada's-Legal-Cannabis-Industry_CDPE-UofT-Policy-Brief_Final.pdf

Mattick, Richard P et al, "Methadone Maintenance Therapy Versus No Opioid Replacement Therapy for Opioid Dependence (Review)" (2009) 2009:3 Cochrane Database Syst Rev CD002209.

McNeil, Ryan et al, "Negotiating Place and Gendered Violence in Canada's Largest Open Drug Scene" (2014) 25:3 Int J Drug Policy 608 at 609.

Milloy, M-J et al, "Increased Prevalence of Controlled Viremia and Decreased Rates of HIV Drug Resistance Among HIV-Positive People Who Use Illicit Drugs During a Community-Wide Treatment-as-Prevention Initiative" (2015) 62:5 Clinical Infectious Disease 640.

Mulgrew, Ian, "B.C. Cannabis Police 'Blink,' and Reverse their Stance on Evidence," *Vancouver Sun* (19 February 2020), online: vancouversun.com/opinion/columnists/ian-mulgrew-cannabis-police-blink-and-reverse-their-stance-on-evidence.

Nichol, Emily, Karen Urbanoski & Bernie Pauly, *A Peer-Run Cannabis Substitution Program: Experiences and Outcomes Over the First Year* (Victoria, BC: Canadian Institute for Substance Use Research, 2020), online: solidvictoria.org/wp-content/uploads/2021/02/SOLID_CSP-Report_First-Year-Experiences-and-Outcomes_September-8_-2019.pdf

Nicholson, Bailey & Lisa Steacy, "Vancouver Council Votes to Slash Sky-High Fees for Cannabis Retailers," *City News Vancouver* (18 February 2021), online: www.citynews1130.com/2021/02/18/vancouver-cannabis-retail-fees/.

Nixon, Rob, *Slow Violence and the Environmentalism of the Poor* (Cambridge: Harvard University Press, 2011) at 15.

Nosyk, B et al, "Proportional Hazards Frailty Models for Recurrent Methadone Maintenance Treatment" (2009) 170:6 American J Epidemiology 783.

Owusu-Bempah, Akwasi & Alex Luscombe, "Race, Cannabis and the Canadian War on Drugs: An Examination of Cannabis Arrest Data by Race in Five Cities" (2020), 91 Intl J Drug Policy.

Paperny, Anna Mehler, "Canada Considering Drug Decriminalization to Fight Overdose Crisis," *Reuters* (29 January 2021), online: www.reuters. com/article/us-health-coronavirus-canada-drugs/canada-considering-drug-decriminalization-to-fight-overdose-crisis-idUSKBN29Y2FM.

Paul, Braedon et al, "'Something That Actually Works': Cannabis Use Among Young People in the Context of Street Entrenchment" (2020) 15:7 PLoS One e0236243.

Pauly, Bernie, et al, "'If I Knew I Could Get that Every Hour Instead of Alcohol, I Would Take the Cannabis': Need and Feasibility of Cannabis Substitution Implementation in Canadian Managed Alcohol Programs" (2021) 18 Harm Reduction J 65 at 78.

Peles, Einat et al, "Similarities and Changes Between 15- and 24-Year Survival and Retention Rates of Patients in a Large Medical-Affiliated Methadone Maintenance Treatment (MMT) Center" (2018) 185 Drug & Alcohol Dependence 112.

Potter, Andrew & Weinstock, Daniel, eds, *High Time: The Legalization and Regulation of Cannabis in Canada* (Kingston and Montreal: McGill-Queen's University Press, 2019).

Rankin, Jim, Sandro Contenta & Andrew Bailey, "Toronto Marijuana Arrests Reveal 'Startling' Racial Divide," *Toronto Star* (6 July 2017), online: www. thestar.com/news/insight/2017/07/06/toronto-marijuana-arrests-reveal-startling-racial-divide.html.

Reporting in Indigenous Communities, "Communities" (last visited 24 July 2022), online: indigenousreporting.com/2016/communities/.

Robertson, Leslie & Dara Culhane, eds, *In Plain Sight: Reflections on Life in the Downtown Eastside* (Vancouver: Talenbooks, 2005).

Romo, Vanessa, "LA County DA Moves to Dismiss 66,000 Marijuana-Related Convictions," *NPR* (14 February 2020) online: www.npr. org/2020/02/14/806132895/la-county-da-moves-to-dismiss-66-000-marijuana-related-convictions.

Rotermann, Michelle, "What Has Changed Since Cannabis Was Legalized?" (2020) 31:2 Health Rep 11 at 16.

Schatz, Donna, "Unsettling the Politics of Exclusion: Aboriginal Activism and the Vancouver Downtown Eastside" (Paper prepared for the Annual Meeting of the Canadian Political Science Association, Session M10(b) Beyond Statistics: Urban Indigenous Politics. Concordia University, Montreal, 3 June 2010), online: www.cpsa-acsp.ca/papers-2010/ Schatz.pdf.

Seron, Carroll, "Commentary: The Two Faces of Law and Inequality: From Critique to the Promise of Situated, Pragmatic Policy" (2016) 50:1 Law & Society Review 9 at 10.

Seron, Carroll & Susan S Silbey "Profession, Science and Culture: An Emergent Canon of Law and Society Research" in Austin Serat, ed, *The Blackwell Companion to Law & Society* (Malden, MA: Blackwell Publishing, 2004) 51.

Statistics Canada, "Aboriginal Population Profile, 2016 Census," (last modified 19 July 2019), online: www12.statcan.gc.ca/census-recensement/2016/.

Stilman, Jacob, "Is Legalization a War on Drugs by the Back Door?" in Potter & Weinstock, *High Time, supra* note 7, 99 at 100.

Strain, Eric C et al, "Moderate- Vs High-Dose Methadone in the Treatment of Opioid Dependence: A Randomized Trial" (1999) 281:11 JAMA 1000.

Transform Drug Policy Foundation, "Drug Decriminalisation in Portugal: Setting the Record Straight" (last visited 24 July 2022), online: transformdrugs.org/assets/files/PDFs/Drug-decriminalisation-in-Portugal-setting-the-record-straight.pdf

Truth & Reconciliation Commission of Canada, *Truth & Reconciliation Commission Of Canada: Calls To Action* (Winnipeg: The Truth and Reconciliation Commission of Canada, 2015) online: www2.gov.bc.ca/assets/gov/british-columbians-our-governments/indigenous-people/aboriginal-peoples-documents/calls_to_action_english2.pdf

Tyndall, Mark W et al, "Impact of HIV Infection on Mortality in a Cohort of Injection Drug Users" (2001) 28:4 JAIDS 351.

UNODC, *World Drug Report 2017: Maps & Tables*, online: UNODC www.unodc.org/wdr2017/en/maps-and-graphs.html.

Valleriani, Jenna et al, "The Emergence of Innovative Cannabis Distribution Projects in the Downtown Eastside of Vancouver, Canada" (2020) 79 Int J Drug Policy 102737.

Vancouver City Council, "Motion: Cannabis as an Alternative to Opiates and More Dangerous Drugs on the Downtown Eastside" (26 June 2019), online: council.vancouver.ca/20190626/documents/cfsc3.pdf.

Vancouver Coastal Health, *Response to the Opioid Overdose Crisis in Vancouver Coastal Health* (Vancouver: Vancouver Coastal Health, 2018), online: www.vch.ca/Documents/CMHO-report.pdf.

VANDU, "Mission Statement" (last visited 25 July 2022), online: vandureplace.wordpress.com/history/.

Voon, Pauline et al, "Denial of Prescription Analgesia Among People Who Inject Drugs in a Canadian Setting" (2015) 34:2 Drug & Alcohol Rev 221.

Voon, Pauline et al, "Pain as a Risk Factor for Substance Use: A Qualitative Study of People Who Use Drugs in British Columbia, Canada" (2018) 15:1 Harm Reduction J 35.

Voon, Pauline et al, "Self-Management of Pain Among People Who Inject Drugs in Vancouver" (2014) 4:1 Pain Management 27.

Wenger, Laura et al, "The Phenomenon of Low-Frequency Heroin Injection Among Street-Based Urban Poor: Drug User Strategies and Contexts of Use" (2014) 25:3 IJDP.

White, Erik, "3 Years Ago You Could Only Buy Legal Weed on First Nations, Now Some Say the Industry Needs a 'Red Market,'" *CBC News* (26 February 2021), online: www.cbc.ca/news/canada/sudbury/ontario-first-nations-cannabis-1.5927412.

Wong, Todd, *2019 Downtown Eastside Local Area Profile* (Burnaby: Simon Fraser University, 2019).

Worley, Scot & Akwasi Owusu-Bempah, "Race, Ethnicity, Corie and Criminal Justice in Canada" in Anita Kalantry-Crompton, ed, *Race, Ethnicity, Crime and Criminal Justice In The Americas* (London, UK: Palgrave Macmillan, 2012) 11.

Young, Margot, "Insite: Site and Sight (Part 1—Insights on Insite)" (2011) 19:3 Const Forum Const 87.

Notes

1   We use the scientific term "cannabis" throughout, but the colloquial term "marijuana" is also used to refer to cannabis in certain quotes and source material.

2   See, e.g., Larry Campbell, Neil Boyd & Lori Culbert, *Vancouver's Downtown Eastside and the Fight for Its Future* (Vancouver: Greystone Books, 2009); see also Leslie Robertson & Dara Culhane, eds, *In Plain Sight: Reflections on Life in the Downtown Eastside* (Vancouver: Talenbooks, 2005); see also Travis Lupick, "The Vancouver Area Network of Drug Users Looks Back on 20 Years Fighting for Human Rights" (4 September 2017), online: www.straight.com/news/959286/vancouver-area-network-drug-users-looks-back-20-years-fighting-human-rights.

3   See, e.g., Travis Lupick, *Fighting for Space: How a Group of Drug Users Transformed One City's Struggle with Addiction* (Vancouver: Arsenal Pulp Press, 2018) [Lupick, *Fighting for Space*]. Lupick provides a detailed account of how PWUD and community activists in Vancouver's Downtown Eastside successfully lobbied the city to implement and expand harm reduction services.

4   See Alana Klein, "Harm Reduction Works: Evidence and Inclusion in Drug Policy and Advocacy" (2020) 28 Health Care Anal 404.

5   See, e.g., Centre for Addiction and Mental Health, *Cannabis Policy Framework* (Toronto: CAMH, 2014).

6   See Alana Klein, "What Jurisdiction of Harm Reduction: Cannabis Policy Reform under Canadian Federalism," [Klein, "Jurisdiction"] in Andrew Potter & Daniel Weinstock, eds, *High Time: The Legalization and Regulation of Cannabis in Canada* (Kingston and Montreal: McGill-Queen's University Press, 2019) [Potter & Weinstock, *High Time*].

7   See John Braithwaite, *Regulatory Capitalism: How It Works, Ideas for Making It Work Better* (Cheltenham: Edward Elgar, 2008) at 8, as cited in Ely Aaronson & Gil Rothschild-Elyassi, "The Symbiotic Tensions of the Regulatory–Carceral State: The Case of Cannabis Legalization" (2021) 15:S1 Regulation and Governance S23, online: onlinelibrary.wiley.com/doi/pdf/10.1111/rego.12394 [Aaronson & Rothschild-Elyassi, "Symbiotic Tensions"].

8   See Aaronson & Rothschild-Elyassi, "Symbiotic Tensions," *supra* note 8, at 3.

9   *Ibid* at 4.

10   *Ibid* at 5.

11   *Ibid* at 4.

12   *Ibid* at 6.

13   See Carroll Seron, "Commentary: The Two Faces of Law and Inequality: From Critique to the Promise of Situated, Pragmatic Policy" (2016) 50:1 Law & Society Review 9 at 10. Of course, there are other significant critiques of the new cannabis laws than the ones we discuss. For example, concern has been expressed about the "financialization" of cannabis access: that the model is one that favours a non-diverse group of elite market entrepreneurs: see John Akpata, "Prometheus Re-Bound" (1 March 2018) online: www.policyalternatives.ca/publications/monitor/prometheus-re-bound.

14   See Carroll Seron & Susan S Silbey "Profession, Science and Culture: An Emergent Canon of Law and Society Research" in Austin Serat, ed, *The Blackwell Companion to Law & Society* (Malden, MA: Blackwell Publishing, 2004) 51, as quoted in Seron, *supra* note 14 at 11.

15   See Aaronson & Rothschild-Elyassi, "Symbiotic Tensions," *supra* note 8 at 7.

16   Simple possession, production and supply were criminalized. See Akwasi Owusu-Bempah, Alex Luscombe & Brandon M Finlay, "Unequal Justice: Race and Cannabis Arrests in the Post-Legal Landscape" in Potter & Weinstock, *High Time*, *supra* note 7, 114, at 112.

17   SOC 1923 c 22.

18   See Andrew Potter, "In Praise of Political Opportunism, or, How to Change a Policy in Only Fifty Years" in Potter & Weinstock, *High Time*, *supra* note 7, 9 at 9 [Potter, "In Praise of Political Opportunism"].

19   See Health Canada, *Canadian Tobacco, Alcohol and Drugs (CTADS) Survey: 2017 Detailed Tables* (Ottawa: Health Canada, 2018), online: www.canada.ca/en/health-canada/services/canadian-tobacco-alcohol-drugs-survey/2017-summary/2017-detailed-tables.html#t16.

20   Approximately 15% of the Canadian population aged 15–64 used cannabis in 2010; the third-highest annual prevalence based on countries' most recent estimates, as reported by the United Nations Office on Drugs and Crime in 2017: see UNODC, *World Drug Report 2017: Maps & Tables*, online: www.unodc.org/wdr2017/en/maps-and-graphs.html.

21   Prime Minister Pierre Elliott Trudeau, the current Prime Minister's father, had expressed support in 1977 for relaxation of laws against cannabis use. The Throne Speech from his government had contained a call for decriminalization to the extent of removing jail sentences as a response for individual possession: see Potter, "In Praise of Political Opportunism," *supra* note 19 at 14. The lone outlier here is Stephen Harper's federal government (2006 to 2015), which pointedly adopted an American style "war on drugs"; see Rachel Browne & Arthur White, "Harper Is Waging A War On Drugs In Canada—And Scientists Say He's Clueless" (18 December 2015) online: www.vice.com/en/article/43mv99/harper-is-waging-a-war-on-drugs-in-canada-and-scientists-say-hes-clueless.

22   See P James Giffen, Shirley Endicott & Sylvia Lambert, *Panic and Indifference: The Politics of Canada's Drug Laws* (Ottawa: Canadian Centre on Substance Abuse, 1991) at 571, quoted in Jean-François Crépault, "Legalize It (But Don't Advertise It): The Public Health Case for Cannabis Legalization" in Andrew Potter & Daniel Weinstock, eds, *High Time: The Legalization and Regulation of Cannabis in Canada* (Kingston and Montreal: McGill-Queen's University Press, 2019) 79 [Crépault].

23   *Ibid* at 90.
24   See Magdalena Cerdá & Beau Kilmer, "Uruguay's Middle-Ground Approach to Cannabis Legalization" (2017) 42 Int J Drug Policy 118 at 118.
25   See Crépault, *supra* note 23, at 86.
26   See Transform Drug Policy Foundation, "Drug Decriminalisation in Portugal: Setting the Record Straight" (last visited 24 July 2022), online: transformdrugs.org/assets/files/PDFs/Drug-decriminalisation-in-Portugal-setting-the-record-straight.pdf.
27   See Crépault, *supra* note 23 at 86.
28   See Alana Klein "Criminal Law and the Counter-Hegemonic Potential of Harm Reduction" (2015) 38 Dalhousie LJ 447 (this article discusses the contested significance of the notion of harm reduction).
29   *Canadian Charter of Rights and Freedoms*, Part 1 of the *Constitution* Act, 1982, being Schedule B to the *Canada Act* 1982 (UK), 1982, c 11.
30   [2000] OJ No 2787, 188 DLR (4th) 385 (CA) *[Parker]*.
31   *Ibid* at para 10.
32   SOR/2001-227. After a successful constitutional challenge in *Allard v Canada*, 2016 FC 236 *[Allard]*, these regulations were replaced by the *Access to Cannabis for Medical Purposes Regulations*, SOR/2016-230 in August 2016.
33   SC 1996, c 19.
34   Although, notably, the Supreme Court of Canada upheld the criminalization of recreational use of cannabis as constitutional: see *R v Malmo-Levine*; *R v Caine*, 2003 SCC 74; see also *R v Clay*, 2003 SCC 75.
35   See, e.g., *R v Smith*, 2015 SCC 34; see also Allard, *supra* note 33.
36   See Jacob Stilman, "Is Legalization a War on Drugs by the Back Door?" in Potter & Weinstock, *High Time, supra* note 7, 99 at 100 [Stilman, "Back Door"].
37   See Potter, "In Praise of Political Opportunism," *supra* note 19 at 16.
38   See Malcolm G Bird, "Legalized Cannabis in Canada: Federalism, Policy, and Politics" in Potter & Weinstock *High Times, supra* note 7, 22 at 23 [Bird, "Legalized Cannabis"].
39   The legislation is due for a three-year review in Autumn 2021. For an overview of outstanding issues, some of which are discussed in this chapter, see Ian Austen, "2 Years After Legalizing Cannabis, Has Canada Kept Its Promises?" (last modified 18 April 2021), online: www.nytimes.com/2021/01/23/world/canada/marijuana-legalization-promises-made.html.
40   See Andrew Potter & Daniel Weinstock, "Introduction" [Potter and Weinstock, "Introduction"], in Potter and Weinstock, *High Time, supra* note 7, 3 at 3.
41   *Ibid* at 5.
42   *Ibid* at 3.
43   *Ibid* at 6.
44   See Crépault, *supra* note 23 at 82.
45   See Stilman, "Back Door," *supra* note 37 at 100.
46   See Potter and Weinstock, "Introduction," *supra* note 41 at 4.
47   SC 2018, C. 16 *[Cannabis Act]*.
48   For the government summary of these purposes and the legislative provisions, see Government of Canada, "Cannabis Legalization and Regulation" (last visited 24 July 2022), online: www.justice.gc.ca/eng/cj-jp/cannabis [Government of Canada, "Cannabis Legalization"].
49   In some provinces and territories cannabis can be bought online from federally licensed producers.
50   For more precise details, see Government of Canada, "Cannabis Legalization," *supra* note 49.

51   See *Cannabis Act, supra* note 48, s 8.

52   See *Cannabis Act, supra* note 48, s 10.

53   See Klein, "Jurisdiction," *supra* note 7 at 136.

54   See Bird, "Legalized Cannabis," *supra* note 39 at 23.

55   See Jared Wesley, "Cannabis Legalization and Colonial Legacies" [Wesley, "Colonial Legacies"], in Potter and Weinstock, *High Time, supra* note 7, 35 at 37.

56   See Government of Canada, "Cannabis Laws and Regulations, Authorized Cannabis Retailers In The Provinces And Territories," (last modified 26 October 2022), online: www.canada.ca/en/health-canada/services/drugs-medication/cannabis/laws-regulations/provinces-territories.html.

57   See Potter and Weinstock, "Introduction," *supra* note 41 at 4.

58   See Wesley, "Colonial Legacies," *supra* note 56 at 44.

59   See Klein, "Jurisdiction," *supra* note 7 at 136.

60   SBC 2018, c 29; see also, *Cannabis Distribution Act,* SBC 2018, c 28.

61   See City of Vancouver, "Cannabis Retail Store Business Licence: Approved Locations" (last visited 24 July 2022), online: vancouver.ca/doing-business/cannabis-retail-dealer-business-licence.aspx.

62   In 2015, Vancouver adopted a bylaw that would allow the regulated sale of medical cannabis, where retailers paid a $33,000 licensing fee that would be used to help the city cover the cost of regulating and policing the local, federally unsanctioned industry.

63   See Canadian Press, "'Our Own Grey Areas': First Nations Navigate Hazy Cannabis Retail Jurisdictions" (26 April 2021), online: www.blueline.ca/our-own-grey-areas-first-nations-navigate-hazy-cannabis-retail-jurisdictions/   [Canadian Press, "Our Own"].

64   Estimates vary. See, e.g., Cecilia Benoit, Dena Carroll & Munazi Chaudhry "In Search of a Healing Place: Aboriginal Women in Vancouver's Downtown Eastside" (2003) 56 Soc Science & Medicine 821 at 824; see also Reporting in Indigenous Communities, "Communities" (last visited 24 July 2022), online: indigenousreporting.com/2016/communities/.

65   See Statistics Canada, "Aboriginal Population Profile, 2016 Census," (last modified 19 July 2019), online: www12.statcan.gc.ca/census-recensement/2016/dp.

66   See Jesse Donovan, "Canada Must Respect Indigenous Cannabis Laws" (1 August 2019), online: policyoptions.irpp.org/magazines/august-2019/canada-must-respect-indigenous-cannabis-laws/ [Donovan].

67   *Ibid.*

68   For discussion and history of this, see First Nations Tax Commission, "First Nations Cannabis Jurisdiction Update: June 2018" (26 June 2018) online: fntc.ca/first-nation-cannabis-jurisdiction; see also Canadian Press, "Our Own", *supra* note 64; see also Erik White, "3 Years Ago You Could Only Buy Legal Weed on First Nations, Now Some Say the Industry Needs a 'Red Market,'" *CBC News* (26 February 2021), online: www.cbc.ca/news/canada/sudbury/ontario-first-nations-cannabis-1.5927412 [White, "Some Say"].

69   See Truth & Reconciliation Commission of Canada, *Truth & Reconciliation Commission of Canada: Calls to Action* (Winnipeg: The Truth and Reconciliation Commission of Canada, 2015), online: www2.gov.bc.ca/assets/gov/british-columbians-our-governments/indigenous-people/aboriginal-peoples-documents/calls_to_action_english2.pdf, recommendation #42.

70   The Pheasant Rump Nakota Nation in Saskatchewan has passed its own *Traditional Medicinal Plants Act,* regulating possession and sale of cannabis on their reserve: see Donovan, *supra* note 67.

71   The field research that formed the basis of this chapter was conducted by Stephanie Lake under the supervision of M-J Milloy and supervisory committee members Jane Buxton, Thomas Kerr, and Zach Walsh.

72   See British Columbia Coroners Service, *Illicit Drug Overdose Deaths in BC: Findings of Coroners' Investigations*, (Victoria, BC: Ministry of Public Safety and Solicitor General, 27 September 2018), online: www2.gov.bc.ca/assets/gov/birth-adoption-death-marriage-and-divorce/deaths/coroners-service/statistical/illicitdrugoverdosedeathsinbc-findingsofcoronersinvestigations-final.pdf.

73   See British Columbia Coroners Service, *Illicit Drug Toxicity Deaths in BC, January 1, 2010—November 30, 2020* (Victoria BC: Ministry of Public Safety and Solitor General, 11 February 2021) online: paninbc.ca/wp-content/uploads/2021/02/BC-illicit-drug-deaths-jan1-2010-dec31-2020.pdf.

74   See Vancouver Coastal Health, *Response to the Opioid Overdose Crisis in Vancouver Coastal Health* (Vancouver: Vancouver Coastal Health, 2018), online: www.vch.ca/Documents/CMHO-report.pdf.

75   See Ryan McNeil et al, "Negotiating Place and Gendered Violence in Canada's Largest Open Drug Scene" (2014) 25:3 Int J Drug Policy 608 at 609.

76   See, e.g., Michael Krausz & Kerry Jang, "Lessons from the Creation of Canada's Poorest Postal Code" (2015) 2:3 Lancet Psychiatry e5.

77   See City of Vancouver, "Downtown Eastside Local Area Profile" (2013), online: vancouver.ca/files/cov/profile-dtes-local-area-2013.pdf [City of Vancouver, "2013 Profile"]; see also, Todd Wong, *2019 Downtown Eastside Local Area Profile* (Burnaby: Simon Fraser University, 2019); see also City of Vancouver, "Downtown: Neighbourhood Social Indicators Profile" (2020), online : vancouver.ca/files/cov/social-indicators-profile-downtown.pdf.

78   See City of Vancouver, "2013 Profile", *supra* note 78.

79   See Margot Young, "Insite: Site and Sight (Part 1 - Insights on Insite)" (2011) 19:3 Const Forum Const 87.

80   See Nick Blomley, "Enclosure, Common Right and the Property of the Poor" (2008) 17 Soc Leg Stud 311 at 312 (Blomley describes activism around issues of land, redevelopment and gentrification, but his characterization of the neighbourhood applies equally to poverty and drug use issues).

81   See Lupick, *Fighting for Space, supra* note 4.

82   See Ehsan Jozaghi et al, "Activism and Scientific Research: 20 Years of Community Action by the Vancouver Area Network of Drug Users" (2018) 13:1 SATPP 18.

83   See, e.g., Philippe Lucas et al, "Substituting Cannabis for Prescription Drugs, Alcohol and Other Substances Among Medical Cannabis Patients: The Impact of Contextual Factors" (2015) 35:3 Drug Alcohol Rev 326; see also Kevin F Boehnke et al, "Medical Cannabis Use Is Associated with Decreased Opiate Medication Use in a Retrospective Cross-Sectional Survey of Patients with Chronic Pain" (2016) 17:6 J Pain 739. One high-impact study, in which authors noted a 25% lower overdose death rate in states with medical cannabis laws, is often credited as having catalyzed proliferation of research studies addressing the question of cannabis as a "substitute" for opioids: see Marcus Bacchuber et al, "Medical Cannabis Laws and Opioid Analgesic Overdose Mortality in the United States, 1999-2010" (2014) 174:10 JAMA Internal Medicine 1668.

84   See Jenna Valleriani et al, "The Emergence of Innovative Cannabis Distribution Projects in the Downtown Eastside of Vancouver, Canada" (2020) 79 Int J Drug Policy 102737.

85   VANDU is essentially a drug users union; their mission statement reads: "VANDU is a group of users and former users who work to improve the lives of people who use drugs through user-based peer support and education. VANDU is committed

to increasing the capacity of people who use drugs to live healthy, productive lives. VANDU is also committed to ensuring that drug users have a real voice in their community and in the creation of programs and policies designed to serve them"; see "Mission Statement" (last visited 25 July 2022), online: vandureplace. wordpress.com/history/.

86 See Saša Lakić, "Cannabis Substitution Project Claims Its Free 'Care Packages' Help Opioid Users Kick" (22 March 2018), online: www.vancourier.com/news/ cannabis-substitution-project-claims-its-free-care-packages-help-opioid-users- kick-1.23209946.

87 See Valleriani et al, *supra* note 85 at 3.

88 The High Hopes Cannabis Collective described its mission as "to facilitate the sharing of home-grown cannabis to increase access to cannabis to people who need it most."

89 See Valleriani et al, *supra* note 85.

90 *Ibid.*

91 See Sarah Berman, "Vancouver Projects Give Weed to Curb Overdoses. Police Just Raided One," *The Tyee* (17 November 2020), online: thetyee.ca/News/2020/11/17/ Weed-Curbing-Overdoses/.

92 See, for example, acknowledgment of an informal credit system for marginalized PWUD in Koharu Loulou Chayama et al, "The Role of Cannabis in Pain Management Among People Living with HIV Who Use Drugs: A Qualitative Study" (2021) 40:7 Drug & Alcohol Rev 6.

93 At the time of writing, studies 1 and 2 had been published as peer-reviewed articles, and study 3 was undergoing peer-review.

94 See Stephanie Lake, "Cannabis Use During an Opioid-Related Public Health Crisis: Implications for Therapeutic Advancements and Harm Reduction Initiatives" (PhD Dissertation, University of British Columbia, 2020), online: open.library.ubc. ca/cIRcle/collections/ubctheses/24/items/1.0395368 [Lake, "Cannabis Use During a Public Health Crisis"].

95 See Mark W Tyndall et al, "Impact of HIV Infection on Mortality in a Cohort of Injection Drug Users" (2001) 28:4 JAIDS 351; see also M-J Milloy et al, "Increased Prevalence of Controlled Viremia and Decreased Rates of HIV Drug Resistance Among HIV-Positive People Who Use Illicit Drugs During a Community-Wide Treatment-as-Prevention Initiative" (2015) 62:5 Clinical Infectious Disease 640.

96 The study's methods and results are described in full in its original publication. Stephanie Lake et al, "Characterizing Motivations for Cannabis Use in a Cohort of People Who Use Illicit Drugs: A Latent Class Analysis" (2020) 15:5 PLoS One e0233463 [Lake et al, "Characterizing Motivations"].

97 See Pauline Voon et al, "Self-Management of Pain Among People Who Inject Drugs in Vancouver" (2014) 4:1 Pain Management 27; see also Pauline Voon et al, "Denial of Prescription Analgesia Among People Who Inject Drugs in a Canadian Setting" (2015) 34:2 Drug & Alcohol Rev 221; see also Pauline Voon et al, "Pain as a Risk Factor for Substance Use: A Qualitative Study of People Who Use Drugs in British Columbia, Canada" (2018) 15:1 Harm Reduction J 35.

98 See Committee on the Health Effects of Marijuana, *The Health Effects of Cannabis and Cannabinoids: The Current State of Evidence and Recommendations for Research* (Washington, DC: The National Academies Press, 2017).

99 See Ziva D Cooper et al, "Impact of Co-Administration of Oxycodone and Smoked Cannabis on Analgesia and Abuse Liability" (2018) 43:10 NPP 2046 at 2047.

100 The study's methods and results are described in full in its original publication: see Stephanie Lake et al, "Frequency of Cannabis and Illicit Opioid Use Among

People Who Use Drugs and Report Chronic Pain: A Longitudinal Analysis" (2019) 16:11 PLoS Med e0233463 [Lake et al, "Frequency of Cannabis"].

101 See Vincent P Dole, "A Medical Treatment for Diacetylmorphine (Heroin) Addiction" (1965) 193:8 JAMA 80.

102 See, e.g., Richard P Mattick et al, "Methadone Maintenance Therapy Versus No Opioid Replacement Therapy for Opioid Dependence (Review)" (2009) 2009:3 Cochrane Database Syst Rev CD002209.

103 See, e.g., Eric C Strain et al, "Moderate- Vs High-Dose Methadone in the Treatment of Opioid Dependence: A Randomized Trial" (1999) 281:11 JAMA 1000; see also B Nosyk et al, "Proportional Hazards Frailty Models for Recurrent Methadone Maintenance Treatment" (2009) 170:6 American J Epidemiology 783.

104 See Lester Grinspoon, *Marijuana Reconsidered* (Cambridge: Harvard University Press, 1971), chapter 8.

105 For example, over half of PWUD reported using cannabis to address symptoms of opioid withdrawal: see Cecilia L Bergeria et al, "The Impact of Naturalistic Cannabis Use on Self-Reported Opioid Withdrawal" (2020) 113 J Substance Abuse Treatment 108005.

106 The study's methods and results are described in full in the original paper: see Lake, "Cannabis Use During a Public Health Crisis," *supra* note 95 at 87.

107 This threshold is consistent with previous literature demonstrating improved outcomes at doses around or exceeding 100 mg/day; see, e.g., Leslie Lappalainen et al, "Dose-Response Relationship Between Methadone Dose and Adherence to Antiretroviral Therapy Among HIV-Positive People Who Use Illicit Opioids" (2015) 110:8 Addiction 1330; see also Einat Peles et al, "Similarities and Changes Between 15- and 24-Year Survival and Retention Rates of Patients in a Large Medical-Affiliated Methadone Maintenance Treatment (MMT) Center" (2018) 185 Drug & Alcohol Dependence 112.

108 See Lake et al, "Characterizing Motivations," *supra* note 97 at e0233463-13; see also Lake et al, "Frequency of Cannabis," *supra* note 101 at e0233463-12; see also Lake, "Cannabis Use During a Public Health Crisis," *supra* note 95 at 78.

109 See Valleriani et al, *supra* note 85; see also Braedon Paul et al, "'Something That Actually Works': Cannabis Use Among Young People in the Context of Street Entrenchment" (2020) 15:7 PLoS One e0236243; see also Chayama et al, *supra* note 93.

110 See Laura Wenger et al, "The Phenomenon of Low-Frequency Heroin Injection Among Street-Based Urban Poor: Drug User Strategies and Contexts of Use" (2014) 25:3 IJDP; see also Miriam Boeri et al, "Green Hope: Perspectives on Cannabis From People Who Use Opioids" (2020) Sociological Inquiry; see also Emily Nichol, Karen Urbanoski & Bernie Pauly, *A Peer-Run Cannabis Substitution Program: Experiences and Outcomes Over the First Year* (Victoria, BC: Canadian Institute for Substance Use Research, 2020), online: solidvictoria.org/wp-content/uploads/2021/02/SOLID_CSP-Report_First-Year-Experiences-and-Outcomes_September-8_-2019.pdf.

111 See Lake et al, "Characterizing Motivations," *supra* note 97.

112 See City of Vancouver, "Cannabis Retail Store Business Licence" (2021), vancouver.ca/doing-business/cannabis-retail-dealer-business-licence.aspx.

113 See Vancouver City Council, "Motion: Cannabis as an Alternative to Opiates and More Dangerous Drugs on the Downtown Eastside" (26 June 2019), online: council.vancouver.ca/20190626/documents/cfsc3.pdf>.

114 See Piper Courtenay, "Vancouver's City Council Votes to End Cannabis Prohibition in the Downtown Eastside" (27 June 2019), online: www.canncentral.com/vancouvers-city-council-votes-to-end-cannabis-prohibition-in-the-downtown-eastside.

115 See Dan Fumano, "Regulators Play 'Whac-A-Mole' as Vancouver's Illegal Pot Shops Flourish" (9 January 2021), online: vancouversun.com/cannabis/cannabis-business/regulators-play-whac-a-mole-as-vancouvers-illegal-pot-shops-keep-sprouting.

116 *Ibid*.

117 See Michelle Rotermann, "What Has Changed Since Cannabis Was Legalized?" (2020) 31:2 Health Rep 11 at 16. It is worth noting that many factors that varied across jurisdictions are thought to contribute to faster transition to the legal market, including the availability of legal retail cannabis in the period immediately following legalization. In BC, where cannabis retail is a mix of government- and private-run stores, only one government-run store (Kamloops) was operational on legalization day. Rotermann writes that, according to the 2019 NCS, an estimated 29.4% of Canadian cannabis users reported obtaining all the cannabis they consumed from a legal source. Many consumers obtained cannabis from multiple sources.

118 See Ian Mulgrew, "B.C. Cannabis Police 'Blink,' and Reverse Their Stance on Evidence" (19 February 2020), online: vancouversun.com/opinion/columnists/ian-mulgrew-cannabis-police-blink-and-reverse-their-stance-on-evidence.

119 See Michelle Gamage, "Vancouver Pot Shops Pay Canada's Highest Licensing Fees. They Don't Have a Straight Answer Why" (30 September 2020), online: mugglehead.com/vancouver-retailers-pay-highest-licensing-fees-in-country; see also Bailey Nicholson & Lisa Steacy, "Vancouver Council Votes to Slash Sky-High Fees for Cannabis Retailers" (18 February 2021), online: www.citynews1130.com/2021/02/18/vancouver-cannabis-retail-fees/.

120 See Nicholson, *supra* note 121.

121 See Aaronson & Rothschild-Elyssi, "Symbiotic Tensions," *supra* note 8 at 9.

122 *Ibid* at 9.

123 *Ibid* at 10.

124 See Valleriani et al, *supra* note 85 at 4.

125 Another more recent study supports this observation. Pauly et al found that costs associated with procuring cannabis were difficult, particularly for legal cannabis: "While cannabis is legal in Canada, sourcing and funding cannabis by programs were identified as primary challenges" see Bernie Pauly et al, "'If I Knew I Could Get That Every Hour Instead of Alcohol, I Would Take The Cannabis': Need and Feasibility of Cannabis Substitution Implementation in Canadian Managed Alcohol Programs" (2021) 18 Harm Reduction J 65 at 78.

126 *Ibid*.

127 See Government of Canada, *Canadian Cannabis Survey 2020: Summary* (Ottawa: Cannabis Research and Data, last modified: 12 August 2021), online: www.canada.ca/en/health-canada/services/drugs-medication/cannabis/research-data/canadian-cannabis-survey-2020-summary.html#a6-01.

128 See Government of Canada, Task Force of Marijuana Legalization and Regulation, *Toward The Legalization, Regelation, and Restriction of Access to Marijuana: Discussion Paper*, (Ottawa: Health Systems and Services, 30 June 2016), online: www.canada.ca/en/health-canada/programs/consultation-toward-legalization-regulation-restriction-access-marijuana/discussion-paper-introduction.html.

129 See Valleriani et al, *supra* note 85 at 5.

130 *Ibid* at 2. A detailed description of compassion club operational models is provided in Lynne Belle-Isle, *Cannabis as Therapy for People Living with HIV/AIDS* (Ottawa: Canadian AIDS Society, 2006), online: sagecollection.ca/en/resources/final-report-cannabis-therapy-people-living-hivaids-our-right-our-choice.

131 See Bird, "Legalized Cannabis," *supra* note 39 at 32.

132 *Ibid* at 26.

133 See, e.g., *ibid* at 33.

134 See Crépault, *supra* note 23 at 85.

135 See Owusu-Bempah et al, *supra* note 17 at 114.

136 See Jim Rankin, Sandro Contenta & Andrew Bailey, "Toronto Marijuana Arrests Reveal 'Startling' Racial Divide" (6 July 2017), online: www.thestar.com/news/ insight/2017/07/06/toronto-marijuana-arrests-reveal-startling-racial-divide.html; see also Scot Worley & Akwasi Owusu-Bempah, "Race, Ethnicity, Corie and Criminal Justice in Canada" in Anita Kalantry-Crompton, ed, *Race, Ethnicity, Crime and Criminal Justice in the Americas* (London: Palgrave Macmillan, 2012) 11, as quoted in Crépault, *supra* note 23, at 86.

137 See Crépault, *supra* note 23 at 86; see also Akwasi Owusu-Bempah & Alex Luscombe, "Race, Cannabis and the Canadian War on Drugs: An Examination of Cannabis Arrest Data by Race in Five Cities" (2020) 91 Intl J Drug Policy 102937 [Owusu-Bempah & Luscombe, "Race, Cannabis, and the Canadian War on Drugs"]. Under the criminalization regimes, social harms associated with cannabis criminalization were "highly arbitrary and, in the case of racialized communities, discriminatory and inequitable" see Crépault, *supra* note 23 at 86.

138 See Owusu-Bempah & Alex Luscombe, "Race, Cannabis, and the Canadian War on Drugs," *supra* note 139 at 5. By way of related illustration of discriminatory policing, a 2017 investigation by CBC News found that, in 2016, Indigenous women were nearly 10 times as likely to be street checked as white women. Indigenous people were six times more likely to be stopped. Black individuals were five times more likely: see Stephanie Dubois, "New 'Statement to Police' Card for Indigenous People Released in Alberta" (21 April 2021), online: www.cbc.ca/news/canada/ edmonton/statement-to-police-card-1.5997169.

139 See Crépault, *supra* note 23 at 87.

140 See Daniel Weinstock, "Will Legalization Protect Our kids?" in Potter & Weinstock, *High Time*, *supra* note 7 67 at 70.

141 See Aaronson & Rothschild-Elyassi, "Symbiotic Tensions," *supra* note 8 at 2.

142 See, for example, Vanessa Romo, "LA County DA Moves To Dismiss 66,000 Marijuana-Related Convictions" (14 February 2020) www.npr.org/2020/02/14/ 806132895/la-county-da-moves-to-dismiss-66-000-marijuana-related-convictions.

143 See Government of California, "Cannabis Equity Grants Program for Local Jurisdictions" (2021), online: business.ca.gov/cannabis-equity-grants-program-for-local-jurisdictions/.

144 In this context, "social equity" refers to policy measures that aim to address the discriminatory enforcement of cannabis laws under prohibition, as exemplified by Owusu-Bempah & Alex Luscombe, "Race, Cannabis, and the Canadian War on Drugs," *supra* note 139.

145 The federal government introduced a program to expedite pardons for people previously charged with simple cannabis possession, but the program has been widely criticized for keeping the onus on the individual rather than the government. See, e.g., Chuka Ejeckam, "Clearing Pot Charges From Canadians' Records Would be a Good Start—But It's Not Enough" (24 October 2018) online: www.macleans.ca/opinion/clearing-pot-charges-from-canadians-records-would-be-a-good-start-but-its-not-enough/. Initially, it was estimated that 250,000 Canadians would be eligible, but as of March 2021, the program had issued fewer than 400 pardons: see Patrick Cain, "Fewer Than 400 People Pardoned Under New System for Erasing Old Weed Convictions" (10 March 2021) online: www.ctvnews. ca/canada/fewer-than-400-people-pardoned-under-new-system-for-erasing-old-weed-convictions-1.5341579.

146 See Wesley, "Colonial Legacies," *supra* note 56 at 37.

147 *Ibid* at 46; see also Owusu-Bempah & Alex Luscombe, "Race, Cannabis, and the Canadian War on Drugs," *supra* note 139.

148 See, for example, Donna Schatz, "Unsettling the Politics of Exclusion: Aboriginal Activism and the Vancouver Downtown Eastside" (2010), online: www.cpsa-acsp.ca/papers-2010/Schatz.pdf.

149 See Crépault, *supra* note 23 at 2.

150 For a detailed description of "safe supply" and the proposed ways in which it can be provided, as outlined by PWUD, see Canadian Association of People who Use Drugs, "Safe Supply Concept Document" (2019), online: vancouver.ca/files/cov/capud-safe-supply-concept-document.pdf.

151 See Camille Bains, "Feds Provide $15M to Fund 4 B.C. Pilot Projects Looking into a Safer Drug Supply" (1 February 2021), online: www.cbc.ca/news/canada/british-columbia/feds-provide-15-million-for-safer-bc-drug-supply-1.5896659.

152 See City of Vancouver, *Cannabis as an Alternative to Opiates and More Dangerous Drugs on the Downtown Eastside: Report* (Vancouver: City of Vancouver, 6 October 2020) online: council.vancouver.ca/20201020/documents/r1.pdf [City of Vancouver, "Cannabis as an Alternative"].

153 See Roxanne Egan-Elliott, "Harm-Reduction Group Wants Permission to Give Free Cannabis to Opioid Users" (3 September 2020) online: www.timescolonist.com/news/local/harm-reduction-group-wants-permission-to-give-free-cannabis-to-opioid-users-1.24196929.

154 City of Vancouver, "Cannabis as an Alternative," *supra* note 153.

155 *Ibid.*

156 *Ibid.*

157 *Ibid.*

158 See, e.g., Travis Lupick, "Decriminalization Is Just the Start of Real Reform—and Drug Users Need to Be Part of the Conversation," *The Globe and Mail* (21 August 2020), online: www.theglobeandmail.com/opinion/article-on-decriminalization-lets-hear-from-drug-users; see also Anna Mehler Paperny, "Canada Considering Drug Decriminalization to Fight Overdose Crisis" (29 January 2021), online: www.reuters.com/article/us-health-coronavirus-canada-drugs/canada-considering-drug-decriminalization-to-fight-overdose-crisis-idUSKBN29Y2FM.

159 See Nazlee Maghsoudi et al, "How Diverse Is Canada's Legal Cannabis Industry" (last visited 24 July 2022), online: cdpe.org/wp-content/uploads/dlm_uploads/2020/10/How-Diverse-is-Canada's-Legal-Cannabis-Industry_CDPE-UofT-Policy-Brief_Final.pdf; see Chuka Ejeckam, "The Unbearable Whiteness of Weed: Canada's Booming Cannabis Industry Has a Race Problem" (2 August 2019), online: www.theglobeandmail.com/opinion/article-the-unbearable-whiteness-of-weed/.

160 See Stewart Macauley, "Wisconsin's Legal Tradition" (1994) 24 Gargoyle 6 at 9.

161 See Rob Nixon, *Slow Violence and the Environmentalism of the Poor* (Cambridge, MA: Harvard University Press, 2011) at 15.

CHAPTER 7

This Is Your Country on Cannabis

A Review of Legislation, Testing, and Pharmacology of Legal Cannabis in Canada

Ryan J. P. Pusiak

Canada legalized the recreational sale of cannabis for adults on October 17, 2018, in response to consumer demand for its legalization. This has come with issues along the cannabis supply chain arising from governmental policy, licensed production, and consumer confusion. This chapter offers an overview of the biology of cannabis, legalization, dosing measures, and the variability of cannabis products.

Cannabis

First, a general overview of the cannabis plant and its interaction with humans. *Cannabis sativa* has been used for millennia by humans for medicinal, recreational, spiritual, industrial, and nutritional reasons.[1] Cannabis shares some of the same terpenes (scent molecules) found in plants such as limonene, dominant in lemons, and linalool, dominant in lavender.[2] Cannabinoids, however, are a unique class of phytochemicals (naturally occurring compounds found in plants) found almost exclusively in *Cannabis sativa* (though see).[3] The cannabinoids are responsible for the psychoactive and some of the bioactive effects of cannabis. The highest density of cannabinoids are found within the trichomes of the female inflorescence (the complete flower head).

The most dominant cannabinoids found in the cannabis plant are tetrahydrocannabinol (THC) and cannabidiol (CBD), along with over 60 minor cannabinoids that may have therapeutic potential. THC is primarily responsible for the psycho-euphoric effects (i.e., feeling "high") and adverse effects such as paranoia and delusions in susceptible individuals.[4] Meanwhile, CBD is known for its medicinal properties, such as an anti-psychotic,[5] anti-anxiety,[6] anti-epileptic,[7] and anti-inflammatory agent. However, THC is also therapeutic, for example by improving appetite for those undergoing chemotherapy or patients suffering from AIDS.[8]

Only trace amounts of THC and CBD occur within the cannabis plant; instead, they naturally occur in their acidic forms, THCA and CBDA. This acidic side-chain reduces the bioavailability (e.g., psychoactive properties) of these cannabinoids relative to their neutral forms, THC and CBD.[9] Once heated, however, the acidic group detaches (i.e., decarboxylates), making the cannabinoids bioactive. This decarboxylation step is the reason why cannabis is typically smoked, vaporized, or cooked before being consumed. The effects of cannabis vary based on the concentration (e.g., mg/g) of THC and CBD along with the ratio of cannabinoids (i.e., THC:CBD). THC is responsible for the intoxicating effects of cannabis,[10] whereas products dominant in CBD generally act as an anxiolytic (although the full suite of psychoactive effects associated with both THC and CBD have yet to be established). A simple way to remember the effects of cannabinoids is through the mnemonic THC as The High Cannabinoid and CBD as Calm Back Down.

The endocannabinoid system could explain some of the benefits from cannabis as the cannabinoid receptors are the most abundant G-coupled protein receptor in the central nervous system[11] and are ubiquitous throughout the human body.[12] The endocannabinoid system works by producing endocannabinoids, which bind to one of two cannabinoid receptors and are later degraded. Exogenous cannabinoids (i.e., from cannabis) interact with the cannabinoid receptors within the body, producing effects stronger than the endocannabinoids alone. Furthermore, unlike alcohol or opioids, a person cannot die from over consuming cannabis—rather, they may *feel* like they are dying[13]—because the cannabinoids do not shutdown the part of the brain responsible for breathing.[14]

The selection for different traits in cannabis resulted in two phenotypically distinct groups: high- and low-THC cannabis. High-THC cannabis (i.e., drug-type cannabis) was selected for high levels of THC and is traditionally used for its medicinal, recreational, and spiritual practices.[15] Meanwhile, low-THC cannabis (i.e., hemp), was selected for fibre and food production, and was a popular addition to bird feed in the early twentieth century.[16] Hemp was not selected for THC content (most cultivars <0.3% THC dry weight) and is proportionally higher in CBD. A third lesser-known group of cannabis, ruderalis, is typically found along roadside ditches; it has low levels of either cannabinoids. Cannabis could be classified into sativa and indica. Sativa strains are said to grow tall and lanky with an uplifting high, while indica strains have a short stature with sedative effects. Cannabis users report having different effects between indica and sativa; however, there is little chemical difference between these two groups of cannabis.[17]

A more precise way to categorize cannabis could be based on its THC:CBD ratio, where type I is THC-dominant, type II is balanced between THC and CBD, and type III is CBD-dominant.[18] While THC and CBD each have their own unique medicinal properties, the illicit market has seen a demand for greater amounts of THC in cannabis products. For example, average cannabis in the mid-1990s had approximately 40 mg/g (i.e., 4%) THC, while average cannabis in the mid-2010s had 120 mg/g (i.e., 12%) THC.[19]

The cannabis from the 1970s was even less potent than the 1990s, ranging from 0% to 3% THC.[20] In contrast, cannabis sampled in 2015 from licensed testing facilities report THC values over 25% in some cases.[21] Perhaps the shift from outdoor to indoor covert grow-operations and selective breeding regimens explains this dramatic increase in THC.[22] However, demand for higher THC content comes at a cost to greater THC variability within a single harvest of illicit cannabis.[23]

Due to the lack of quality control/quality assurance (QCQA) oversight, selection for more potent cannabis and greater variability of THC between harvests could be most harmful to the consumer (especially medical-cannabis users). When cannabis was prohibited, consumers were generally unaware of the amount of THC and the THC:CBD ratio,[24] along with the potential contaminants on or within their cannabis products. Legalization and regulation of cannabis are one solution to provide a consistent cannabis product to consumers.

Quality Control/Quality Assurance and Accessibility of Cannabis: From Legislation to the Consumer

Canada was the second country to legalize cannabis for recreational use. The Canadian government's three main goals for legalizing cannabis were to ensure safe products for Canadians, reduce use among minors, and reduce the proceeds to the illicit market.[25] In theory, government oversight and regulation of legal cannabis provide rigorous control and product testing, all lacking in the illicit market, of course. However, the legal market is not without issue as recalls have been issued for improperly labelled cannabis products[26] and security breaches with online cannabis transactions.[27] These scenarios could reduce consumer trust and strengthen the illicit cannabis market.[28] Legal cannabis can work if there is a cohesive partnership among government agencies, licensed producers, and consumers as each are integral to the cannabis supply chain.

Legislation

The Canadian government opted for a two-phase approach to legalizing the recreational use of cannabis products via the Cannabis Act[29] and cannabis regulations.[30] In October 2018, flower, oil, and tincture cannabis were permitted to be sold. There was no limit on the THC potency of flower cannabis, although it is generally less than 30 percent THC dry weight.[31] In some provinces, cannabis sales were limited to online transactions until physical (brick-and-mortar) stores were opened. In October 2019, the sale of concentrate, topicals, and edible products went forward. The limit on edible products was set at 10 mg THC per package, while there is no upper limit of CBD per package.[32]

The slow release of approved products allowed for adjustments in legislation. This helped to tease apart the effects of having some or all cannabis products available.[33] The top-down approach permitted greater government control and QCQA oversight, and provided a safer supply to consumers compared with a prohibition or decriminalized approach to selling cannabis.

Having less government oversight might result in a higher risk for contamination, lot-to-lot inconsistency, and improperly labelled edible products.[34] Legal cannabis, however, is tested for potency and contaminants.[35] The legal limits on the potency of edible cannabis mitigates the harms of accidental or over consumption, which might occur in jurisdictions with greater potency limits on edibles. The

10 mg THC per package limit, along with public education about the effects of these products,[36] should reduce health care costs associated with accidental consumption by minors and reduce the risk of drug-impaired driving.[37] The Cannabis Act prohibits the sale of products containing a mixture of cannabis and alcohol (ethanol concentration <0.5w/w or limit of 7.5 g ethanol tincture), tobacco, and/or caffeine (max. of 30 mg natural caffeine permitted).[38] Routes of consumption must not harm the user (e.g., abrasion to the skin, taken through the eye or via injection), though smoking is arguably harmful. The goal of these regulations is to focus on consumer safety.

The rollout of legalizing cannabis had some issues. Provinces had their own regulations in place as to how cannabis was sold. Provinces such as Newfoundland and Labrador had physical stores, while others such as Ontario began legal sales online. For online sales, customers had to input their credentials (e.g., name and address) and pay electronically. There have been rumours suggesting that the sales of legal cannabis are tracked and could result in issues when crossing international borders; however, there is insufficient evidence to suggest that this information is easily accessible to border security.[39] Furthermore, within weeks of legalization there was a security breach of 4,500 customers from the province's online retailer of recreational cannabis.[40] Another unforeseen issue with the two-stage framework was the consumer demand for an array of cannabis products that were not legalized until late 2019. This *hypothetically* provided an avenue for the continued illicit online sales of concentrates, topicals, and edibles.

Issues associated with illicit cannabis sale usually revolve around the QCQA of illicit vape cartridges[41] and concentrates.[42] Regulated vaping products must undergo rigorous product testing before being sold to consumers, whereas unregulated, thus illicit, products do not. Furthermore, the term "vaping" is used as a catchall statement for an e-cigarette containing nicotine, known as electronic nicotine delivery system;[43] vape pens and cartridges with THC; and vaping using a vaporizer (i.e., a device that decarboxylates cannabis using heat, thus making it bioavailable without combustion), each of which could lead to consumer confusion and catchy media headlines.[44] For example, researchers tested the effects of smoked vs. herbal vaporized cannabis flower.[45] That study was later cited by another researcher reporting on a young male who entered a psychosis after inhaling an illicit THC vape pen (i.e., cannabis concentrate).[46] The former experimenter used herbal cannabis from the US National Institute on Drug Abuse at known concentrations, while the latter researcher reported on illicit concentrate use. Having a clear definition of vaping, such as differentiating legal versus illicit, nicotine versus THC, and concentrate versus flower, could mitigate misinterpretations of data. However, please note that some herbal vaporizers are equipped to handle vape cartridges—adding to the confusion.[47] Finally, the difference in QCQA between legally regulated and illicit vape products should be clearly defined in any regulation pertaining to the harms of vaping.

Product Testing and Creation

Under the current cannabis regulations, individuals can grow up to four plants per adult for their own personal use. However, only licensed producers (LPs) of cannabis are permitted to sell to licensed retailers (provincial restrictions apply). The initial start-up cost and approval process for the licensing, production, and product testing of cannabis is expensive. The LP must adhere to the government oversight for production practices, product testing, and hire a quality-assurance person that has experience in cannabis product testing.[48]

Product testing is one way to ensure a safe product is being sold to consumers. Each batch of product must be tested for fertilizer and pesticide residue, the presence of heavy metals (and metalloids), microbes, and the amount of THC and CBD. Additional product testing could include terpenes (i.e., odour profile) that would provide customers with more product information. In contrast, the illicit market has limited product testing and claim to have high levels of THC in their products.[49] This could result in improper dosing and adverse effects. Legal packages must include proper documentation for cultivation and packaged-on dates.[50] Moreover, LPs must practice recall scenarios and retain the records of recalls for 25 years.[51] There are also strict regulations pertaining to the production and sales of cannabis products, along with proper disposal procedures.[52]

During the first three years of legalization, however, it appeared that most cannabis consumed in Canada was not coming from the LPs but from unregulated sources.[53] Prior to the second-wave of legalization, in October 2019, the thriving illicit cannabis market was selling cannabis products (e.g., edibles and vape cartridges) that were not yet available from regulated sources and had THC contents that were well above the proposed legal limits.[54] Furthermore, it is unknown if illicit products actually contain the level of THC mentioned on the label.[55] In Canada, there are also strict requirements for childproof and plain packaging, making it less attractive to minors. Meanwhile, illicit cannabis companies have attractive (usually non-childproof) packaging with various banned flavours or forms of product.[56] The LPs were also not permitted to advertise their products. However, illicit cannabis ads were commonplace on various social media sites.[57] Not only did the illicit market have a wide range of products but they were also undercutting the price of cannabis. While legal cannabis sold for $10.30/g in the fourth quarter of 2019, illicit cannabis sold for on average $5.73/g.[58] This could nudge people to continue to purchase illicit cannabis based on the price alone. To adjust for this, the price for legal cannabis has since dropped, which may explain why half of the cannabis purchased in 2020 was from a legal source.[59]

Consumer Protection: Safe Supply

The legalization of cannabis came in part from consumer demand for a safer alternative to illicit cannabis, followed by greater social acceptance of its use.[60] The multitude of cannabis products available (e.g., flower, topical, edible, concentrates) allows customers to purchase a product that suits their needs. In addition, customers may order cannabis through a legal online retailer (where applicable), offering anonymity from members of the community.[61] Alternatively, customers could go to a physical store where they can pay cash (less traceable) and can ask questions about cannabis products.[62]

Although there are strengths associated with legal cannabis (both as a product and policy), there are some weaknesses that should be addressed. Consumer trust could be one example, where cannabis consumers may initially trust their original, quasi-legal or illicit source over novel legally regulated cannabis. Likewise, legal cannabis might not be available in the dosage desired, the consumer may believe that their current source is superior to legal sources, and/or they may not have experienced any issues with their original source. Furthermore, the customer might be wary of legal cannabis as there has been a growing number of recalls for cannabis products, ranging from inaccurate measurements of THC to the presence of mould on edible products.[63] In contrast, there are no recalls in the unregulated cannabis market—where products could have more contaminants and inaccurate (if any) labelling.[64] There is also a legal purchasing limit of 30 g of cannabis flower from licensed stores, which might not be enough for people who have difficulty accessing a cannabis store. This includes medical patients who may require more of a particular product and/or those in communities with no cannabis stores. However, in 2019, 45% of Canadians lived within 10 km of a regulated cannabis store.[65] In contrast to the purchasing limits of legal cannabis, there is no advertised purchasing limit for at-home use of alcohol and tobacco products in Canada. Perhaps limiting the amount of alcohol and tobacco that could be purchased at a given time could be adopted as a public health measure, or, alternatively, simply abolish the purchasing limit for cannabis.

Upon legalization in 2018, illicit sales were still on the rise because illicit websites offered a wide array of products at lower prices and with no purchasing limit. These illicit cannabis products had varying levels of QCQA (e.g., contaminant and potency testing) and no government approval or oversight.[66] Edible products were also well above the maximum 10 mg/dose. Moreover, there were wholesale prices exceeding the 30 g limit set by the government, and these sites typically have loyalty reward programs. Even with new classes of cannabis lawfully available, the economic (price and dose) incentive to purchase from an illicit seller remains alluring.

Dosing and Bio-Equivalency

With the array of cannabis products available, it would be useful to be able to compare the psychoactive effects among the various products available to customers. As at the time of writing, there is no defined dose of cannabis and no equivalency for what a dose means among products.[67] However, the National Institute on Drug Abuse has set 5 mg as a standard dose of cannabis for research.[68] One approach is to create a bio-equivalency table among products, first to describe the onset times and, second, to state an equivalent dose (at a set concentration) of flower cannabis. Bio-equivalency is defined as two or more substances having the same concentration in the body over time.[69] Any deviation between these products is a change in bio-equivalency. For example, the concentration of THC in the body is different whether the cannabis is an edible product or was inhaled.[70]

Cannabis is typically inhaled, reducing the onset time of cannabis's psychoactivity and providing users an opportunity to self-titrate an appropriate dose. Although flower is the most popular type of cannabis purchased,[71] there are still harmful compounds present in cannabis smoke (e.g., pyrolytic [carcinogenic] compounds) that are absent in vaporized cannabis.[72] In contrast, other researchers demonstrate that there is no temporal link between cannabis smoke and cancer.[73] Similar to tobacco, the temporal link between smoking and lung cancer might take a few decades to hash out. Moreover, there have been anti-smoking campaigns aimed at reducing tobacco/cigarette use and motions for a smoke-free Canada[74]—and this movement would likely transfer to smoked cannabis. Although edible cannabis, it should be noted, is not without consequence. The psychoactive effects after consuming edible cannabis (via the digestive tract) are delayed and may result in adverse effects from over consumption.[75] For example, the onset of inhaled cannabis is 5 minutes, peaking at 15–20 minutes, and lasting 2–3 hours, while the onset of edible cannabis is 30–90 minutes, peaking at 2–3 hours, and lasting 4–12 hours.[76] Therefore, it is more challenging to dose edible cannabis due to its delayed effects, whereas inhaling cannabis is easier to dose but comes at a potential risk of lung injury.

In order to reduce harm, setting a dose for cannabis could help consumers expect similar effects across products. For example, if someone occasionally smokes flower cannabis containing 200 mg/g THC, then what would be an equivalent dose of edibles to achieve the same level of intoxication without adverse effects? The maximum level of THC in an edible is 10 mg THC per package, so would the consumer aim for 7.5 mg THC? How does flower compare with vape cartridges or other forms of concentrates? If a company claims their vape pen administers 2.5 mg from the vape cartridge on every inhalation,[77] then how does this compare to a 0.5 g joint with 100 mg THC? It is not surprising to know that there is little published research comparing the pharmacology of various cannabis products to one another (vaporized concentrates, smoked flower/concentrates, edibles, oils, topicals, toothpaste, suppositories, etc.). Yet, these products remain available to both recreational and medical consumers, with varying levels of guidance.

In contrast to cannabis, alcohol has a defined dose (in Canada) set at 17.05 mL of pure alcohol (i.e., ethanol), the equivalent found in 341 mL of beer at 5%, 142 mL of wine at 12%, and 43 mL of spirits at 40%. This way consumers can assess an equivalent dose and anticipate a similar effect among drinks.[78] The standard also helps set the social reference pricing for alcohol (the price below which alcohol cannot be sold to consumers), where higher-potency alcohol beverages are taxed at a higher rate.[79] Taxing higher-potency cannabis flower and concentrates could reduce risk of adverse effects, although this would best be monitored to ensure consumers are not transitioning back to unregulated markets.[80]

Defining a standard dose of cannabis could be useful as a public health approach and mitigate adverse reactions.[81] Yet the main advice given by legal cannabis retailers, along with some scholars and medical professionals, is to "start low and go slow"—without any defined standard dose.[82] Do you consume a tenth of a 10 mg edible or one puff (2.5 mg) from a vape pen at 85% THC, over 1 hour versus 4 hours versus 24? What about oils, sprays, or topicals? In theory, there should have been evidence-based guidelines for the appropriate dosing for medical patients since the approval of cannabis for medicinal use in 2001. Thus far, the general advice from Health Canada's guide for medical-cannabis use for medical practitioners is to advise patients to use the lowest possible dose to achieve a therapeutic effect.[83] The 2018 guidance from Health Canada comes with a disclaimer indicating that there is no established standard dose for medical cannabis because every individual reacts differently to cannabis. The complexity of cannabis (e.g., percentage of THC/CBD, THC:CBD, batch variability), user experience with cannabis, and individual differences in their endocannabinoid system, makes it exceedingly difficult to provide an accurate population-wide recommended dose of cannabis.[84] There have been attempts to accurately dose cannabis products in the pharmaceutical industry through products such as Sativex[85] and Epidiolex.[86] Setting a dose of cannabis across products is a critical knowledge gap that should be addressed in partnership with the government, industry, and consumers.

The labels of flower cannabis originally contained only the percent dry weight of THC and CBD on the label.[87] Moreover, it must also contain the total amount of THC and CBD; that is, 0.877 x [THCA] + [THC] = total THC, and 0.877 x [CBDA] + [CBD] = total CBD. Once the new products (e.g., edibles, topicals) were regulated in 2019, flower cannabis packaging then had to include the milligrams per gram of THC and CBD, and could also contain the percentage of THC and CBD. At first glance, this might be confusing to customers as a strain with 20% THC might be sold as 200 mg/g.[88] Moreover, this has apparently led to the recall of various products as the percent THC was incorrectly labelled as 20.5 mg/g—thus underestimating the potency by a factor of 10 (e.g., 20.5 mg/g labelled but it is actually 205 mg/g).[89] When changes like this happen, it is important to inform consumers and explain the rationale for changing the labels. The labelling change for flower cannabis to mg/g may actually act as the first step toward bio-equivalency among products, though the pharmacology among products is still unknown.

Bio-equivalency starts in the product. Putting together a simple table comparing the average amount of THC per class of product is a good first step, along with the estimated onset time and duration of psychoactive effects. Researchers might then give a survey to customers when they purchase cannabis. With such data, researchers could formulate what experiments should be conducted to accurately assess the bio-equivalency of cannabis products. A comparative infographic could thus be created toward informing customers of the duration and intensity of a given cannabis product. Taken a step further, combining product information with user preferences would unequivocally enhance the consumer experience.[90]

Variability of THC in Cannabis Products

Plants can greatly vary in the quantity of phytochemicals produced due to environmental, genetics, or epigenetic conditions.[91] Cannabis is no exception as cannabinoid levels can be altered given various methods of cultivation and processing.[92]

Strain Credibility

The term "strain" is typically used to describe microorganisms, not plants.[93] Regardless, strains are the standard protocol when categorizing cannabis—without any consensus among growers on what defines a strain. If there was a lineage for a particular strain, then there might be some credibility in the pedigree of such strains. However, written accounts of breeding lineages are rare due to the risks of having these records confiscated by law enforcement or competing growers.[94]

Traditionally, cannabis has been classified into sativa and indica types, though recent research suggests that there is no statistical difference in cannabinoid content between these categories of cannabis.[95] Terpenes are chemicals responsible for the odour of cannabis and might be a better predictor on how to categorize cannabis.

Elzinga and colleagues analyzed terpene profiles of various cannabis strains and found that OG strains tend to be different from Kush
strains.[96] Although, the names OG and Kush could mean something
different based on where and how they were grown.

Even under a legal model of cannabis regulation, there is no
penalty for selling an incorrectly labelled strain in Canada. In the
Netherlands, THC content from the same strain varied greatly both
between and within cannabis storefronts.[97] This could lead to consumer confusion as they may be expecting certain psychoactive
effects from a particular strain, but if they receive a different strain
with the same strain name, other effects might occur. In Canada,
there has only been one voluntary recall due to the improper labelling
of strain names, although this is likely not an isolated occurrence.[98]

One solution for the improper labelling of strains could be to
create cultivars. Cultivars are cultivated varieties of plants that have
consistent traits among individuals and across generations.[99] This
cultivar approach is not impossible for high-THC cannabis as there
is a list of approved cultivars for hemp (i.e., low-THC cannabis).[100]
However, there must be an established definition for each of the
high-THC cultivars in question and this could be challenging as
there are differences among the definition (or lineage) for certain
strains of cannabis.[101]

Cultivation and Processing

Some of the variability within strains might be partially explained
by the way the cannabis flower has been cultivated and processed.[102]
In attempts to recreate an illicit cannabis grow operation, Knight and
colleagues found there to be inconsistency in the potency of cannabis
grown under the same conditions from the same clonal mother.[103]
Cloning cannabis is a process to ensure greater consistency among
plants—a stem from an unmatured female cannabis plant is cut and
propagated to maturity.[104] Even with clonal propagation, it is likely
that the difference in production practices may explain why variability exists. Moreover, post-production processing (e.g., trimming,
drying, and curing flower) could influence the levels of THC in the
final product.[105]

The lack of a variability range results in the LPs (licensed producers) announcing voluntary recalls on improperly analyzed cannabis flower and include the corrected values of THC.[106] This can be
costly for LPs to issue the recall as it results in lost time, revenue, and

credibility. Moreover, if there is no penalty for improperly labelled levels of THC in flower cannabis, then why would an LP issue a recall? Less than three years into legal cannabis there have been 15 recalls for inaccurate THC analysis.[107] Currently, there is no limit on THC variability within flower cannabis, though it has been proposed that a 20% variability limit is reasonable.[108]

Instead of focusing on the variability within the strain, another approach would be to focus on the chemistry and categorize the cannabis post-harvest and processing.[109] Categories must be created and named, along with a set variability range for each of the plant compounds. Using strain names may help the transition toward this approach so as to avoid consumer confusion. If enough LPs accept the definition and thresholds for groups of cannabis, then the rates of variability would be reduced as the chemical profile will define the category rather than the category being defined by its alleged lineage.

Machine learning, coupled with the chemical analysis, could streamline the categories of cannabis, where the computer model can quickly categorize cannabis based on levels of cannabinoids (even beyond THC and CBD) and terpenes for cannabis flower.[110] Physical appearance (e.g., size, density, colour of the flower) could also be included in the computer model for these varieties. Once the chemical analysis for the particular plant is complete, then it could be binned into a particular chemical variety. This would make for an easier transition from strain to cultivar and would reduce variability within the strains as the cannabis industry moves toward a more consistent product. Some of these ideas have already been patented and utilize user data along with objective chemical analysis to arrange products on user preference.[111] Creating a network combining user-guided structured decision making and chemical analysis could improve user/product outcomes and mitigate adverse effects with over-consumption, thus reducing harm.

Consumer Consideration

The new classes of cannabis products typically use an extract or concentrate of cannabis, and producers mix this extract or concentrate into their own product (e.g., edibles, topicals, oral sprays). Though the chemistry of these extracts and concentrates can be accurately measured, there are additional challenges to adding these extracts to another product, especially if they are produced at non-licensed facilities (such as at home).

If the home cook is using homegrown cannabis flower to create their product, then they would likely be uncertain of the quantity of THC per gram of cannabis. The unknown potency of cannabis is then decarboxylated (making the cannabinoids more bioactive), adding more uncertainty with the level of decarboxylation (e.g., partially or fully decarboxylated). If heated too long, the THC might be vaporized off of the cannabis and, therefore, would not be present in the final product.[112] The bioactive cannabinoids are typically extracted using a carrier oil (e.g., medium-chain triglyceride oil or olive oil) or high-potency alcohol, though the level of THC in the liquid would be unknown. The oil is added to a product and is sometimes baked. When making candy edibles, the concentrate is dissolved in carrier liquid (e.g., oil or melted candy) and then is applied to candy. Uneven spraying or mixing of the cannabis concentrate could produce hotspots and lead to inaccurate dosing. Moreover, when calculating THC in confections, there is a matrix of carbohydrates, fats, and proteins that could interfere with the pharmacology of the cannabinoids. Furthermore, replicating the exact process and achieving the same results every time is very unlikely due to the variability introduced in every step of manufacturing these types of products. All this variability could result in the over consumption of an edible product due to inaccurate dosing.

There are multiple areas where sources of error could arise in the production of homemade cannabis products. Therefore, the established protocols from LPs coupled with the upper limits of THC set at 10 mg/discrete unit are safeguards against over/accidental consumption of cannabis products.[113] Moreover, precise extraction protocols and testing the cannabis extract or concentrate will improve accuracy in the final product and ensure complete decarboxylation without vaporization (i.e., cannabinoids are not vaporized off). There is improved consistency between products and batches when produced at the industrial level used by most LPs (e.g., using industrial mixers to form a homogenous mixture between samples). Finally, there is less variability due to the well-documented source and chemistry of the cannabis product.

Chemical Analysis

Legally produced cannabis products must be tested for THC potency but initially there was no validated method for quantifying THC. The LP could create and validate their own method for these tests in an analytical testing facility. Alternatively, the LPs could send their product to a testing facility. This means that the variability in the amount of THC in a particular product (or flower) could vary among testing facilities if they have different analytical methodology.[114] This could lead to biases as an LP could use multiple analytical techniques (post-production) in order to achieve the "correct" level of THC to fit a given product. Alternatively, the LP could send their product to various third-party testing facilities and select the results that best suit their product, considering that the testing facilities use different analytical techniques to test for THC.[115] However, if there were validated testing methodologies from a reputable source that could be used industry wide, then the variability of THC between labs would likely decrease.

Third-party testing facilities, with industry-wide, validated testing protocols, should reduce the cost and bias of testing cannabis products. The testing facility could also accept cannabis from home growers who want to test their product for levels of cannabinoids, terpenes, and contaminants. This would greatly reduce the harm toward the cannabis user as it provides an objective chemical overview of the product's contents. However, this approach would only work if there were approved and validated methods from a governing body that can ensure inter-lab consistency. Therefore, testing cannabis via independent third-party testing facilities that use validated methods, which are approved by a governing body would reduce biases among LPs. This approach is already used in the supplement industry and is promising to reduce the number of tainted supplements.[116]

Cannabis products, excluding flower, must fall within a range of THC, which changes with potency of the product, or else the product cannot be sold.[117] Cannabis flower, however, has no variability threshold. This means that flower cannabis labelled at 10% THC could be between 0% and 30% THC. A 20% variability threshold, as proposed by the United States Pharmacopeia, which sets standards for medicines and supplements, means that 10% THC cannabis flower could range from 8% to 12% THC.[118] A governing body could also set a threshold on the THC variability in flower cannabis. The lack of a threshold has some LPs issuing recalls for products due to improper analysis and labelling of a product. For example, one product had the correct level of THC but mislabelled CBD at 0.4% when the corrected value is <0.07%.[119] It is unlikely that this minute difference in CBD will elicit a different psychoactive experience. In contrast, there was another recall where the labelled THC was 0.3%, while the actual amount was 20.66%.[120] This could be harmful for the naive user who is seeking a low-THC cannabis product.

How Does Inaccurate Analysis Impact Taxation?

Some food and beverages have compositional standards outlined in the Canadian Food and Drugs Act.[121] This includes various types of alcohol (e.g., beer, wine, vodka). Alcoholic beverages that do not have a compositional standard are considered unstandardized and follow a different set of labelling requirements. Adopting and applying the compositional standard approach to the categories of cannabis would permit a legal definition for cannabis products. Once these standardized products are established, then subsequent taxation for these products could be equivalent based on their level of THC (e.g., 2 mg, 5 mg, or 10 mg THC per dose) and, perhaps, route of administration (smoked versus edible). Alternatively, the government could tax all products the same or set prices, which is similar to nicotine-based vaping liquid, whereby the price of a product is similar regardless of the amount of nicotine present. However, customers may select a higher-potency product considering it costs the same as a lower-potency one.

Currently, the taxation for all cannabis products (except flower) in Canada are based on the amount of THC (in mg) found in the product.[122] If the THC analysis overestimates the actual amount of THC in the product, then the LP will pay more taxes. However, if the THC analysis underestimates the level of THC, then the LP will pay lower taxes. One solution is to set the tax based on the category and mass of product being sold. This is already the case for flower cannabis, where taxation is based on the mass of the flower instead of the quantity of THC.[123] Cannabis products (excluding flower) tend to contain other ingredients, such as carrier oils, sugars, etc. Therefore, setting taxes based on the weight of a product would likely shift the market to manufacture products that weigh less and have proportionally more THC. Simply taxing based on the potency of the product could help favour less-potent products that would (in theory) result in fewer adverse effects—similar to the social reference pricing for alcohol.[124] This would be a challenging task if there is no bio-equivalency or knowledge of the pharmacology of various cannabis products.

Purchasing Limits

The purchasing limits for cannabis products is just as confusing as cannabis taxation. The government set the public possession and purchasing limit at 30 g dried cannabis flower. However, since there are more products than just flower, the government also had to devise an equivalency based on the weight of the product—not based on the total THC of the product (see table 7.1). It would be sensible to follow the logic used for taxing cannabis, whereby taxation is based on the amount of THC in the product.

TABLE 7.1. Possession Limits for Products that Contain Cannabis[*]

Class of Cannabis	Equivalent to 1g dried cannabis	Possession limit
Dried cannabis	1 g	30 g
Fresh cannabis	5 g	150 g
Solids containing cannabis	15 g	450 g
Non-solids containing cannabis	70 g	2100 g
Cannabis concentrate	0.25 g	7.5 g
Cannabis plant seed	1	30 seeds

* See *Cannabis Act*, supra note 25.

Source: Cannabis Act 2018, Schedule 3 subsection 2(4).

The current regulations for possession and purchasing limits need some rehashing. For example, if cannabis flower contains 200 mg/g THC, then the 30 g limit would contain 6,000 mg THC per 30 g flower. The greatest difference on purchasing limits for cannabis products is between bath bombs (solids containing cannabis) and oral sprays (non-solid containing cannabis). If a bath bomb contains 140 mg THC and weighs 150 g, then the legal purchasing limit is 3 units as this would be the "equivalent" of 30 g of dried cannabis (though it only contains 420 mg THC/3 units—not 6,000 mg/30 g THC). In theory, producers could reduce the final weight of their product, while keeping THC at a fixed amount, so as to facilitate a greater number of units sold per transaction. This strategy is apparent when it comes to oral sprays. For example, a 20 ml bottle of oral spray contains 500 mg THC/bottle and has a purchasing limit of 110 bottles. Therefore, the purchase would contain over 55,000 mg of THC, which is almost 10 times the limit of THC from 6,000 mg/30 g cannabis flower.

If the limits for possession and purchasing cannabis products were based on a set amount of THC (e.g., 6,000 mg THC), then this would eliminate the difference in the amount of THC being purchased at a single time between products. In contrast, there are no purchasing limits on tobacco or alcohol within Canada. If the cannabis purchase limit does not change, then this would be an excellent opportunity to advertise and set purchasing and possession limits of tobacco and alcohol products in Canada. [125]

Future Directions and Conclusions

Moving forward, all parties involved in the legal cannabis industry should consider the following. First, there should be a defined standard dose of cannabis and clearly defined bio-equivalency among products. Dosing cannabis should have been established 20 years ago, when cannabis was legalized for medical purposes. Second, categorizing the cannabis flower based on its chemistry would reduce the level of variability within types of cannabis as the flower would be categorized based on its phytochemical profile instead of its lineage (where lineages are unknown due to the prohibition of cannabis). The use of machine learning and user-preference data can help consumers select a product that is best for them, with a reduced likelihood of adverse effects. Homemade products can vary in level of THC, even if the cannabis is legally purchased. Therefore, LPs should highlight their QCQA protocols as a less harmful approach to various cannabis products.

Perhaps most importantly, there is no publicly available government validated cannabis testing methodology. This results in various analytical methods being used by various labs in order to test for levels of THC—resulting in variability among testing facilities. Verified third-party testing facilities could reduce bias among LPs. Furthermore, all cannabis products, except for flower, have variability limits in order to reduce harm. Cannabis flower should follow suit, with a variability limit at 20%. With no variability limit, customers are uncertain of the THC (and/or CBD) potency in their flower product with wide ranges of THC.

Finally, there should be a call for compositional standards for cannabis products, so consumers know that there is a legal definition of a given product. Either alter or abolish the purchase limits of cannabis products as the limits are not based on the amount of THC, rather they are based on the weight of the product. This could be adapted to limiting the amount of THC (in milligrams) purchased from each of the categories instead of the weight of the product (disregarding the amount of THC).

In conclusion, *Cannabis sativa* is a notorious plant, which has a unique and rich history with humans. Canada legalized the recreational use of cannabis in 2018, providing safer alternatives with goals to reduce proceeds to organized crime, reduce use among minors, and provide a safer supply of cannabis to Canadians. The two-stage approach to legalization had some benefits, such as teasing apart the effects of permitting various cannabis products, and some drawbacks, such as ephemeral illicit cannabis retailers filling the void for novel products and lower prices. The illicit cannabis products likely do not follow the strict QCQA product-testing protocols that LPs follow and could be harmful to the consumer. Legal cannabis, however, has seen online security breaches and recalls on products, which may nudge consumers to illicit market. The wide array of cannabis products available can have various consequences, making it challenging to determine a standard dose for each type. Canada, being the first G7 country to legalize cannabis, can be a leader in cannabis policy and cannabis science by addressing these and other concerns. This is Canada on cannabis.

References

Legislation

Cannabis Act, SC 2018, c 16.
Cannabis Regulations, SOR/2018-144.
Food And Drugs Act, RSC 1985, c F-27.
Food and Drugs Regulation, CRC, c 870.

Publications

Alchin, David R, "'Vaping Psychosis': Ultra-Acute Onset of Severe, Persisting and Unusual Psychotic Symptoms Following First-Time Cannabis Vaping in a Previously Well Individual" (2020) 54:8 Australian & New Zealand J Psychiatry 848.

Bell, Cameron et al, "Butane Hash Oil Burns Associated with Marijuana Liberalization in Colorado" (2015) 11:4 J Medical Toxicology 422.

Boira, Herminio & Antonio Blanquer, "Environmental Factors Affecting Chemical Variability of Essential Oils in *Thymus piperella* L" (1998) 26:8 Biochemical Systematics & Ecology 811.

CADTH, "What Are Bioavailability and Bioequivalence?" (2012), online: www.cadth.ca/sites/default/files/pdf/What_Are_Bioavailability_and_ Bioequivalence_e.pdf

Campbell, Lesley G, Steve GU Naraine & Jaimie Dusfresne, "Phenotypic Plasticity Influences the Success of Clonal Propagation in Industrial Pharmaceutical Cannabis Sativa" (2019) 14:3 PloS one e0213434.

Canada Revenue Agency, *EDN55 Calculation of Cannabis Duty and Additional Cannabis Duty On Cannabis Products* (Ottawa: Canada Revenue Agency, September 2018), online: www.canada.ca/en/revenue-agency/services/ forms-publications/publications/edn55/calculation-cannabis-duty- additional-cannabis-duty-cannabis-products.html.

——, *EDN60 Calculation Of Cannabis Duty And Additional Cannabis Duty On Cannabis Oil, Edible Cannabis, Cannabis Extracts And Cannabis Topicals* (Ottawa: Canada Revenue Agency, April 2019), online: www.canada. ca/en/revenue-agency/services/forms-publications/publications/edn60/ calculation-cannabis-duty-additional-cannabis-duty-cannabis-oil- cannabis-edibles-extracts-topicals.html.

Canadian Centre on Substance Use and Addiction, "Social Reference Pricing for Alcohol FAQs" (2017), online: www.ccsa.ca/social-reference-pricing- alcohol-faqs.

Childs, Emma, Joseph A Lutz & Harriet de Wit, "Dose-Related Effects of Delta- 9-THC on Emotional Responses to Acute Psychosocial Stress" (2017) 177 Drug & Alcohol Dependence 136.

Citti, Cinzia et al, "Pharmaceutical and Biomedical Analysis of Cannabinoids: A Critical Review" (2018) 147 J Pharmaceutical & Biomedical Analysis 565.

Correa, Ginni, "Advertising Illicit Marijuana on Social Media" (4 February 2020), online: www.addictioncenter.com/community/advertising-marijuana- social-media.

Cox, Chelsea, "The Canadian Cannabis Act Legalizes and Regulates Recreational Cannabis Use in 2018" (2018) 122:3 Health Policy 205.

de la Fuente, Alethia et al, "Relationship Among Subjective Responses, Flavor, and Chemical Composition Across More than 800 Commercial Cannabis Varieties" (2020) 2:1 J Cannabis Research 1.

Degenhardt, F, F Stehle & O Kayser, "The Biosynthesis of Cannabinoids" in Victor R Preedy, ed, *Handbook of Cannabis and Related Pathologies* (Cambridge, MA: Academic Press, 2017) 13.

Di Marzo Vincenzo, "Targeting the Endocannabinoid System: To Enhance or Reduce?" (2008) 7:5 Nature Reviews Drug Discovery 438.

Dosist, "Dosist" (last visited 26 July 2022), online: dosist.com/dose-pens.

Duff, Cameron et al, "A Canadian Perspective on Cannabis Normalization Among Adults" (2012) 20:4 Addiction Research & Theory 271.

Eichner, Amy K et al, "Essential Features of Third-Party Certification Programs for Dietary Supplements: A Consensus Statement" (2019) 18:5 Current Sports Medicine Reports 178.

ElSohly, Mahmoud A et al, "Changes in Cannabis Potency Over the Last 2 Decades (1995–2014): Analysis of Current Data in the United States" (2016) 79:7 Biological Psychiatry 613.

Elzinga, Sytze et al, "Cannabinoids and Terpenes as Chemotaxonomic Markers in Cannabis" (2015) 3:4 Natural Products Chemistry & Research 181.

Freeman, Daniel et al, "How Cannabis Causes Paranoia: Using the Intravenous Administration of Δ 9-Tetrahydrocannabinol (THC) to Identify Key Cognitive Mechanisms Leading to Paranoia" (2015) 41:2 Schizophrenia Bull 391.

Freeman, Tom P & Valentina Lorenzetti, "'Standard THC Units': A Proposal to Standardize Dose Across All Cannabis Products and Methods of Administration" (2020) 115:7 Addiction 1207.

Gieringer, Dale, Joseph St. Laurent & Scott Goodrich, "Cannabis Vaporizer Combines Efficient Delivery of THC with Effective Suppression of Pyrolytic Compounds" (2004) 4:1 J Cannabis Therapeutics 7.

Glasser, Allison M et al, "Overview of Electronic Nicotine Delivery Systems: A Systematic Review" (2017) 52:2 American J Preventive Medicine e33.

Got Leaf, "Online Cannabis Retailers in Canada" (last visited 26 July 2022), online: gotleaf.ca/online-dispensaries/.

Government of Canada, "Healthy Canadians: Recalls & Alerts: Search: 'Cannabis,'" (last visited 26 July 2022), online: recalls-rappels.canada.ca/en/search/site?search_api_fulltext="cannabis".

Green, Bob, David Kavanagh & Ross Young, "Being Stoned: A Review of Self-Reported Cannabis Effects" (2003) 22:4 Drug & Alcohol Rev 453.

Hammond, David & Samantha Goodman, "Knowledge of Tetrahydro-cannabinol and Cannabidiol Levels Among Cannabis Consumers in the United States and Canada" (2020) 7:3 Cannabis and Cannabinoid Research 345.

Hammond, David, "Communicating THC Levels and 'Dose' to Consumers: Implications for Product Labelling and Packaging of Cannabis Products in Regulated Markets" (2021) 91 Intl J Drug Policy 102509.

Hanuš, Lumír Ondřej et al, "Phytocannabinoids: A Unified Critical Inventory" 33:12 Natural Product Reports 1357.

Hazekamp, Arno & JT Fischedick, "Cannabis-From Cultivar to Chemovar" (2012) 4:7-8 Drug Testing & Analysis 660.

Hazekamp, Arno, Katerina Tejkalová & Stelios Papadimitriou, "Cannabis: From Cultivar to Chemovar II — A Metabolomics Approach to Cannabis Classification" (2016) 1:1 Cannabis and Cannabinoid Research 202.

Health Canada, Information for Health Care Professionals: Cannabis (Marihuana, Marijuana) and the Cannabinoids (Ottawa: Health Canada, October 2018), online : www.canada.ca/content/dam/hc-sc/documents/services/drugs-medication/cannabis/information-medical-practitioners/information-health-care-professionals-cannabis-cannabinoids-eng.pdf.

———, "Recalls and Safety Alerts: Tweed Inc. Recalls One Lot of LBS Sunset (Indica) Dried Cannabis," (7 March 2019), online: healthycanadians.gc.ca/recall-alert-rappel-avis/hc-sc/2019/69256r-eng.php.

———, "Recalls and Safety Alerts: Aphria Inc. Recalls One Lot of Good Supply Royal Highness Dried Cannabis," (29 October 2019), online: www.healthycanadians.gc.ca/recall-alert-rappel-avis/hc-sc/2019/71407r-eng.php.

———, "Recalls and Safety Alerts: Medical Cannabis by Shoppers Drug Mart Inc. Recalls One Lot of WeedMD's Pedro's Sweet Sativa Dried Cannabis," (20 November 2020), online: healthycanadians.gc.ca/recall-alert-rappel-avis/hc-sc/2020/74363r-eng.php [Recall, Nov 2020].

———, *Canadian Cannabis Survey 2020: Summary* (Ottawa: Health Canada, 21 December 2020), online: www.canada.ca/en/health-canada/services/drugs-medication/cannabis/research-data/canadian-cannabis-survey-2020-summary.html.

———, "List of Approved Cultivars for the 2021 Growing Season: Industrial Hemp Varieties Approved for Commercial Production" (19 April 2021), online: www.canada.ca/en/health-canada/services/drugs-medication/cannabis/producing-selling-hemp/commercial-licence/list-approved-cultivars-cannabis-sativa.html.

Hecht, Peter, *Weed Land: Inside America's Marijuana Epicenter and How Pot Went Legit* (Berkley: University of California Press, 2014).

Hillig, Karl W & Paul G Mahlberg, "A Chemotaxonomic Analysis of Cannabinoid Variation in Cannabis (Cannabaceae)" (2004) 91:6 American J Botany 966.

International Society for Horticulture Science, *International Code of Nomenclature For Cultivated Plants*, 9th ed, (International Society for Horticultural Science, 2016), online: www.ishs.org/scripta-horticulturae/international-code-nomenclature-cultivated-plants-ninth-edition.

Jikomes, Nick & Michael Zoorob, "The Cannabinoid Content of Legal Cannabis in Washington State Varies Systematically Across Testing Facilities and Popular Consumer Products" (2018) 8:1 Scientific Reports 1.

Jikomes, Nickolas et al, "System for Selection of Regulated Products" U.S. Patent Application No. 16/228, 197.

Karschner, EL et al, "Subjective and Physiological Effects After Controlled Sativex and Oral THC Administration" (2011) 89:3 Clinical Pharmacology & Therapeutics 400.

Knight, Glenys et al, "The Results of an Experimental Indoor Hydroponic Cannabis Growing Study, Using the 'Screen of Green'(Scrog) Method — Yield, Tetrahydrocannabinol (THC) and DNA Analysis" (2010) 202:1-3 Forensic Science Intl 36.

Leweke, FM et al "Cannabidiol Enhances Anandamide Signaling and Alleviates Psychotic Symptoms of Schizophrenia" (2012) 2:3 Translational Psychiatry e94.

MacCallum, Caroline A & Ethan B Russo, "Practical Considerations in Medical Cannabis Administration and Dosing" (2018) 49 European J Internal Medicine 12.

Mahamad, Syed et al, "Availability, Retail Price and Potency of Legal and Illegal Cannabis in Canada After Recreational Cannabis Legalisation" (2020) 39:4 Drug & Alcohol Rev 337.

Marchitelli, Rosa, "Copycat Pot Edibles That Look Like Candy Are Poisoning Kids, Doctors Say," CBC News (25 January 2021), online: www.cbc.ca/news/canada/british-columbia/cannabis-gummies-poisonings-kids-illegal-sites-1.5879232.

Melamede, Robert, "Cannabis and Tobacco Smoke Are Not Equally Carcinogenic" (2005) 2:1 Harm Reduction J.

Pax Canada, "Dual Use Vaporizer" (last visited 26 July 2022), online: ca.pax.com/products/pax-3?variant=32024009408625.

Pertwee, Roger G, "Cannabinoid Pharmacology: The First 66 Years" (2006) 147:S1 British J Pharmacology S163.

Pusiak, Ryan JP, Chelsea Cox & Cory S Harris, "Growing Pains: An Overview of Cannabis Quality Control and Quality Assurance in Canada" (2021) 93 Intl J Drug Policy 103111.

Russo, Ethan B, "Taming THC: Potential Cannabis Synergy and Phytocannabinoid-Terpenoid Entourage Effects" (2011) 163:7 British J Pharmacology 1344.

———, "Beyond Cannabis: Plants and the Endocannabinoid System" (2016) 37:7 Trends in Pharmacological Sciences 594.

———, "The Case for the Entourage Effect and Conventional Breeding of Clinical Cannabis: No 'Strain,' No Gain" (2019) 9 Frontiers In Plant Science 1969.

Sarma, Nandakumara D et al, "Cannabis Inflorescence for Medical Purposes: USP Considerations for Quality Attributes" (2020) 83:4 J Natural Products 1334.

Savoie, Alexandra, "Cannabis Purchases, Privacy and the Canada—U.S. Border Background Paper" (16 April 2019), online: lop.parl.ca/sites/PublicWebsite/default/en_CA/ResearchPublications/201913E.

Sekar, Krithiga & Alison Pack, "Epidiolex as Adjunct Therapy for Treatment of Refractory Epilepsy: A Comprehensive Review with a Focus on Adverse Effects" (2019) 8 F1000 Research.

Small, Ernest, Cannabis: A Complete Guide (CRC Press, 2016).

Small, Ernest, HD Beckstead & Allan Chan, "The Evolution of Cannabinoid Phenotypes in Cannabis" (1975) 29 Economic Botany 219.

Smoke-Free, "Physicians for a Smoke-Free Canada" (last visited 26 July 2022), online: smoke-free.ca/.

Spindle, Tory R et al, "Acute Effects of Smoked and Vaporized Cannabis in Healthy Adults Who Infrequently Use Cannabis: A Crossover Trial" (2018) 1:7 JAMA Network Open e184841.

Statistics Canada, *The Retail Cannabis Market in Canada: A Portrait of the First Year* (Ottawa: Statistics Canada, 11 December 2019), online: www150.statcan.gc.ca/n1/pub/11-621-m/11-621-m2019005-eng.htm.

——, *The Daily, Stats Cannabis Data Availability: Crowdsourced Cannabis Prices, Fourth Quarter 2019*, (Ottawa: Statistics Canada, 23 January 2020), online: www150.statcan.gc.ca/n1/en/daily-quotidien/200123/dq200123c-eng.pdf?st=i4TzoSgZ.

——, *What Has Changed Since Cannabis Was Legalized* (Health Report), by Michelle Rotermann (Ottawa: Statistics Canada, 19 February 2020), online: www150.statcan.gc.ca/n1/en/pub/82-003-x/2020002/article/00002-eng.pdf?st=2WULQWne.

Taschwer, Magdalena, and Martin G. Schmid. "Determination of the Relative Percentage Distribution of THCA and Δ9-THC in Herbal Cannabis Seized in Austria–Impact of Different Storage Temperatures on Stability" 254 (2015) Forensic Science International 167-171.

University of Victoria: Canadian Institute for Substance Use Research, "Convert Your Drinks into Standard Drink Sizes" (last visited 26 July 2022), online: aodtool.cfar.uvic.ca/index-stddt.html.

Vandrey, Ryan et al, "Cannabinoid Dose and Label Accuracy in Edible Medical Cannabis Products" (2015) 313:24 JAMA 2491.

Vuong, Oriena, "Canada Post Data Breach Affected 4,500 Customers, OCS Says," *Global News* (7 November 2018), online: globalnews.ca/news/4639742/ocs-canada-post-hacked/.

Warf, Barney, "High Points: An Historical Geography of Cannabis" (2014) 104:4 Geographical Rev 414.

Zuardi, Antonio W et al "Inverted U-Shaped Dose-Response Curve of the Anxiolytic Effect of Cannabidiol During Public Speaking in Real Life" (2017) 8:3 Frontiers in Pharmacology 259.

Notes

1   See Barney Warf, "High Points: An Historical Geography of Cannabis" (2014) 104:4 Geographical Rev 414 [Small, "High Points"]; see also Ernest Small, "Evolution and Classification of Cannabis Sativa (Marijuana, Hemp) in Relation to Human Utilization" (2015) 81:3 Botanical Rev 189.

2   See Ethan B Russo, "Taming THC: Potential Cannabis Synergy and Phytocannabinoid-Terpenoid Entourage Effects" (2011) 163:7 British J Pharmacology 1344.

3   See F Degenhardt, F Stehle & O Kayser, "The Biosynthesis of Cannabinoids" in Victor R Preedy, ed, *Handbook of Cannabis and Related Pathologies* (Academic Press: 2017) 13.

4   See Daniel Freeman et al, "How Cannabis Causes Paranoia: Using the Intravenous Administration OfΔ 9-Tetrahydrocannabinol (THC) to Identify Key Cognitive Mechanisms Leading to Paranoia" (2015) 41:2 Schizophrenia Bull 391.

5   See FM Leweke et al "Cannabidiol Enhances Anandamide Signaling and Alleviates Psychotic Symptoms of Schizophrenia" (2012) 2:3 Translational Psychiatry e94.

6   See Antonio W Zuardi et al "Inverted U-Shaped Dose-Response Curve of the Anxiolytic Effect of Cannabidiol During Public Speaking in Real Life" (2017) 8 Frontiers in Pharmacology 259.

7   See Lumír Ondřej Hanuš et al, "Phytocannabinoids: A Unified Critical Inventory" 33:12 Natural Product Reports 1357.

8   See Caroline A MacCallum & Ethan B Russo, "Practical Considerations in Medical Cannabis Administration and Dosing" (2018) 49 European J Internal Medicine 12.

9   See Cinzia Citti et al, "Pharmaceutical and Biomedical Analysis of Cannabinoids: A Critical Review" (2018) 147 J Pharmaceutical & Biomedical Analysis 565.

10 See Emma Childs, Joseph A Lutz & Harriet de Wit, "Dose-Related Effects of Delta-9-THC On Emotional Responses to Acute Psychosocial Stress" (2017) 177 Drug &Alcohol Dependence 136; see also Bob Green, David Kavanagh & Ross Young, "Being Stoned: A Review of Self-Reported Cannabis Effects" (2003) 22:4 Drug & Alcohol Rev 453.

11 See Ethan B Russo, "Beyond Cannabis: Plants and the Endocannabinoid System" (2016) 37:7 Trends in Pharmacological Sciences 594.

12 See Roger G Pertwee, "Cannabinoid Pharmacology: The First 66 Years" (2006) 147:S1 British J Pharmacology S163; see also Vincenzo Di Marzo, "Targeting the Endocannabinoid System: To Enhance or Reduce?" (2008) 7:5 Nature Reviews Drug Discovery 438.

13 See Ernest Small, *Cannabis: A Complete Guide* (CRC Press: 2016).

14 *Ibid* at 314.

15 See Small, "High Points," *supra* note 1.

16 See Ernest Small, HD Beckstead & Allan Chan, "The Evolution of Cannabinoid Phenotypes in Cannabis" (1975) 29 Economic Botany 219 [Small, "Evolution"].

17 See Sytze Elzinga et al, "Cannabinoids and Terpenes as Chemotaxonomic Markers in Cannabis" (2015) 3:4 Natural Products Chemistry & Research 181.

18 See Small, "Evolution," *supra* note 16; see also Karl W Hillig & Paul G Mahlberg, "A Chemotaxonomic Analysis of Cannabinoid Variation in Cannabis (Cannabaceae)" (2004) 91:6 American J Botany 966. Note: Hillig uses the term chemotype (chemical type), while Small used the term phenotype. To avoid confusion between terms I use the word type to describe these three categories.

19 See Mahmoud A ElSohly et al, "Changes in Cannabis Potency Over the Last 2 Decades (1995–2014): Analysis of Current Data in the United States" (2016) 79:7 Biological Psychiatry 613.

20 See Small, "Evolution," *supra* note 16.

21 See Nick Jikomes & Michael Zoorob, "The Cannabinoid Content of Legal Cannabis in Washington State Varies Systematically Across Testing Facilities and Popular Consumer Products" (2018) 8:1 Scientific Reports 1 [Jikomes, "Cannabinoid"].

22 See Glenys Knight et al, "The Results of an Experimental Indoor Hydroponic Cannabis Growing Study, Using the 'Screen of Green' (SCROG) Method Yield, Tetrahydrocannabinol (THC) and DNA Analysis" (2010) 202:1-3 Forensic Science Intl 36.

23 *Ibid.*

24 David Hammond & Samantha Goodman, "Knowledge of Tetrahydrocannabinol and Cannabidiol Levels Among Cannabis Consumers in the United States and Canada" (2020) 7:3 Cannabis and Cannabinoid Research 345.

25   See *Cannabis Act*, SC 2018, c 16.

26   See Government of Canada, "Healthy Canadians: Recalls & Alerts: Search: 'Cannabis,'" (last visited 26 July 2022), online: recalls-rappels.canada.ca/en/search/site?search_api_fulltext="cannabis" [Government of Canada, "Healthy Canadians: Recalls"].

27   See Oriena Vuong, "Canada Post Data Breach Affected 4,500 Customers, OCS Says," *Global News* (7 November 2018), online: globalnews.ca/news/4639742/ocs-canada-post-hacked/.

28   See Chelsea Cox, "The Canadian Cannabis Act Legalizes and Regulates Recreational Cannabis Use in 2018" (2018) 122:3 Health Policy 205.

29   See *Cannabis Act, supra* note 25.

30   SOR/2018-144 [*Cannabis Regulation*].

31   See Jikomes, "Cannabinoid," *supra* note 21.

32   See *Cannabis Regulation, supra* note 30.

33   See Ryan JP Pusiak, Chelsea Cox & Cory S Harris, "Growing Pains: An Overview of Cannabis Quality Control and Quality Assurance in Canada" (2021) 93 Intl J Drug Policy 103111.

34   *Ibid;* see also Ryan Vandrey et al, "Cannabinoid Dose and Label Accuracy in Edible Medical Cannabis Products" (2015) 313:24 JAMA 2491.

35   See *Cannabis Regulation, supra* note 30; see also Pusiak, *supra* note 33.

36   See David Hammond, "Communicating THC Levels and 'Dose' to Consumers: Implications for Product Labelling and Packaging of Cannabis Products in Regulated Markets" (2021) 91 Intl J Drug Policy 102509.

37   See *Cannabis Regulation, supra* note 30; see also Pusiak, *supra* note 33.

38   See *Cannabis Act, supra* note 25.

39   See Alexandra Savoie, "Cannabis Purchases, Privacy and the Canada—U.S. Border Background Paper" (16 April 2019), online: lop.parl.ca/sites/PublicWebsite/default/en_CA/ResearchPublications/201913E.

40   See Vuong, *supra* note 27.

41   See David R Alchin, "'Vaping Psychosis': Ultra-Acute Onset of Severe, Persisting and Unusual Psychotic Symptoms Following First-Time Cannabis Vaping in a Previously Well Individual" (2020) 54:8 Australian & New Zealand J Psychiatry 848.

42   Cameron Bell et al, "Butane Hash Oil Burns Associated with Marijuana Liberalization in Colorado" (2015) 11:4 J Medical Toxicology 422; see also Ottawa Police, "Ongoing Police and Fire Operation On Renaud Road" (25 March 2021), online: www.ottawapolice.ca/Modules/News/index.aspx?page=2&newsId=7d00f83d-982b-4ff2-87ab-c3977be6a53e.

43   See Allison M Glasser et al, "Overview of Electronic Nicotine Delivery Systems: A Systematic Review" (2017) 52:2 American J Preventive Medicine e33.

44   See Dale Gieringer, Joseph St. Laurent & Scott Goodrich, "Cannabis Vaporizer Combines Efficient Delivery of THC with Effective Suppression of Pyrolytic Compounds" (2004) 4:1 J Cannabis Therapeutics 7.

45   See Tory R Spindle et al, "Acute Effects of Smoked and Vaporized Cannabis in Healthy Adults Who Infrequently Use Cannabis: A Crossover Trial" (2018) 1:7 JAMA Network Open e184841.

46   See Alchin, *supra* note 41.

47   See Pax, "Dual Use Vaporizer" (last visited 26 July 2022), online: ca.pax.com/products/pax-3?variant=32024009408625.

48   See *Cannabis Regulations, supra* note 30.

49   See Syed Mahamad et al, "Availability, Retail Price and Potency of Legal and Illegal Cannabis in Canada After Recreational Cannabis Legalisation" (2020) 39:4 Drug & Alcohol Rev 337 [Mahamad, "Retail"]; see also Vandrey, *supra* note 34.

50   See *Cannabis Regulations, supra* note 30.

51   *Ibid.*

52   *Ibid.*

53   See Statistics Canada, *What Has Changed Since Cannabis Was Legalized* (Health Report), by Michelle Rotermann (Ottawa: Statistics Canada, 19 February 2020), online: www150.statcan.gc.ca/n1/en/pub/82-003-x/2020002/article/00002-eng.pdf?st=2 WULQWne [Rotterman].

54   See Mahamad, "Retail," *supra* note 49.

55   *Ibid.*

56   See Rosa Marchitelli, "Copycat Pot Edibles that Look Like Candy Are Poisoning Kids, Doctors Say" (25 January 2021), online: www.cbc.ca/news/canada/british-columbia/cannabis-gummies-poisonings-kids-illegal-sites-1.5879232.

57   See Ginni Correa, "Advertising Illicit Marijuana on Social Media" (4 February 2020), online: www.addictioncenter.com/community/advertising-marijuana-social-media/.

58   See Statistics Canada, *The Daily, StatsCannabis Data Availability: Crowdsourced Cannabis Prices, Fourth Quarter 2019*, (Ottawa: Statistics Canada, 23 January 2020), online: www150.statcan.gc.ca/n1/en/dailyquotidien/200123/dq200123c-eng.pdf?st=i4TzoSgZ.

59   See Rotermann, *supra* note 53.

60   See Cameron Duff et al, "A Canadian Perspective on Cannabis Normalization Among Adults" (2012) 20:4 Addiction Research & Theory 271.

61   See Got Leaf, "Online Cannabis Retailers in Canada" (last visited 26 July 2022), online: gotleaf.ca/online-dispensaries/.

62   See Pusiak, *supra* note 33.

63   See Government of Canada, "Healthy Canadians: Recalls,", *supra* note 26.

64   See Vandrey, *supra* note 34; see also Mahamad, "Retail," *supra* note 49.

65   See Statistics Canada, *The Retail Cannabis Market in Canada: A Portrait of the First Year* (Ottawa: Statistics Canada, 11 December 2019), online: www150.statcan.gc.ca/n1/pub/11-621-m/11-621-m2019005-eng.htm.

66   See Marchitelli, *supra* note 56.

67   See Hammond, *supra* note 36.

68   See Tom P Freeman & Valentina Lorenzetti, "'Standard THC Units': A Proposal to Standardize Dose Across all Cannabis Products and Methods of Administration" (2020) 115:7 Addiction 1207.

69   See CADTH, "What Are Bioavailability and Bioequivalence?" (2012), online: www.cadth.ca/sites/default/files/pdf/What_Are_Bioavailability_and_Bioequivalence_e.pdf.

70   See Small, *supra* note 1; see also Health Canada, *Information for Health Care Professionals: Cannabis (Marihuana, Marijuana) and the Cannabinoids*, (Ottawa: Health Canada, October 2018) online: www.canada.ca/content/dam/hc-sc/documents/services/drugs-medication/cannabis/information-medical-practitioners/information-health-care-professionals-cannabis-cannabinoids-eng.pdf   [Health Canada, *Information*].

71   See Health Canada, *Canadian Cannabis Survey 2020: Summary*, (Ottawa: Health Canada, 21 December 2020) online: www.canada.ca/en/health-canada/services/drugs-medication/cannabis/research-data/canadian-cannabis-survey-2020-summary.html.

72   See Gieringer, *supra* note 44.

73   See Robert Melamede, "Cannabis and Tobacco Smoke Are Not Equally Carcinogenic" (2005) 2:1 Harm Reduction J 1.

74   See Smoke-Free, "Physicians for a Smoke-Free Canada" (last visited 26 July 2022), online: smoke-free.ca/.

75   See Health Canada, *Information, supra* note 70.

76   *Ibid* at table 4: Comparison Between Cannabis and Prescription Cannabinoid Medications.

77   See Dosist, "Dosist" (last visited 26 July 2022), online: dosist.com/dose-pens.

78   See University of Victoria, Canadian Institute For Substance Use Research, "Convert Your Drinks into Standard Drink Sizes" (last visited 26 July 2022), online:: aodtool.cfar.uvic.ca/index-stddt.html.

79   See Canadian Centre on Substance Use and Addiction, "Social Reference Pricing for Alcohol FAQs" (2017), online: www.ccsa.ca/social-reference-pricing-alcohol-faqs [Canadian Centre on Substance Use].

80   See Cox, *supra* note 28.

81   See Freeman, *supra* note 68.

82   See MacCallum, *supra* note 8.

83   See Health Canada, *Information, supra* note 70.

84   *Ibid*.

85   See EL Karschner et al, "Subjective and Physiological Effects After Controlled Sativex and Oral THC Administration" (2011) 89:3 Clinical Pharmacology & Therapeutics 400.

86   See Krithiga Sekar & Alison Pack, "Epidiolex as Adjunct Therapy for Treatment of Refractory Epilepsy: A Comprehensive Review with a Focus on Adverse Effects" (2019) 8 F1000 Research.

87   See *Cannabis Regulations, supra* note 30.

88   See Hammond, *supra* note 36.

89   See Government of Canada, "Healthy Canadians: Recalls," *supra* note 26.

90   See Nickolas Jikomes et al, "System for Selection of Regulated Products" U.S. Patent Application No. 16/228, 197 [Jikomes, Patent].

91   See Herminio Boira & Antonio Blanquer, "Environmental Factors Affecting Chemical Variability of Essential Oils In *Thymus piperella* L" (1998) 26:8 Biochemical Systematics & Ecology 811.

92   See Knight, *supra* note 22.

93   See Ethan B Russo, "The Case for the Entourage Effect and Conventional Breeding of Clinical Cannabis: No 'Strain,' No Gain" (2019) 9 Frontiers in Plant Science 1969.

94   See Peter Hecht, *Weed Land: Inside America's Marijuana Epicenter and How Pot Went Legit* (Berkley: University of California Press, 2014).

95   See Elzinga, *supra* note 17; see also Arno Hazekamp, Katerina Tejkalová & Stelios Papadimitriou, "Cannabis: From Cultivar to Chemovar II—A Metabolomics Approach to Cannabis Classification" (2016) 1:1 Cannabis and Cannabinoid Research 202 [Hazekamp, "Metabolomics"].

96   See Elzinga, *supra* note 17.

97   See Hazekamp, "Metabolomics," *supra* note 95.

98   See Health Canada, "Recalls and Safety Alerts: Medical Cannabis by Shoppers Drug Mart Inc. Recalls One Lot of WeedMD's Pedro's Sweet Sativa Dried Cannabis," (20 November 2020), online: healthycanadians.gc.ca/recall-alert-rappel-avis/hc-sc/2020/74363r-eng.php [Recall, Nov 2020].

99   See International Society for Horticulture Science, *International Code of Nomenclature for Cultivated Plants*, 9th ed, (International Society for Horticultural Science, 2016), online: www.ishs.org/scripta-horticulturae/international-code-nomenclature-cultivated-plants-ninth-edition.

100 See Pusiak, *supra* note 33; see also Health Canada, *List of Approved Cultivars for the 2021 Growing Season: Industrial Hemp Varieties Approved for Commercial Production* (Ottawa: Health Canada, 19 April 2021) online: www.canada.ca/en/health-canada/services/drugs-medication/cannabis/producing-selling-hemp/commercial-licence/list-approved-cultivars-cannabis-sativa.html.

101 See Pusiak, *supra* note 33.

102 *Ibid.*

103 See Knight, *supra* note 22.

104 See Lesley G Campbell, Steve GU Naraine & Jaimie Dusfresne, "Phenotypic Plasticity Influences the Success of Clonal Propagation in Industrial Pharmaceutical Cannabis Sativa" (2019) 14:3 PloS one e0213434.

105 *Ibid*; see also Knight, *supra* note 22.

106 See Recall, Nov 2022, *supra* note 98.

107 *Ibid.*

108 Nandakumara D Sarma et al, "Cannabis Inflorescence for Medical Purposes: USP Considerations for Quality Attributes" (2020) 83:4 J Natural Products 1334.

109 See A Hazekamp & JT Fischedick, "Cannabis-From Cultivar to Chemovar" (2012) 4:7-8 Drug Testing & Analysis 660; see also Hazekamp, "Metabolomics," *supra* note 95.

110 See Alethia de la Fuente et al, "Relationship Among Subjective Responses, Flavor, and Chemical Composition Across More than 800 Commercial Cannabis Varieties" (2020) 2:1 J Cannabis Research 1.

111 See Jikomes, Patent, *supra* note 90.

112 Taschwer, Magdalena, and Martin G. Schmid. "Determination of the Relative Percentage Distribution of THCA and Δ9-THC in Herbal Cannabis Seized in Austria–Impact of Different Storage Temperatures on Stability." Forensic Science International 254 (2015): 167–171.

113 See *Cannabis Regulations, supra* note 30.

114 See Jikomes, "Cannabinoid," *supra* note 21; see also Pusiak, *supra* note 33.

115 See Jikomes, "Cannabinoid," *supra* note 21.

116 See Amy K Eichner et al, "Essential Features of Third-Party Certification Programs for Dietary Supplements: A Consensus Statement" (2019) 18:5 Current Sports Medicine Reports 178.

117 See *Cannabis Regulations, supra* note 30.

118 See Sarma, *supra* note 108.

119 See Health Canada, "Recalls and Safety Alerts: Tweed Inc. Recalls One Lot of LBS Sunset (Indica) Dried Cannabis," (7 March 2019), online: healthycanadians.gc.ca/recall-alert-rappel-avis/hc-sc/2019/69256r-eng.php.

120 See Health Canada, "Recalls and Safety Alerts: Aphria Inc. Recalls One Lot of Good Supply Royal Highness Dried Cannabis," (29 October 2019), online: www.healthycanadians.gc.ca/recall-alert-rappel-avis/hc-sc/2019/71407r-eng.php. However, this strain is known to have between 170-240 mg/g therefore, the purchaser might see the typical range prior to purchase.

121 See *Food And Drugs Act*, RSC 1985, c F-27; see also *Food and Drugs Regulation*, CRC, c 870.

122 See Canada Revenue Agency, *EDN60 Calculation of Cannabis Duty and Additional Cannabis Duty on Cannabis Oil, Edible Cannabis, Cannabis Extracts and Cannabis Topicals* (Ottawa: Canada Revenue Agency, April 2019) online: www.canada.ca/en/revenue-agency/services/forms-publications/publications/edn60/calculation-cannabis-duty-additional-cannabis-duty-cannabis-oil-cannabis-edibles-extracts-topicals.html.

123 See Canada Revenue Agency, *EDN55 Calculation of Cannabis Duty and Additional Cannabis Duty on Cannabis Products* (Ottawa: Canada Revenue Agency, September 2018) online: www.canada.ca/en/revenue-agency/services/forms-publications/publications/edn55/calculation-cannabis-duty-additional-cannabis-duty-cannabis-products.html.

124 See Canadian Centre on Substance Use, *supra* note 79.

125 See *Cannabis Act, supra* note 25.

CHAPTER 8

Preventing Perverse Effects of Public Health Policy Is also Harm Reduction

Potential Risks in Some Tobacco-Control Interventions for Indigenous Peoples

Marewa Glover

Me haere I te manukāwhaki, kaua e whakaupa
ki te riri, kia whai mōrehu.

(Be clever, don't prolong the fighting, let us be
survivors. That is, the wise chief ideally seeks to
achieve victory quickly with minimal losses.)

Māori proverb

In 2015, an estimated 6.4 million people worldwide died prematurely from largely preventable tobacco-smoking-related diseases, representing 11.5% of global deaths.[1] This death toll was expected to rise in subsequent years reflecting upward trends in smoking prevalence and population growth.[2] The risk of dying from a smoking-related disease is associated with years of smoking daily. There is also a dose-response relationship, meaning the greater the consumption of smoke, the higher the risk.[3] But smoking cessation works to reduce the risk, with most of the risk reduction occurring within the first five years of abstinence.[4]

In 2004, the electronic cigarette (e-cigarette) was launched as a non-combustible and thus lower-risk alternative to smoking tobacco. An e-cigarette contains a battery-powered heating element that transforms a liquid mix of propylene glycol, vegetable glycerin, nicotine, water, and flavouring into an aerosol intended for inhalation; this action is referred to as vaping. (For the purposes of this chapter, vaping refers to the use of nicotine-containing vaporizer products.) Vaping has been estimated to be 95 percent safer than smoking tobacco.[5] Vaping has proved popular, with an estimated 68 million users globally as of 2020.[6]

In 2014, another non-combustible tobacco product succeeded at market, the class of which is referred to as "heated tobacco products" (HTPs). While the technology is not new, previous iterations of the product had failed to attract and hold consumers. The new class of HTPs contain a battery and software that regulates the heating time and time between uses. Small highly engineered "sticks" containing tobacco and other substances such as propylene glycol (a fairly inoffensive chemical compound) are inserted into the device and heated to a point just below combustion to avoid creating smoke. Nicotine in the tobacco is released by the heating and forms, along with the other carrier constituents, an aerosol intended for inhalation. On a risk hierarchy, HTP use is estimated to represent a slightly higher risk than vaping but still falls within a low-risk range compared to smoking conventional cigarettes.[7] As of 2020, an estimated 20 million people worldwide used HTPs.[8]

These two risk-reduced products (RRPs) extended the range of non-combustible alternatives to smoking tobacco, which include smokeless oral and nasal tobacco products. Some of these are established RRPs (such as Swedish snus, a type of snuff) and some have a different set of health risks (such as chewing products that combine tobacco with other potentially toxic substances).[9] A third novel non-combustible product that surged in popularity recently are snus-like tobacco-free oral pouches containing cellulose fibre impregnated with nicotine (similar to nicotine-replacement therapy products in risk, at 98 percent safer than smoking).[10] As of 2020, an estimated 10 million people use risk-reduced smokeless or snus products.[11]

Most users of the relatively novel RRPs (excluding snus) have switched from smoking tobacco. Given that the risk to health reduces quickly after smoking cessation, new estimates of the global smoking-related death toll are now needed. It would also need to be recalculated for subgroups, several of which the World Health Organization

(WHO) recognises are being "left behind," including Indigenous Peoples, people with mental-health conditions, and the 2SLGBTQ+ community.[12]

The current and projected smoking-related mortality and morbidity burden varies widely by country, ethnicity, sex, and socio-economic status. Access to RRPs and medical and social supports to use RRPs also varies. Few countries allow people who smoke to have access to the full range of RRPs. Disinformation designed to discourage any tobacco or nicotine use, regardless of the risk relative to smoking, is also increasing as a major barrier to smoking cessation.[13] Smoking-cessation support is both inconsistently available, internationally and within countries, and varies in efficacy.[14]

What Is Being Done to Reduce Smoking-Related Harm

The WHO's Framework Convention on Tobacco Control (FCTC),[15] the so-called global tobacco treaty, oversees tobacco-control strategies worldwide. Though the FCTC includes harm reduction as a prevention strategy, the current focus of the FCTC-directed sector has narrowed to achieving "the tobacco endgame;"[16] that is, eliminating all tobacco use.

Some countries have adopted a prohibitionary approach and aspire to eliminate the consumption of tobacco products and use of nicotine products. For example, Finland has banned e-cigarettes. Such a move could ironically delay reduction of smoking-related harm, especially since evidence mounts that vaping is twice as effective as nicotine-replacement therapies at assisting abstinence from smoking.[17] Other countries, such as Iceland, allow access to the full range of RRPs. The United Kingdom and New Zealand allow HTPs and vaping but prohibit the sale of lower-risk oral nicotine products.

Experts on tobacco control in countries with advanced tobacco-control programs are worried, however. Despite nearly six decades of anti-smoking campaigns, restrictions, and eye-watering rises in taxation on tobacco, smoking-cessation rates had remained relatively low (until the introduction of vaping and, in Japan, HTPs). In some countries, smoking prevalence had plateaued. The frustration is triggering calls for increasingly regressive interventions.[18] There are calls for ever greater taxation on targeted products; increased restrictions on the manufacture, import, and sale of targeted products; removal of product constituents or characteristics to make use as unpleasant as possible, or to castrate the function altogether by reducing nicotine to useless levels;[19] imposition of sinking-lid restrictions on retailers and/ or on customers (such as banning sales to people born after a certain year) to phase out sales; and increased policing and penalization of consumers who fail to align their product use with new laws.

Little consideration is given to the perverse consequences. One is the shift to co-opting police and the judicial system to enforce compliance with the smoke- or tobacco-free ideal (a "policing public health" approach).[20]

A tactic of tobacco-free-world campaigners is to raise outrage toward the tobacco industry, continue the denormalization of smoking, intensify pressure on politicians, and sway young people and public opinion generally, particularly via social media.[21] This approach is based on an Anglo-European disease model that frames the tobacco industry as the vector of tobacco-related morbidity. People who use the targeted products are framed as victims who have been fooled by the industry, and if they cannot stop the aberrant behaviour when advised to, they are perceived to be educationally and or mentally deficient. They are pathologized as weak-willed or lacking self-esteem. If treatment fails them, they are framed as recalcitrant, resistant, or remote.

Particularly disturbing are the intensified infantilizing claims that human beings do not attain the intellectual capacity to be able to decide if they should or should not smoke until some as-of-yet established age in adulthood. This claim was used to set the minimum age for tobacco purchase in New Zealand at 16, then 18, and in some countries it is 21. This tactic mimics the character of pseudo-scientific racism that was employed to justify European colonization of countries and Indigenous populations. One particularly pernicious narrative was that Indigenous Peoples were less evolved and, thus, childlike. The history on the application of craniometry (measuring peoples' skulls) that was used to degrade the Sámi people of northern Europe is one such example.[22] It is jarring to see some European/Western tobacco-control researchers exploiting a similar type of argument: that younger adults who smoke tobacco are not really adults, they should be treated as minors, and thus older adults (who have surpassed the nebulous 30- or 40-year-old measure of brain maturation) should paternalistically protect these vulnerable "youngsters" from tobacco.

One rationale for the New Zealand government's smoke-free 2025 proposals is that they are required to "protect" Māori (the Indigenous people of New Zealand) and children (no other groups are identified) "to the greatest extent practicable."[23] The Treaty of Waitangi,[24] the country's founding document, was invoked in a token way, disparaged in some quarters as a "selective endorsement of rights."[25] It is a short phrase representing an expedient interpretation of a part of the New Zealand Crown's obligations under the Treaty of Waitangi extracted to justify what European tobacco companies want. Any critique of the approach is dismissed by applying a utilitarian imperative that focuses on achieving health improvement for a majority, even if a minority might be harmed.

The principles of tobacco harm reduction are outlined first. Then three projects are drawn upon to illustrate three potential perverse effects of tobacco-control strategies on Māori: (1) the amount of tobacco excise tax the New Zealand government extracts from Māori versus non-Māori purchasers of tobacco, (2) passage of the first law in New Zealand that could result in people who smoke being fined, and (3) an increase in aggravated robberies of corner stores for tobacco.

Indigenous Peoples

There are over 476 million Indigenous people in the world, living across more than 100 countries. Collectively, about 6 percent of the world's population is Indigenous. Who is Indigenous is determined by those groups who have self-identified as Indigenous, and that they were the predominant people resident and holding sovereignty in a geographical area prior to a different ethnic group settling in and dominating.

The WHO has warned that Indigenous Peoples are being "left behind" by countries implementing the FCTC.[26] Our 2021 investigation into smoking prevalence among Indigenous Peoples confirms this is the case. We found that only five FCTC countries (New Zealand, United States, Canada, Australia, Fiji) monitor or report on smoking among Indigenous populations within their modern colonial-state boundaries.[27] In New Zealand, the United States, Canada, and Australia, smoking prevalence has historically been, and remains, disproportionately higher among Indigenous Peoples.

Harm Reduction

Harm reduction are acts that an individual undertakes or that are socially promoted, such as wearing a bicycle helmet. Behavioural choices are believed to result from a complex interplay of personal, familial, historical, cultural, social, and economic determinants. The converse would be viewing behavioural choices as medically pathological due to some biochemical or psychological hiccup causing diversion from some (culturally prescribed) norm.

Dignity, respecting others as having the same status as a human being, is a key tenet of harm reduction.[28] As such, harm reduction does not tend to support strategies that express and propagate a belief in "human biosocial inequality";[29] that is, that some people are biologically, socially, or culturally superior to others, and that by stint of their skin colour, ethnicity, or religion, for example, they should be recognised as having a higher status in society, and that they should determine what behaviours are appropriate or inappropriate. Harm reduction supports person-centred and person-directed change. It favours a bottom-up approach rather than authoritarian intervention.[30] In practice, harm reduction typically is non-judgmental and avoids labelling people (e.g., calling individuals "addicts"). Stigmatizing people, inciting discrimination against groups of people, and marginalizing them is antithetical to a harm reduction approach. One task of harm reduction work, in fact, is to challenge the social injustices that result from such strategies.

Harm reduction is about supporting people to protect and attain as good a state of well-being as they can, given their circumstances. It is believed that adults know best what state of well-being they want, and what they can do to achieve that. Expecting all people to immediately and completely refrain from drug use, gambling, unsafe sexual behaviour, etc., is not realistic. However, there is no consensus on one single approach to harm reduction, especially as some supporters of prohibition, or eventual abstinence endorse more conservative goals within harm reduction.[31] Thus, harm reduction is pragmatic rather than intransigent about achieving prohibition.[32] Support to reduce risk rather than coercion is offered to access education, skill development, or other resources the person identifies as desired. This can seem at odds with a reductionist focus on eradicating illness.

Within the context of reducing the health risks of tobacco products some support access to RRPs, but only as a temporary step toward the prohibition of all tobacco and nicotine use. Writing from a critical harm reduction perspective, I of course support the reduction of smoking- or tobacco-related disease and premature deaths, but I do not support strategies that do nothing to change socially unjust determinants of smoking or, worse, that increase marginalization and poverty among the very people tobacco control claim they seek to help.

Perverse Effects of Tobacco-Control Policies: Three Examples

Anti-smoking messaging began in New Zealand in the late 1960s, following the US surgeon general's 1964 report warning that smoking kills. The first national stop-smoking campaign did not occur until the 1980s. New Zealand became the first country to pass a comprehensive smoke-free law aimed at reducing smoking-related morbidity and mortality in 1990. Several amendments have added further restrictions on smoking and on the advertising, sale, and distribution of tobacco products. The tobacco excise tax has also been regularly increased.

In 1992, smoking prevalence among people aged 15 and over was 27 percent in New Zealand,[33] but this statistic obscures vast disparities by ethnicity and sex. About 50 percent of Māori smoked. After 60 years of government intervention to reduce tobacco smoking, with the intensified effort from 1990, smoking prevalence among people aged 15 years and up has only halved (to 13.4 percent in 2019–2020), but disparities remain, with smoking among Māori disproportionately higher at 31.4 percent.[34]

Tax: Continuing the Extraction
of Wealth from Indigenous Peoples

The mantra that taxing tobacco is one of the most effective methods of reducing tobacco use is widely promulgated. To combat the economist classification that the tax is a regressive measure, some people in tobacco control promote the narrative that instead taxing tobacco is "pro-poor"[35] or "pro-health equity," even while admitting that poverty could worsen for low-income people who continue to smoke.[36]

Due to the excise tax on tobacco, New Zealand has the highest-priced cigarettes relative to income in the world.[37] Quantification of the tobacco tax by ethnicity, taken in 2018, revealed that a dispro-portionately high amount of tax was being extracted from Māori adults (15 years and over). Though they made up less than one-fifth (517,000, or 18 percent) of the European/Other adult (15 years and over) population (2.8 million), Māori tobacco expenditure was just under half of the European/Other tobacco expenditure.[38] Of the NZ$1 billion (C$897 million) Māori total expenditure on tobacco, NZ$569 million (C$510 million) was excise tax, and a further NZ$153 million (C$137 million) was goods-and-services tax. That is, just one year of tax extracted from Māori via tobacco purchases was NZ$723 million (C$648 million).

To put this in context, over the same period of time since New Zealand's world-leading Smoke-Free Environments Act was passed in 1990, aggregate expenditure on Treaty of Waitangi settlements to Indigenous tribes for treaty breaches[39] was NZ$2.2 billion (C$1.9 bil-lion), an amount equivalent to just three years of the tobacco excise tax paid by Māori people who smoke.

Almost two hundred years since British colonization, Māori are still over-represented among the lowest income groups,[40] and have the highest rates of unemployment[41] and imprisonment.[42] There are many other determinants of smoking that Māori women particularly are disproportionately negatively affected by that help to explain why they have the highest smoking rates at 35 percent (in 2019/20), over three times the rate of New Zealand European/Other women at 11.5 percent.[43]

The taxes on tobacco cause a significant loss of income for young Māori women who smoke. In 2017, smoking prevalence was 30 percent and 45 percent among Māori women aged 18 and 24 years respective-ly.[44] Using these figures, an estimated NZ$9 million (C$8 million) of the government tax taken from tobacco in 2018, including the goods-and-services tax, came from Māori women aged 18 years, and NZ$11 million (C$9.8 million) came from Māori women aged 24.[45] This is disproportionately higher than that extracted from any other ethnic or age group in New Zealand.

Sara Greene's legal immobility theory of poverty explains how government policies, such as taxation, contribute to a "mechanism through which poverty is perpetuated and upward socioeconomic mobility is stunted."[46] New Zealand's excise-tax policy on tobacco contributes to rendering Māori immobilized, financially suppressed, and locked in poverty. There is nothing "pro-poor" or "pro-health equity" about the tobacco tax for young Māori women, many of whom are mothers of young children.

Using Judicial Charges, Fines, and Incarceration to Discourage Smoking

New Zealand has extensive environmental bans on smoking in indoor spaces such as office buildings and schools, public transport, and restaurants and bars. Many city councils have banned smoking in outdoor town centres, parks, sports grounds, beaches, and areas outside restaurants or cafes, though this is rarely enforced. Some employers such as hospitals and universities, extended the ban to encompass their outdoor grounds.

Once vaping became widespread, many institutions and businesses classified vaping as smoking. It was not until the Smokefree Environments and Regulated Products (Vaping) Amendment Act took effect in November 2020 that bans on smoking were legally to be applied to vaping and "smokeless" products (HTPs).[47]

The government had previously passed the Smoke-free Environments (Prohibiting Smoking in Motor Vehicles Carrying Children) Amendment Act, banning smoking in a motor vehicle, whether moving or stationary, and in any vehicle having a person under the age of 18. The act came into effect in May 2020 with an educational (no-fine) period, after which people caught breaching the law would receive a NZ$50 (C$44.88) fine.[48] This is the first law in New Zealand that imposes a fine on a person smoking (or vaping). Previous fines associated with smoking in a prohibited area were imposed on the organization or business that failed to enforce the ban.

This law signalled an ideological shift on several levels. A moral imperative took precedence and the need for scientific evidence to support the introduction of the law was abandoned. The preceding three decades of environmental bans on smoking and mass media campaigns promoting smoke-free homes and cars had almost completely eliminated smoking in homes and cars, especially when children were present. If a person smoked in a vehicle with a child present, they were often from marginalized groups, which had the least exposure to health-promotion messages.

Further, this law was the first environmental smoking ban that required individuals to implement and enforce it within their private property. But as smoking was banned in more and more outdoor areas, and campaigns incited public opprobrium toward people smoking, people's private spaces, such as their cars, had increasingly become a place they could smoke free of the risk of being abused for doing so.

Most alarming, from a harm reduction perspective, this was the first tobacco-control law that co-opted police resources to enforce a ban on smoking. The law also extended police powers by giving them the right to stop or inspect any vehicle if they suspected that a person under aged 18 was being exposed to tobacco smoke or vapor. Further fines could be imposed if people would not give their name, address, and age. Additional costs could accrue if the initial fine was not paid. Though uncommon in New Zealand, being incarcerated for unpaid fines can occur if people have other offences. Outstanding fines and a warrant can result in loss of up to half of a person's social assistance payment. Thus, not being able to pay a "low-level" fine can begin a chain of negative consequences that depreciate the very economic and social determinants that, in turn, increase the likelihood of smoking. This is how "legal immobility" functions.[49]

The likelihood that people fined under the Smoke-free Environments (Prohibiting Smoking in Motor Vehicles Carrying Children) Amendment Act will be disproportionately Māori women is high. Not only because Māori women have the highest smoking rates but Māori are disproportionately targeted by police, punished, and imprisoned by the justice system.[50] More than half of the people incarcerated in New Zealand are Māori, though they make up only 15 percent of the population. Of women incarcerated, 63 percent are Māori.[51] Māori women in their late teens to early twenties are twice as likely to receive a police-court proceeding.[52]

The creation of laws aimed at criminalizing Indigenous Peoples and the use of police "were an important part of the pioneering structure."[53] It became an embedded colonial practice. Several laws in New Zealand's history were specifically designed to force Māori to assimilate or conform to European ways, such as the Ordinance to Prohibit the Sale of Spirits to Natives of 1847. Reform of the liquor law ending the different treatment of Māori did not occur until 1948.[54] The ban on smoking in cars when minors are present is not worded to *target* Māori—that would be a breach of New Zealand's Human Rights Act. But it is a tripwire laid across the path of Māori. Proportionately more Māori will be tripped up by it, their fall will be that much harder, and their recovery that much slower.

Tobacco Robberies

Creating a law that Indigenous Peoples are more likely to fall foul of is one way tobacco control contributes to worsening the economic and social determinants of smoking among Indigenous Peoples. Another unintended consequence of tobacco-control policies in New Zealand, the increased demand for illicit tobacco, poses several other risks.

The taxes on tobacco have raised the price so high that tobacco was being likened to gold.[55] As of January 2021, a pack of 20 cigarettes cost NZ$32 (C$28.20) on average. Several other tobacco-control policies have progressively reduced adaptations people were using to get more puffs per dollar. The minimum pack size is 20 cigarettes, or 30 g of loose tobacco (an even heftier upfront cost of NZ$50. The tax on loose tobacco was raised to "equalize" the tax per gram to stop people switching to hand rolling cigarettes. In November 2014, duty-free allowances on tobacco brought into New Zealand by overseas travellers (aged 18 and over) was reduced to no more than 50 cigarettes or 50 g. Bringing tobacco on behalf of someone else was already illegal, but with this regulatory change enforcement became more stringent. In addition, a duty-free concession on gifts of tobacco (valued less than NZ$110) sent by mail from overseas was removed. Growing tobacco for own use (giving or selling to others was forbidden) is uncommon because of the time, effort, and difficulty involved. Still, the dry weight allowed to be grown for personal use was reduced from 15 kg to 5 kg per year. Furthermore, New Zealand has strict border controls, effectively limiting the amount of illicit tobacco that is smuggled in.

Most likely a result of these interventions, spates of robberies of convenience stores for tobacco were reported in 2016–2017.[56] Of a total of 572 such news reports over 2009–2018, 336 were published in 2016–2017. Many of the robberies were aggravated. They occurred more frequently in lower socio-economic areas and, when offenders were described, it was predominantly males.[57]

Some equity implications for Māori of this robbery phenomenon are that Māori disproportionately live in lower socio-economic neighbourhoods. Robberies of community-based stores, especially those involving violence, can trigger a cascade of detrimental effects on community health and social cohesion, such as increased residential transience as people flee to safer neighbourhoods (or those who can afford to).

In one study I led, of the characteristics of the robberies, we did not analyse the ethnicity of offenders as reporters tended to group Māori and Pacific Islanders together. Given the disproportionate socio-economic context in which Māori find themselves, it is likely that some disenfranchised young Māori males would have been enticed to cash in on the increased demand for cheaper tobacco.

The Promise of UNDRIP

There is resonance between a critical harm reduction approach and the principles set out in the United Nations Declaration on the Rights of Indigenous Peoples (UNDRIP).[58]

In common is a recognition that all people are equal and have the right to be different, identify differently, and be respected as such. Policies based on or promoting that some ethnic groups are biologically or culturally superior are rightly considered unjust. There is further recognition of historical events and their impacts, and respect for self-determination.

UNDRIP states that Indigenous Peoples "have the right not to be subjected to forced assimilation or destruction of their culture."[59] This is relevant to assessing the perverse effects of tobacco-control policies because the current direction of tobacco control propagates an ethnocentric European/Western analysis, a consequence of which is that other culturally specific analyses are disregarded as incorrect or improper.

Many of the beliefs and principles of behaviour of the European/ Western tobacco-control sector radically conflicts with family- and tribal-centred ecological-based Indigenous perspectives. For example, the Western reductionist approach singles out the individual as the principal unit of autonomous power, thus one to focus on and control. Indigenous cultures variously respect and nurture individual "power," but individual authority and right to decide is understood to occur within the (genetically related) collective that individuals are members of. Cultural beliefs and *tikanga* (cultural protocols) guide personal choices and policy choices toward outcomes that support individuals and, consequently, the collective to thrive. Thus, Indigenous perspectives centre on relatedness, respect, love, reciprocity, and duty. Strategies for protecting the survival of the collective are arrived at via participatory processes. In stark contrast, the European/Western (ethnocentric) tobacco-control sector is completely disconnected from people who smoke and from their communities and contexts. The voices of people who smoke (or vape) and their advocates are not represented; in fact, they are forbidden from, for example, contributing in any way to FCTC policy development and review.

The FCTC is top-down, paternalistic, and has no compassion for people who smoke. Denormalization of tobacco and particularly, smoking tobacco, has been endorsed as a central aim of the FCTC, [60] despite critics' concerns about the damaging effects of using stigma to turn public attitudes against smoking and "the smoker."[61] Denormalizing smoking messages and policies intend to ridicule and evoke shame or embarrassment in people who cannot quit. For example, banning filters in cigarettes so that people who do smoke have to fashion a filter from scrap.[62] The FCTC wants people to be reduced to undignified acts, such as having to collect butts off the street, or commit illegal acts, such as buying black-market tobacco. This is a form of structural violence and punishment, and a further example of how the legal system is using "gratuitous management" to infantilize smokers.[63] An approach rooted in compassion, would not remove access to nicotine-containing products overnight (by instituting a nationwide limit of .05 mg nicotine per gram of tobacco, for example), forcing hundreds of thousands of people to go into nicotine withdrawal. The FCTC should seek to understand why people smoke and turn its attention to reducing those determinants, or at least lessening the influence of those determinants. But, as one Māori woman participating in our Voices of the 5% study said about the people pushing the harshest smoke-free 2025 policies, "they are boneless."[64] In the Māori language, the word for "bones" is kōiwi, and the word iwi means "tribe." Boneless in this context means without human structure, such as a tribal or similar institution with ethics and principles guiding reciprocal obligation to others.

Similar to the "nothing about us, without us" call by consumers in harm reduction movements, Indigenous Peoples have the right to maintain their own decision-making institutions and participate in decision making about matters that affect them. They have the right to determine and influence priorities and strategies concerning their health. That is, states strategically choose who they will "consult," preferring Indigenous representatives and organizations that work for them, are funded by them, or are in other ways dependent upon government funding or contracts. This can include university students or junior academics training under, and dependent upon, European professors. Contrary views are neutralized. Genuinely independent research, by Māori for Māori, is blocked if it might expose governmental neglect. Indigenous researchers who do not parrot European/Western narratives are "cancelled," so that knowledge about what is really occurring for Māori is suppressed.[65] Because of actions like these, Māori are not necessarily fully informed about the potentially perverse effects of proposed tobacco-control policies, as is their right.

Indigenous Peoples have the right, under UNDRIP, to develop knowledge based upon their traditional beliefs, and they have the right to develop and trial tradition-informed healing interventions, say for smoking cessation, for example. Despite, evidence that many by Māori/for Māori interventions trialled over the last 30 years were attractive to Māori, were feasible, and were potentially effective, only smoking-cessation interventions based upon Western theories of behavioural change receive backing. Contravening this Indigenous right, the New Zealand Ministry of Health is proposing to restrict the delivery of training in smoking cessation to one (Western-based) ministry-approved course, and messages on how to stop smoking will be restricted to ministry-approved statements, which only authorized people will deliver. This would suppress the delivery of Māori knowledge-based smoking-cessation training or delivery.

Conclusion

Using criminal law, even low-level infringement notices, to deter tobacco use is antithetical to harm reduction.[66] It creates discursive and administrative mechanisms to reframe people who smoke tobacco, or use other targeted products, as "offenders," morally deficient, and therefore less deserving of rights (such as the right to be treated with dignity), and more deserving of punishment, such as harsher taxes, increased inconvenience to access the product, removal of pleasurable product features, and, most damaging, increased social exclusion and sanctioned discrimination, such as denying jobs, housing, and medical treatment.

The perverse effects of such policies, including cascading and longer-term effects, for Indigenous Peoples must be projected. The affected consumers and other stakeholders, such as the public and politicians, need to be informed of these risks and given sufficient time to deliberate decisions.

Policies must be assessed for alignment with local and international rights instruments such as UNDRIP and human-rights laws. If tobacco-control policies breach these, or perpetuate unjust social inequities, they should not be implemented.

We now have a range of tobacco and nicotine RRPs that represent no more risk to health than many other day-to-day activities. There is no extraordinary need to single these out for prohibition. The focus should be on informing people who use high-risk tobacco products of the RRPs, and supporting them to switch. The billions of dollars spent chasing the endgame, regardless of the perverse consequences, could then be rerouted to attend to other critical priorities.

As the opening Māori proverb advises, let us work to stop unnecessary deaths due to high-risk tobacco use, but let it not be a pyrrhic victory. Let us be clever about it and not cause unnecessary deaths as a consequence. Forgetting ethics, forsaking compassion, will do far greater damage to our humanity. We have strategies that value all people equally, are humane, and equitably deliver the chance to survive—we should commit to these first.

Disclosures

Dr. Glover's Centre of Research Excellence: Indigenous Sovereignty & Smoking was funded June 2018 through August 2024 with a grant from Global Action to End Smoking (formerly known as the Foundation for a Smoke-Free World) an independent, U.S. nonprofit 501(c)(3) grantmaking organization, accelerating science-based efforts worldwide to end the smoking epidemic. Through September 2023, the organization received charitable gifts from PMI Global Services, Inc ("PMI") while operating as an entirely independent entity. In October 2023, the organization ended its prior funding agreement with PMI. Global Action has since adopted a formal policy that it will not seek or accept funding from any industry that manufactures tobacco products or non-medicinal nicotine products. Global Action played no role in the conception, design, analysis, editing or approval of the Centre's studies or publications. The contents, selection, and presentation of facts, as well as any opinions expressed, are the sole responsibility of the author and should not be regarded as reflecting the positions of Global Action to End Smoking. Glover (some 10 years ago) received fees from pharmaceutical companies for consultancy in regard to cessation medicines. She has not received research funding from any tobacco or vaping company, and neither she nor the Centre have any commercial interests in any smoking cessation programs or aids or nicotine or tobacco products. A special note of thanks goes to Kyro Selket for research assistance.

References

Legislation

New York State *Tobacco Product Waste Reduction Act* to take effect from January 1, 2022.

Smoke-free Environments (Prohibiting Smoking in Motor Vehicles Carrying Children) Amendment Act (NZ), 2020/19.

Smokefree Environments and Regulated Products (Vaping) Amendment Act (NZ), 2020/62.

Publications

Beaglehole, Robert et al, "A Tobacco-free World: A Call to Action to Phase Out the Sale of Tobacco Products by 2040" (2015) 385:9972 Lancet at 1011.

Blakely, Tony et al, "Health, Health Inequality, and Cost Impacts of Annual Increases in Tobacco Tax: Multistate Life Table Modeling in New Zealand" (2015) 12:7 PLoS Medicine e1001856.

Centre of Research Excellence: Indigenous Sovereignty and Smoking, "Voices of the 5%" (last accessed 22 July 2022), online: voicesofthe5percent.nz/home.

Chan, Gary et al, "A Systematic Review of Randomized Controlled Trials and Network Meta-analysis of E-cigarettes for Smoking Cessation" (2021) 119 Addictive Behaviours 106912.

Christoffel, Paul, "Story: Liquor Laws" (last modified 15 December 2014), online: teara.govt.nz/en/liquor-laws.

Clarke, Elizabeth et al, "Snus: A Compelling Harm Reduction Alternative to Cigarettes" (2019) 16:1 Harm Reduction J 1.

Ernst & Young & Parthenon, "Smoking Cessation Products and Services Global Landscape Analysis" (2018).

GBD 2015 Tobacco Collaborators, "Smoking Prevalence and Attributable Disease Burden in 195 Countries and Territories, 1990–2015: A Systematic Analysis from the Global Burden of Disease Study 2015" (2017) 389 Lancet 1885.

Glover, Marewa & Kyro Selket, *Smoking Prevalence Among Indigenous Peoples of the World* (Auckland: Centre of Research Excellence: Indigenous Sovereignty & Smoking, 2021).

Glover, Marewa et al, "Price Hikes, Crime Fad or Political Football? What Caused a Spike in Store Robberies for Cigarettes in New Zealand: Analysis of News Reports (2009-2018)" (2021) 20:3 Safer Communities.

Glover, Marewa et al, "Store Robberies for Tobacco Products: Perceived Causes and Potential Solutions" (2021) 6:4 J Community Safety & Wellbeing 191.

Glover, Marewa, Pooja Patwardhan & Kyro Selket, "Tobacco Smoking in Three 'Left Behind' Subgroups: Indigenous, the Rainbow Community and People with Mental Health Conditions" (2020) 20:3 Drugs Alcohol Today 263.

Greene, Sara, "A Theory of Poverty: Legal Immobility" (2019) 96:4 Washington U LR 753.

Huang, Jidong et al, "Changing Perceptions of Harm of E-cigarette vs Cigarette Use Among Adults in 2 US National Surveys from 2012 to 2017" (2019) 2:3 JAMA Network Open e191047.

Jha, Prabhat & Richard Peto, "Global Effects of Smoking, or Quitting and of Taxing Tobacco" (2014) 370:1 New England J Medicine 60.

Knowledge Action Change, Burning Issues: Global State of Tobacco Harm Reduction, by Harry Shapiro, (London: Knowledge-Action-Change, 2020), online: gsthr.org/resources/item/burning-issues-global-state-tobacco-harm-reduction-2020.

Latu, Alex & Albany Lucas, "Discretion in the New Zealand Criminal Justice System: The Position of Māori and Pacific Islanders" (2008) 12:1 J South Pacific L 84.

McNeill, Ann et al, Vaping in England: 2021 Evidence Update Summary (London, UK: Public Health England, February 2021), online: www.gov.uk/government/publications/vaping-in-england-evidence-update-february-2021/vaping-in-england-2021-evidence-update-summary.

Mead, Tania, A Justice System for Everyone (New Zealand: Just Speak, 2020), online: www.justspeak.org.nz/ourwork/justspeak-idi-research-a-justice-system-for-everyone.

Melbøe, Line et al, "Ethical and Methodological Issues in Research with Sami Experiencing Disability" (2016) 75:1 Intl J Circumpolar Health 31656.

Murkett, Rachel, Megyn Rugh & Belinda Ding, "Nicotine Products Relative Risk Assessment: A Systematic Review and Meta-Analysis" (2020) 9 F1000Research 1225.

New Zealand Department of Corrections, Hōkai Rangi. Ara Poutama Aotearoa Strategy: 2019-2024 (Wellington, NZ: Department of Corrections, 2019), online:www.corrections.govt.nz/__data/assets/pdf_file/0003/38244/Hokai_Rangi_Strategy.pdf.

New Zealand Ministry of Business, Innovation and Employment, Māori Labour Market Trends—December 2020 Quarter (Unadjusted) (Wellington, NZ: Ministry of Business, Innovation and Employment, 2020), online: www.mbie.govt.nz/dmsdocument/13559-maori-in-the-labour-market-december-2020-quarter-unadjusted.

New Zealand Ministry of Health, *New Zealand Health Survey Annual Data Explorer* (Wellington, NZ: Ministry of Health, 2020), online: minhealthnz. shinyapps.io/nz-health-survey-2019-20-annual-data-explorer/_w_ c21e7ba1/#!/explore-topics.

——, "Proposals for a Smokefree Aotearoa 2025 Action Plan" (2021), online: consult.health.govt.nz/tobacco-control/smokefree2025-actionplan/.

——, *Tobacco Products: The Public Health Commission's Advice to the Minister of Health 1993-1994* (Wellington, NZ: Public Health, 1994).

Rée, Gerald, *Policing Public Health in Queensland, 1859-1919* (PhD Thesis, Griffith University, 2010), online: research-repository.griffith.edu.au/ bitstream/handle/10072/367309/Ree_2010_02Thesis.pdf?sequence=1.

Roe, Gordon, "Harm Reduction as Paradigm: Is Better than Bad Good Enough? The Origins of Harm Reduction" (2005) 15:3 Critical Public Health 243.

Selak, Vanessa et al, "Ethnic Differences in Cardiovascular Risk Profiles among 475,241 Adults in Primary Care in Aotearoa, New Zealand" (2020) 133:1521 New Zealand Medical J 14.

Siddharth, Prince, *Quantifying Māori Spend on Tobacco, Alcohol and Gambling* (Wellington, NZ: New Zealand Institute of Economic Research, 2019), online: coreiss.com/assets/Tobacco%20Alcohol%20Gambling%20Tax%20 Take%202018_NZIER%20Report.pdf.

Single, Eric, "Defining Harm Reduction" (1995) 14:3 Drug Alcohol Rev 287.

Stanley, Elizabeth & Riki Mihaere, "The Problems and Promise of International Rights in the Challenge to Māori Imprisonment" (2019) 8:1 Intl J for Crime, Justice and Social Democracy 1.

Te Uepū Hāpai i te Ora (the Safe and Effective Justice Advisory Group), *He Waka Roimata: Transforming our Criminal Justice System* (Wellington, NZ: Ministry of Justice, 2019), online: www.justice.govt.nz/assets/Documents/ Publications/he-waka-roimata.pdf.

United Nations Declaration on the Rights of Indigenous Peoples, 13 September 2007, A/61/L.67 and Add.1.

World Health Organization, *WHO Framework Convention on Tobacco Control* (Geneva: World Health Organization, 2003), online: www.who.int/fctc/ text_download/en/.

——, *WHO Global Report on Trends in Prevalence of Tobacco Smoking 2000–2025*, 3rd ed (Geneva: World Health Organization, 2019) 39.

Wu, Daphne et al, "Impact of Cigarette Tax Increase on Health and Financing Outcomes in Four Indian States" (2020) 4:49 Gates Open Research.

Notes

1   See GBD 2015 Tobacco Collaborators, "Smoking Prevalence and Attributable Disease Burden in 195 Countries and Territories, 1990–2015: A Systematic Analysis from the Global Burden of Disease Study 2015" (2017) 389 Lancet 1885.

2   See Prabhat Jha & Richard Peto, "Global Effects of Smoking, or Quitting and of Taxing Tobacco" (2014) 370:1 New England J Medicine 60.

3   *Ibid.*

4   See GBD 2015, *supra* note 1 at 1.

5   See Ann McNeill et al, *Vaping in England: 2021 Evidence Update Summary* (London, UK: Public Health England, February 2021), online: www.gov.uk/government/publications/vaping-in-england-evidence-update-february-2021/vaping-in-england-2021-evidence-update-summary.

6   See Knowledge Action Change, *Burning Issues: Global State of Tobacco Harm Reduction* by Harry Shapiro (London, UK: Knowledge-Action-Change, 2020), online: gsthr.org/resources/item/burning-issues-global-state-tobacco-harm-reduction-2020.

7   See Rachel Murkett, Megyn Rugh & Belinda Ding, "Nicotine Products Relative Risk Assessment: A Systematic Review and Meta-Analysis" (2020) 9 F1000Research 1225.

8   See Knowledge Action Change, *supra* note 6 at 6.

9   See Elizabeth Clarke et al, "Snus: A Compelling Harm Reduction Alternative to Cigarettes" (2019) 16:1 Harm Reduction J 1.

10   See Murkett et al, *supra* note 7 at 7.

11   See Knowledge Action Change, *supra* note 6 at 6.

12   See Marewa Glover, Pooja Patwardhan & Kyro Selket, "Tobacco Smoking in Three 'Left Behind' Subgroups: Indigenous, the Rainbow Community and People with Mental Health Conditions" (2020) 20:3 Drugs Alcohol Today 263.

13   See Jidong Huang et al, "Changing Perceptions of Harm of E-cigarette vs Cigarette Use Among Adults in 2 US National Surveys From 2012 to 2017" (2019) 2:3 JAMA Network Open e191047.

14   See Ernst & Young & Parthenon, "Smoking Cessation Products and Services Global Landscape Analysis" (2018), online: www.smokefreeworld.org/wp-content/uploads/2019/06/ey-p_smoking_cessation_landscape_analysis_key_findings.pdf.

15   See World Health Organization, *WHO Framework Convention on Tobacco Control* (Geneva: WHO, 2003), online: iris.who.int/bitstream/handle/10665/42811/9241591013.pdf?sequence=1.

16   See Robert Beaglehole et al, "A Tobacco-Free World: A Call to Action to Phase Out the Sale of Tobacco Products by 2040" (2015) 385:9972 Lancet at 1011.

17   See Gary Chan et al, "A Systematic Review of Randomized Controlled Trials and Network Meta-Analysis of E-cigarettes for Smoking Cessation" (2021) 119 Addictive Behaviours 106912.

18   See Beaglehole, *supra* note 16 at 16.

19   See New Zealand Ministry of Health, "Proposals for a Smokefree Aotearoa 2025 Action Plan" (2021), online: consult.health.govt.nz/tobacco-control/smokefree2025-actionplan/ [Smokefree NZ 2025].

20   See Gerald Rée, *Policing Public Health in Queensland, 1859-1919* (PhD Thesis, Griffith University, 2010), online : research-repository.griffith.edu.au/bitstream/handle/10072/367309/Ree_2010_02Thesis.pdf?sequence=1.

21   See Beaglehole, *supra* note 16 at 16.

22   See Line Melbøe et al, "Ethical and Methodological Issues in Research with Sami Experiencing Disability" (2016) 75:1 Intl J Circumpolar Health 31656.

23   See Smokefree NZ 2025, *supra* note 19 at 19.

24   The *Treaty of Waitangi*, British Crown and Māori, 6 February 1840, is an agreement between Māori tribes and the Crown, which established that the British would establish governance in partnership with Māori. Māori tribes would retain their right to self-determination over their own affairs, land and resources, culture,

beliefs and other "taonga" (treasures); Māori could expect to be recognized as equal citizens in law; and different religious or spiritual beliefs would be respected.

25   See Elizabeth Stanley & Riki Mihaere, "The Problems and Promise of International Rights in the Challenge to Māori Imprisonment" (2019) 8:1 Intl J for Crime, Justice and Social Democracy 1.

26   See World Health Organization, *WHO Global Report on Trends in Prevalence of Tobacco Smoking 2000–2025*, 3rd ed (Geneva: World Health Organization, 2019) 39.

27   See Marewa Glover & Kyro Selket, *Smoking Prevalence Among Indigenous Peoples of the World* (Auckland: Centre of Research Excellence: Indigenous Sovereignty & Smoking, 2021).

28   See Eric Single, "Defining Harm Reduction" (1995) 14:3 Drug Alcohol Rev 287.

29   See Rée, *supra* note 20 at 19.

30   See Gordon Roe, "Harm Reduction as Paradigm: Is Better than Bad Good Enough? The Origins of Harm Reduction" (2005) 15:3 Critical Public Health 243.

31   *Ibid.*

32   See Single, *supra* note 28 at 23.

33   See New Zealand Ministry of Health, *Tobacco Products: The Public Health Commission's Advice to the Minister of Health 1993-1994*, (Wellington, NZ: Public Health Commission, 1994).

34   See New Zealand Ministry of Health, *New Zealand Health Survey Annual Data Explorer* (Wellington, NZ: Ministry of Health, 2020), online: minhealthnz.shinyapps.io/nz-health-survey-2022-23-annual-data-explorer/_w_256caccd/ - !/home.

35   See Daphne Wu et al, "Impact of Cigarette Tax Increase on Health and Financing Outcomes in Four Indian States" (2020) 4:49 Gates Open Research.

36   See Tony Blakely et al, "Health, Health Inequality, and Cost Impacts of Annual Increases in Tobacco Tax: Multistate Life Table Modeling in New Zealand" (2015) 12:7 PLoS Medicine e1001856.

37   See Marewa Glover et al, "Price Hikes, Crime Fad or Political Football? What Caused a Spike in Store Robberies for Cigarettes in New Zealand: Analysis of News Reports (2009-2018)" (2021) 20:3 Safer Communities.

38   Prince Siddharth, *Quantifying Māori Spend on Tobacco, Alcohol and Gambling* (Wellington, NZ: New Zealand Institute of Economic Research, 2019), online: coreiss.com/assets/Tobacco%20Alcohol%20Gambling%20Tax%20Take%202018_NZIER%20Report.pdf.

39   The *Treaty of Waitangi, supra* note 24, was the founding document of New Zealand, in which Māori tribal chiefs and the British Crown agreed upon the parameters of British settlement. Treaty settlements seek to compensate tribes, historical grievances resulting from Crown breaches of the Treaty of Waitangi. Compensation can include financial payments along with the return of confiscated land.

40   See Vanessa Selak et al, "Ethnic Differences in Cardiovascular Risk Profiles Among 475,241 Adults in Primary Care in Aotearoa, New Zealand" (2020) 133:1521 New Zealand Medical J 14.

41   See New Zealand Ministry of Business, Innovation and Employment, "Māori Labour Market Trends—December 2020 Quarter (Unadjusted)" (Wellington, NZ: Ministry of Business, Innovation and Employment, 2020), online: www.mbie.govt.nz/dmsdocument/13559-maori-in-the-labour-market-december-2020-quarter-unadjusted.

42   See New Zealand Department of Corrections, *Hōkai Rangi. Ara Poutama Aotearoa Strategy: 2019-2024* (Wellington, NZ: Department of Corrections, 2019), online: www.corrections.govt.nz/__data/assets/pdf_file/0003/38244/Hokai_Rangi_Strategy.pdf.

43 See Ministry of Health Survey, *supra* note 34 at 29.

44 See Siddharth, *supra* note 38 at 33.

45 *Ibid.*

46 See Sara Greene, "A Theory of Poverty: Legal Immobility" (2019) 96:4 Washington U LR 753.

47 See *Smokefree Environments and Regulated Products (Vaping) Amendment Act* (NZ), 2020/62.

48 See *Smoke-free Environments (Prohibiting Smoking in Motor Vehicles Carrying Children) Amendment Act* (NZ), 2020/19.

49 See Greene, *supra* note 46 at 42.

50 See Alex Latu & Albany Lucas, "Discretion in the New Zealand Criminal Justice System: The Position of Māori and Pacific Islanders" (2008) 12:1 J South Pacific L 84; see also Stanley, *supra* note 25.

51 See Te Uepū Hāpai i te Ora (the Safe and Effective Justice Advisory Group), *He Waka Roimata: Transforming Our Criminal Justice System* (Wellington, NZ: Ministry of Justice, 2019), online: www.justice.govt.nz/assets/Documents/Publications/he-waka-roimata.pdf.

52 See Tania Mead, *A Justice System for Everyone* (New Zealand: JustSpeak, 2020), online: www.justspeak.org.nz/ourwork/justspeak-idi-research-a-justice-system-for-everyone.

53 See Roe, *supra* note 30 at 360.

54 See Paul Christoffel, "Story: Liquor Laws" (last modified 15 December 2014), online: teara.govt.nz/en/liquor-laws.

55 See Marewa Glover et al, *Store Robberies for Tobacco Products: Perceived Causes and Potential Solutions* (2021) 6:4 J Community Safety & Wellbeing 191.

56 *Ibid* at 37.

57 *Ibid.*

58 See *United Nations Declaration on the Rights of Indigenous Peoples*, 13 September 2007, A/61/L.67 and Add.1.

59 *Ibid* at 57.

60 See Voigt, Kristin, "'If You Smoke, You Stink.' Denormalisation Strategies for the Improvement of Health-Related Behaviours: The Case of Tobacco" In: Strech, D., Hirschberg, I., Marckmann, G. (eds) Ethics in Public Health and Health Policy. Public Health Ethics Analysis, vol 1. Springer, Dordrecht, 2013, pp. 47–61. https://doi.org/10.1007/978-94-007-6374-6_4.

61 See Brewis, Alexandra & Amber Wutich, *Lazy, Crazy, and Disgusting: Stigma and the Undoing of Global Health* (Baltimore: Johns Hopkins University Press, 2019.

62 See, e.g., the New York State *Tobacco Product Waste Reduction Act* to take effect from January 1, 2022.

63 See Greene, *supra* note 46.

64 See Centre of Research Excellence: Indigenous Sovereignty and Smoking, "Voices of the 5%" (last accessed 22 July 2022), online: voicesofthe5percent.nz/home (this is an in-depth qualitative longitudinal (2020-2025) study aimed at understanding why people do not want to or cannot quit smoking, despite the increasingly punishing tobacco control programme being implemented in New Zealand.

65 See Stanley, *supra* note 25 at 4-5.

66 See Single, *supra* note 28 at 23.

CHAPTER 9

Regulating Harm Reduction Claims Under the Canadian Tobacco and Vaping Products Act and the US Family Smoking Prevention and Tobacco Control Act

Sam F. Halabi

As a matter of individual and public health, the authorization of tobacco products for purposes of "harm reduction" is fraught with risk. On the one hand, there is arguably no more lethal invention than the combustible cigarette. It killed 100 million people over the course of the twentieth century and is projected to kill one billion this century—mainly in poorer countries.[1] Viewed this way, *any* movement by tobacco users away from combustible cigarettes to other forms of tobacco consumption are preferable.

On the other hand, harm reduction has been part and parcel of a massive, decades-long, deadly fraud perpetrated upon the consuming public. As early as the 1920s and 1930s, the American Tobacco Company and Philip Morris used claims by physicians that their cigarettes caused less health irritation. "Authors of reviews and commentaries have noted that menthol cigarettes were described in ads during the 1940s and early 1950s as 'healthier.'"[2] The use of descriptors like "light," "ultra-light," "mild," along with associated colour and package schemes, was similarly part of an orchestrated effort to lead people—often the young, women, or both—to believe that it was possible to smoke a less harmful cigarette. The result was addiction, illness, and death on a massive scale.

Recent tobacco-control legislation in Canada and the United States acknowledges this dilemma. The 2018 Tobacco and Vaping Products Act[3] in Canada and the 2009 Family Smoking Prevention and Tobacco Control Act[4] in the United States are the major statutes regulating harm reduction tobacco devices in the two countries and the claims that can be made about them. Those statutes, in turn, establish regulatory mechanisms for tobacco manufacturers to submit for approval, such as statements for the promotion of non-cigarette tobacco products claiming "harm reduction" relative to cigarette use. While this chapter focuses on the use of so-called vaping products, regulatory approvals in the United States have included entirely smokeless products as well.

This chapter analyzes these laws, their regulatory review mechanisms, and identifies strengths and weaknesses in each regime as part of a broader effort to make "harm reduction," "modified risk," or "modified exposure" claims protective of individual and public health. It argues that, based on a comparison of Canadian and US approaches, the important steps are to (1) ensure that regulatory review agencies and related advisory boards are free from tobacco-industry influence, (2) require that review processes be informed by extensive public commentary, and (3) scrutinize not only evidence submitted with product-claims applications but the corporate relationships behind those applications.

"Modified Risk" and "Harm Reduction" in the Tobacco Context

Harm reduction may be defined as "a strategy that lowers total tobacco-related mortality and morbidity despite continued exposure to tobacco-related toxicants."[5] Harm reduction seeks to "encourage less risky behaviors" by implementing "a range of practical policies, regulations, actions, and strategies that reduce health risks by providing safer forms of products/substances." Harm reduction can take the form of "behavioral methods, nicotine replacement therapies, or so-called 'safer' cigarettes manufactured by the tobacco industry to reduce daily cigarette consumption."[6]

The controversy surrounding modified risk and harm reduction in the tobacco industry centres around how they may harm individuals, particularly younger consumers, who do not yet use tobacco products and how they benefit current, addicted users of tobacco products. On one hand, there are "clear reasons to assume these nicotine-containing products have risks for public health, because they may be appealing to non-smokers, particularly adolescents."[7] Labelling these products as "modified risk" or "harm reduction" may result in an increase of "the number of dual users" of these products and cigarettes, as well as an increase in "the number of non-smokers using tobacco products after getting addicted to nicotine from smokeless tobacco."[8] Users, particularly adolescents, equate these "safer" products as "safe."[9]

On the other hand, harm reduction strategies are asserted to be "necessary to help those incapable of breaking their dependence on tobacco" as the promotion of these "treatments" could "increase autonomy among those least able to control their own health behaviors."[10] Using "novel, purportedly less hazardous tobacco products" as a harm reduction strategy aims to "disassociat[e] nicotine from the ancillary carbon monoxide and myriad carcinogens of smoking," allowing an individual to "retain addictive behaviors while limiting their concomitant harms."[11] While the healthiest option is not using tobacco at all, these less hazardous products could be a workable approach for individuals who are "addicted to nicotine and [are] unwilling or unable to quit smoking."[12]

The bulk of drug-regulatory authority is focused on so-called modified risk, a classification that, so far, is requested for an already marketed product.[13] Marketing these products as modified risk in Canada and the United States requires authorization by Health Canada or the Food and Drug Administration (FDA), respectively, that the product will, or is expected to, benefit the health of the population as a whole.[14] This, however, does not mean the products are "safe" because "[a]ll tobacco products are potentially harmful and people who do not use them should not start."[15]

Modified Risk and Harm Reduction Promotion in Action: Vaping in Canada and the United States

One of the most important forms of tobacco consumption asserted to potentially be of value for harm reduction is vaping products, also known as e-cigarettes, e-vaporizers, or electronic nicotine delivery systems. These are battery-operated devices that people use to inhale an aerosol, which typically contains nicotine (though not always), fla-vouring, and other chemicals.[16] E-cigarettes are smokeless and con-tain a replaceable nicotine cartridge, an atomizer that vaporizes the nicotine and various secondary chemical ingredients, and a battery that powers the device.[17]

A "vaping product" is defined in section 2 of the Canadian Tobacco and Vaping Products Act as

> (a) a device that produces emissions in the form of an aerosol and is intended to be brought to the mouth for inhalation of the aerosol; (b) a device that is designated to be a vaping product by the regulations; (c) a part that may be used with those devices; and (d) a substance or mixture of substances, whether or not it contains nicotine, that is intended for use with those devices to produce emissions.

E-liquids, including zero-nicotine e-liquid, fall within this definition. In the United States, vaping products are deemed "tobacco products" under the more broadly worded statute.

Vaping products are more popular than traditional tobacco prod-ucts among young people and are the most commonly used form of nicotine among youth in Canada and the United States.[18] Research suggests that e-cigarettes appeal to youth and young people because they may believe vaping is less harmful than smoking.[19] Many teens do not know that vaping cartridges contain nicotine.[20] E-cigarettes are also generally less expensive than conventional ones.[21]

In the United States, despite legal prohibitions, the potential bene-fits of e-cigarettes and other vaping products—health and otherwise—have been frequently emphasized in advertisements, including the freedom to smoke in a wider range of spaces, a lack of smell or toxic chemicals, the absence of the social stigma around cigarette smoking, cost savings, and health advantages to smokers and to their family members, primarily related to the content of tobacco smoke emissions.[22]

Many vaping products look and feel like traditional cigarettes and theoretically could satisfy psychological and behavioural stimuli for smokers.[23] Evidence points to nicotine vaping products as signifi-cantly less harmful than combustible cigarettes and they may play a role in achieving cessation.[24] Harm reduction advocates argue that e-cigarettes could meet the needs of some ex-smokers by substituting physical, psychological, social, cultural, and identity-related aspects of tobacco addiction, thus preventing relapse.[25]

Similarly in Canada, the potential health benefits of using vaping products have been primarily focused on harm reduction benefits and their potential as smoking-cessation devices.[26] Tobacco use is still the leading preventable cause of disease and premature death in Canada.[27] "[N]icotine-containing e-cigarettes may be a less harmful nicotine product, containing fewer carcinogens than combustible cigarettes and other tobacco products," thus "nicotine-containing e-cigarettes may be a product that could help smokers reduce their health risks, and may help them quit."[28]

Those claims are contested, and even if shown to enjoy significant evidentiary support later, they must be balanced against the risks of allowing the promotion of *any* product that contains nicotine.[29] The maximum benefit from using nicotine vaping products as a harm reduction tool is realized *only* if smokers *completely* quit smoking rather than using them as a partial substitute, since even low-level smoking still confers substantial health risk.[30] A single vaping cartridge, such as an extra-strength one, could hold the amount of nicotine that is equivalent to an entire pack of cigarettes or more, and there is tremendous variation in the composition, strengths, and flavouring of available nicotine liquids.[31] While it is true that e-cigarettes may expose individuals to fewer toxic chemicals than combustible cigarettes, electronic cigarettes may be as addictive.[32]

Moreover, research suggests associations between the dual use of e-cigarettes and smoking with cardiovascular disease.[33] As an entirely separate risk, vaping products have been shown to cause lung injuries and death for reasons related to the content of their liquid and smoke.[34] As of 21 January, 2020, the US Centers for Disease Control and Prevention confirmed 60 deaths in patients with e-cigarette/vaping-associated lung injury (EVALI). Data from patient reports and product testing show THC-containing e-cigarette or vaping products, particularly from informal sources like friends, family, or in-person or online dealers, are linked to most cases of EVALI.[35]

A 2015 US Surgeon General report shows that about 40 percent of young e-cigarette users had never smoked regular tobacco previously, and early evidence suggests that vaping might serve as an introductory product for preteens and teens who then go on to use other nicotine products.[36] Another study suggests that vaping nicotine might actually encourage cigarette smoking in adolescents.[37] A 2015 report of the House of Commons Standing Committee on Health also addressed this similar "gateway effect"—the possibility that children (and generally non-smokers) will initiate nicotine use with electronic nicotine delivery systems (ENDS) at a rate greater than expected if ENDS did not exist, as well as the possibility that once addicted to nicotine through ENDS children will switch to cigarette smoking.[38] It also identified advertising of e-cigarettes targeted to youth as a significant concern.[39]

Facing these problems, both Canada and the United States have taken regulatory actions to address the rise in youth vaping and to protect the public, especially the younger generation, from the risk of nicotine addiction and other vaping-related harms.[40]

Canadian and US Approaches to Harm Reduction and Modified Risk: Canada

Tobacco and Vaping Products Act

The Tobacco and Vaping Products Act (TVPA) was enacted on May 23, 2018, to regulate the manufacture, sale, labelling, and promotion of tobacco and vaping products sold in Canada.[41] The TVPA creates a new legal framework to protect young people from nicotine addiction and tobacco use, while allowing adults access to vaping products as a less harmful alternative to smoking.[42]

The TVPA prohibits the promotion of a vaping product, including by means of the packaging, in a manner that suggests its use may convey a health benefit or by comparing health effects arising from the use of the product with those arising from the use of a tobacco product.[43] This prohibition aims to prevent the public from being deceived or misled with respect to the health hazards of using vaping products.[44] It also seeks to protect young persons and non-users of tobacco products from inducements to use vaping products.[45] Health Canada proposed to make exceptions to this prohibition by having regulations set out a selection of authorized statements regarding the relative health risks of vaping products, as well as the conditions upon which manufacturers, retailers, and others could use these statements in product promotions.

Scientific Advisory Board on Vaping Products

Under the TVPA, Health Canada, in collaboration with the Canadian Institutes of Health Research, established the Scientific Advisory Board on Vaping Products to review the scientific literature on the potential health benefits and harms of vaping products, including statements that accurately reflect the evidence on the use of vaping products versus combustible cigarettes, and provide recommendations on the federal legislative framework for vaping products.[46] The mandate of the board is to monitor and analyze scientific evidence around the benefits and harms of vaping products and inform Health Canada of emerging evidence, and make position statements that accurately reflect the evidence on the use of vaping products versus combustible cigarettes. From the review of the emerging evidence, the board will assess the net public health impact of current federal approaches to regulating vaping products, and provide advice and recommendations to Health Canada officials on whether to further restrict or liberalize the regime established as part of the TVPA.[47]

The 10-member advisory board includes scientists, researchers, academics, and health professionals with expertise in a range of disciplines, including clinical medicine, population and public health, and basic and biomedical science.[48] No member of the board represents industry interests.[49] The board can have 8 to 12 members. The executive secretary, in consultation with the chair, may adjust the number of members from time to time to ensure the appropriate range of knowledge, expertise, experience, and perspectives.[50]

Members are recruited through a targeted nomination process, co-led by Health Canada and the Canadian Institutes of Health Research.[51] The recruitment process supports broad representation across appropriate disciplinary, geographic, gender, and cultural dimensions.[52] As for disciplines, membership should include two to three experts in biomedical/basic science, three to five experts in clinical/individual-level benefits, and three to five experts in population and public health benefits/harms.[53]

Exclusion from consideration for membership includes candidates with affiliations with the tobacco or vaping industry within the last ten years, which increases the chance that no member of the board represents industry interests.

Health Canada's Proposed Harm Reduction Statements

On September 4, 2018, Health Canada released a list of seven proposed promotional statements aimed at accurately communicating the harm reduction potential of vaping products.[54] This "List of Statements for Use in the Promotion of Vaping Products" invited public comment and stated an objective of preventing consumers from being misled about the health hazards of vaping.[55] The statements would be expressed in clear terms to ensure that tobacco users are better informed about the relative health effects of vaping:

1. If you are a smoker, switching completely to vaping is a much less harmful option;
2. While vaping products emit toxic substances, the amount is significantly lower than in tobacco smoke;
3. By switching completely to vaping products, smokers are exposed to a small fraction of the 7,000 chemicals found in tobacco smoke;
4. Switching completely from combustible tobacco cigarettes to e-cigarettes significantly reduces users' exposure to numerous toxic and cancer-causing substances;
5. Completely replacing your cigarette with a vaping product will significantly reduce your exposure to numerous toxic and cancer-causing substances;
6. Switching completely from smoking to e-cigarettes will reduce harms to your health; and
7. Completely replacing your cigarette with an e-cigarette will reduce harms to your health.[56]

These statements intend to accurately communicate the harm reduction potential of vaping products. Six contain the word "completely," a term that is critical to the truthfulness and public health benefit of the legislative effort but which may be ignored or neglected by consumers.

Health Canada announced its Vaping Products Promotion Regulations on July 8, 2020,[57] which set out additional measures to further restrict the promotion of vaping products to youth under the TVPA, such as requiring a warning statement (e.g., "vaping products contain nicotine, a highly addictive chemical") on all advertisements for vaping products.[58]

Fontem Ventures, an e-vapour technology company that produces leading e-cigarette brand blu, filed comments with Health Canada on its proposed list of statements.[59] The company supported the use of this type of warning statement under the TVPA, emphasizing their value to adults in making an "informed choice," but argued against "exaggerating" risks to deter use.[60] Fontem recommended changing the last statement to "Vaping is likely to be much less harmful than smoking."[61]

Fontem's comments were representative of industry positions generally. The head of corporate affairs with JTI-Macdonald, which sells the Logic e-cigarette brand, said in 2019 that the government's proposal was "a step in the right direction," and supported "any initiative that would give adult smokers the information they need."[62] Daniel David, president of the Vaping Industry Trade Association, said he was encouraged by Health Canada's proposal, stating that it was their right to market directly to adult smokers and vapers using harm reduction statements.[63]

Conversely, public health experts argued that promoting harm reduction claims would exacerbate the unfolding vaping crisis.[64] The critical problem with vaping product advertisement is that it reaches youth, ex-smokers, and non-smokers.[65] Additionally, physicians, researchers, and health organizations expressed concerns about allowing companies to make such claims, seeing it as a critical misstep because such statements down play the risks of e-cigarettes and could encourage young people to vape.[66] Indeed, there are mounting concerns about the danger of e-cigarettes given an outbreak of vaping-related lung illness.[67] Health groups said that e-cigarettes also pose long-term health risks and that Health Canada should move to quickly ban advertising as a way of protecting young people.[68]

The United States

Family Smoking Prevention and Tobacco Control Act

The Family Smoking Prevention and Tobacco Control Act (the Tobacco Control Act) was signed into law on June 22, 2009,[69] granting the FDA authority to regulate the manufacture, distribution, and marketing of tobacco products.[70] The Tobacco Control Act made it illegal for companies to market their products as being less risky to US consumers, except where specifically authorized by the FDA.[71] In 2016, the FDA finalized a rule that extends its regulatory authority to all tobacco products, including e-cigarettes and other ENDS, hookah (waterpipe) tobacco, pipe tobacco, cigars, and nicotine gels.[72]

Specifically, the Tobacco Control Act restricts tobacco marketing and sales to youth.[73] In addition, the Tobacco Control Act prohibits tobacco companies from making reduced-harm claims like "light," "low," "mild," or similar descriptors without obtaining a "modified risk tobacco product order" from the FDA.[74]

An application for modified risk tobacco product (MRTP) can be submitted by any person seeking an FDA modified risk order, under section 911 of the Federal Food, Drug, and Cosmetic Act.[75] The FDA's evaluation of the scientific information in an application, recommendations from the Tobacco Product Scientific Advisory Committee, public comments, and other information made available to the agency will all be considered to make a final decision on whether to grant a modified risk order letter.[76] Excluding information regarding trade secrets or that is otherwise confidential commercial information, by law the FDA must make MRTP applications available for public comment and refer MRTP applications to the Tobacco Product Scientific Advisory Committee.[77]

An MRTP application must demonstrate to the FDA that the proposed MRTP will, or is expected to, benefit the health of the US population as a whole, including adults and children, as well as tobacco users and non-users.[78] The FDA recognizes that tobacco products exist on a continuum of risk, with combustible cigarettes being on the most harmful end and other ways to consume nicotine being less harmful.[79] To meet the MRTP standard, tobacco companies must show, among other things, that proposed modified risk information about a product, including claims about reduced harm or risk of tobacco-related disease or reduced exposure to a substance, are supported by scientific evidence and that consumers can adequately understand the information.[80] A granted MRTP allows a tobacco company to market the product using information about the health risks, which can include a comparison to other tobacco products.[81]

Tobacco Product Scientific Advisory Committee

The Tobacco Product Scientific Advisory Committee (TPSAC) consists of 12 members who are selected from individuals knowledgeable in the fields of medicine, medical ethics, science, or technology involving the manufacture, evaluation, or use of tobacco products.[82] Members serve for overlapping terms of up to four years.[83] The TPSAC includes nine technically qualified voting members: physicians, dentists, scientists, or health-care professionals practising in the area of oncology, pulmonology, cardiology, toxicology, pharmacology, addiction, or any other relevant specialty.[84] Among those voting members, one is an officer or employee of a state, local or federal government, and the final voting member is a representative of the general public.[85] In addition, there are three non-voting members who are identified with industry interests: large-sized tobacco manufacturers, tobacco growers, and small-sized tobacco manufacturers.[86] Records show that the three non-voting members have used their participation to steer relevant deliberations over tobacco-control policies under the FDA's authority.[87]

The TPSAC reviews and evaluates safety, dependence, and health issues relating to tobacco products and provides appropriate advice, information, and recommendations to the FDA.[88] Besides submitting reports or recommendations on applications submitted by a manufacturer for an MRTP, the TPSAC also considers and provides recommendations on other tobacco-related topics, such as the impact of the use of menthol in cigarettes on public health, including such use among children and other racial and ethnic minorities.[89]

MRTP Approved by the FDA

Swedish Match USA

On October 22, 2019, the FDA granted the first modified risk orders to Swedish Match USA, allowing it to market eight types of snus products under the brand name General, with the claim: "Using General Snus instead of cigarettes puts you at a lower risk of mouth cancer, heart disease, lung cancer, stroke, emphysema, and chronic bronchitis."[90] Although Swedish Match was the official applicant, it had gathered much of its evidence through a joint venture with Philip Morris, the world's biggest tobacco company.[91] According to the FDA, scientific evidence showed that exclusive use of General smokeless-tobacco products poses lower risks than cigarette smoking for many of the major causes of tobacco-related disease.[92] Additionally, the FDA previously determined that the levels of two potent cancer-causing chemicals (N-nitrosonornicotine and nicotine-derived nitrosamine ketone) in these General snus products are lower than those in most other smokeless-tobacco products sold in the United States, and when used exclusively, General's products may pose lower risk of oral cancer.[93]

The FDA also said that the modified risk claim did not make non-users of tobacco more likely to buy the products, because Swedish Match submitted scientific evidence showing that non-users of tobacco, including young adults, did not intend to buy any of its eight snus products.[94] Nevertheless, the FDA stated that the use of these products still poses increased health risks compared to not using tobacco, and that there are no safe tobacco products.[95] Although the FDA did not find evidence of minors using snus, it has taken steps to further limit the likelihood that youth will start using General's products by requiring Swedish Match to restrict youth access and exposure to the marketing of snus, particularly via websites and social media.[96] These modified risk orders are product-specific and limited to five years.[97]

Gerry Roerty, vice-president and general counsel at Swedish Match, saw the granted orders as "a huge accomplishment for public health in the U.S. and another step toward realizing our vision of a world without cigarettes" because it provides its users with "a risk-reducing alternative."[98]

The FDA's decision certainly gives the tobacco industry hope that tobacco companies can win regulators' permission to advertise new tobacco products as less harmful alternatives to smoking cigarettes.[99] An analyst at Jefferies, an investment bank, viewed this decision as positive for the industry since it showed that the FDA is committed to allowing MRTP products on the market, and it could also comfort consumers as they question the safety of e-cigarettes.[100] Similarly, Wells Fargo analysts wrote that the FDA's authorization is good news for the broader tobacco/nicotine industry as it demonstrates the FDA's commitment to a continuum of risk strategy and provides a viable pathway for manufacturers. The ability to make a modified risk claim in tobacco is "a real game changer" for tax regimes because FDA approval meant that lower-risk products would be taxed less.

However, health-advocacy organizations such as the American Lung Association, the American Academy of Pediatrics, and the American Heart Association submitted testimony to the FDA arguing against modified risk claims.[101] They argued that "there was insufficient evidence on the impact of the marketing of General Snus with modified risk claims on the increased likelihood of tobacco use initiation by non-users, particularly by kids."[102] The evidence suggested that adults would not quit cigarettes but instead would use snus in addition to cigarettes.[103]

Philip Morris International

Philip Morris International submitted its MRTP applications in December 2016 seeking authorization to market its "heat-not-burn" IQOS tobacco product with three flavours of Marlboro HeatSticks.[104]

Its MRTP contains three claims: (1) a reduced risk claim ("Switching completely from cigarettes to the IQOS system can reduce the risks of tobacco-related diseases"), (2) a second reduced risk claim ("Switching completely to IQOS presents less risk of harm than continuing to smoke cigarettes"), and (3) a reduced exposure claim ("Switching completely from cigarettes to the IQOS system significantly reduces your body's exposure to harmful and potentially harmful chemicals").[105]

On July 7, 2020, the FDA issued exposure modification orders to Philip Morris for IQOS and determined that IQOS does not currently meet the standard for marketing with reduced-risk claims but can be marketed with a reduced-exposure claim.[106] It allows the company to claim that the IQOS system heats tobacco but does not burn it; this significantly reduces the production of harmful and potentially harmful chemicals; and studies have shown that switching completely from conventional cigarettes to IQOS significantly reduces your body's exposure to harmful or potentially harmful chemicals.[107]

"Data submitted by the company shows that marketing these particular products with the authorized information could help addicted adult smokers transition away from combusted cigarettes and reduce their exposure to harmful chemicals, but only if they completely switch."[108] Tobacco executives and investment banking firms celebrated the approval.[109]

However, several organizations, including the Campaign for Tobacco-Free Kids, the American Cancer Society Cancer Action Network, the American Heart Association, the American Lung Association, and the Truth Initiative (a non-profit organization that seeks to eliminate tobacco use) released a joint statement, arguing that the FDA put kids and public health at risk.[110] The FDA acknowledged in its decision that the impact on youth of allowing IQOS to be marketed as a modified risk product was still unclear. Further, it argued that the FDA's decision created a real danger that people, particularly kids, "will falsely believe that IQOS has been proven to present a lower health risk and that kids will be exposed to marketing that portrays IQOS, a highly addictive tobacco product, as an appealing, cool alternative to cigarettes, in much the same way as e-cigarettes."[111]

Even before the FDA made its July designation, health advocates published an article arguing the FDA should not authorize Philip Morris to market IQOS with claims of reduced risk or reduced exposure.[112] The article provided ten reasons why the FDA should deny the application, including the proposed reduced risk MRTP claims for IQOS are not supported by the data, the proposed reduced exposure claim is false and misleading, and its proposed reduced exposure claim will be misunderstood by consumers.[113] For example, it noted that the Tobacco Control Act explicitly requires an applicant for an MRTP order to demonstrate that the product "as actually used" exposes consumers to substantially reduced exposures to harmful substances. However, Philip Morris failed to adequately consider dual use, which is the likelihood that IQOS users will use conventional cigarettes, e-cigarettes, and/or other tobacco products at the same time, which is the predominant use pattern. Studies have shown that dual use of IQOS with conventional cigarettes could lead to negative public health impacts, and current IQOS users were more likely to smoke conventional and/or e-cigarettes rather than switching completely to IQOS.[114]

Conclusion

Efforts at harm reduction pose an enormous public health dilemma for lawmakers. On the one hand, non-combustible cigarettes may help current users quit tobacco consumption altogether, a win for both individual and public health. On the other, harm reduction claims are practically as old as the combustible cigarette itself, which means that the claims have a century-long history of being used to deceive people into either initiating tobacco consumption or consuming tobacco in harmful ways.

The experience to date in Canada and the United States suggests that the latter risk is materializing. The only two products that have received harm reduction claim authorization in the United States are either partially or wholly tied to Philip Morris, and both authorizations were accompanied by significant ambiguities in the scientific case. For Canada, the regulatory approach differs and it is too early to tell how the proposed harm reduction statements might affect its population. As has been argued in this chapter, allowing harm reduction will almost always be risky, but risks may be reduced by removing all tobacco-industry influence from deliberations, allowing significant public commentary—especially from public health researchers—to guide regulatory processes, and remaining attentive not only to the information within the four corners of a harm reduction claimant's application but to the corporate and ownership interests behind it.

References

Blaha, Michael Joseph, "5 Vaping Facts You Need to Know" (last visited 29 July 2022), online: www.hopkinsmedicine.org/health/wellness-and-prevention/5-truths-you-need-to-know-about-vaping.

Campaign for Tobacco-Free Kids et al, Press Release, "FDA Puts Kids, Public Health at Risk by Allowing Philip Morris to Market IQOS Heated Cigarette as Modified Risk Tobacco Product" (7 July 2020), online: www.tobaccofreekids.org/press-releases/2020_07_07_fda-iqos-risk.

Centers for Disease Control and Prevention, "Outbreak of Lung Injury Associated with the Use of E-Cigarette, or Vaping, Products" (25 February 2020), online: www.cdc.gov/tobacco/basic_information/e-cigarettes/severe-lung-disease.html [perma.cc/Q4NU-WYWN].

Chaffee, Benjamin W, Shannon Lea Watkins & Stanton A Glantz, "Electronic Cigarette Use and Progression from Experimentation to Established Smoking" (2018) 141:4 Pediatrics e20173594.

Chowdhury, Azim & Keller and Heckman, "Canada's New Regulatory Framework for Vaping Products" (9 October 2018), online (blog): www.thecontinuumofrisk.com/2018/10/canadas-new-regulatory-framework-vaping-products/.

Christensen, Jen, "Smokeless Tobacco Company Can Advertise Snus as Less Risky than Cigarettes, FDA Says," *CNN Health* (22 October 2019), online: www.cnn.com/2019/10/22/health/snus-health-claims-smokeless-tobacco-fda-bn/index.html.

Erku, Daniel et al, "Nicotine Vaping Products as a Harm Reduction Tool Among Smokers: Review of Evidence and Implications for Pharmacy Practice" (2020) 16:9 Research in Soc Administrative Pharmacy 1272.

Glantz, Stanton A, "FDA Should Not Authorize Philip Morris International to Market IQOS with Claims of Reduced Risk Or Reduced Exposure" (23 February 2020), online: tobacco.ucsf.edu/fda-should-not-authorize-philip-morris-international-market-iqos-claims-reduced-risk-or-reduced-exposure.

Halabi, Sam, "Modified Risk Tobacco Products and Preemption" (2011) FDLI Update Magazine.

——, "The Scope of Preemption Under the Family Smoking Prevention and Tobacco Control Act" (2016) 71:2 Food & Drug LJ 300.

Hammond, David et al, "Prevalence of Vaping and Smoking Among Adolescents in Canada, England, and the United States: Repeat National Cross Sectional Surveys" (2019) 365:l2219 BMJ.

Health Canada, *Proposals for the Regulation of Vaping Products* (Ottawa: Health Canada, 31 August 2017), online: www.canada.ca/en/health-canada/programs/consultation-regulation-vaping-products/proposals-regulate-vaping-products.html.

———, "Terms of Reference: Scientific Advisory Board on Vaping Products," (13 April 2018), online: www.canada.ca/en/health-canada/corporate/about-health-canada/public-engagement/external-advisory-bodies/vaping-products/terms-of-reference.html [perma.cc/N6XZ-6RYR].

———, "Final Vaping Products Promotion Regulations (VPPR)" (9 July 2020), online: www.canada.ca/en/health-canada/news/2020/07/final-vaping-products-promotion-regulations-vppr.html.

———, "Scientific Advisory Board on Vaping Products," (26 January 2021), online: www.canada.ca/en/health-canada/corporate/about-health-canada/public-engagement/external-advisory-bodies/vaping-products.html [perma.cc/QZ7P-MWYC].

House of Commons, Standing Committee on Health, *Vaping: Toward a Regulatory Framework for E-Cigarettes* (report), 41-2, No 9 (10 March 2015) (Chair: Ben Lobb).

LaVito, Angelica, "FDA Permits Swedish Match to Advertise Snus Smokeless Tobacco as Less Harmful than Cigarettes," *CNBC* (22 October 2019), online: www.cnbc.com/2019/10/22/fda-authorizes-swedish-match-to-advertise-snus-as-less-harmful-than-cigarettes.html.

Lempert, Lauren Kass & Stanton Glantz, "Analysis of FDA's IQOS Marketing Authorisation and Its Policy Impacts" (2020) 30:4 Tobacco Control 413.

Meier, Benjamin Mason & Donna Shelley, "The Fourth Pillar of the Framework Convention on Tobacco Control: Harm Reduction and the International Human Right to Health" (2006) 121:5 Public Health Reports 494 at 495.

National Center for Health Research, "NCHR's Comments on Modified Risk Tobacco Product Application for Camel Snus" (30 December 2020), online: www.center4research.org/nchrs-comments-on-modified-risk-tobacco-product-application-for-camel-snus/ [perma.cc/7J69-H6EX].

National Institute on Drug Abuse, "Vaping Devices (Electronic Cigarettes) DrugFacts" (January 2020), online: www.drugabuse.gov/publications/drugfacts/vaping-devices-electronic-cigarettes [perma.cc/3MV4-K39V].

Notley, Caitlin et al, "The Unique Contribution of E-Cigarettes for Tobacco Harm Reduction in Supporting Smoking Relapse Prevention" (2018) 15:31 Harm Reduction J 1.

Osei, AD et al, "Association Between E-Cigarette Use and Cardiovascular Disease Among Never and Current Combustible-Cigarette Smokers" (2019) 132:8 American J Medicine 949.

Paradise, Jordan, "Electronic Cigarettes: Smoke-Free Laws, Sale Restrictions, and the Public Health" (2014) 104:6 American J Public Health e17.

Rising, Joshua & Lori Alexander, "Marketing of Menthol Cigarettes and Consumer Perceptions" (2011) 9:1 Tobacco Induced Diseases.

Swedish Match, Press Release, "FDA Designates General Snus as Less Harmful Alternative to Cigarettes" (22 October 2019), online: www.swedishmatch.

com/Media/Pressreleases-and-news/News/fda-designates-general-snus-as-less-harmful-alternative-to-cigarettes/.

Tobacco Reporter, "FDA Grants IQOS Exposure Claim" (8 July 2020), online (blog): tobaccoreporter.com/2020/07/08/fda-grants-iqos-modified-exposure-claim.

US Food & Drug Administration, "The Facts on the FDA's New Tobacco Rule" (16 June 2016), online: www.fda.gov/consumers/consumer-updates/facts-fdas-new-tobacco-rule [perma.cc/XZ9F-YMWE].

——, "Light, Low, Mild or Similar Descriptors" (19 January 2018), online: www.fda.gov/tobacco-products/labeling-and-warning-statements-tobacco-products/light-low-mild-or-similar-descriptors [perma.cc/WQF8-84UK].

——, "FDA Grants First-Ever Modified Risk Orders To Eight Smokeless Tobacco Products" (22 October 2019), online: www.fda.gov/news-events/press-announcements/fda-grants-first-ever-modified-risk-orders-eight-smokeless-tobacco-products.

——, "Tobacco Products Scientific Advisory Committee" (12 November 2019), online: www.fda.gov/advisory-committees/committees-and-meeting-materials/tobacco-products-scientific-advisory-committee [perma.cc/97TC-6H2W].

——, "Think E-Cigs Can't Harm Teens Health?" (30 April 2020), online: www.fda.gov/tobacco-products/public-health-education/think-e-cigs-cant-harm-teens-health#references.

——, "Family Smoking Prevention and Tobacco Control Act—An Overview" (3 June 2020), online: www.fda.gov/tobacco-products/rules-regulations-and-guidance/family-smoking-prevention-and-tobacco-control-act-overview [perma.cc/NQZ8-X8X3].

——, "Modified Risk Tobacco Products" (1 December 2020), online: www.fda.gov/tobacco-products/advertising-and-promotion/modified-risk-tobacco-products [perma.cc/ET79-4EN3].

Ventures, Fontem, "Response to Health Canada's Proposed List of Statements for Use in the Promotion of Vaping Products" (17 September 2018), online: www.fontemscience.com/wp-content/uploads/2018/09/2018-09-17-fontem-ventures-canada-comment-on-proposed-statements.pdf.

Weeks, Carly, "Health Canada Considers Allowing E-Cigarette Companies to Promote Harm-Reduction Benefits," *The Globe and Mail* (17 October 2019) online: www.theglobeandmail.com/canada/article-health-canada-considers-allowing-e-cigarette-companies-to-promote-harm/.

——, "How the Vaping Industry Is Targeting Teens—And Getting Away with It," *The Globe and Mail* (16 November 2019), online: www.theglobeandmail.com/canada/article-vaping-advertising-marketing-investigation/.

Werner, Angela K et al, "Hospitalizations and Death Associated with EVALI," (2020) 382.

World Health Organization, "Tobacco" (27 May 2020), online: www.who.int/news-room/fact-sheets/detail/tobacco.

Notes

1   See World Health Organization, "Tobacco" (27 May 2020), online: www.who.int/news-room/fact-sheets/detail/tobacco [perma.cc/X8KJ-YRHV].

2   See Joshua Rising & Lori Alexander, "Marketing of Menthol Cigarettes and Consumer Perceptions" (2011) 9:1 Tobacco Induced Diseases.

3   SC 1997, c 13.

4   21 USC 301 (2009).

5   See Benjamin Mason Meier & Donna Shelley, "The Fourth Pillar of the Framework Convention on Tobacco Control: Harm Reduction and the International Human Right to Health" (2006) 121:5 Public Health Reports 494 at 495 [Fourth Pillar].

6   *Ibid.*

7   See National Center for Health Research, "NCHR's Comments on Modified Risk Tobacco Product Application for Camel Snus" (30 December 2020), online: www.center4research.org/nchrs-comments-on-modified-risk-tobacco-product-application-for-camel-snus/ [perma.cc/7J69-H6EX].

8   *Ibid.*

9   *Ibid.*

10   Fourth Pillar, *supra* note 5 at 494.

11   *Ibid.*

12   *Ibid* at 495.

13   See US Food and Drug Administration , "FDA Authorizes Modified Risk Tobacco Products" (4 May 2020), online: www.fda.gov/tobacco-products/advertising-and-promotion/fda-authorizes-modified-risk-tobacco-products [perma.cc/9T5D-AE9X] ["FDA Authorizes Modified Risk Tobacco Products"].

14   *Ibid.*

15   *Ibid.*

16   See National Institute on Drug Abuse, "Vaping Devices (Electronic Cigarettes) DrugFacts" (January 2020), online: www.drugabuse.gov/publications/drugfacts/vaping-devices-electronic-cigarettes [perma.cc/3MV4-K39V] ["Vaping Devices"].

17   See Jordan Paradise, "Electronic Cigarettes: Smoke-Free Laws, Sale Restrictions, and the Public Health" (2014) 104:6 American J Public Health e17.

18   See David Hammond et al, "Prevalence of Vaping and Smoking Among Adolescents in Canada, England, and the United States: Repeat National Cross Sectional Surveys" (2019) 365:l2219 BMJ; see also "Vaping Devices," *supra* note 16; see also Michael Joseph Blaha, "5 Vaping Facts You Need to Know" (last visited 29 July 2022), online: www.hopkinsmedicine.org/health/wellness-and-prevention/5-truths-you-need-to-know-about-vaping [perma.cc/QF5D-F6VC] ["5 Vaping Facts"].

19   See US Food & Drug Administration, "Think E-Cigs Can't Harm Teens Health?" (30 April 2020), online: www.fda.gov/tobacco-products/public-health-education/think-e-cigs-cant-harm-teens-health#references.

20   See "Vaping Devices," *supra* note 16.

21   See "5 Vaping Facts," *supra* note 18.

22   See Paradise, supra note 17.

23   *Ibid.*

24   See Daniel Erku et al, "Nicotine Vaping Products as a Harm Reduction Tool Among Smokers: Review of Evidence and Implications for Pharmacy Practice" (2020) 16:9 Research in Soc Administrative Pharmacy 1272.

25   See Caitlin Notley et al, "The Unique Contribution of E-Cigarettes for Tobacco Harm Reduction in Supporting Smoking Relapse Prevention" (2018) 15:31 Harm Reduction J 1.

26 See House of Commons, *Standing Committee on Health, Vaping: Toward a Regulatory Framework For E-Cigarettes* (report), 41-2, No 9 (10 March 2015) (Chair: Ben Lobb) [*Vaping: Toward a Regulatory Framework*].

27 *Ibid.*

28 *Ibid.*

29 See Paradise, *supra* note 17.

30 See Erku, *supra* note 24.

31 See Paradise, *supra* note 17.

32 See "5 Vaping Facts," *supra* note 18.

33 See AD Osei et al, "Association Between E-Cigarette Use and Cardiovascular Disease Among Never and Current Combustible-Cigarette Smokers" (2019) 132:8 American J Medicine 949.

34 *Ibid.*

35 See Centers for Disease Control and Prevention, "Outbreak of Lung Injury Associated with the Use of E-Cigarette, or Vaping, Products" (25 February 2020), online: www.cdc.gov/tobacco/basic_information/e-cigarettes/severe-lung-disease. html [perma.cc/Q4NU-WYWN].

36 See "5 Vaping Facts," *supra* note 18; see also "Vaping Devices," *supra* note 16.

37 See Benjamin W Chaffee, Shannon Lea Watkins & Stanton A Glantz, "Electronic Cigarette Use and Progression from Experimentation to Established Smoking" (2018) 141:4 Pediatrics e20173594.

38 See *Vaping: Toward a Regulatory Framework, supra* note 26.

39 *Ibid.*

40 See *Tobacco and Vaping Products Act, supra* note 3; see also *Vaping: Toward a Regulatory Framework, supra* note 26.

41 See *Tobacco and Vaping Products Act, supra* note 3.

42 *Ibid.*

43 See Health Canada, *Proposals for the Regulation of Vaping Products* (31 August 2017), online: online www.canada.ca/en/health-canada/programs/consultation-regulation-vaping-products/proposals-regulate-vaping-products.html [perma.cc/U9BR-4A5S].

44 *Ibid.*

45 *Ibid.*

46 See Health Canada, "Scientific Advisory Board on Vaping Products," (26 January 2021), online: www.canada.ca/en/health-canada/corporate/about-health-canada/public-engagement/external-advisory-bodies/vaping-products.html [perma.cc/ QZ7P-MWYC] ["Scientific Advisory Board on Vaping Products"]; see Health Canada, "Terms of Reference: Scientific Advisory Board on Vaping Products," (13 April 2018), online: www.canada.ca/en/health-canada/corporate/about-health-canada/public-engagement/external-advisory-bodies/vaping-products/terms-of-reference.html [perma.cc/N6XZ-6RYR] ["Terms of Reference"].

47 See "Terms of Reference," *supra* note 46.

48 See "Scientific Advisory Board on Vaping Products," *supra* note 46.

49 See "Terms of Reference," *supra* note 46.

50 *Ibid.*

51 *Ibid.*

52 *Ibid.*

53 *Ibid.*

54 See Azim Chowdhury & Keller and Heckman, "Canada's New Regulatory Framework for Vaping Products" (9 October 2018), online (blog): www.thecontinuumofrisk. com/2018/10/canadas-new-regulatory-framework-vaping-products/[perma.cc/A7QN-FY7V] ["Canada's New Regulatory Framework for Vaping Products"].

55   See Fontem Ventures, "Response to Health Canada's Proposed List of Statements for Use in the Promotion of Vaping Products" (17 September 2018), online: www. fontemscience.com/wp-content/uploads/2018/09/2018-09-17-fontem-ventures-canada-comment-on-proposed-statements.pdf [perma.cc/L2TB-ZDA8] [Fontem Response]; see also *ibid*.

56   *Ibid*.

57   SOR 2020-143.

58   See Health Canada, "Final Vaping Products Promotion Regulations (VPPR)," (Ottawa: Health Canada, 9 July 2020), online: www.canada.ca/en/health-canada/news/2020/07/final-vaping-products-promotion-regulations-vppr.html [perma.cc/7W8M-VZJ4].

59   *Ibid*.

60   *Ibid*.

61   See Fontem Response, *supra* note 55.

62   See Carly Weeks, "Health Canada Considers Allowing E-Cigarette Companies to Promote Harm-Reduction Benefits" (17 October 2019) online: www.theglobeandmail.com/canada/article-health-canada-considers-allowing-e-cigarette-companies-to-promote-harm/ [perma.cc/KCH4-3KE9] ["Health Canada Considers"].

63   *Ibid*.

64   See Carly Weeks, "How the Vaping Industry Is Targeting Teens—And Getting Away with It" (16 November 2019), online: www.theglobeandmail.com/canada/article-vaping-advertising-marketing-investigation/ [perma.cc/WJ3S-6WCU].

65   *Ibid*.

66   See "Health Canada Considers," *supra* note 62.

67   See Angela K Werner et al, "Hospitalizations and Death Associated with EVALI," (2020) 382 New England J Medicine 1589 ("Vitamin E acetate, an additive sometimes used in THC-containing products, is strongly linked to the EVALI outbreak; however, evidence is not sufficient to rule out the contribution of other chemicals of concern, including chemicals in either THC-containing or non-THC-containing products.").

68   *Ibid*.

69   See *supra*, note 4.

70   See US Food and Drug Administration, "Family Smoking Prevention and Tobacco Control Act—An Overview" (3 June 2020), online: www.fda.gov/tobacco-products/rules-regulations-and-guidance/family-smoking-prevention-and-tobacco-control-act-overview [perma.cc/NQZ8-X8X3] ["Family Smoking Prevention"].

71   See "FDA Authorizes Modified Risk Tobacco Products," *supra* note 13.

72   See US Food and Drug Administration, "The Facts on the FDA's New Tobacco Rule" (16 June 2016), online: www.fda.gov/consumers/consumer-updates/facts-fdas-new-tobacco-rule [perma.cc/XZ9F-YMWE].

73   See "Family Smoking Prevention," *supra* note 70.

74   *Ibid*; see also US Food and Drug Administration, "Light, Low, Mild or Similar Descriptors" (19 January 2018), online: www.fda.gov/tobacco-products/labeling-and-warning-statements-tobacco-products/light-low-mild-or-similar-descriptors [perma.cc/WQF8-84UK].

75   See US Food and Drug Administration, "Modified Risk Tobacco Products" (1 December 2020), online: www.fda.gov/tobacco-products/advertising-and-promotion/modified-risk-tobacco-products [perma.cc/ET79-4EN3].

76   *Ibid*.

77   *Ibid*.

78   See "FDA Authorizes Modified Risk Tobacco Products," *supra* note 13.

79 See Angelica LaVito, "FDA Permits Swedish Match to Advertise Snus Smokeless Tobacco As Less Harmful Than Cigarettes" (22 October 2019), online: www.cnbc. com/2019/10/22/fda-authorizes-swedish-match-to-advertise-snus-as-less-harmful-than-cigarettes.html [perma.cc/4ZJA-LN4N] ["FDA Permits Swedish Match"]; see also "FDA Authorizes Modified Risk Tobacco Products," *supra* note 13.

80 See "FDA Authorizes Modified Risk Tobacco Products," *supra* note 13.

81 See US Food and Drug Administration, "Tobacco Products Scientific Advisory Committee" (12 November 2019), online: www.fda.gov/advisory-committees/ committees-and-meeting-materials/tobacco-products-scientific-advisory-committee [perma.cc/97TC-6H2W] ["Tobacco Products Scientific Advisory Committee"].

82 *Ibid.*

83 *Ibid.*

84 *Ibid.*

85 *Ibid.*

86 *Ibid.*

87 See Sam Halabi, "Modified Risk Tobacco Products and Preemption" (2011) FDLI Update Magazine.

88 See "Tobacco Products Scientific Advisory Committee," *supra* note 81.

89 *Ibid.*

90 *Ibid.*

91 See Sam Halabi, "The Scope of Preemption Under the Family Smoking Prevention and Tobacco Control Act" (2016) 71:2 Food & Drug LJ 300.

92 *Ibid.*

93 *Ibid.*

94 *Ibid.*

95 *Ibid.*

96 *Ibid.*

97 See US Food and Drug Administration, "FDA Grants First-Ever Modified Risk Orders to Eight Smokeless Tobacco Products" (22 October 2019), online: www.fda.gov/news-events/press-announcements/fda-grants-first-ever-modified-risk-orders-eight-smokeless-tobacco-products [perma.cc/VJY6-9N8E].

98 See Swedish Match, Press Release, "FDA Designates General Snus as Less Harmful Alternative to Cigarettes" (22 October 2019), online: www.swedishmatch. com/Media/Pressreleases-and-news/News/fda-designates-general-snus-as-less-harmful-alternative-to-cigarettes/ [perma.cc/C3VW-JS9E].

99 See "FDA Permits Swedish Match," *supra* note 79.

100 See Angelica Levito, "FDA Permits Swedish Match To Advertise Snus Smokeless Tobacco as Less Harmful than Cigarettes" (22 October 2019), online: www.cnbc. com/2019/10/22/fda-authorizes-swedish-match-to-advertise-snus-as-less-harmful-than-cigarettes.html (quoting Jefferies analyst Owen Bennett).

101 See Jen Christensen, "Smokeless Tobacco Company Can Advertise Snus As Less Risky Than Cigarettes, FDA Says" (22 October 2019), online: www.cnn. com/2019/10/22/health/snus-health-claims-smokeless-tobacco-fda-bn/index.html [perma.cc/N88J-ML7V] ["Smokeless Tobacco Company Can Advertise"].

102 *Ibid.*

103 *Ibid.*

104 See Stanton A. Glantz, "FDA Should Not Authorize Philip Morris International to Market IQOS with Claims of Reduced Risk Or Reduced Exposure" (23 February 2020), online: tobacco.ucsf.edu/fda-should-not-authorize-philip-morris-international-market-iqos-claims-reduced-risk-or-reduced-exposure [hperma.cc/85N2-DNYK] ["FDA Should Not Authorize"].

105 *Ibid.*

106 See Tobacoo Reporter, "FDA Grants IQOS Exposure Claim" (8 July 2020), online (blog): tobaccoreporter.com/2020/07/08/fda-grants-iqos-modified-exposure-claim [perma.cc/M4E7-HKDQ].

107 *Ibid.*

108 *Ibid.*

109 *Ibid.*

110 See Campaign for Tobacco-Free Kids et al, "FDA Puts Kids, Public Health at Risk by Allowing Philip Morris to Market IQOS Heated Cigarette as Modified Risk Tobacco Product" (7 July 7 2020), online: <www.tobaccofreekids.org/press-releases/2020_07_07_fda-iqos-risk> [perma.cc/C7A5-E33B].

111 *Ibid.*

112 See "FDA Should Not Authorize," *supra* note 104.

113 *Ibid.*

114 See Lauren Kass Lempert & Stanton Glantz, "Analysis of FDA's IQOS Marketing Authorisation and Its Policy Impacts" (2020) 30:4 Tobacco Control 413.

CHAPTER 10

From First Puffs to Policy

A Non-Apology for 32 Years of Substance Use

Alex Clarke

By way of disclosure, my advocacy in support of access to safer nicotine products comes purely from my experience of switching from cigarettes to vaping in 2013. Prior to getting involved with vaping, I had no experience in policy work, government relations, lobbying, law, or public health. I started advocating on a voluntary basis and I am currently serving as the paid CEO of the Consumer Advocates for Smoke-free Alternatives Association (CASAA). CASAA is a US-based non-profit organization with a grassroots membership of more than 250,000 people. While CASAA accepts donations from industry stakeholders, we do not take direction from or speak on behalf of businesses. Nearly everyone serving on CASAA's board, past and present, switched from smoking to vaping or some other safer alternative. We are involved in this fight because harm reduction is saving our lives, and everyone deserves the same opportunity we have had to learn about safer nicotine products and experience the benefits of switching from combustion.

I am offering the following personal history of smoking, other substance use, and my recovery from both as a qualifier and to illustrate that relationships with nicotine and other drugs do not happen magically overnight. The road to habituation, dependence, and addiction is a process, which is not accurately communicated by campaigns against smoking and nicotine use. Accordingly, the public is suffering from a lack of contextualized information that could be helpful in implementing more meaningful policies and supporting people in making healthier choices.

· · ·

By way of background, I smoked my first hundred cigarettes before I turned 14 years old. My dad smoked, my grandfathers smoked, and my cool aunt and uncle smoked. My paternal grandmother quit in the early 1980s, which was certainly helpful to her talents as a singer and vocal coach. Out of her four grandchildren, I am the only one who smoked into adulthood.

I grew up in predominantly White suburban America, with stops in the Southeast, the Midwest, and, finally, the Northeast. I have wanted for nothing my entire life except for maybe an easy answer to the question "where are you from?" Other than the seemingly random uprooting from one place to another, I enjoyed an idyllic childhood, ripe with access to education and opportunity.

I started experimenting with drugs when I was 13 years old, and my progression moved along a continuum of convenience. Cigarettes and alcohol were the most accessible substances because my dad smoked and both parents drank, conservatively. After stealing and smoking regular light cigarettes from my dad, I purchased my first pack for under $2 at a shady neighbourhood grocery located a few blocks from my junior high school. It was a pack of menthols, and I might have purchased them knowing that my friends would not ask to smoke them. It was the only pack of menthols I bought until after I turned 18.

As I began experimenting with cigarettes, I also chose to try other drugs, such as cannabis and LSD. Similar to my experience with smoking, using other drugs was a matter of curiosity, convenience, and enjoying the sensations of altered states. Having friends with older siblings who had connections to sellers was, for lack of a better term, helpful.

I started smoking regularly when I started driving, at 16. Even though I knew that smoking was harmful, having badgered my dad for years with anti-smoking talking points, I adopted the habit as a means to cope with anxiety behind the wheel. As it turned out, I wanted to drive more than I wanted to not smoke.

By the time I turned 18, I was obsessed with both driving and smoking. I organized my life around being able to do both as often as possible.

I delivered food and took spontaneous road trips with friends. "Of course I'll drive!" I would say, "just let me grab a carton of cigarettes."

Over the next 12 years, I floated almost rudderless through colleges and took jobs involving steering wheels. I also prioritized substance use over almost everything else in my life. My ability to use—primarily alcohol—became a daily benchmark of success. No matter what else happened over the preceding 24 hours, as long as I could afford enough alcohol to be drunk, it was a success.

By the end of my 30th trip around the sun, I checked into a 12-step-based drug and alcohol treatment program. I turned 31 while I was there and completed the program three months later. Patients were offered the option to quit smoking, but without the assistance of nicotine-replacement therapy (NRT) or prescription medication. Instead, a Nicotine Anonymous meeting was available every Wednesday evening. I declined the offer as counselors also suggested that dealing with one vice at a time may be a better, gentler strategy. After all, relapsing to alcohol was a more immediate threat to my survival. Moreover, therapists were aware that making smoking cessation a condition of treatment may discourage people from sticking with the program, or even taking the first step toward seeking help.

Now, with the exception of some interesting "near beer" brands, I have not consumed alcohol in nearly 15 years. But through thick and thin during early recovery, my relationship with cigarettes endured. Even though I currently do not smoke tobacco, cigarettes are woven into the fabric of my life. Whiffs of second-hand smoke and the smell of smoky upholstery evoke pleasant memories of visiting my grandparents' house. A cigarette freshly lit off a car lighter instantly transports me to our 1979 Buick LeSabre ("the Green Bomb") en route to the beach for summer vacation. My wonderful childhood is inextricably linked to the sights, sounds, and smells associated with smoking.

Similar to my experience with recovery from substance use disorder, my transition to smoke-free nicotine products required me to replace harmful, self-destructive rituals with new, less risky practices and products. Perhaps there will come a day when I no longer have an interest in nicotine, but until then, I am sliding down the continuum of risk and currently enjoy flavourful, smoke-free alternatives to combustible tobacco. Specifically, Swedish snus is my go-to tobacco of choice. Whether it is marking time, relaxing, giving my mouth something to do, or elevating my focus on a particular task, I experience benefits from consuming nicotine.

Refuge in Self-Destruction and
Harm Reduction as a Bridge to Self-Care

Following my successful completion of inpatient treatment for substance-use disorder, the time came for me to incorporate all the therapy and education I had been exposed to into my daily life, outside of a bubble. But while treatment provided tools for staying away from alcohol and other drugs, my general sense of self-worth continues to suffer. For many years following treatment, smoking was my last means of self-harm, usually prompted by failure or rejection. Sometimes a deep draw on a cigarette was an attempt at receiving a larger dose of soothing nicotine. Other times it was a conscious effort to make sure the smoke reached deep into my lungs, where it could do the most harm. In the absence of defeat, I live with internalized anti-drug and -tobacco messaging and a perception that I am easily identified as a morally deficient drug user.

I found comfort in self-destruction. As I understand and experience it, self-harm can be an act of reclaiming agency—not necessarily rebellious self-destruction (although I will admit that my self-harm was also an open defiance of every coercive campaign ostensibly designed to motivate me to want a healthier life). Whereas external forces determining the direction of my life seem immovable and unavoidable, the act of smoking or getting blackout drunk enabled me to beat them to the punch. In other words, "they can't hurt me any more than I'm hurting myself; I win."

When I decided to give vaping a try, I had three motivations: seeing someone who smoked like me using the products successfully (completely switching), affordability compared to cigarettes (if the marketing statement about pack-equivalency was true), and my first experience with vaping was more enjoyable and less of a hassle than smoking. For a brief and fleeting moment, I felt like I was finally doing something right by switching from smoking to vaping.

While I experienced a confidence boost knowing that my motivations to switch were not entirely extrinsic, I admit to wondering how my deep-seated tendency toward self-destruction would manifest now that slow suicide was off the table. But in the eight years since I switched to vaping, I have slowly oriented my habits, diet, and activity in a more positive and healthy direction.

I still live with internalized messages about deviance and substance use, but I am better equipped to identify those messages as misleading and dishonest. In general, thoughts of dying early make me feel sad, but sadness does not have the warm fuzziness it used to. I am more patient with myself now, and I owe some of that to building off the confidence I experienced from switching away from smoking. Thoughts of being resigned to failure are quieter.

Switch to Quit

Prior to switching to vaping completely in 2013, my first exposure to e-cigarettes occurred in 2008 at a truck stop along I-78, in New Jersey. An e-cigarette display case was on the counter next to the register and the products looked cheap. I think what offended me the most was that they imitated cigarettes, right down to the glowing tip. I immediately pegged them as a scam. I was skeptical and ignorant about how these devices could deliver the nicotine I was accustomed to, and confident that e-cigarettes were even worse than smoking. It would be five more years until I became curious about vapour products. In hindsight, I wish more information was featured alongside the products I saw in 2008. My decision to switch might have happened sooner.

I describe my transition to vaping as near miraculous and accidental. Although I qualify as "motivated" to quit following years of using NRT, prior to trying e-cigarettes I experienced failure in using NRT exclusively. As a result, I resigned myself to continuing to smoke, and expected cigarettes to be with me until my predictable early death. But after trying vaping, I made the mental switch away from smoking within eight hours of purchasing an e-cigarette, and I completely transitioned three days later. In spite of my immediate enthusiasm following my first full day of vaping, it took me at least two weeks to feel certain that I would be able to stick with the products long term. During those first two weeks, I leaned on nicotine gum to make up for what vaping did not seem to be delivering. I was also unsure if I was using the product correctly. While it was clear to me that I was receiving a dose of nicotine, the effect was noticeably milder, or slower than what I was accustomed to with smoking.

I turned to YouTube and message boards like Electronic Cigarette Forum for instruction and advice. Through these community-driven resources, I quickly learned it was not my fault that the products were not meeting my expectations, but that nicotine delivered by way of vaping was different from what I was accustomed to with smoking.

If I wanted to more closely replicate my experience with cigarettes, I would need to upgrade to more powerful devices and use higher concentrations of nicotine. For reference, the e-liquid products available to me in 2013 ranged in nicotine concentrations from unknown to 36 milligrams per millilitre (or 3.6 percent).

Vaping found me at the best possible time in the evolution of the products. In 2013, the industry underwent a massive shift from small, underpowered devices to larger "mods" with bigger batteries offering more power and life. There was a gold rush into the space as opening up a retail location or scaling up hobbyist e-liquid-making into a multi-million-dollar manufacturing operation did not require massive capital investment. The diversity of vapour products exploded, and for the next three years hype around new products drove enthusiasm and adoption among people who are underserved by traditional smoking-cessation strategies and anti-tobacco campaigns.

Aside from the seemingly limitless array of options, and an almost biological drive to keep up with the Joneses, a simple truth provides the foundation for all the excitement around vaping—these products are working where prescriptive smoking-cessation strategies fail. Vaping and the broader tobacco harm reduction movement are enabling hope for millions of people previously resigned to "quit or die."

Peer-to-Peer Support in the Unlikeliest of Places

Prior to switching to vaping, my experience with the social aspects of tobacco retail was limited to infrequent purchases at one of America's oldest brick-and-mortar tobacco stores, in Lancaster, Pennsylvania. Demuth's, no longer an active tobacco shop,[1] always seemed to have one or two regular customers hanging around, chatting with the person behind the counter about everything from local politics to whatever the hot new TV show was. Of course, it was also a place to discuss the pros and cons of various tobacco products and exhibit one's skill for discerning them. As a young adult, it was baffling to me why anyone would spend more than 30 minutes to peruse, purchase, and discuss something like tobacco, and it took quitting smoking for me to fully recognize the social aspect of tobacco use as part of its utility.

In 2014, I finally spent some time sitting on a couch in a vape shop, socializing with other vapers. We shared our preferences for certain devices and e-liquids in tandem with our stories about switching. It became clear to me that vape shops, like the tobacco shops before it, were a temporary escape from the home, or office, or home office. They are an oasis where people can tune out the stressors of the world and just focus on our enthusiasm for the products.

Vape shops are also one of the best places for people new to vaping to learn about the products, and to hear from others about their success with switching away from cigarettes. This voluntary sharing of transition stories reminds me of profound experiences in treatment where something as simple as someone reminding me that I was not alone snapped me out of obsessing over using or dwelling on feelings of hopelessness. I am still excited that people are offering this support to one another without prodding or supervision. We genuinely want people who smoke to succeed with switching from cigarettes.

It may not be immediately obvious to people hanging around a vape shop that they are likely doing double-duty between enjoying some leisure time and helping people quit smoking. While most conversations start with a new vaper asking about which products might work for them, they typically end with encouragement and open offers of support. If one flavour or nicotine strength does not meet their needs, new customers are invited to come back and try something different. Like smoking, finding the right combination of device and liquid takes time—ideally, less time than it took to habituate smoking.

Conclusion

I started smoking because I was curious about drugs. I continued smoking because I enjoyed it and nicotine provided me noticeable relief from anxiety. In turn, I quit smoking because I was curious about a new, potentially safer delivery device. I continue using nicotine because I enjoy its pleasurable effects and it still provides relief. While some argue that any utility from habitual nicotine use is limited to managing withdrawal symptoms, using tobacco products is not strictly about consuming a drug. The ritual itself is a source of comfort, distraction, marking time, and simply enjoying a variety of flavours—and in places where nicotine use has not been banished to the curb, it is a pro-social experience as well.

One of the more endearing—and arguably promising—vape shop models is reminiscent of the old tobacco shop. Customers are invited to relax with comfy chairs, couches, and maybe a television. On

Saturdays, some shops are tuning into the CASAA Live podcast that I host alongside board member Logan Evans and member coordinator Kristin Knoll-Marsh. In the best cases, shops are honestly informing their customers about low-risk alternatives to smoking while encouraging them to engage in discussion about nicotine policy with policy-makers. (While FDA regulations in the United States prohibit *marketing* statements that include therapeutic or modified risk claims, the same restrictions do not apply to statements made by way of lobbying or other legislative engagement. Moreover, consumers are free to share their knowledge, opinions, and experiences with safer nicotine products.)

Vape shops are valuable touchpoints for health and safety information.[2] But the trend in policies promoted by wealthy anti-smoking organizations and public health officials is moving toward shutting these environments down in favour of a tightly controlled distribution scheme for products that people are expected to feel bad about using. While the vapour industry and the community that built it may have an image problem (some of it of our own making), that is not a good enough reason to choke off the space we can use to mature.

Looking toward the future, the recent past provides both words of dire warning and reasons for hope. TVALI, which stands for THC-vaping-associated lung injury—a suggested replacement for the inappropriately named and methodically repeated EVALI, or e-cigarette/vaping-associated lung injury—affecting more than 2,807 people in 2019, and killing 68, is a horrific example of injuries and death attributable to prohibition and imbalanced regulations.[3] At the same time, considering the potential scale of the vitamin E acetate-adulterated illegal THC cartridges that were headed to underground sellers, it was surprising that, eventually, fewer than three thousand people were affected.[4] Of course, we may also come to understand that the misinformation on the evening news, championed by officials in front of statehouses, and enshrined in meeting minutes and statute, is leading to avoidable injuries.

While the nation was gripped by fear of fruity-flavoured USB drives, the Utah Department of Health took a step toward acknowledging the aforementioned utility of specialty vape shops when it enacted emergency rule R384-418.[5] Although the rule erroneously prohibited sales of flavoured e-cigarettes (and might have resulted in people returning to smoking), it required a warning posted at all tobacco retailers clearly alerting customers about contaminated cannabis products. The required warning specifically informed people that "[v]aping unregulated THC is dangerous to your health. A lung disease related to vaping unregulated THC has recently hospitalized dozens of Utahns and caused several deaths nationwide."[6] Rather than using the warning as a means to discourage people from vaping nicotine, the health department acknowledged that the most effective way to communicate with people who are more likely to be affected by the tainted cannabis products was to *tell them the truth* and meet them where they are, at vape shops.

Decades of anti-tobacco campaigns deserve credit for pushing smoking prevalence into a steady decline, but there appears to be a point of diminishing returns when it comes to the prohibitionist approach. Similarly to pushing one's fist into sand, increasing force only results in more resistance after progressing a couple of centimetres down. While the lion's share of effort in anti-tobacco activism is devoted to programming young people to resist nicotine use, those of us who are no longer eligible for salvation by prevention strategies are left to feel broken, unwanted, and branded as walking billboards for evil. I think there is only so much of this treatment that we are willing to accept before exploring different and positive solutions on our own.

References

Legislation

US, R384-418, Electronic-Cigarette Mandatory Warning Signage and Sale Restrictions, Utah, 2019 (enacted).

Publications

Centers for Disease Control and Prevention, "Outbreak of Lung Injury Associated with the Use of E-Cigarette, or Vaping, Products" (25 February 2020), online: www.cdc.gov/tobacco/basic_information/e-cigarettes/severe-lung-disease.html [perma.cc/Q4NU-WYWN].

Downs, David, Dave Howard & Bruce Barcott, "Journey of a Tainted Vape Cartridge: From China's Labs to Your Lungs" (24 September 2019), online: www.leafly.com/news/politics/vape-pen-injury-supply-chain-investigation-leafly.

Utah Department of Health & Human Services, "Emergency Rule to Address Vaping-related Illnesses" (2 October 2019), online: health.utah.gov/featured-news/emergency-rule-to-address-vaping-related-illnesses.

Notes

1   See The Demuth Museum, "Demuth Tobacco Shop" (last visited 29 July 2022), online: www.demuth.org/tobacco-shop.

2   See Utah Department of Health & Human Services, "Emergency Rule to Address Vaping-related Illnesses" (2 October 2019), online: health.utah.gov/featured-news/emergency-rule-to-address-vaping-related-illnesses.

3   See Centers for Disease Control and Prevention, "Outbreak of Lung Injury Associated with the Use of E-Cigarette, or Vaping, Products" (last modified 3 August 2021), online: www.cdc.gov/tobacco/basic_information/e-cigarettes/severe-lung-disease.html.

4   See David Downs, Dave Howard & Bruce Barcott, "Journey of a Tainted Vape Cartridge: From China's Labs to Your Lungs" (24 September 2019), online: www.leafly.com/news/politics/vape-pen-injury-supply-chain-investigation-leafly.

5   See US, R384-418, Electronic-Cigarette Mandatory Warning Signage and Sale Restrictions, Utah, 2019 (enacted).

6   *Ibid* at 4.

Health and Society

Series editor: Sanni Yaya

Health occupies a central place in public debate, and the *Health and Society* series provides a space for dialogue on different fields of expertise (sociology, psychology, political science, biology, nutrition, medicine, nursing, human kinetics, and rehabilitation sciences), generating new insights into health matters from individual as well as global perspectives on population health. The principal domains explored in *Health and Society* are hospitals, communities, medicine, social policies, medico-sanitary institutions, and health systems.

Previous titles in the *Health and Society* collection

Frédéric Mérand and Jennifer Welsh, eds., *The Afterworld: Long Covid and International Relations*, 2024.

Robert J. Flynn, Meagan Miller, Tessa Bell, Barbara Greenberg, and Cynthia Vincent, *Young People in Out-of-Home Care: Findings from the Ontario Looking After Children Project*, 2023.

Lloyd Hawkeye Robertson, *The Evolved Self: Mapping an Understanding of Who We Are*, 2020.

Sylvie Frigon, ed., *Dance: Confinement and Resilient Bodies / Danse : Enfermenent et corps résilients*, 2019.

Martin Rovers, Judith Malette, and Manal Guirguis-Younger, eds., *Touch in the Helping Professions: Research, Practice and Ethics*, 2018.

Serge Brochu, Natacha Brunelle, and Chantal Plourde, *Drugs and Crime: A Complex Relationship. Third revised and expanded edition*, 2018.

Marie Drolet, Pier Bouchard, and Jacinthe Savard, eds., *Accessibility and Active Offer: Health Care and Social Services in Linguistic Minority Communities*, 2017.

Isabelle Perreault and Marie Claude Thifault, eds., *Récits inachevés : Réflexions sur les défis de la recherche qualitative*, 2016.

Mamadou Barry and Hachimi Sanni Yaya, *Financement de la santé et efficacité de l'aide internationale*, 2015.

For a complete list of the University of Ottawa Press titles, please visit:
www.Press.uOttawa.ca

www.ingramcontent.com/pod-product-compliance
Lightning Source LLC
Chambersburg PA
CBHW071412290326
41932CB00047B/2636